SOCIOLOGY

A BIOSOCIAL INTRODUCTION

SOCIOLOGY
A BIOSOCIAL INTRODUCTION

Rosemary L. Hopcroft
University of North Carolina at Charlotte

Paradigm Publishers
Boulder • London

Published in the United States by Paradigm Publishers, 3360 Mitchell Lane, Suite E, Boulder, CO 80301 USA.

Paradigm Publishers is the trade name of Birkenkamp & Company, LLC, Dean Birkenkamp, President and Publisher.

Library of Congress Cataloging-in-Publication Data

Hopcroft, Rosemary L. (Rosemary Lynn), 1962–
Sociology : a biosocial introduction / Rosemary L. Hopcroft.
p. cm.
Includes bibliographical references and index.
ISBN 978-1-59451-801-0 (pbk. : alk. paper)
1. Sociology. 2. Sociobiology. I. Title.
HM585.H66 2010
301—dc22

2010002191

978-1-59451-801-0 (paperback : alk. paper)

Printed and bound in the United States of America on acid-free paper that meets the standards of the American National Standard for Permanence of Paper for Printed Library Materials.

Designed by Cindy Young and Typeset by Scratchgravel Publishing Services.

14 13 12 11 10 1 2 3 4 5

This book is dedicated to those who taught me much of what is in it: Herbert Costner, Vaughn Grisham, George Homans, Margaret Levi, Rodney Stark, Pierre van den Berghe, and Joseph Whitmeyer.

contents in brief

contents

list of photos

list of figures

list of tables

preface for students and teachers

Integrating biology into sociology—sociology for the 21st century

THIS TEXT IS INTENDED for introduction to sociology courses. Unlike other introduction to sociology texts, it presents a *biosocial* introduction to sociology. It integrates mainstream sociology with a scientifically informed model of an evolved, biological human actor. My goal for **students** is to have them understand that all social phenomena are a product of the interaction of the nature of individuals with the social context—never one or the other, always *both*. The goal for **instructors** is to give them a textbook in which the inclusion of biology strengthens and enhances the sociological approach.

THE BIOSOCIAL APPROACH

Since the decoding of the human genome at the close of the 20th century, the discovery of the genetic bases of a variety of social behaviors has proceeded apace. The historic divide between sociology and biology is no longer tenable. In this new textbook, I do three things:

1. Firmly link the discipline of sociology to the other life sciences by grounding the discipline in a solid understanding of humans as an evolved, biological species.
2. Show how this linking can be done effortlessly, with little change to sociological theories and the traditional sociological foci on the importance of group dynamics, roles, norms, class, institutions, and culture. In fact, I show how the sociological perspective flows naturally out of a grounding in an evolved, biological actor, as humans evolved to be a fundamentally social species. Yet despite this grounding in the concept of the *individual* as an evolved actor, this does not mean that

there is no disagreement in sociological theories at the level of the *group*. There are disagreements between and among sociological theories on occasion, and where appropriate I discuss those disagreements.

Instructors should find that the integration of the biosocial perspective does not radically change their usual approach to teaching introduction to sociology. All the standard tools of sociological analysis and the primary subject areas of sociology are covered in the text. The primary difference in topics covered is the addition of a chapter on human biology and evolved predispositions.

3. Link the biosocial approach to a comparative approach to each topic. It is important to see the flexibility of humans in different historical and material contexts. This aspect of the text owes a great debt to Gerhard Lenski's pioneering efforts in his text *Human Societies*. Human biology may be universal, but human social behavior differs substantially depending on the historical time period and cultural setting. Thus, information on a variety of different types of societies in different time periods is presented. A global perspective is utilized when appropriate.

I think that this new approach will make sociology both more interesting and sensible to students. Rather than just restating the obvious—for example, the statement that norms differ from group to group and are important—this textbook shows how norms differ and, perhaps more important, how they do not differ. A grounding of sociology in biology illuminates what is typical in human social life, but it does not negate the great variety of human social life. Nor does it negate the reality of group phenomena in shaping social life, as well as the complexity of social processes in human societies. I hope to strike a balance between revealing and understanding the typical patterns of human social life, with a proper respect for the complexity and contingency of human social life. Far from genetic determinism, I show how the biological underpinnings of social behavior flexibly give rise to the great richness and variety of the human social tapestry. Both culture and biology are given their due. In all cases, I link the text to the most recent sociological research on the topics.

A SCIENTIFIC APPROACH

This biosocial approach is firmly embedded in a mainstream, positivist methodology and a belief in the importance of testing any kind of theoretical ideas with empirical data. Such data may be qualitative or quantitative. Key to all science (including social science) is not the particular way we collect data or the type of data we collect but, rather, that the data help us support or falsify hypotheses. The results of these tests in turn help us to achieve the general goal of developing better explanations (theories) of phenomena. Just as in other sciences, points of difference between sociological theories must be amenable to adjudication by the evidence. Accordingly, this text points out areas of genuine debate between contemporary sociological theories.

Given the scientific approach, this text omits sociological thinking on topics (e.g., the conflict and functional perspectives once staples of introduction to sociology texts) that does not lend itself to empirical testing of any kind. Such thinking is not helpful for understanding the evidence-based, hypothesis-testing style of contemporary sociological research. Hence, this text works better as an introduction to sociology as it currently exists than many other previous texts.

I believe these enhancements of the traditional introduction to sociology text—a grounding in a biosocial conception of the actor, a comparative approach, and a commitment to the empirical testing of sociological theories—work to highlight the strengths of sociology as an academic discipline and the strengths of the sociological approach. Sociology is a relatively young discipline more full of promise than ever before. I hope this text makes that clear to students.

FEATURES OF THE TEXT

In the Textbook

Feature	*Benefit*
Textboxes	These offer examples and specific elaborations of concepts in the text.
Running Glossary Terms	Found in the margins near a term's first use, these provide instant definitions of new ideas and concepts.
Maps	These connect data and information to geography and spatial orientation.
Tables and Figures	These carefully crafted portrayals of data reinforce the text's commitment to a scientific approach to sociology.
Photographs and Illustrations	Chosen for visual interest, these illustrate points made in the book as well.
Chapter Conclusions	Essential for student comprehension and review, these are among the best of any text pedagogy.
References	Offered on a chapter-by-chapter basis to facilitate student research and further exploration

On the Web

PowerPoint slides for lectures are available. They include the tables and figures of the text and also extend key concepts. These are created by the author and can be requested by professors from the publisher.

In the Instructor's Manual

Useful guides and tips for professors on teaching each chapter:

- Test Bank (Multiple Choice and True/False)
- Discussion/Essay Questions
- In-class activities and worksheets to assist learning
- Movie suggestions

ORGANIZATION OF THE TEXT

The organization of this text is slightly different from other introduction to sociology texts. The first chapter is an introduction to what sociology is all about—the scientific study of human society. The next chapters describe and explain *analytical concepts* crucial to sociological analysis. These are organized from the more micro to more macro concepts as follows: biology, culture, networks and groups, institutions, and demography. These are the basic concepts that are used repeatedly in the chapters that follow.

In the substantive chapters on various topics of sociological research, my goal has been to cover the basic descriptive facts of an area first and then briefly cover the major sociological explanations of these facts. To some extent, the sociological research reviewed consists of the "greatest hits" of sociology. These topics generally proceed from microsociological topics to macrosociological topics, with the exception of stratification. This topic is so central to sociology that it is placed earlier in the text than a strict micro to macro ordering would dictate.

If instructors want to retain a more standard order of chapters, the chapters can be taught in the following order:

Introduction to Sociology

1. Chapter 1: What Do Sociologists Do?

Foundations of Society

2. Chapter 2: Biology: One Human Nature
3. Chapter 3: Culture: Socialization, Norms, and Roles
4. Chapter 7: Microsociology
5. Chapter 4: Social Groups: Social Networks, Kin Groups, Classes, Organizations, Status Groups, and Political Groups
6. Chapter 14: Crime and Violence

Social Inequality

7. Chapter 9: Social Stratification
8. Chapter 10: Global Inequality
9. Chapter 11: Contemporary Gender Inequality
10. Chapter 12: Race and Ethnicity

Institutions

11. Chapter 5: Institutions: The Architecture of Society
12. Chapter 16: Economic Sociology
13. Chapter 8: Sociology of the Family
14. Chapter 13: Sociology of Religion
15. Chapter 15: Biosociology of Health

Social Change

16. Chapter 6: Demography
17. Chapter 17: Sociology of the Environment
18. Chapter 18: Political Sociology and Social Movements

Last, I thank the following people, who have made valuable comments on parts or all of the text: Saul Brenner, Yang Cao, Shelley Colvin, Jeff Davis, François Neilson, Elizabeth Stearns, Joseph Whitmeyer, Mark Whitmeyer, and Sophie Whitmeyer. All these people have helped me produce a better book than I would have produced by myself. Of course, any errors are mine alone.

about the author

Rosemary L. Hopcroft is Associate Professor of Sociology at the University of North Carolina at Charlotte. She has published widely in the areas of Comparative and Historical Sociology and Evolution, Biology, and Society in journals that include the *American Sociological Review, American Journal of Sociology*, and *Social Forces.* Her PhD in Sociology is from the University of Washington in Seattle, and the sociological methodology and evolutionary approach to human behavior she learned there have long influenced her teaching and research. As a teacher, she has found that an evolutionary approach helps her students make sense of sociology and its research findings. A native of Australia, she has lived in the United States since 1981. She loves skiing and traveling with her husband, who is also a sociologist, and her children.

FEEDBACK FOR THE AUTHOR

The author and the publisher's office would love to hear your feedback, comments, or suggestions about the book. Should you as a professor or student wish to share ideas for ways to improve this text for future editions, please write to Paradigm's College Marketing Department at jessicap@paradigmpublishers.com. The author may be contacted at rlhopcro@uncc.edu.

INTRODUCTION

WHAT DO SOCIOLOGISTS DO?

1

THE CHAIR OF THE SOCIOLOGY department was talking with another member of the faculty about what he said when people asked him what sociologists study: "Whatever they want!" he said. As an independent-minded 21-year-old at the time, that response helped me decide to go into the field of sociology. However, his statement is not entirely true. You do have the freedom to focus on a great many different subjects in sociology, but there are boundaries. You can't study chemistry or physics, for example. What you do study is groups of people—people in friendship groups, families, organizations, and societies. But wait, you might say. Lots of people study people in groups. Novelists and writers do. Journalists do. Historians do. Ordinary people do in everyday life. Does this mean that everyone is a sociologist? The famous economist Joseph Schumpeter once joked that this was the case. He said that he was planning to write a "sociological novel" in his old age, and that he had even once done fieldwork for the book: He rode the subway back to work! "This, he reported, had been a very interesting experience, and what was more, when he came to writing his sociological novel he was going to do it again" (Samuelson, 1951, p. 98).

In a way, it is true that everyone is a sociologist in that everyone is interested in social groups (their own in particular). So what makes professional sociologists different? Do they really just ride the subway (or some equivalent)? The answer is this: *Sociologists study people in groups using the scientific method.* Society is made up of many groups. The smallest group is the dyad—two people. The dyad is one level of analysis for sociologists. A **level of analysis** is the primary unit the researcher is studying. Sociologists studying dyads and larger groups often collect information about individuals, so the lowest level of analysis for sociologists is the individual. At

Level of analysis The primary unit the researcher is studying (e.g., individual, dyad, family, state, and country).

FIGURE 1.1 Levels of analysis in sociological research.

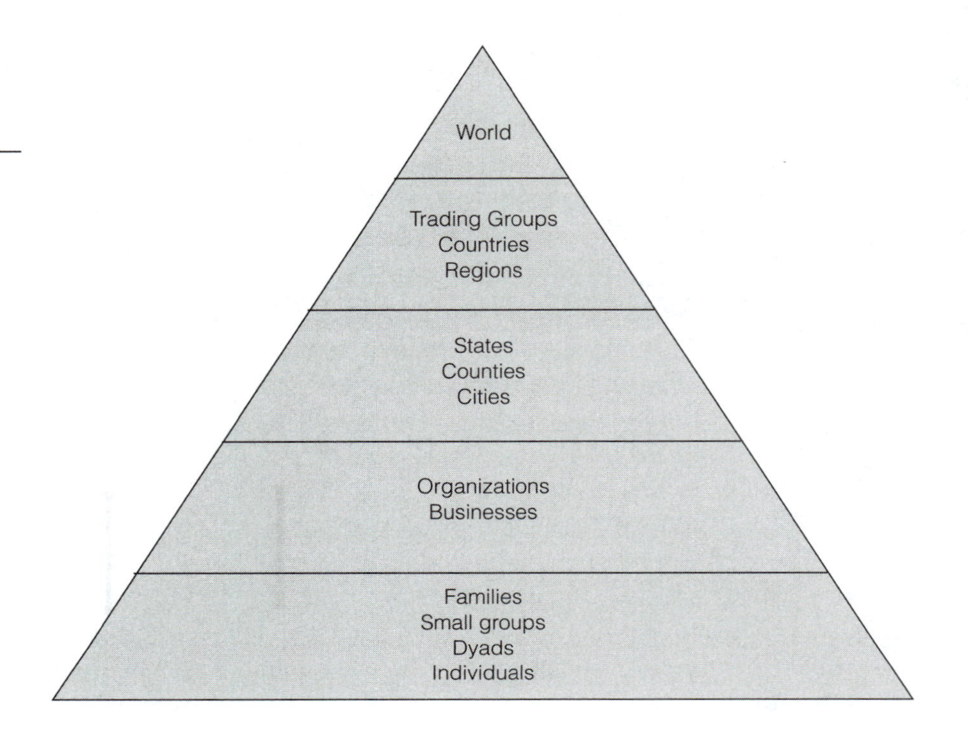

the next highest level of analysis after dyads, we have groups of more than two people, which include friendship groups and families. Then we have groups of people in businesses and organizations, geographically based groups such as counties and states, and, finally, at the highest level of analysis we have countries and then the entire world. You can imagine this as a pyramid of groups with the smallest at the bottom and the whole world at the top (Figure 1.1). This is the subject matter of sociology. Sociologists study all these groups, and they do so using the scientific method.

THE SCIENTIFIC METHOD AND SOCIOLOGICAL INVESTIGATION

So what is the scientific method? You probably have learned about the scientific method in other science courses. The scientific method consists of following the steps in the wheel of science (Figure 1.2). The wheel shows the steps of developing a theory about a particular phenomenon, drawing a hypothesis from the theory, testing it (observation), and then drawing conclusions relevant for your theory. You can actually start at any point on the wheel, but the important point is that no matter where you start,

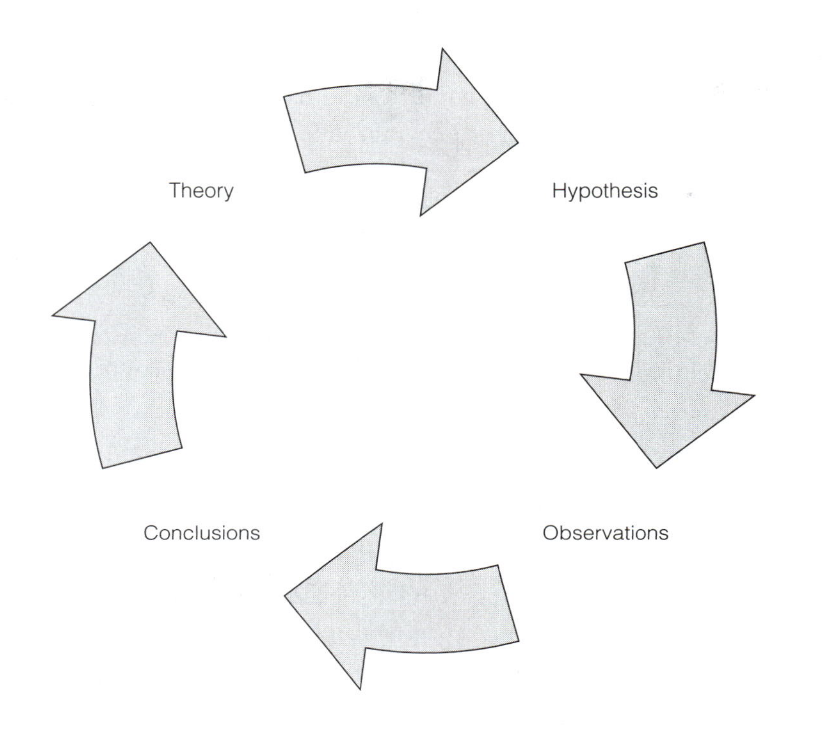

FIGURE 1.2 Wheel of science.

you complete one full circle of the wheel. You could begin with an observation. For instance, you could observe that people in one country seemed happier than people in another country. Then you could develop a theory about why that might be so, draw a hypothesis from it, and test it. Based on the results of the test, you would draw conclusions about the theory. Is it supported? Is it falsified? Or you could begin with a theory of why people tend to be happy, draw a hypothesis from it, test it, and then draw conclusions. For example, one early sociological theorist, Emile Durkheim (1858–1917), wanted to explain why suicide rates varied from country to country. He theorized that more individualistic (egoistic) societies would have more suicide than less individualistic societies. He thought that people in more individualistic societies would be less socially integrated (have fewer connections to other people) than people in less individualistic societies and, therefore, they would be less happy and more likely to kill themselves. From this he hypothesized that because Protestantism promoted individualism more than did Catholicism, then predominantly Protestant countries would be less socially integrated and therefore have higher suicide rates than predominantly Catholic countries. He then tested this hypothesis by collecting information about suicide rates in Protestant and Catholic countries. He found that, indeed, Protestant countries did have higher suicide rates than Catholic countries, and then he generalized these results as support for his theory of suicide.

The Role of Theory

Theory is at the top of the wheel of science because theory is central to all science, including social science. Unlike scholars in disciplines such as history and journalism, sociologists seek to explain the social world by developing general explanations, or theories, of particular social phenomena. Whereas a historian might seek to describe a revolution, a sociologist wants to explain why, when, and how revolutions occur.

Since theory is so important, we had better define it more explicitly. **Theories** are explanations of particular social phenomena. They are made up of a series of propositions. A **proposition** gives the relationship between two factors or characteristics that vary from case to case of whatever we are studying. Propositions can be general or specific. The specific propositions are derived from the more general propositions, and they must be testable.

Theories Explanations of particular social phenomena. They are made up of a series of propositions.

Proposition A proposition gives the relationship between two factors or characteristics that vary from case to case of whatever is being studied.

Durkheim's theory, as a set of propositions, looks like this:

1. In any country, the suicide rate varies with the degree of individualism (egoism). As individualism increases, so does the suicide rate.
2. The degree of individualism varies with the incidence of Protestantism. That is, as the incidence of Protestantism increases, the degree of individualism increases.
3. Given propositions 1 and 2, the suicide rate in a country varies with the incidence of Protestantism. The higher the incidence of Protestantism, the higher the suicide rate.

The final, testable specific proposition or hypothesis (3) is deduced from the more general propositions (1 and 2). That is, if proposition 1 and proposition 2 are true, then proposition 3 must be true. In all cases, the most specific proposition becomes the hypothesis. This hypothesis can be tested by collecting the appropriate data—in this case, data on Protestantism and suicide for a number of regions or countries.

Durkheim tested his theory by collecting data on suicide rates in Protestant and Catholic regions (Durkheim, 1897/1997). He found evidence to support his hypothesis that Protestant regions had higher suicide rates than

Catholic regions. However, it turns out that Durkheim conveniently overlooked some regions in which the Catholic suicide rate was higher than the Protestant suicide rate. Last, there was the glaring exception of England—a Protestant nation that had a low suicide rate. Durkheim tried to explain away England by pointing to the fact that the Anglican church was something like the Catholic church. Unfortunately, many English people were not Anglicans at all but, rather, belonged to other (non-Anglican) Protestant denominations. So in hindsight, we can see that Durkheim's theory of suicide was not entirely correct. This in turn has led to revisions of the original theory. Other studies, for example, show that it is not so much the type of religion but religious commitment that helps prevent suicide, and that, in general, the modernization and development of a country promotes suicide (Stack, 1983). Note that it took nearly 100 years to fully revise Durkheim's findings—a testimony to how slow the production of scientific knowledge can be.

Theories and Beliefs

The most important thing about theory is that it can generate a testable hypothesis that can be supported or falsified with data. If a statement cannot generate a testable hypothesis and therefore cannot be tested, it is not a theory; it is a belief. For example, the statement "there is a god" is not a theory; it is a belief. So is the statement "there is no god." No data can prove that god does or does not exist, so the statements "there is a god" and "there is no god" are beliefs, not theories. If you cannot falsify a theory, it is not a true theory.

Sociological Theories at Different Levels of Analysis

Because of the wide variety of social groups, sociological theories come at all levels of analysis corresponding to the layers of the pyramid in Figure 1.1. Some theories are about individuals in small groups, and we call them *social psychological* theories. There are other theories about families, organizations, and countries. Some sociologists formalize their theories into mathematical models. These theories differ, and there is disagreement on their merits by many sociologists. However, all these theories, if they are any good at all, have the following characteristics.

1. They all generate testable hypotheses.
2. Theories at different levels of analysis are compatible with each other. That is, propositions of a theory at one level of analysis (e.g., society) do not contradict propositions of a theory at a lower level of analysis (e.g., the small group).

Methods

Sociologists must collect data to test their hypotheses. This is the observation part of the wheel of science. We observe the social world to see if our predictions are supported or not supported. Observation can take place in many ways. The gold standard for testing hypotheses is the *experimental method.* With experiments, you randomly assign cases to different groups, the experimental and control groups. The experimental group undergoes the experimental manipulation, whereas the control group does not. The experimental manipulation is a change in the factor you believe to be the important causal factor. In Durkheim's theory of suicide, this factor was the country's religion. The two groups are compared, and any difference in the group outcomes is attributed to the experimental manipulation. For ethical reasons, there is a limit to how much you can experimentally manipulate individuals. If you are studying large groups of people, then it is impossible to do an experiment. For example, with Durkheim's theory of suicide, it would have been impossible to randomly assign countries to experimental and control groups and then manipulate the predominant religious affiliation of each country. For this reason, experimental methods are generally confined to social psychology or microsociological research. (**Microsociological research** is research that has individuals and small groups as the units of analysis.) All experimental research using human subjects must be approved by a review board of the university or institution whose charge it is to thoroughly vet research designs to ensure that participants will not be harmed in any way by their participation in the research.

Microsociological research Research that has individuals and small groups as the units of analysis.

For sociologists studying larger groups, other methods they can use include *field research*, or ethnographic research, in which a researcher visits the group under study and physically observes what goes on in the group. Field research was particularly popular in the early years of sociology, as the preceding joke from Schumpeter suggests. It continues to be the primary methodology used in the discipline of anthropology. In contemporary sociology, sociologists often study large societies that are too big to observe directly. To study such mass societies, other methods besides field research must be used. These methods include *survey research*, in which a researcher surveys a group to find answers to a variety of questions and then analyzes the results. *Analysis of existing data* from government records (or other existing records) is another way sociologists can study very large groups of people. Both survey research and analysis of existing data lend themselves to the use of statistical methods that enable the researcher to make inferences about large populations.

Conclusions and Generalization

After collecting data, sociologists must then draw a conclusion in which they determine whether the data support or do not support their hypotheses. They then must determine what this means for their theory. Is the theory supported? Or is the theory falsified? Or is the theory neither supported nor falsified? Based on this, the theory may need to be revised, or alternative tests of the theory may need to be developed. Ultimately, new hypotheses will be generated, and the whole process will begin again.

Positivism

This approach to research and theory in sociology is called *positivism*. Positivism is the view, first, that social phenomena can be studied like any other phenomena. Second, to do this, social science must follow the scientific method. By these criteria, sociological research and theory must be (1) objective and (2) ethically neutral.

Objective means that the conclusions arrived at as the result of inquiry and investigation are independent of the race, color, creed, occupation, nationality, religion, moral preferences, and political predispositions of the investigator. *Ethically neutral* means that the scientist, in his or her professional capacity, does not take sides on issues of moral or ethical significance. As a scientist, the sociologist is not interested in what is good or evil but only in what is true or false. In 1957, Bierstedt expressed this as follows:

> Sociology is a categorical, not a normative, discipline; that is, it confines itself to statements about what is, not what should or ought to be. As a science, sociology is necessary silent about questions of value; it cannot decide the directions

> in which society ought to go, and it makes no recommendations on matters of social policy. This is not to say that sociological knowledge is useless for purposes of social and political judgment, but only that sociology cannot itself deal with problems of good and evil, right and wrong, better or worse, or any others that concern human values. It is this canon that distinguishes sociology, as a science, from social and political philosophy and from ethics and religion. (Bierstedt, 1957, p. 11)

PITFALLS OF STUDYING OURSELVES

What Bierstedt said is all well and good, but sociologists, like psychologists and other social scientists, are studying people like themselves. Despite the intent to be objective, the values and beliefs of the researcher may interfere with the observation process, and the researcher may see what he or she wants to see. This poses problems for all scientists. For example, a famous scientist named Robert Millikan received the Nobel prize in 1923 in part for work he did measuring the charge of the electron. No one knew it at the time, but Millikan's value for the charge on the electron was slightly off (because he had the incorrect value for the viscosity of air). Yet the error was not caught immediately. Over time, as different researchers measured the charge on the electron, every measurement got a little bit higher than the preceding measurement. It was not until many years later that the correct charge on the electron was determined.

So why didn't they discover that the measurement was incorrect right away? Apparently what happened was that new researchers, when they got a measurement a great deal higher than Millikan's, thought something must be wrong with their measurement. Millikan was a great man—how could his measurement be in error? So they would look for and find a reason why something was wrong with their measurement. If they got a number close to Millikan's value, they did not look so hard. So they eliminated the numbers that were too far off and only reported the numbers that were close to Millikan's, or at least the last reported measurement. That is why the measurements gradually increased in value over time, until finally the correct charge on the electron was reported.

Researchers measuring the charge on the electron were seeing what they wanted to see (the measurement that they expected), not the real measurement. The same sort of thing happens in sociology. Researchers may see what they want to see, not what is actually there. They may do this consciously or unconsciously, for career reasons because they think no one will believe them otherwise, because they do not want to offend people, and so on. This is what makes doing social science especially difficult.

There are other problems unique to the social sciences. In chemistry, for instance, molecules are not going to try to deceive the person looking at them through the microscope, but people may try to deceive a social scientist. Molecules are not going to try to avoid being studied, but people may. There are few ethical restraints on how we can study molecules, but there are many ethical restraints on how we can study people.

The Postmodern Critique

The 1980s and 1990s saw the development of a school of thought known as *postmodernism.* Postmodernism suggests that because researchers are embedded in a particular culture (their own), complete objectivity is impossible. Postmodernism was a movement that emerged in the social sciences, as well as philosophy, art, music, literature, and other areas. Leading postmodernists have been scholars such as Jacques Derrida and Jean-Francois Lyotard in France.

Postmodernists suggest that since we are all trained to adopt the assumptions and values of a particular society, we cannot see our own society, or any society, as it really is because we have no independent standpoint from which to look at it. Therefore, postmodernists reject the idea of value-free social science as impossible, and they suggest that it is impossible to be entirely objective and ethically neutral. This means that there are no truly objective "facts." All knowledge that we thus consider "factual" is in reality just one worldview among many possible. In fact, some postmodernists see that all past science and social science reflects the biased perspective of white men. Some contemporary feminists also share this approach.

Thus, the postmodern approach questions all accepted truths and all social rules, including the set of rules (that we have described) of positivism, which are now seen as products of the dominant, white male perspective. "Deconstruction" is the name given to this process of dismantling of dominant perspectives and revealing them for what they are—the biased point of view of one particular group.

A Response to the Postmodernist Critique

The postmodern critique alerts us to the difficulties of objectivity in the social sciences, yet the critique is not without its own problems. First, if we take the postmodern critique to the extreme and accept that there are no objective facts that anyone can see, then the entire scientific endeavor would break down completely. If there is no objective truth that people can see, then no approach can reveal the truth, including postmodernism. That is, if there is no objective truth, then what postmodernists say cannot be the objective truth because there is no objective truth to reveal. So should all scientists give it up and get real jobs?

No. Even though different people do see things differently, this does not mean there are no objective facts, social or otherwise, that can be discovered by the scientific approach—that is, by testing hypotheses. In fact, the scientific method is designed to minimize the effects of investigator biases and discover these objective facts. Remember the example of Robert Millikan and the charge on the electron? Yes, it is true that the early researchers allowed themselves to be biased by the great man's findings. But eventually, over time, researchers following the scientific method found the correct answer. So although we can accept that we all have biases and find it difficult to be objective, by following the scientific method and holding up our hypotheses to the flame of empirical testing, sooner or later truth will come out.

The Need for Comparative Research

The postmodern critique correctly points out that all social scientists are influenced by the values and assumptions of their own culture. Given this, it is useful for social scientists to do cross-cultural, comparative research and study a variety of different societies. In this way, the individual researcher may be able to uncover his or her own culturally based assumptions about the social phenomena in question. For example, a researcher may be convinced that there is only one way for a particular social group to be organized and find, by examining other societies, that this is not the case.

There are many other reasons for social scientists to examine more than one society. Research comparing different societies can help us understand what is common and what is not common in human societies and discover the patterns and trends in human societies. This book takes an explicitly comparative perspective on the various topics of sociology. For example, the chapter on the family examines not only how families are organized in the contemporary United States but also how they are organized in other industrialized countries as well as in preindustrial societies. Similarly, the chapter on crime and violence examines crime and violence not only in the United States, but also in other countries.

Reactivity

Similar to a postmodern critique is the claim that in doing social research, we ourselves change the social processes we are studying, so therefore what we report is not what would have gone on if we had not studied it. This is called the problem of *reactivity*. A famous example of reactivity is the so-called Hawthorne effect, where researchers found that they improved productivity in a factory just by watching the workers work. In a series of experiments at the Hawthorne Plant of the Western Electric Company in Cicero, Illinois, from 1927 to 1932, researchers led by Harvard Business School professor Elton Mayo changed a variety of work conditions (pay, light levels, humidity, rest breaks, and so on) for company workers. They found that brighter lighting caused worker productivity to increase, lower lighting caused worker productivity to increase—in fact, every change they made caused worker productivity to increase, even a change back to the original conditions. The researchers concluded that it was the process of watching the workers work that was changing productivity, not the experimental changes (Mayo, 1933).

Because of the problems created by reactivity, we have to be careful that our interventions do not change the behaviors we are observing. A very large part of the choice of research methodology involves choosing ways to minimize reactivity. **Unobtrusive methods** are those methods that have been particularly chosen to limit or eliminate reactivity. Unobtrusive methods include collecting information on behavior that has already happened or watching subjects without their awareness. This must be subject to ethical guidelines, of course.

Unobtrusive methods Those methods that have been particularly chosen to limit or eliminate reactivity.

Values and the Effects of Social Research

Some scholars believe that some research is best avoided if the results of the research may have negative effects. These scholars suggest that even if some things are true, they are best left unsaid. For example, many feminists protest against studies examining sex differences, especially sex differences in psychology and behavior. The feminist fear is that if there are sex differences, and these are publicized, then this will lead to further discrimination against women. Another example is that of the response to the book *Time on the Cross: The Economics of American Slavery* by the economic historians Robert Fogel and Stanley Engerman. In the book, they showed how American slavery was a money-making enterprise. As a result, they were criticized for praising slavery.

The response to these kinds of critique must be as follows. First, there is always a danger that scientific findings will be misused or have negative outcomes. The ability to split the atom caused the devastation at Hiroshima during World War II. However, were the scientists wrong in learning how to split the atom? Certainly, learning how to split the atom has been useful for mankind in other ways. Second, the principles of free speech and academic freedom require that all types of research be allowed to flourish, even research into topics that others might view as objectionable. That being said, as a practical matter, there may be reasons for the individual researcher to choose not to study a particular topic given the prevailing political climate.

Ethics and Social Research

It is important to note that all research on humans must always be ethical and not be the cause of harm or any other negative consequences to the people involved, both in the present and in the future. This precludes all research that reveals private or personal information about a person without his or her consent or research that causes emotional or physical pain to the participants. In most cases, research participants must give their informed consent to the researchers before they participate in any research. Human subjects review boards at universities exist to ensure that all research carried out at universities fits these criteria.

Such oversight cannot prevent possible misuse of research findings in the future, however. Yet if researchers can anticipate the likely misuse of their research findings, they should take steps to minimize the likelihood of this happening.

THE SOCIOLOGICAL PERSPECTIVE

Durkheim is rightly considered one of the fathers of sociology because he was one of the first to examine how the social context influenced that most individual of all decisions—the decision to take one's own life. This is the essence of the sociological perspective: examining people as situated in a social context and understanding their actions and behaviors as a result of that social context. That social context is made up of many factors—an individual's position in a social network; his or her culture, religion, group, and institutional setting; and the prevailing demography of the society.

This does not mean that individual psychology and human nature do not influence how individuals respond to their social context. Our fundamentally social nature, for instance, is the reason why individuals who feel isolated or alienated from the group are often so miserable. The sociologists' ability to generalize about groups of people results from the fact that most people respond in similar ways to similar situations. This is because we all share the same fundamental human nature. We all become miserable when we feel excluded from the group, we all do not like to be put down or insulted, and we all want to think that our children have opportunities in life. Of course, we are not all exactly the same. Some individual personalities may be particularly prone to feeling alienated. Each person's behavior is a result of a complex interplay of their biological predispositions and the environment he or she inhabits.

Edvard Westermarck was one of the first to examine the effects of this complex interaction between human nature and the social context on behavior. Westermarck's research showed that children who are raised together between the ages of birth and 6 years tend not to be sexually attracted to each other as adults. He figured that there was a crucial period during which the brain learned to reject intimate peers as prospective mates. Thus, Westermarck showed how the brain is prepared to be and is responsive to the social environment: The social setting influences the biological (the brain) and then in turn the biological affects the social (mate selection). Research since then suggests Westermarck's conclusion was correct, and the effect is called the Westermarck effect in his honor. In the Israeli kibbutzim, research has shown that nonrelated children who were brought up in the same children's houses tended not to marry each other as adults (Shepher, 1983; see Box 1.1 on page 16). At the same time, brothers and sisters who are separated at birth and who are not raised

BOX 1.1
THE ISRAELI KIBBUTZIM CHILDREN'S HOUSES

The Israeli kibbutzim were first established in Israel in the early 20th century as an attempt to create a utopian, egalitarian society. To liberate women for work outside the home, all children (at least in the early years of the kibbutzim) were raised entirely in children's houses. This meant that all children of approximately the same age were grouped together in the same house, where they slept, ate, played, and went to school. Since the 1970s, however, all children of the kibbutz live at home, and the children's houses are only used during the day. Today there are approximately 269 kibbutzim in Israel that are home to approximately 120,000 people (Eylon, 2001).

PHOTO 1.1 Israeli children attend art class at a kindergarten in Israel's oldest kibbutz, Deganya Alef, on the shores of the Sea of Galilee on April 1, 2008. Source: Menahem Kahana/AFP/Getty Images.

together often find each other attractive as adults, much to their distress (Campbell, 2006).

Why Study Sociology?

Sociology is useful because we as humans are a highly social species. As Michael S. Gazzaniga states, "Understanding being social is fundamental to understanding the human condition" (2008, p. 112). What we do is greatly influenced by our social setting, so understanding an individual's friends and family and his or her social setting is crucial to understanding that person's behavior. This is the great sociological insight and why sociology is useful to anyone who wants to understand group phenomena. This is useful in all endeavors in life, whether it be in business (e.g., marketing), architecture and design, finance and economics, education, politics, etc. We can design better public policies if we understand what contexts work and what contexts do not work to produce the social behaviors we prefer.

Understanding how we ourselves are influenced by our social setting can help us understand ourselves better. C. Wright Mills called this the "sociological imagination." The sociological imagination is the ability to understand how private troubles reflect public issues. For example, say you are having trouble getting a job. It may be that you do not have the correct skills or connections to get a good job. Or, if you were part of the echo boom (people born in the 1980s and 1990s), it may be because there are so many people in your age bracket that competition for jobs is stiffer than normal.

Sociology does not excuse the individual, however. Social contexts influence, but do not determine, how we live our lives. We have free will, and we almost always have choices. If we find ourselves in a tight job market, for example, we can choose to try harder to get those skills that will make us competitive.

Nor does human nature excuse what a person does, even though it can also help us understand our own behavior. For example, everyone in the world has a natural predisposition to enjoy sweets, salts, and fats. This can explain why many people in the modern world have difficulty controlling their weight, despite the fact that being overweight is bad for one's health. But this does not mean that we are at the mercy of our own tastes. We can choose not to indulge our taste for sweets, fats, and salts. We can even choose to go on a diet if we want.

What sociology does for us is to help us understand our own actions, as well as the actions of others. That understanding is helpful for us all, whatever we do in life.

ORGANIZATION OF THE BOOK

Part II examines the foundations of human social life. We examine the evolutionary origins of the human species and the implications of this legacy for our shared human nature. Next, we examine the process of human growth, development, and socialization into a particular culture. The next few chapters examine basic characteristics of human groups—the social networks that often form the core of a social group, the different types of naturally occurring human groups (based on family, economic, and political interests), as well as the institutional systems that structure group life. Last, we examine an overview of human demography and the implications of demographic characteristics for group dynamics.

Part III discusses sociological research and knowledge in various areas, from the study of the smallest social groups (dyads and small groups) to the study of the largest social groups (whole societies).

REFERENCES

Bierstedt, Robert. 1957. *The Social Order: An Introduction to Sociology*. New York: McGraw-Hill.

Campbell, Anne. 2006. "Feminism and Evolutionary Psychology." Pp. 63–100 in *Missing the Revolution: Darwinism for Social Scientists*, edited by Jerome H. Barkow. Oxford: Oxford University Press.

Durkheim, Emile. 1997. *Suicide*. New York: Free Press. [Original work published 1897]

Eylon, Lili. 2001. "Kibbutz, Then and Now." *Architecture Week*, 29 August.

Gazzaniga, Michael S. 2008. *Human. The Science behind What Makes Us Unique*. New York: HarperCollins.

Mayo, Elton. 1933. *The Human Problems of an Industrial Civilization.* New York: Macmillan.

Samuelson, Paul A. 1951."Schumpeter as a Teacher and Economic Theorist." *Review of Economics and Statistics* 33(2), 98–103.

Shepher, Joseph. 1983. *Incest: A Biosocial View.* New York: Academic Press.

Stack, Steven. 1983. "The Effects of Religious Commitment on Suicide: A Cross-National Analysis." *Journal of Health and Social Behavior* 24, 362–374.

FUNDAMENTALS OF SOCIOLOGY

To understand social life *in any social group or society, we must understand five factors: human* biology, *the* culture *(including technology) of the society, the nature of* social groups *in the society and the* social networks *that are often at their core, plus the formal* institutions *and* demography *of the society. We also have to understand the specialized sociological lingo, or jargon, that sociologists use. For example,* culture *refers to the totality of norms, values, beliefs, behavior, and material objects that form a people's way of life. A* social network *is the pattern of ties or connections between individuals or groups.* Institutions *are the formal and informal rules and laws that govern a society.* Demography *refers to characteristics of the population such as its distribution among age and sex groups.*

The next five chapters discuss what sociologists and others have learned about each of these factors. This is important to know before we discuss specific topics of sociological research in Part III because often this research assumes knowledge of these factors. In the following chapters, human biology is discussed first because basic human biology is a constant across all societies. Biology is the foundation, but there is a constant process of dynamic feedback between all these factors. Thus, for example, a society's institutions can have implications for that society's groups and social networks, demography, culture, and individual biology; at the same time, individual biology has implications for a society's groups and social networks, demography, culture, and institutions.

BIOLOGY
One Human Nature

2

EVOLUTION OF THE HUMAN SPECIES

The human species is the product of evolution by natural selection. In the process of natural selection, there is selection for those genes (or gene constellations) associated with those traits that work to improve the survival prospects of the organism in a particular environment. Those traits (and associated genes) that do not work to improve the survival prospects of the organism in a particular environment die out. Thus, all living organisms have been selected for traits that in the evolutionary past enabled their ancestors to successfully survive and reproduce. Natural selection is not the only process involved in evolution (other processes include genetic drift), but it is likely the most important one.

For each particular organism, the evolutionary past is referred to as the environment of evolutionary adaptedness, and for humans this is considered to be Africa during the Pleistocene, where modern humans first emerged as a species (Bowlby, 1969). All humans inherit traits that were adaptive for our ancestors in Africa during the Stone Age. The human species left Africa approximately 50,000 years ago and then spread out through the Middle East into Europe, eastward toward Asia and Australia, and over the Bering Straits to the Americas (Figure 2.1). After that time, there was some local evolution that particularly affected traits such as skin color and eye shape that adapted each human group to the ecological conditions in their new homes. For example, early humans who migrated into northwestern Europe faced selection pressures for lighter skin. The cloudy conditions of northwestern Europe are not ideal for the synthesis of vitamin D, and darker skinned individuals would have been more likely to suffer vitamin D deficiency and associated poor health. Thus, lighter skinned individuals would have been healthier and outreproduced darker skinned individuals

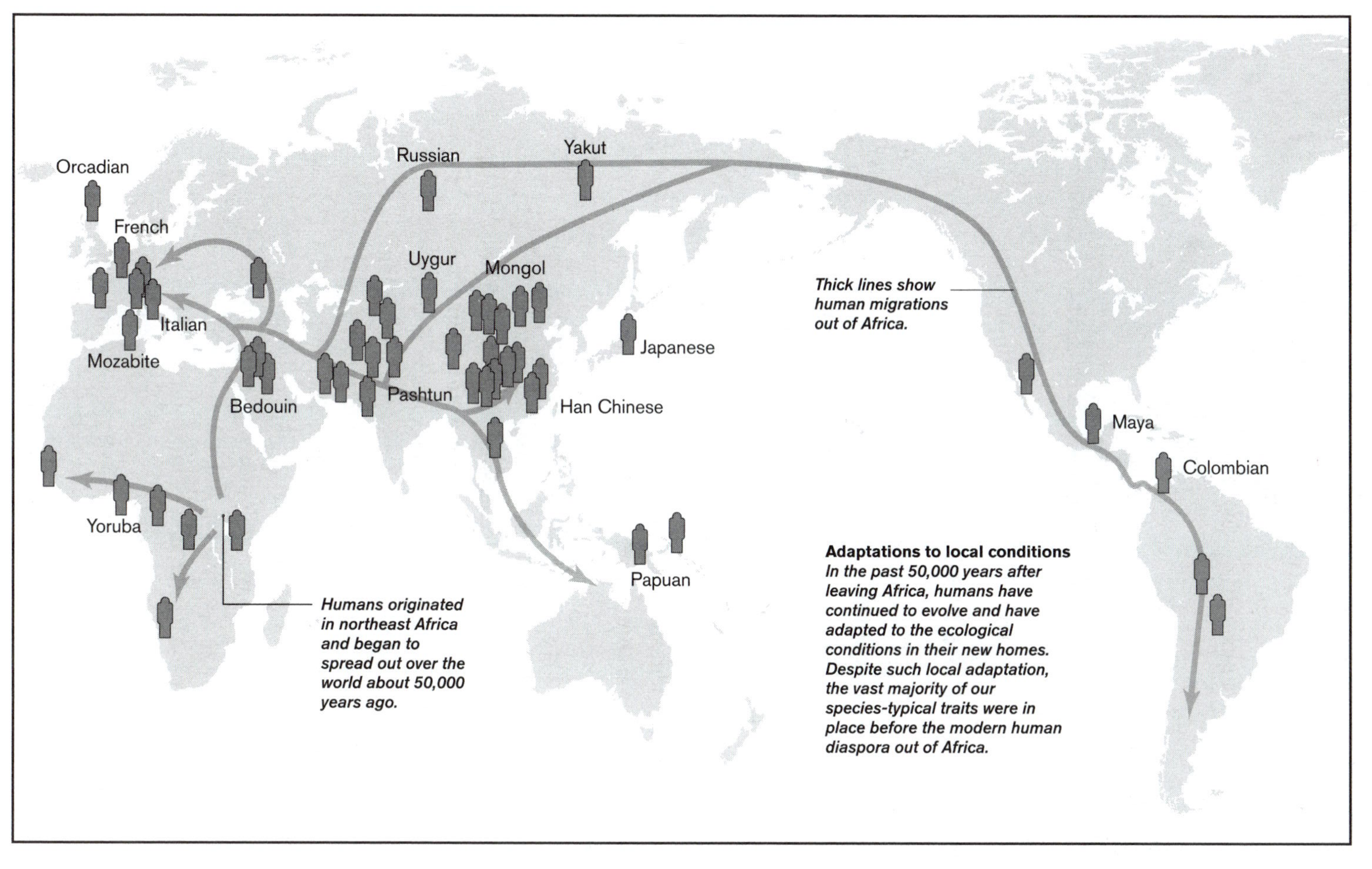

FIGURE 2.1 Human migrations out of Africa.

Source: Adapted from Nicholas Wade, *New York Times,* June 26, 2007.

until lighter skin was the dominant skin color in northwestern Europe. Despite such local selection, the vast majority of our species-typical traits were in place before the modern human diaspora out of Africa.

EVOLVED PREDISPOSITIONS

There is selection for both physiological traits (e.g., skin color) and behavioral traits (e.g., food-getting preferences and practices). For example: all people have a preference for sweets, fats, and salts. This is because in Africa during the Pleistocene, sweets, fats, and salts were essential to the human diet but were rare and difficult to come by. At the same time, environmental conditions were unpredictable, and there was sometimes scarcity due to war or famines, or ill health due to epidemics. Our ancestors who consumed as many sweets and fats as possible when they were available were more likely to be healthy and also store energy as fat and, as a result, were more likely to be able to survive periods of scarcity and periods of epidemic. Thus, there was selection for this food preference, and so we all inherit a preference for sweets, fats, and salts. This predisposition is no longer healthful, however. In a modern environment, these substances are no longer in short supply, and so our preferences for sweets, fats, and salts contribute to making us overweight.

Selection for behavioral traits is really selection for the genes that underlie the behavioral traits. Genes do not specify behavior directly but encode for molecular products that build the brain and govern its functioning (Robinson, Fernald, and Clayton, 2008). As discussed later, there are genetic differences between individuals that also influence behavior. Furthermore, the situation and environment (including the social environment) are always crucially important in shaping both the expression of genes and the brain functions involved. It is a two-way street. This is discussed later in this chapter and in Box 2.1.

Selfish Behavior

Given that individuals who were somewhat self-interested in the evolutionary past were more likely to survive and reproduce than other individuals, there was likely selection for a human psychology that encourages individuals to follow their own interests. In the evolutionary past, individual

BOX 2.1
GENES AND SOCIAL BEHAVIOR: A TWO-WAY STREET

Brain development, brain activity, and behavior all depend on both inherited and environmental influences, and there is increasing evidence that social information can alter brain gene expression and behavior. The following figure shows some of these feedback effects:

Dotted and solid **black** lines: Genes influence development of the organism and brain function, both of which in turn influence social interactions.

Short dashed, dotted, and solid **gray** lines: Social interactions influence development of the organism and brain gene expression, and they can even have long-term effects on the individual genome.

Long dashed **gray** lines: Social interactions over evolutionary time can influence the genome by shaping the natural selection of gene variants.

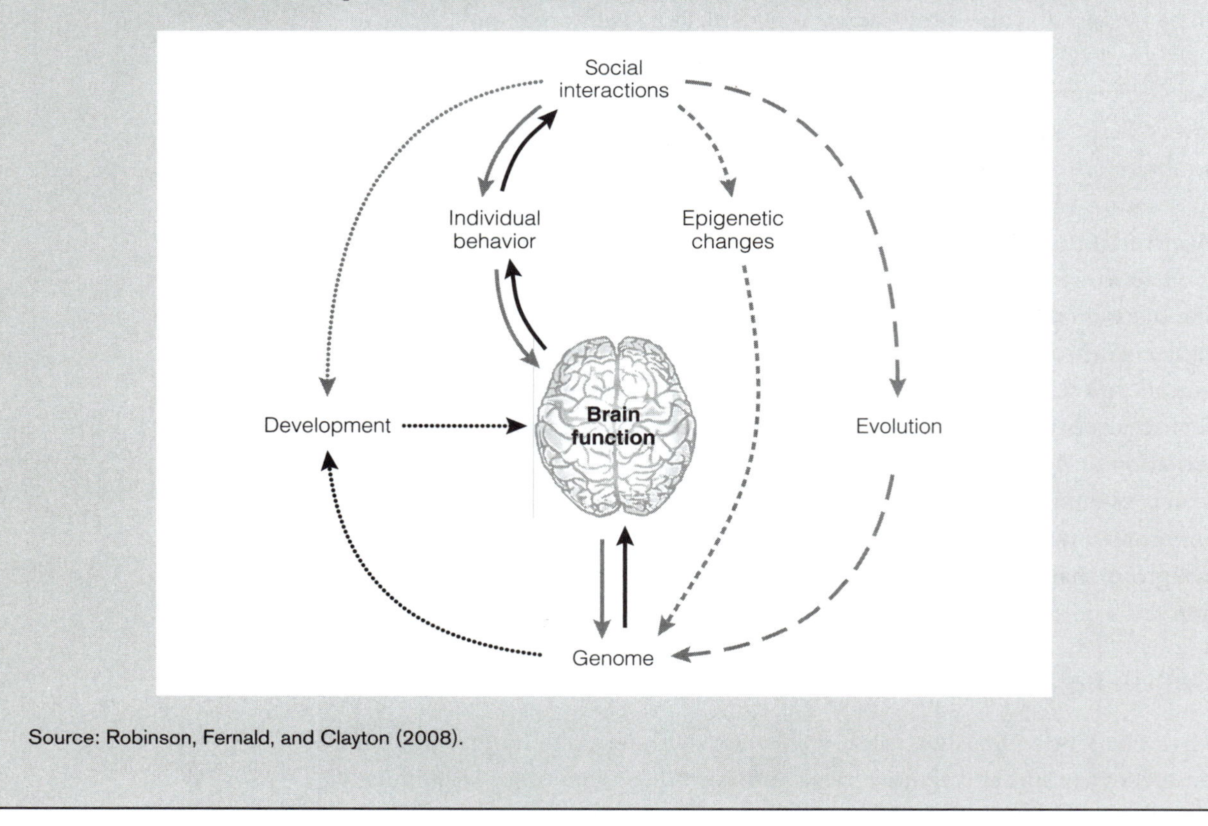

Source: Robinson, Fernald, and Clayton (2008).

interests likely included interests in having **material resources** such as food and shelter as well as interests in having **social status** because both would have helped our ancestors survive and reproduce. Material resources such as food and shelter were important for obvious reasons. High social status within the group was important because it would have provided access to more or better resources, helped an individual find a high-quality mate, and helped ensure the well-being of children.

Material resources Resources such as food and shelter.

Social status A person's position in a social hierarchy; honor or prestige within the social group.

Thus, humans are likely to be predisposed to be self-interested and to pursue both material resources and social status. The idea that individuals follow their own interests whatever they might be is the basis of the entire discipline of economics. Economics typically focuses on material interests and resources such as money, although social status is equally if not more important for individuals. The importance of social status for individuals is reflected in the speed with which people form status hierarchies when put together in a small group (Fisek and Ofshe, 1970). Usually, people can determine others' status and their own status in the group hierarchy in just a few minutes (Kalma, 1991).

Reciprocal Altruism

Humans needed more than food, shelter, and social status to survive in the evolutionary environment. Africa during the Stone Age was a dangerous place, including the dangers of snakes, poisonous insects, disease, wild animals, and hostile neighbors. People needed the help of others in the group to deal with these dangers. One important basis of cooperation in the group is likely to have been **reciprocal altruism**—you do me a favor and I will do you a favor. Reciprocal altruism is found in all known human societies and is an important basis of sociality. (It is also an important basis of sociality in many other species as well.) By helping each other out, people can do better in a group than they can on their own. Hence, there would have been selection for a predisposition for people to return favors, and there is evidence that this is the case. The "Golden Rule" of doing unto others as they do to you is found in all human societies. Most human economies are also based on the principle of reciprocal altruism. Goods and services are traded for other goods or services or, in a more sophisticated economy, some form of money. Trust that people will honor their debts and deliver goods or payment as agreed is crucial to the working of the economic system (Seabright, 2005).

Reciprocal altruism The exchange of services or favors between individuals—"You scratch my back and I'll scratch yours."

Kin-based altruism Behaving altruistically to those who share your genes.

Altruism Treating others well for no immediate reward.

Kin-Based Altruism

Not all evolved behavior is likely to be self-centered, however. One behavioral trait that successfully helped the ancestors of most species to successfully reproduce in most environments is **altruism** toward kin (often referred to as *kin selection*). Individuals who in the evolutionary past were predisposed to help their genetic relatives left more descendants and genetic relatives than did individuals who were not so predisposed; hence, there was selection for traits that predisposed individuals to help their genetic kin (Hamilton, 1964). This includes a cognitive or psychological bias toward kin.

This means that, on average, people will be altruistic to people who share their genes. Individuals are also likely to cooperate with individuals who share their genetic interests because those people are also likely to be altruistic to those who share their genes. For example, parents who share genetic interests in their joint children typically cooperate with each other in parenting those children.

For this reason, most people in most societies help their biological children and also help their partners help their joint biological children. They are likely to be unconscious of the inclusive fitness arguments discussed previously, however. People are likely to be aware of the fact that they helped their children because they loved them, because they thought that was their job as a parent, or that they self-identified as good parents. The average person looking at his or her newborn does not think to himself or herself, "I am going to love you and help you as much as I possibly can because you share 50% of my genes." But nevertheless, the behaviors and feelings are automatic, triggered by a cascade of hormones and other biochemicals.

Gender Asymmetry in Parenting

The principle of altruism to one's genetic relatives has implications for sex differences in parenting behaviors. This is because of sexual reproduction. Among sexually reproducing species (such as our own), one sex typically shoulders a greater burden of the biological cost of parenting. In our species, as in many others, it is the female. The female provides the larger (and rarer) gamete and must bear the biological costs of carrying a fetus to term, undergoing childbirth, and the physiological costs of nursing. (Remember that throughout human evolutionary history, breast-feeding was the only way of feeding a baby.) The male's biological contribution to the offspring is by comparison trivial—a few of the tiny and abundant male gametes (the difference in size of male and female gametes is called anisogamy). What this means is that from a biological standpoint, the female's investment in any child is much greater than the male's investment. The higher costs of childbearing for females mean that each child represents a greater proportion of total possibilities for reproduction for the female than for the male (Trivers, 1972). For the female, then, from a biological perspective each child is more precious than for the male.

Evolutionary biologists suggest that these differences in reproductive interests lead to different behaviors with regard to mating and parenting behavior. In some species, this means no male investment in offspring at all. In our species, as in some others in which males do offer parental care, it is in the reproductive interests of the female to find a mate who is both willing and able to invest in nonbiological ways in her offspring. This means that there has been selection for distinct male and female psychologies when it comes to mating and parenting.

First, given greater female "sunk costs" in a child, women are expected to mostly follow a "mom" strategy. That is, they are going to stick around and invest in children, and they are only going to abandon offspring in extreme situations. For men, it will also be in their reproductive interests to invest in children because their children share 50% of their genes. Thus, men also are likely to follow a "dad" strategy at least some of the time. However, because men have less invested in each child, they have another viable strategy to get their genes into the next generation. They can father a large number of children in which they invest very little. Although children without an investing father are less likely to do well, some are likely to survive and prosper, hence ensuring the passing on of the father's genes. So the "love 'em and leave 'em" strategy, or "cad" strategy, is a viable reproductive strategy for a man. Hence, a father's commitment and investment in his children is less certain than a mother's.

These different parenting strategies encourage males and females to have different mate preferences. Women are likely to be more interested in committed and high-status mates than are men because commitment and high status indicate that the man will be both willing and able to invest in any potential offspring. They are also going to be interested in males who can provide resources to future children and are stable and dependable enough to continue to invest in children in the future. In addition, for each of their precious children, women are going to be looking for the best second set of genes they can find. These characteristics do not necessarily all come in the same person. Women may be forced to make a choice between dependability and good genes or between resources and high status, for example.

Men are likely to be more interested in youth and beauty in a mate because these are correlates of the ability to bear children (Buss, 1989). There would have been strong selection against traits that encouraged male sexual interest in older and hence less fertile mates. Males are also likely to be very interested in females who are faithful. For men there exists the problem of paternity certainty—that is, uncertainty about whether their partner's children are in fact their own. For this reason, an unfaithful spouse or partner is a reproductive disaster for an investing male because he will be spending time and resources investing in some other person's child. We can expect strong selection for males to be very interested in the sexual behavior of their mates. Men who were tolerant of an unfaithful partner are not our ancestors.

Implications of Gender Asymmetry: Sex Differences in Mate Choice and Family Roles

These predispositions are manifest in *norms* for mate choice and norms for sex roles in families across human societies (Lopreato and Crippen, 2002). A **norm** is what is expected or typical in a particular circumstance. These norms are influenced by a society's technology, material resources, and history. Women are less likely to be interested in the resources a man can bring to the family if she can provide substantial resources on her own, for instance. Nevertheless, some universal patterns appear.

Norm What is expected or typical in a particular circumstance.

David Buss's (1989) study of 37 cultures finds that in all of these cultures, women are more interested in the financial prospects of a prospective marriage partner than are men. Men, on the other hand, are more interested in the physical beauty of a prospective marriage partner. In all human cultures, men prefer younger mates, whereas women prefer older (and more established) mates. Women also have a stronger preference than men for a high-status mate. There is also evidence that tall and athletic men are preferred by women. Buss's study showed that all people want a kind, intelligent, and loving person as a long-term marriage partner.

There is also evidence that women have stronger psychological ties binding them to their children than do men. Mothers are much less likely to abandon their children than are fathers. In all human societies, women have the primary responsibility for the care of young children. They also have the primary responsibility for activities that often have children as primary beneficiaries—cooking, cleaning, and housekeeping. Different male and female psychologies mean that in general, fathers and mothers play different social and emotional roles in the family. A **role** is the set of typical behaviors expected of a person in a particular social position. Typically, the mother spends more time with her children and is the warmer and more intimate parent, whereas the father spends less time with his children and is the cooler and more distant parent.

Role The set of typical behaviors expected of a person in a particular social position.

Some of the earliest literary records show this division of labor in the household. Consider the following example from Classical Greece, 2,500 years ago:

> Calonice: It's hard for women, you know. To get away. There is so much to do. Husbands to be patted and put in good tempers: Servants to be poked out: children washed or soothed with lullays or fed with mouthfuls of pap.
>
> —From the *Lysistrata*, in the *Complete Plays of Aristophanes* (1962, Bantam, New York)

Perhaps even more telling is when people have tried to radically change sex roles in the family. The Israeli kibbutzim initially tried to eradicate them entirely. The nuclear family unit was done away with. Children were raised in communal children's houses. Meals were prepared in communal kitchens. Men and women were given the option of pursuing whatever occupation in the kibbutz they wanted. With time, however, things began to revert to familiar patterns. First, the women pushed to allow their children to stay with them at night and not in the children's houses. Although there was resistance to this at first (by the men!), eventually the children's houses became day cares where children only stayed during the day rather than places for the full-time care of children. Women were disproportionately likely to choose work in the children's houses, the kitchens, or the laundry than were the men. Many of them did not want to be too far away from their children during the day, and working in the children's houses, kitchen, and laundry meant they could visit their children at lunchtime (Shepher, 1983).

INDIVIDUAL DIFFERENCES

These patterns and norms do not apply to everyone in a society. Not all family members are altruistic to each other. Some groups of biological kin are abusive and dysfunctional. Some mothers kill or abandon their children (Hrdy, 1999). Not all men marry younger women. Some women are very happy to be the sole or primary earners in their families. But these cases are comparatively rare and do not reflect the average.

People differ in personality characteristics and can have idiosyncratic preferences and behaviors. Some of these differences are genetically based. Guo et al. (2008) studied genetic and survey data for 1,100 males from the National Longitudinal Study of Adolescent Health. Their research found that certain genes predispose individuals to serious and violent delinquent behaviors. The environment was also important (family and school environment and whether or not friends were delinquent). Not everyone with the genetic predisposition for delinquent behaviors actually became delinquent, and some people without the genetic predisposition became delinquent. Nevertheless, those individuals with the gene in question were more likely to be delinquent than those individuals who lacked the gene, all else being equal.

Studies of identical twins reared apart show that a great many other social behaviors are influenced by genes (Freese, 2008), including aggressiveness, altruism toward others, church attendance, conscientiousness, criminal behavior, divorce, educational attainment, acceptance of modern art, occupational attainment, parenting behavior, and smoking. Once again, if you have the genes predisposing you to one of those behaviors, you may not actually behave that way. However, you are more likely to behave that way than someone who does not have those genes.

Hormones and Behavior

Hormones are part of our evolved biological makeup and also influence behavior. Hormones are important regulators of a variety of biological processes. The neurohormone oxytocin, for example, has been implicated in bonding between mothers and infants. This hormone works the same way in all mammals (Box 2.2). Changing levels of hormones (naturally or artificially) has consequences. For example, changing individual levels of testos-

BOX 2.2
NEUROPEPTIDES OXYTOCIN AND VASOPRESSIN AND SOCIAL BEHAVIOR

Neuropeptides are biochemicals that act as neurotransmitters in the brain or as neurohormones that activate other receptors in the brain. Neuropeptides have emerged as central players in the regulation of social cognition and behavior. Research has focused on members of the oxytocin/vasopressin family. Versions of these biochemicals have existed for at least 700 million years and have been identified in many species, including hydra, worms, insects, and vertebrates. They also exist in humans. Research has identified roles for these peptides in personality, trust, altruism, social bonding, and the ability to infer the emotional state of others.

Oxytocin influences human female sexual behavior, lactation, and maternal attachment. Oxytocin is released during lactation and evolved to facilitate maternal bonding, but in humans and some other animals it may also be involved in pair bonding.

Vasopressin is involved in male reproduction and behavior, and it mediates a variety of male-typical social behaviors, including aggression and territoriality. Genetic variations on the AVPR1A locus that influence vasopressin receptors have been directly associated with differences in personality traits, the onset of reproduction, and social interactions such as the experience of marital problems. AVPR1A variants have also been associated with autism (Donaldson and Young, 2008).

terone changes individual spatial abilities (Kimura, 1999). On average, men have higher spatial ability (the ability to rotate objects in one's head) than women. However, men who undergo sex change operations and are given female hormones see their spatial abilities decline; conversely, women who are given testosterone see their spatial abilities improve.

Hormones are also involved in feedback effects. Men who win competitive sports (even chess) see an increase in their testosterone levels, whereas men who lose see a decrease in their testosterone levels. These elevated levels of testosterone in winners may then serve to improve performance, accounting for the winner's streak (Mazur and Booth, 1998). These effects of winning and losing even extend to people who watch sports. In the 1994 World Cup in which Brazil beat Italy, the Brazilian fans who watched the match on TV saw a rise in testosterone after the game, whereas the Italian fans who watched the match saw a decline (Dabbs and Dabbs, 2000).

THE IMPORTANCE OF THE SITUATION

All human predispositions work in conjunction with environmental conditions. Thus, although mothers generally are devoted to their children, there are some situations in which they might be persuaded to kill their own children. For example, in many hunting and gathering groups, if a second child was born too soon after the first child was born, the mother would kill the second child. This is because she could not adequately feed and care for two children simultaneously, so it was better that one die and one live than have both potentially die. There are many circumstances in which people are likely to override their predispositions.

Sometimes predispositions work in different directions, and people have to make choices about the best way to go. For example, this often occurs when selecting a mate. A woman may be confronted by the choice between a stable, dependable "dad" type of suitor or a devastatingly handsome "cad" type of suitor. A man may be confronted with a choice between a pliant, controllable woman who would be a devoted wife or a beautiful, independent woman whose affections are uncertain.

OTHER EVOLVED PREDISPOSITIONS

The predispositions described previously are universal. Many others have been described, including fear of snakes, landscape preferences, and liking of music. The ones most relevant to sociology include predispositions toward religion and magic, ethnocentrism, male sexual jealousy, violent aggression in males, and deference behavior in females. These predispositions are most relevant to *social* behavior, the subject matter of sociologists. Of course, you could argue that a predisposition toward liking music is important to social behavior; nevertheless, I focus here on predispositions most relevant to the topics sociologists have studied extensively, such as religion, race and gender inequality, and family violence.

As with the evolved predispositions previously discussed, all these predispositions work in conjunction with environmental conditions and the social context of the individual. There are also differences among individuals.

Religion and Magic

In addition to predispositions toward reciprocal altruism and kin selection, discussed previously, many have argued that we have innate predispositions toward religious beliefs and behavior. There are two versions of this argument: (1) Religious beliefs and behavior are promoted by predispositions that originally evolved for a different purpose, and (2) religious behavior is directly promoted by predispositions toward religiosity that were adaptive in the evolutionary environment. Nevertheless, it is clear that however they evolved, religious beliefs are universal, and they are important to understanding human social behavior. All societies have some sort of religious practices and/or beliefs in the supernatural. In many societies, religion is central to the operation of the society; in others, such as the secular societies of Western Europe, religion is much less important.

History matters as to what religion or spiritual practices a population adopts. Societies with more complex technologies are more likely to subscribe to monotheistic religions (including Christianity, Judaism, and Islam) with formal churches, professional priests, and religious hierarchies, whereas societies with less complex technologies are more likely to subscribe to animistic beliefs (beliefs in spirits) and ancestor worship, and they are unlikely to have formal churches, priests, and religious hierarchies.

Dislike of Out-Groups and Ethnocentrism

Human history is full of conflicts between groups. Racial, ethnic, and religious groups have gone to war with each other, tried to exterminate each other, and enslaved each other. Prejudice and discrimination against people based on race, ethnic group, or religious affiliation have been only too common. Pierre van den Berghe (1991) suggests that dislike of out-groups, or ethnocentrism, is innate and is an extension of inclusive fitness to the larger kinship group. That is, people in an in-group are likely to intermarry and are likely to have intermarried in the past and, therefore, are more likely to be related to each other than to people in an out-group. This was certainly the case in the evolutionary environment, where groups would have been small and would have consisted mostly of related people. By favoring members of the in-group, a person is favoring those who are likely to share his or her genes. There would have been selection for this behavioral trait because people with this trait would have left more genetic descendants than people without the trait. Given this, it is likely that all people have an innate tendency to be ethnocentric—that is, favor one's own in-group over others.

Such kin group favoritism can even work in groups bonded by fictitious kinship and groups that cannot possibly share any kinship ties. Joseph Whitmeyer (1997) has shown that as long as the in-group is a currently endogamous group—that is, people always marry within the group—in-group favoritism will help an individual's genetic descendants. Through intermarriage, the grandchildren and great-grandchildren of group members are very likely to share kin ties. Thus, helping in-group members helps the parents and grandparents of your future relatives and therefore indirectly supports your own genetic stock.

Research supports the idea that in-group favoritism may be innate. For example, experiments show that we are more likely to trust people who look like us. Experiments also show that people very readily sort themselves into in-groups and out-groups with little encouragement and then proceed to discriminate against each other (see Chapter 12). As with all predispositions, this is subject to the constraints of the situation. Certain situations and social environments will exacerbate this predisposition, and other situations and social environments will suppress it. Thus, although common, ethnocentrism is not inevitable.

Male Sexual Jealousy

Male interest in monitoring the sexual behavior of their mates is often displayed as sexual jealousy. Most men are made extremely uncomfortable by the thought of their spouse or partner having sex with another person. Women are also uncomfortable with this, but evidence suggests that women are even more uncomfortable with the thought of their spouse or partner falling in love with another woman (Buunk et al., 1996). Although the sex difference in sexual jealousy differs across cultures, in all cases men are more likely to be sexually jealous than women (Figure 2.2). These tendencies reflect the different reproductive interests of men and women, with men being most concerned that their partners be faithful, whereas women are most concerned that their partners not abandon them and their offspring (or potential offspring).

The man's relatives are also interested in his wife's sexual behavior because they want to make sure the man (who shares their genes) is not cuckolded. So the man's relatives are likely to help him in the task of monitoring his wife's sexual behavior. Even the woman's own relatives, who are interested in making sure the wife and her children continue to receive her husband's investments, are likely to help monitor her sexual behavior. They know that if she strays, she and her children (their relatives) are likely to be

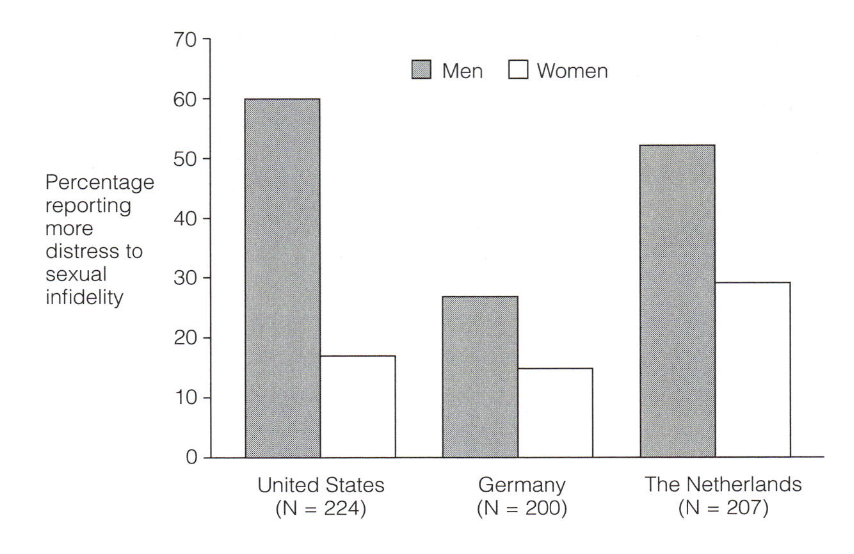

FIGURE 2.2 **Percentage of subjects reporting that they would be more distressed by imagining their partner enjoying passionate sexual intercourse with another person than by imagining their partner forming a deep emotional attachment to that person. Results are shown separately for men and women from the United States, Germany, and The Netherlands.**

Source: Buunk et al. (1996).

deprived of the husband's support. People are likely to be unaware of their own motivations and the evolved nature of these motivations, and they may explain their own behavior to themselves in terms people are more familiar with: values, norms, roles, "family honor," "face," etc. The methods for the control of female sexuality do vary from group to group, but in all societies the ultimate goal is the same—the control of female sexuality to give men paternity certainty.

In all species in which the female bears the young and both parents invest in offspring, males face the problem of cuckoldry and investing in offspring that are not their own. Yet human societies, particularly premodern, agricultural societies, often involve greater oppression of women than is typical of other species. Smuts (1995) suggests that this may be a result of increased male efforts to control the sexuality of their mates, given the context of high male parental investment typical of agricultural societies. If social customs dictate that the wife lives with the husband's family, this means that the woman is also deprived of the support of her own relatives and friends. At the same time, males have the advantage of the presence of their own relatives and friends.

In societies with a great deal of economic inequality, male concern with paternity certainty is greatest because they have the most invested in children (e.g., bequests of property and position) and more to lose if those investments are misplaced. Such concerns typically lead to the creation of a great variety of practices and ideologies intended to create male control and female subordination. These include direct attempts to control female sexuality such as use of close observation and chaperoning of women, purdah (veiling), female seclusion, and confinement to the home. They also include cruder forms of sexual control, such as the use of chastity belts, female "circumcision," and infibulation. Female circumcision and infibulation are discussed in Chapter 8. Female circumcision (clitoridectomy) consists of the cutting out of the woman's clitoris so sex is no longer pleasurable for her; infibulation consists of the sewing up of the vagina so sex is impossible. Needless to say, both operations are painful and dangerous, yet millions of women still routinely undergo these operations every year, mostly in Africa, but in some other regions as well.

There are also indirect attempts at controlling women's behavior and sexuality through practices such as foot binding (the Chinese practice of binding a baby girl's feet, resulting in stunted foot growth), tolerance of wife beating, and institutional rules preventing women from owning property or obtaining an education. These practices restrict the freedom of women to go where they want and earn their own livelihoods.

Another consequence of male sexual jealousy is male discomfort with wives who have greater status and resources than themselves. What many have termed threats to male ego may be (not necessarily conscious) threats to the male's reproductive interests. A woman who has greater status and resources than her husband threatens his reproductive interests because she may find a higher-status mate more to her liking. Furthermore, she is less dependent and therefore her behavior is less controllable than that of a lower status female.

As with all predispositions, the predisposition toward greater male sexual jealousy is an average tendency. It differs from person to person. It is also dependent on the situation to a great extent. Circumstances can make a normally nonjealous person jealous, and vice versa. As noted previously, the extent of male sexual jealousy also depends on the culture of the society. A predisposition is only a predisposition—it may or may not be expressed in beliefs and behavior.

Violent Aggression in Males

Male sexual jealousy also frequently fuels wife abuse and wife beating. Wife killing is often a result of fulfilling threats aimed at controlling and confining

FIGURE 2.3 Age-specific rates of homicide victimization within legal marriages for (open bars) women killed by their husbands ($n = 528$) and (solid bars) men killed by their wives ($n = 124$), Canada, 1974–1983. Age-related variations in spousal homicide victimization are significant for wives (χ^2 [DF = 9] = 44.2, $P < 0.001$), but not for husbands (χ^2 [DF = 9] = 10.6, $P > 0.3$).

Reproduced from Daly and Wilson (1998).

wives. This typically occurs just after the woman has left the man. Young wives are more likely to be the victims because they are the most reproductively valuable, and therefore husbands are most at risk of losing them to other men (Daly and Wilson, 1998; Figure 2.3).

Although a small percentage of all homicides are men killing women, most male violent aggression is aimed at other men (see Chapter 14). Whereas women are also aggressive, males are much more likely to express their aggression violently. Violent behavior is often triggered by altercations over petty issues. Often, the reason is one man's attempt to "save face" or defend his honor. Sometimes violence is committed in the course of another crime, such as robbery. Violence can be seen as a risky way of obtaining status and resources. Young men who have less risky methods of obtaining status and resources are less likely to use violence. As a result, violence among young men is most common among those without other legitimate means of obtaining status and resources—the unemployed and low socioeconomic status youths. Evidence suggests that employment deters young men from violence. Finding a mate does also. Married men are much less likely to be involved in violent crime than unmarried men (Gottfredson and Hirschi, 1990). Men also age out of violent crime, partly because older men are more likely to be established than younger men.

It is likely that the male willingness to use violent aggression is an evolved predisposition. First, the male hormone testosterone is implicated in violence (Book, Starzyk, and Quinsey, 2001). Second, obtaining status and resources is more essential for a man in finding a mate than for a woman in finding a mate. Males who were willing to take risks (e.g., using violent behavior) to obtain status and resources in the evolutionary environment were more likely to find a mate and therefore leave descendants; hence, there would likely have been selection for risk-taking behavior in males. Every year thousands of young men die in car accidents, violent altercations, and other accidents as a result of risk-taking behavior. Far fewer young women die in car accidents and violent altercations than do young men. Young men often pay much higher car and life insurance premiums than young women for this reason.

Deference Behavior

All societies have norms of male dominance and female deference in mixed-sex interactions. Even in our own society, in which norms of gender equity are espoused, experimental research shows that young women continue to defer to young men in mixed-sex interactions, all else being equal. Even in games, girls defer. A study of boys and girls playing dodgeball showed that high-skill girls were inhibited when playing with boys, especially low-skill boys (Weisfeld, Weisfeld, and Callaghan, 1982). The boys, on the other hand, played better when playing with the girls. This was particularly true of the low-skill boys. When quizzed about their behaviors afterward, neither the boys nor the girls were aware of the changes in their own behavior.

Female deference to males, and lack of male deference to females, is likely an evolved predisposition. In the evolutionary environment, female deference would have advertised youth and controllability, characteristics highly valuable to prospective long-term mates. Females who exhibited these traits would have found higher-status long-term mates, their children would have had advantages in surviving and reproduction, and as a result there would have been selection for these traits. On the other hand, male lack of deference would have signaled high status, a trait desirable to prospective mates. Males who exhibited this trait would have found higher quality (young and healthy) mates as a result, and hence there would have been selection for this trait in males.

Given that there was selection for deference behaviors because they aided in finding a long-term mate, it seems likely that they would diminish and be of less consequence in older individuals. For women past the age of menopause, this trait could no longer have been selected for and so it is likely that the trait is lessened or absent in older women. Evidence suggests that generally women do become more assertive as they age. They are also given much more freedom in society at large. In all societies, the status of women increases when they are past childbearing age. In many societies, postmenopausal women are given the status of "honorary men." Even in Muslim societies, where younger women are made to wear the veil and are not allowed to go out in public places unchaperoned, older women are free to not wear the veil, go out in public by themselves, and are even free to pursue public office.

FREE WILL AND THE NATURALISTIC FALLACY

The predispositions described previously are universal to the human species. However, listing them in this way does not condone the behaviors involved. It is important to avoid the **naturalistic fallacy**—that is, "if it is natural then it has to be good." We can understand that a predisposition for liking sweets and fats is natural without suggesting that this preference is good and should be indulged. Even though the preference exists, we can avoid acting on the preference. We can avoid keeping sweet or high-fat snacks in the house and make sure our diet is low in fat, sugar, and salt. Similarly, we can note that fathers often spend less time and effort in parental care than mothers but not suggest that this situation is ideal.

Naturalistic fallacy The idea that if it is natural it has to be good.

People can learn to second-guess their predispositions and override them. In fact, people do this on a daily basis. Every time you tell yourself not to do something because "it is only a superstition," you are overriding a predisposition. Every time you refrain from eating a whole bag of chips when you really want to do so you are overriding a predisposition. Every time you tell yourself to be broad-minded when encountering an unusual cultural practice you are overriding a predisposition. In fact, much of socialization is teaching people to override many of their innate predispositions. That is, people are taught not to be selfish, greedy, and so on for the good of the group. Societies do this in different ways. In some societies, dislike of another ethnic group is promoted, not suppressed, or wife beating is tolerated and sometimes even advocated. Socialization and how it differs from culture to culture is the topic of the next chapter.

CONCLUSION

In this chapter, we examined evolved behavioral predispositions that all people share. They are predispositions for selfish behavior, reciprocal altruism, kin-based altruism, and gender asymmetry in parenting, as well as predispositions toward beliefs in religion and magic, ethnocentrism, male sexual jealousy, violent aggression in males, and deference behaviors that differ by sex. This list is not exhaustive of all human predispositions, but they are an important part of explaining common patterns in human social life. Human biological predispositions are one component of the explanation. Now let's discuss the next component: culture.

REFERENCES

Book, Angela S., Katherine B. Starzyk, and Vernon L. Quinsey. 2001. "The Relationship between Testosterone and Aggression: A Meta-Analysis." *Aggression and Violent Behavior* 6(6), 579–599.

Bowlby, John. 1969. *Attachment and Loss. Volume 1: Attachment.* New York: Basic Books.

Buss, David M. 1989. "Sex Differences in Human Mate Preferences: Evolutionary Hypotheses Tested in 37 Cultures." *Behavioral and Brain Sciences* 12, 1–49.

Buunk, Bram P., Alois Angleitner, Victor Oubaid, and David M. Buss. 1996. "Sex Differences in Jealousy in Evolutionary and Cultural Perspective: Tests from The Netherlands, Germany and the United States." *Psychological Science* 7, 359–363.

Dabbs, J. M. Jr., and M. G. Dabbs. 2000. *Heroes, Rogues, and Lovers: Testosterone and Behavior.* New York: McGraw-Hill.

Daly, Martin, and Margo I. Wilson. 1998. "The Evolutionary Social Psychology of Family Violence." Pp. 431–456 in *Handbook of Evolutionary Psychology*, edited by Charles Crawford and Dennis L. Krebs. Mahwah, NJ: Lawrence Erlbaum.

Donaldson, Zoe R., and Larry J. Young. 2008. "Oxytocin, Vasopressin, and the Neurogenetics of Sociality." *Science* 322, 900–904.

Fisek, M. H., and R. Ofshe. 1970. "The Process of Status Evolution." *Sociometry* 33, 327–346.

Freese, Jeremy. 2008. "Genetics and the Social Science Explanation of Individual Outcomes." *American Journal of Sociology* 114, 1–35.

Gottfredson, Michael R., and Travis Hirschi. 1990. *A General Theory of Crime*. Stanford, CA: Stanford University Press.

Guo, Guang, Michael E. Roettger, and Tianji Cai. 2008. "The Integration of Genetic Propensities into Social-Control Models of Delinquency and Violence among Male Youths." *American Sociological Review* 73, 543–568.

Hamilton, W. D. 1964. "The Genetical Evolution of Social Behavior." *Journal of Theoretical Biology* 7, 1–52.

Hrdy, Sarah. 1999. *Mother Nature.* New York: Ballantine.

Kalma, A. 1991. "Hierarchisation and Dominance Assessment at First Glance." *European Journal of Social Psychology* 21, 165–181.

Kimura, Doreen. 1999. *Sex Differences in Cognition.* Cambridge, MA: MIT Press.

Lopreato, Joseph, and Timothy Crippen. 2002. *Crisis in Sociology: The Need for Darwin*. New Brunswick, NJ: Transaction.

Mazur, A., and A. Booth. 1998. "Testosterone and Dominance in Men." *Behavioral and Brain Sciences* 21, 353–363.

Robinson, Gene E., Russell D. Fernald, and David F. Clayton. 2008. "Genes and Social Behavior." *Science* 322, 896–900.

Seabright, Paul. 2005. *The Company of Strangers. A Natural History of Economic Life.* Princeton, NJ: Princeton University Press.

Shepher, Israel. 1983. *The Kibbutz: An Anthropological Study*. Norwood, PA: Norwood Editions.

Smuts, Barbara. 1995. "The Evolutionary Origins of Patriarchy." *Human Nature* 6(1), 1–32.

Trivers, R. 1972. "Parental Investment and Sexual Selection." Pp. 136–179 in *Sexual Selection and the Descent of Man, 1871–1971,* edited by Bernard Campbell. Chicago: Aldine.

van den Berghe, Pierre. 1991. *The Ethnic Phenomenon.* New York: Elsevier.

Weisfeld, Carol Cronin, Glenn E. Weisfeld, and John W. Callaghan. 1982. "Female Inhibition in Mixed-Sex Competition among Young Adolescents." *Ethology and Sociobiology* 3, 29–42.

Whitmeyer, Joseph M. 1997. "Endogamy as a Basis for Ethnic Behavior." *Sociological Theory* 15(2), 162–178.

CULTURE

Socialization, Norms, and Roles

3

IN JANUARY 2002 RORY STEWART walked across Afghanistan, a predominantly Muslim country. Along the way, he had the following conversation, begun by Abdul Haq:

> "How much does it cost to buy a wife in England?"
> "But you are already married."
> "I want a second wife."
> "Nothing. You don't have to pay in England."
> "Then why don't I just go to England and get one for free instead of paying five thousand dollars here?"
> "No reason," I said.
> Abdul Haq looked at me suspiciously.
>
> —Stewart (2004, p. 117)

Abdul Haq is suspicious because Stewart is describing a marriage practice very different from his own. England is a modern, industrialized society in which men and women have similar rights, and there is no bride price custom (purchase of a wife from her parents). Monogamy is the law—no one can have more than one wife at a time. Afghanistan is a premodern, poor, agrarian society in which men and women have very different rights, and there is a bride price custom (payments to the parents of the bride). Afghanistan is also a Muslim country, and under Islamic law men may have up to four wives at once (see Photo 3.1).

Although the biological nature of all humans leads us to expect certain universals across human societies, there is also a great deal of cultural variation, and that variation must be learned. As a small child, Rory Stewart learned the marriage practices of his **culture,** just as Abdul Haq learned the marriage practices in his culture. In this chapter, we discuss how children learn a language, develop a self, and are socialized into their own society and culture.

Culture The totality of norms, values, beliefs, behavior, and material objects that form a people's way of life.

PHOTO 3.1 Faiz Mohammed, 40, and Ghulam Haider, 11, sit in her home prior to their wedding in rural Damarda Village, Afghanistan, on September 11, 2005. In Afghanistan, approximately 57% of all girls are married before they reach the legal minimum age of 16. One of the reasons Afghanistan has such a high maternal mortality rate is because of pregnancies in 10- to 14-year-old girls. Source: © Stephanie Sinclair/VII Photo Agency.

In the second half of the chapter we learn how the subsistence technology of a society is an important shaper of a society's culture. The cultures of agricultural societies such as Afghanistan have more in common with each other than with the cultures of industrial societies such as England. Conversely, cultures in industrial societies such as England, the United States, and Germany tend to have more in common with each other than with cultures in agricultural societies such as Afghanistan. For example, buying a bride is a common cultural practice in poor agricultural societies such as Afghanistan, whereas it is rare in rich industrial societies such as England and the United States.

BIOLOGICAL BASES OF CULTURAL LEARNING

Language Acquisition

A fully developed language is a human universal. All humans instinctively learn a language starting as toddlers. Of course, the language they learn depends on the social group in which they are raised. A baby raised in the United States will learn English, and a baby raised in Japan will learn to speak Japanese. There does seem to be a window of time during which humans are predisposed to learn a language, after which language acquisition becomes difficult if not impossible. This is suggested by the case of the boy, Victor of Aveyron, who grew up in the wilds of France without learning language. He was found in 1897 at the age of approximately 9. Three years later, he agreed to be cared for by people, but he never managed to learn more than a few words (Gazzaniga, 2008, p. 222). There is other evidence that the "language acquisition device" shuts down as we grow older. Immigrant children can learn to speak the language of their new country without an accent if they arrive before approximately age 15. After age 15, they will learn the language of the new country but are likely to always have a pronounced foreign accent.

There is also evidence that hand gestures are tightly connected to language, which is why individuals often gesture when they speak. The speech center is located in the left hemisphere of the brain, the same side that controls the motor movements of the right side of the body (Gazzaniga, 2008, p. 62). Hand gestures (of both left and right hands) also appear to be governed by the left side of the brain. The tendency to use gestures is innate and often unconscious. Blind people gesture as they speak at the same rate as sighted people and in the same way. Deaf people also learn to speak with their hands and not just in a sign language they are taught. Isolated communities of deaf people will develop their own set of hand gestures with their own syntax. People talking on the phone use hand gestures even though the person they are speaking to cannot see them. Just as people learn different languages, however, people in different cultures learn different hand gestures and learn different ways to use hand gestures. In some cultures (e.g., Italy) hand gestures are used prominently, whereas in other cultures (e.g., Sweden) hand gestures are used sparingly.

How do babies learn language? Initially, babies do not understand any words, but they do understand tones. Babies are particularly attracted to "motherese," nonsense language in sing-song tones that people in all cultures

Mirror neurons Neurons in the brain that fire when a person performs an activity or expresses an emotion and when a person sees another person performing the same activity or expressing the same emotion.

tend to use when addressing a baby. Later, before they are 2 years old, they begin to understand what the words mean. How do they do this? Imitation seems key, and part of the way this occurs involves the **mirror neuron** system present in the brains of all individuals. Giacomo Rizzolatti, Leonardo Fogassi, and Vittorio Gallese (2004) first discovered mirror neurons in monkeys in 1996. These researchers found that when a monkey performs an action, these mirror neurons fire. They also fire when a monkey merely *sees* another monkey perform the same action. Humans also appear to have these mirror neurons, and they are highly important in learning, imitation, and, as we shall see, empathy. You can think of learning language as following a pattern such as this: Mom offers me a dark brown substance and says something that sounds like "chocolate" as she does so. When I try it, I find that I really like that stuff, so I am keenly attentive when she says chocolate. My mirror neurons fire, helping me to imitate mom's physical actions when she says the word chocolate, and lo and behold, I can say the word chocolate. At first I may not say it correctly, so mom very helpfully repeats the word, my mirror neurons practice it, and then I try to say it. Then I say it a lot, hoping she understands that I really want some more of it.

Mirror neurons are involved in more than just language learning. University of Washington psychologists Andrew Meltzoff and M. Keith Moore (1977) were the first to show that newborn babies imitate facial expressions (e.g., sticking a tongue out). Other research has confirmed that babies imitate facial expressions accurately from the age of 42 minutes to 72 hours. A researcher will stick out a tongue; the baby will stick out a tongue. By the age of 3 or 4 months, children understand the meaning of what is being copied and will only copy it if they want to. Much later, children imitate more than just facial expressions; they imitate all the behaviors of people they see around them. Imitation becomes role play, and it is an important mechanism of socialization into a society and culture. So small children act out different roles they observe—as mom, dad, doctor, shop assistant, waiter, teacher, and so on. In short, mirror neurons are involved in both learning a language and learning how our social world works.

SOCIAL INTERACTION AND THE DEVELOPMENT OF THE SELF

Before role play can begin in earnest, however, an important development must occur (generally between the ages of approximately 3 and 4 years). Children not only learn to imitate but also learn to be able to see things from another person's point of view. Children at this age can pass the "false belief" test; that is, they learn that other people may have false beliefs. There are various versions of this test, but it goes something like the following "Sally and Ann" test: Sally and Ann are in a room being watched by the subject. The subject watches while Sally hides candy in one of two identical containers with Ann watching. Ann places a mark on the box that holds the candy as the subject watches. Then Ann leaves the room. While Ann is gone, Sally switches the containers and puts the candy in the unmarked container. When Ann comes back into the room, the subject is asked: "Which container will Ann pick to find the candy?" Children older than age 4 or 5 years understand that Ann will pick the wrong container (the marked container) because she has a false belief, whereas younger children will think she will pick the correct (unmarked) container containing the candy. Children who can pass the false belief test are said to have developed a **"theory of mind mechanism."** They understand that others can think differently from themselves and that those beliefs can be false.

Theory of mind mechanism
A mechanism in the brain that allows understanding of the thoughts, beliefs, and intentions of others.

Differentiating between ourselves and others, and what we believe and what others believe, is key to developing a sense of self. The early sociologist George Herbert Mead (1863–1931) described this process as follows: We develop a notion of the self by understanding how we and our intentions/goals/beliefs differ from others and their intentions/goals/beliefs. We can imagine how another will respond to our behavior. At this point, we begin to see ourselves as others see us—we can take the role of the "other." This has important implications for our self-image. Charles Horton Cooley (1864–1929) described this as the "looking glass self"—a self based on how we understand others see us. We do not necessarily have to accept others' view of us, but even our understanding of that discrepancy helps us understand who we are.

Development of the Self

Psychologists Kihlstrom and Klein (1997) suggest that there are four categories of self-knowledge:

1. A concept of ourselves accompanied by an explanation of how we got to be the way we are. For example, "I am self-sufficient because I have always had to take care of myself."

BOX 3.1
BEHAVIORAL GENETICS RESEARCH

Behavioral genetics research examines the genetic origins of both mental illness and personality and behavioral traits. This kind of research often utilizes twins, particularly twins who are reared apart. The research takes advantage of the fact that identical twins share 100% of their genes in common, yet if they are reared apart, their home environments while they were growing up were different. This allows researchers to separate the genetic effects on personality from the environmental effects on personality. One of the largest of these studies is the Minnesota Twin Study conducted by psychologists at the University of Minnesota. They found that traits such as intelligence, as well as mental illnesses such as schizophrenia and depression, have a substantial genetic component. Sociologists have used the techniques of behavioral genetics to examine the genetic correlates of a variety of social behaviors, including severe delinquency (Guo, Roettger, and Cai, 2008) and dropping out of school (Shanahan et al., 2008).

2. Self as narrative: our life story, according to ourselves. For example, "I grew up in a city and have always been a city girl."
3. Self as image: details about face, body, and gestures. For example, "I am tall, dark, and handsome, and have good reflexes."
4. Personality traits, memories, and experiences. For example, "I have always had a way with the ladies" and "I don't like celery."

Michael Gazzaniga (2008) suggests that the brain gets lots of information about oneself from others and from the environment, and the left brain "interpreter" puts it all together as a sense of self. Some of this information is determined by our genetic endowment. Not everyone is born with genes that allow them to become tall, dark, and handsome. Behavioral genetics research also suggests that many personality traits (e.g., boldness or shyness) are inherited (see Box 3.1).

Our sense of self is also influenced by our life experiences, including our social experiences. You don't know if you are shy or bold if you never encounter strangers. You don't know you don't like celery if you have never tasted celery. You can't know you have a way with the ladies if you live in a society in which young men and women are strictly segregated. One's experience of relationships also influences our sense of self. An experience of warm, loving, enduring relationships leaves a different imprint on a person's sense of self than an experience of cold, short-lived relationships. Who those relationships were with also matters. Were those people bookish? Athletic? Computer geeks? Also, one's experience of having social status in social relationships matters. **Social status** refers to a person's position in a social hierarchy. A person who has always found him- or herself at the bottom of the social heap has a different self concept than a person who has always found him- or herself at the top of the social heap. Likewise, losing status and gaining status both influence one's sense of self. In her book *No Two Alike*, Judith Rich Harris (2006) suggests that these are the things (past relationships and status acquisition) that make even identical twins, who share all their genetic inheritance, distinctive as individuals.

Social status A person's position in a social hierarchy; honor or prestige within the social group.

Strangely enough, family environment does not seem to make as much difference as we usually think, at least for personality traits. The family environment is that created by the family in which a person grows up. Most of the similarity in personality between people in the same family can be accounted for by the genetic inheritance they share. Much of the rest is attributed to nonshared environment—that is, not the family environment but, rather, the environments (in school, at play, at work, with friends, etc.) the child finds him- or herself in as he or she goes through life.

ROLES

By understanding others' point of view we can also act out roles. As discussed in Chapter 2, a role is the behavior expected of someone in a particular social position. You have a cut finger and you believe I am a doctor. You expect me to do something about your finger. Once again, we do not have to accept that the role is who we really are, but we understand that someone in that social position is supposed to act that way. Roles also have different statuses or rankings within the group. A person who can tell other people what to do usually has high status, and a person who must do what others tell him or her to do usually has low status. Who gets to play the high-status person (teacher, doctor, or parent) is often very important in children's games. Status remains important to people throughout their lives.

Goffman: Performing Social Roles

For children, the cast of characters in their lives is limited to parents, siblings, relatives, classmates, teachers, and a few others. Yet each child does not play the same role with this cast of others. Judith Rich Harris, in her book *The Nurture Assumption* (1998), notes how the same child will often play a very different role at home in the family than at school with his or her friends. At home, the child may have the role of the eldest child, the bossy one who tells the younger children what to do. At school, in his or her peer group, that same child may not be bossy at all—quite the opposite.

Later, the cast of characters includes bosses, subordinates, co-workers, and so on. However, the status of these people remains important: their position in the group—who can tell others what to do and who cannot. Erving Goffman studied both social roles and **role performance**, which he defined as "the actual conduct of an individual in [a] position." He noticed that in modern societies we typically have to shift from role to role, and to facilitate that transition we use props—the appropriate clothing and accessories, for instance. Thus, we take on one role at work, one role at home, and yet another role with our friends at a party. Goffman particularly studied how people use scenery, props, costumes, and behavior in their role performances. So when people go to work, they typically dress the part—in conservative clothes with a briefcase or a sensible bag. At home, people often dress more casually and more comfortably. At a party, people often dress in splashier clothes: Women wear heels and carry sparkly purses, and men wear their dressier pants and jackets. People also play roles together. Thus, co-workers will form a team in interacting with customers and clients. Husbands and wives will form a team when disciplining a child or hosting a dinner party.

Role performance The actual conduct of an individual in a position.

Goffman also pointed out that in many roles we have both *frontstage* behaviors and *backstage* behaviors. Thus, we have one set of behaviors for use in our on-stage role in front of our clients or customers and another set of behaviors we use when in the presence of our co-workers and friends. With our clients and customers, we are typically polite and accommodating, whereas with our co-workers and friends we are more relaxed and casual. Sometimes the difference in frontstage and backstage behaviors can be quite dramatic. Photos 3.2 and 3.3 of concentration camp guards show the guards' backstage behaviors. On stage, these people were responsible for putting thousands of people to death. Backstage, they listened to music and ate blueberries.

PHOTO 3.2 Nazi officers and female auxiliaries of the concentration camp Auschwitz pose on a wooden bridge in Solahütte, June 21, 1944. During this time, the gas chambers at Auschwitz were operating at maximum efficiency. Source: United States Holocaust Memorial Museum.

PHOTO 3.3 Female auxiliaries and SS officer Karl Hoecker sit on a fence railing in Solahütte eating bowls of blueberries, June 21, 1944. Source: United States Holocaust Memorial Museum.

Mirror Neurons and Empathy

We have seen that learning to see things from other people's point of view is important in learning roles. Learning to take the perspective of the other is a developmental stage all normally developing children experience. Autistic children, however, never pass the false belief test, and as a result their ability to function socially is severely hampered. Autistic children do not play pretend and do not act out roles the way normal children do. Because they can never understand how another person sees the world, they can never fully understand why others do what they do, and as a result, the social world is a very confusing place for them.

Mirror neurons are involved in seeing things from another person's perspective and empathy—learning to feel what others are feeling. If we see someone take a bad fall, we wince. If we see someone who is sad, we often feel sad ourselves. These are our mirror neurons at work, mimicking the emotional states of the person we are watching. Therefore, to a certain extent, we really do feel others' pain. Some people do this to a greater extent than others. In an experiment involving volunteer couples, couples were placed in a **functional magnetic resonance imaging scanner,** and one was given a painful shock to the hand while the other watched. The scans showed that both the observer and the person experiencing the pain had activity in the anterior cingulate, the area of the brain associated with the emotional perception of pain. Experiments show that the subjects who rated themselves as more empathetic were more likely to experience brain activity in the anterior cingulate than others (Gazzaniga, 2008, p. 170). As one might expect, autistic children show deficits in the mirror neuron system (Dapretto et al., 2006).

Functional magnetic imaging scanner Machine that measures the change in blood flow related to neural activity in the brain or spinal cord.

One wonders if the Nazi concentration camp guards had deficits in their mirror neuron systems. In fact, one of the reasons for the creation of the death camps and gas chambers in the first place was to create a more impersonal way of executing thousands of people. In the beginning, the Nazis used cruder techniques of lining people up and shooting them, but many German soldiers balked at shooting defenseless men, women, and children (Mak, 2007). It was easier to get these soldiers and other underlings to herd people into gas chambers. Denying the essential humanity of the victims was another way Nazis overcame the natural human tendency to empathy. As discussed in Chapter 12, such denials of the enemy group's humanity are common in group conflict.

SOCIETAL DIFFERENCES IN ROLES AND CULTURE

All individuals learn about their society and how it functions, and also how to function as part of that society, through imitation and role playing. We all start out with the same equipment, but depending on the society in which we grow up, that will have very different results. The society in which we grow up affects the language and culture we learn and the roles we play on a day-to-day basis. Clearly, what one learns differs greatly from society to society. Of great importance as a shaper of a society's roles and culture is how people go about making a living—getting food to eat and shelter from the elements. We call this the **subsistence technology** of the society. Societies with the same subsistence technology have somewhat similar social roles and cultures, whereas societies with different subsistence technologies have very different social roles and cultures.

Subsistence technology How people go about making a living–getting food to eat and shelter from the elements.

See Photos 3.4 and 3.5 of the aboriginal man and the businessman. The roles the aboriginal man played in his life were very different from the roles the man with the cell phone will play in his life. The skills associated with these roles are also very different. The aboriginal man had the role of hunter, which required skills in tracking and killing animals with very simple weapons, and associated skills of living off the land. The man in Photo 3.5 has the role of businessman, which requires skills of negotiation and financial acumen along with familiarity with modern technology such as cell phones and computers. These roles and skills took a long time to learn; as a result, both men would be at a loss to play the other's role without substantial preparation.

THE IMPORTANCE OF SUBSISTENCE TECHNOLOGY

The societies with the simplest subsistence technology are hunting and gathering societies. Hunting and gathering societies used to cover the earth, but now there are very few such societies (Figure 3.1). During the past century and a half, anthropologists have studied the few remaining groups of hunters and gatherers, including the Australian aborigines and the Bushmen of the Kalahari Desert in southern Africa. Our knowledge of these societies comes from those studies.

In hunting and gathering societies, people survive by hunting wild animals, birds, or fish and gathering wild foodstuffs such as nuts, fruits, berries,

PHOTO 3.4 Simon, an Australian Aborigine of the Yarra Yarra tribe. Source: Portrait of Simon by George Perry, National Library of Australia.

roots, and seeds. In these societies, there are very few roles to take, and they are mostly decided on the basis of age, sex, and kinship status. There is a mother, father, children, and other relatives. Usually there is also a headman of the group, but that is it. There is little occupational specialization, so although someone may be a better toolmaker than others, that is not what

PHOTO 3.5 Businessman at airport. Source: iStockphoto.

they do most of the time. The primary division of labor is between men and women, with men being mostly engaged in activities such as hunting and warfare and women mostly engaged in child care, cooking, and gathering foodstuffs. Anthropologists note that in many of these societies, subsistence activities take up very little time in the day. The rest of the day is left over for

FIGURE 3.1 Time line.

Hunting and gathering societies	**15,000 yrs BP** *Neolithic Revolution* Agriculture begins	**5,000 yrs BP** First agrarian societies	**200 yrs BP** *Industrial Revolution*

BP = Before Present

leisure activities—singing, socializing, and playing. For this reason, these societies have been referred to as the "original affluent societies."

Neolithic Revolution The beginning of agriculture approximately 15,000 years ago.

Horticultural societies are similar to hunting and gathering societies, but food intake is supplemented with foods that are planted in gardens and tended by people. As a result, sometimes these societies are called gardening societies. Horticultural societies first emerged with the **Neolithic Revolution** (the beginning of agriculture) approximately 15,000 years ago. They are still found today scattered in different areas of the world, including the New Guinea Highlands, as well as areas of Africa, Asia, and Central and South America.

In horticultural or gardening societies, there is some specialization, especially by age and sex. Women do much of the gardening work, except for groundbreaking, which is usually performed by men. Each settlement usually comprises several hundred people. There is usually a headman, who is often head of the most extensive family or tribe. There are more status differences between individuals in these societies because the headman and his extended family are often given some special prerogatives and privileges. There is more occupational specialization in these societies, even to the extent of having some people (e.g., headmen or priests) perform some functions full-time. Sometimes there are even slaves—people who are regarded as owned by other people. The larger the horticultural society, the greater these status differences become.

Industrial Revolution The onset of large-scale manufacturing. It is typically dated to 1780 in Europe and slightly later in North America.

Agrarian societies are distinguished from horticultural societies by the use of the plow in agriculture. The plow is a large implement used to turn up the soil to ready it for planting. Plows may or may not have wheels. The plow is typically drawn by some sort of large, domesticated animal—buffalo in Asia and horses and oxen in Europe. Asia, western Europe, and North America were dominated by agrarian societies before the **Industrial Revolution**, or the beginning of large-scale manufacturing industries.

In agrarian societies, there is much greater differentiation of individuals by status and by occupation. The greater productivity of plow agriculture means that agrarian societies tend to be much more populous societies than horticultural societies. Most people live in rural areas on farms, but cities are common. There is pronounced economic specialization and, for the first time, hereditary inequality. Many occupations (priest, scribe, weapon maker, smith, etc.) are full-time occupations, and often these occupations are inherited from father to son (although sometimes from mother to daughter). Slavery is common. Most people in agrarian societies work the land, whether as free or unfree workers.

Ascribed versus Achieved Statuses

In agrarian societies for the first time we see statuses that are ascribed at birth. *Ascribed statuses* are statuses that a person is born into. That is, an individual may be born into a role—an occupation (farmer) or person who is regarded as the property of another (serfs or slaves). Ascribed statuses may be contrasted with *achieved statuses*. These are statuses that one achieves over one's lifetime. There are some achieved statuses in agrarian societies (a successful warrior may take over as monarch, for instance), but many individual statuses are determined at birth.

Where you are born in the status hierarchy in an agrarian society has tremendous influence on how your life is lived. In most agrarian societies, a very small percentage of the population make up the ruling elite. These people live lives of great affluence and much leisure. A very large percentage of the population make up the lower groups, who are often impoverished.

Industrial and Postindustrial Societies

The Industrial Revolution is typically dated to approximately 1780 in Europe and slightly later in North America. This time period ushered in a new kind of society, where much of the goods and services of the society are produced outside of agriculture in industry. In these societies, most people work outside of agriculture, in industry, trade, or services. Whereas in agrarian societies approximately 90% of people live in the country and work the land, in industrial societies only approximately 10% or less do so. Industrial societies are the most populous societies. Most people live in cities and work in factories, businesses, or service industries. There is a great deal of occupational specialization. There is some hereditary inequality but not as much as in agrarian societies. There are many complex groups, including corporations, organizations, and government agencies, and these groups in turn play roles in the larger society. There are a great many possible roles in all these groups.

Norms and Technology

In all societies, there are norms associated with different roles. Norms for various roles differ from society to society, often for historical or other reasons. However, technology also shapes norms. For example, Joan Huber (2007) notes that for much of human history, the only possible food for infants was breast milk. Even in agrarian societies, in which breast milk could be supplemented with cow's milk, breast-feeding would have been extended for many of a child's first years—in fact, up to the age of approximately 4 years in many societies. Thus, the norm for mothers was to breast-feed their infants. In industrialized societies, baby formula was not introduced until after World War II, in the late 1940s and 1950s. For the first time, mothers had an alternative source of food for their infants that was safe and nutritionally complete. Suddenly, norms about breast-feeding changed, and in the United States it became the norm for babies to be bottle-fed. Today, doctors and individuals are more aware of the health benefits of breast-feeding, and norms, at least for some groups, have changed back to breast-feeding (Huber, 2007).

With most norms there is a sense of moral obligation attached. The norms describe not only what people typically do but also what they typically *ought* to do. Thus, when most mothers breast-fed their babies, that was the morally acceptable behavior. When most mothers bottle-fed their babies, that was the morally acceptable behavior. Woe betide those mothers who went against the norm, as they would often be criticized as doing the wrong thing for their babies.

Norms can differ from group to group, and this is typical in a large and diverse society such as our own. Certain groups in today's society (e.g., members of La Leche League) are strong proponents of breast-feeding, whereas other groups and individuals continue to prefer bottle-feeding.

CULTURE

The roles and associated norms are part of a society's or group's culture. **Culture** is the totality of norms, values, beliefs, behavior, and material objects that form a people's way of life. In simpler societies, such as hunting and gathering and horticultural societies, there is usually one predominant culture. In many complex societies (agrarian, industrial, and post-industrial societies), there are often many cultures. There is usually a dominant culture of the larger society or the dominant group in the society, and often there are subcultures—smaller subgroups that function by their own rules.

Culture The totality of norms, values, beliefs, behavior, and material objects that form a people's way of life.

In our own society, there is the dominant American culture and then there are a variety of regional and other subcultures. Thus, within the United States, for example, there are distinctive regional cultures in the South, the Northeast, and the West. Within those regions there are even further divisions—between religious groups, groups of differing national origins, or groups of differing sexual orientation. Even children and teenagers sometimes have their own subcultures.

Culture Shock

Sometimes cultures differ so much from one group or society to the next that a person coming from a different group or society experiences culture shock on first experiencing a new society. For example, when I was 18 years old, I came from Sydney, Australia, to rural Mississippi as an exchange student. I found the accent, manners, and behaviors very different from those to which I was accustomed. Although people in Mississippi spoke the same language as I (English), I often had great difficulty understanding what people said to me. I did not know exactly how I was expected to behave, and I kept making mistakes. For example, in Australian society I had felt very free to explore my environment on my own. Thus, I did the same in the small Mississippi town I found myself in, and one day I wandered into the "wrong" (read poor and black) side of town. I was severely chastised by my (white) host mother, who could not understand why I was wandering around. Furthermore, I felt that my identity had vanished. In my own society, I knew who I was and where I stood relative to others. But I did not understand my place in the new society at all. I knew what I liked doing (including exploring) and in my own society that was OK. Now, my old activities were not always possible and not necessarily OK. Worse, people did things I did not approve of, and they thought that was OK. I got depressed. What I had is a culture shock, and depression is a common way that culture shock is experienced. Eventually, I, like many new immigrants, learned what behaviors were expected of me, and I overcame my dislike of some of the behaviors I had found problematic. I found a new role(s), found my identity in the new society, and became happy again.

Why Do Cultures Differ, Even among Societies That Are Technologically Similar?

Why do cultures differ from society to society? Part of the reason cultures differ is due to the subsistence technology of the society—how most people earn their living. However, although hunting and gathering societies share many cultural commonalities, they differ a lot also. The same is true of all other types of societies, including industrial societies. No one would say that Japan and the United States are culturally the same, even though they share the same industrial/post-industrial subsistence technology. Japanese people work in businesses and drive cars and take trains to work just as Americans do. However, when they get to work, they greet the people they meet by bowing, and Japanese people often take off their shoes before going into their offices; Americans do no such thing. In Japan, women are expected to leave the workforce after they are married; Americans do not expect that. What creates these differences? Sociologists have spilled a lot of ink explaining why cultures differ, and often it is difficult to say exactly why things are done one way in this place and a somewhat different way in another place. The reasons have to do with history—what happened in the past affects what happens in the present. For example, the United States has a history as a frontier society settled primarily (at first) by the English; Japan has a history as a distinctive feudal agrarian society. A feudal society is an agrarian society with a hereditary nobility (often given honorific titles such as prince, duke, or lord) that owns the majority of the land. The land is worked by peasants who may be free or unfree but owe particular obligations to their lord. This means the legacy of status groups is different in Japan and the United States. Japan still has the historical legacy of an emperor and a royal family, whereas the United States has no royalty. Until recently, Japan also had a warrior class—the samurai—and this historical legacy, some argue, has helped shape modern Japanese society. Religious practices in each country are also historically different: The United States was founded by Puritans, whereas Japan is home to Shinto Buddhism. Shinto Buddhism is a distinctive Japanese form of Buddhism that combines ancestor worship and animist beliefs (beliefs in spirits) with Buddhism.

These historical differences can explain some of the difference in culture. **Demography** also makes a difference. The United States started out as a sparsely settled place, and it is still far less densely populated than Japan. Formal **institutions** make a difference: Japanese democracy is not quite the same as American democracy, even though Americans wrote the first democratic Japanese constitution (after World War II).

Demography Characteristics of the population, such as its distribution among age and sex groups.

Institutions The formal rules and laws that govern a society; unwritten and written rules of a social group.

SOCIALIZATION

We learn about our own culture from the people around us. By the time we are adults, most of us have internalized our culture—and it is part of our own personal identity. This process of learning and internalizing our culture is referred to as *socialization*. Some socialization is passive; we learn by watching and copying others around us. These others are referred to as **role models**—people who model the roles present in our society. Other socialization is active. Active socialization is when people deliberately try to teach you information or skills, just as I am attempting with this book. In most societies, important agents of socialization are people's immediate families. Fathers and mothers are important teachers of children in most societies. Other people who are close to us—our friends, peers, brothers and sisters, and other relatives—are also important agents of socialization.

Role models People who model the roles present in a society.

In modern, industrial societies such as our own, agents of active socialization include religious organizations, educational systems, and the state. Religious officials teach the moral precepts by which individuals should live their lives, and educational systems teach a variety of intellectual skills, including abstract thought (e.g., the ability to do complex mathematics), as well as citizenship skills. Workplace colleagues, supervisors, and bosses are also important agents of socialization. You have probably had the experience of beginning a new job and learning from co-workers how things operate in that particular workplace.

CONCLUSION

In this chapter, we have learned about the biological bases of the acquisition of language and culture and the importance of mirror neurons in this process. Mirror neurons help us to understand things from other people's point of view, which is an important basis of learning social roles and becoming socialized into a culture. We also learned that the roles available in a culture differ depending on the subsistence technology of the society. Cultures also differ because of religion, demography, and historical chance and circumstance. This does not mean that cultures are infinitely variable, however. Biology keeps "culture on a leash" so there is never as much cultural variation as there potentially could be. The technology and culture of a society also have implications for the types of groups that emerge in that society, and this is the topic of the next chapter.

REFERENCES

Dapretto, M., M. S. Davies, J. H. Pfeifer, A. A. Scott, M. Sigman, S. Y. Bookheimer, and M. Iacobini. 2006. "Understanding Emotions in Others: Mirror Neuron Dysfunction in Children with Autism Spectrum Disorder." *Nature Neuroscience* 9, 28–30.

Gazzaniga, Michael S. 2008. *Human: The Science behind What Makes Us Unique.* New York: HarperCollins.

Guo, Guang, Michael E. Roettger, and Tianji Cai. 2008. "The Integration of Genetic Propensities into Social-Control Models of Delinquency and Violence among Male Youths." *American Sociological Review* 73, 543–568.

Harris, Judith Rich. 1998. *The Nurture Assumption: Why Children Turn out the Way They Do.* New York: Free Press.

———. 2006. *No Two Alike: Human Nature and Human Individuality.* New York: Norton.

Huber, Joan. 2007. *The Origins of Gender Inequality*. Boulder, CO: Paradigm.

Kihlstrom, J. F., and S. B. Klein. 1997. "Self-Knowledge and Self-Awareness." Pp. 5–17 in *The Self across Psychology: Self-Recognition, Self-Awareness, and the Self Concept*, edited by J. D. Snodgrass and R. L. Thompson. New York: New York Academy of Sciences.

Mak, Geert. 2007. *In Europe: Travels through the Twentieth Century*. New York: Pantheon.

Meltzoff, Andrew N., and M. Keith Moore. 1977. "Facial Imitation in Infants." *Science* 198, 75–78.

Rizzolatti, Giacomo, Leonardo Fogassi, and Vittorio Gallese. 2004. "Cortical Mechanisms Subserving Object Grasping, Action Understanding, and Imitation." Pp. 427–440 in *The Cognitive Neurosciences*, edited by Michael S. Gazzaniga, Vol. 3. Cambridge, MA: MIT Press.

Shanahan, Michael J., Stephen Vaisey, Lance D. Erickson, and Andrew Smolen. 2008. "Environmental Contingencies and Genetic Propensities: Social Capital, Educational Continuation, and Dopamine Receptor Gene DRD21." *American Journal of Sociology* 114(Suppl. 1), S260–S286.

Stewart, Rory. 2004. *The Places in Between*. Orlando, FL: Harcourt.

SOCIAL GROUPS
Social Networks, Kin Groups, Classes, Organizations, Status Groups, and Political Groups

4

IN THIS CHAPTER, WE EXAMINE the social networks (connections between individuals) often found in social groups. Next, we examine the social groups that exist in human societies: kin-based groups, economic groups, status groups, and political groups. These groups are based on different individual interests—genetic interests (kin groups), economic interests (classes and companies), status interests (status groups), and political interests (political groups). People in all societies form groups with kin. In larger and more populous societies, people who have similar economic interests, people who share a common lifestyle, or people who have similar political interests often group together. Whether and how individuals with similar interests coalesce into groups in which the members are linked by social networks differs from society to society.

SOCIAL NETWORKS

In late 2007, New York businessman Bernie Madoff told his two sons that his entire investment business operation was a huge Ponzi scheme. This meant that Madoff was taking money from new investors to pay existing individual investors who wanted their cash back, all the while lying to investors that their money was invested and generating solid rates of return. Such a scheme could only work as long as Madoff could find fresh investors. With the credit crisis and economic downturn of late 2007, creditors were calling for their cash more quickly than Madoff could sign on new investors. As a result, the whole scheme was falling apart. The game was up. Madoff's investors were widely flung around the globe. Some of the investors were other investment companies, such as the Fairfield Greenwich Group; also included were banks, charities, universities, towns, and individuals. All in all, investors lost approximately $50 billion with Madoff (by Madoff's own estimate).

How did all those people come to trust one person with so much money? The *New York Times* (Henriques, 2008, p. A1) explains it as follows: "Initially, he tapped local money pulled in from country clubs and charity dinners, where investors sought him out to casually plead with him to manage their savings so they could start reaping the steady, solid returns their envied friends were getting. Then, he and his promoters set sights on Europe, again framing the investments as memberships in a select club."

Madoff found investors through networks of friends and acquaintances, both in the United States and overseas. Friends, relatives, and acquaintances told their friends, relatives, and acquaintances about the high and steady returns the Madoff funds seemed to offer, and people invested. To many who attended a high school reunion with the Madoffs, "it seemed that the room could be divided into those who had invested with Mr. Madoff and those who were hoping to" (Segal and Cowan, 2009, p. A1).

Social network The pattern of ties or connections between individuals or groups.

The network of Madoff investors is just one example of a **social network** (although most social networks are not used for such criminal ends). Other examples include the network of users of Websites such as Facebook or MySpace, friendship networks, professional networks, hobbyist networks, and kin (family) networks. There are, of course, networks of criminals and terrorists. Networks are at the heart of most social groups (although not all).

Sociologists who study social networks in sociology have found several characteristics of all social networks.

Small World Syndrome

The first characteristic of a social network is what is referred to as the "small world syndrome." People throughout the world are closely connected through networks. (See Box 4.1.)

In 1967, social psychologist Stanley Milgram wanted to test the hypothesis that members of any large social network would be connected to each other through a short chain of acquaintances. To do this, he sent information packets to a few hundred randomly selected individuals in Nebraska and Kansas. Each packet contained a letter detailing the study's purpose (to forward the packet to the target person in Boston) and the name, address,

BOX 4.1
THE KEVIN BACON GAME

The trivia game Six Degrees of Kevin Bacon is based on the concept of the small world phenomenon and rests on the assumption that any actor can be linked through his or her film roles to actor Kevin Bacon. The game requires a group of players to try to connect any film actor in history to Kevin Bacon as quickly as possible and in as few links as possible. The game was created in 1994 by three students at Albright College–Craig Fass, Brian Turtle, and Mike Ginelli. According to an interview with the three in the Spring 1999 issue of the college's magazine, the *Albright Reporter*, they were watching *Footloose* during a heavy snowstorm. When the film was followed by *Quicksilver*, they began to speculate on how many movies Bacon had been in and the number of people he had worked with. In the interview, Brian Turtle said, "It became one of our stupid party tricks, I guess. People would throw names at us and we'd connect them to Kevin Bacon" (Source: Wikipedia). There is an online link to the game at http://www.thekevinbacongame.com.

Ironically, Kevin Bacon was among those who lost money to Bernie Madoff (Rueb, 2008).

and occupation of the target person. First, participants were asked if they knew the target person in Boston on a first-name basis. If so, they were asked to forward the packet directly to that person. If they did not (which was most often the case), they were asked to send the packet on to a friend or relative they knew personally who was most likely to know the target. In all cases, they were asked to sign their name on a roster before they sent the package on. They were also asked to mail a postcard to the researchers at Harvard so that the researchers could track the chain's progression toward the target. When and if the packet eventually reached the target person in Boston, the researchers could examine the roster to count the number of times it had been forwarded from person to person. In addition, for packets that never reached the destination, the postcards helped identify the break point in the chain.

In the end, many packets never did reach the target. A significant problem was that often people refused to pass the packet forward, and thus the packet never reached its destination. Of the packets that did make it to their destination, some would arrive by just 1 or 2 links, whereas others would take as many as 9 or 10. The average path to the target took approximately 5.5 or 6 links between people. Hence, the researchers concluded that people in the United States are separated by approximately six people on average, and hence the term "six degrees of separation" (Travers and Milgram, 1969). A different study conducted an e-mail–based version of the same experiment and found median chain length of 5–7 on a worldwide scale (Dodds, Muhamad, and Watts, 2003; Watts, 2003).

Efficacy of Weak Ties and Structural Holes

Most of the ties that bound the Madoff investors together were weak ties—ties between acquaintances rather than close friends. Most of the ties that bind people together in the "small world" studies are also weak ties. In 1973, Mark Granovetter published an influential article, "The Strength of Weak Ties," in which he made the argument that weak ties are often more important than strong ties at many times in a person's life. This is because close friends know what you already know—acquaintances know what you do not. He supported his argument by showing how people often find jobs not through information from close friends or relatives but through information from acquaintances—"weak ties" (Granovetter, 1974). Think about the last time you got a job—perhaps for the summer. You may have beat the pavement going into all the places you thought might be hiring and asked for a job. Chances are that did not work too well. Or you might have heard through an acquaintance (probably not your best friend) that a place was hiring, and you got there quickly. Chances are that was the job you got.

Related to Granovetter's idea of the strength of weak ties is the notion of *structural holes*. Burt (2004) pointed out that people who link two networks together (at a structural hole) tend to have more influence than people who are only located in one network. This is because they can bring knowledge and ideas from the second network into the first, and vice versa. This is easy to see in the arts. In the visual arts, for instance, the modern artists (e.g., Gauguin, Matisse, Picasso, and many others) who were familiar with the art of Africa, Asia, and elsewhere were able to introduce those styles into European art. As a result, their art was considered both innovative and influential. Other people who are highly influential in a network are those who are central and who are connected to many other people. For example, the people who staff the Democratic or Republican National Committees tend to be highly influential in the Democratic and Republican parties because they have links to Democrats and Republicans throughout the country.

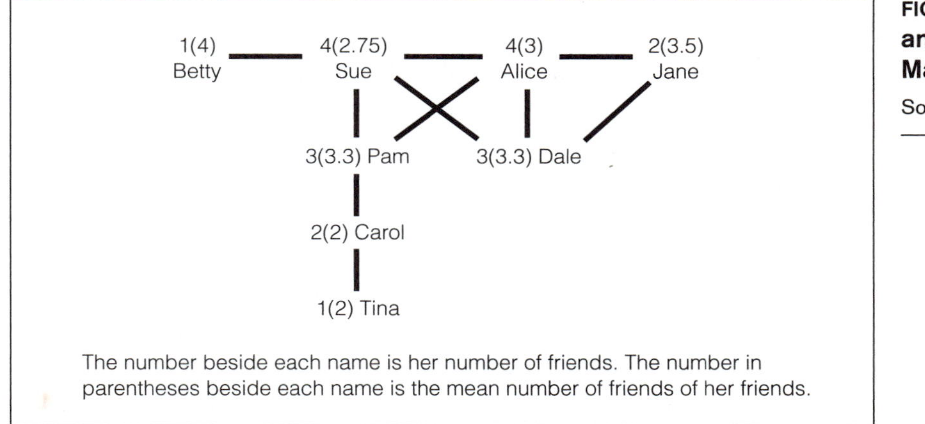

FIGURE 4.1 Friendships among eight girls at Marketville High School.

Source: Feld (1991).

Density and Longevity

Network analysts have found that over time networks tend to become more dense; that is, they tend to contain increasingly more ties (or links) between people in the network. This is because friends of one person often become friends themselves (also known as the principle of **transitivity**; see Cartwright and Harary, 1956; Moody, 1999). The denser a network becomes, the more likely it is to be long lived. Networks with few connections tend not to last very long.

Transitivity A principle from the analysis of social networks that states that friends of one person often become friends themselves.

Why Your Friends Are More Popular Than You

Network analysts have also determined why it is very likely that your friends have more friends than you do. This is because people with lots of friends turn up in more social networks. Thus, it is inevitable that any individual's friendship networks disproportionately include those people with lots of friends, pushing up the average number of your friend's friends. This means that the average number of friends of your friends is typically greater than the number of your own friends.

Look at Figure 4.1. You will notice that in most cases (five of eight), the number of friends each person has is exceeded by the mean (average) number of the friends of his or her friends (number in parentheses). This is because the popular girls Sue and Alice feature in more people's networks than the less popular people.

FAMILIES, CLANS, AND TRIBES

Networks, or ties of acquaintanceship, exist in many social groups but not all. Think of your extended family, including all your cousins, second cousins, parents' relatives, and so on—everyone who is still alive. Probably many of your more distant relatives you could not name and may not have met. Some you may only have heard about in stories your parents or other relatives have told you. It may be that you are well acquainted with all your extended family, but this is fairly rare in a highly mobile society such as the United States. In U.S. society, as in many developed, industrial societies, the extended family is less culturally important than in many other societies. There are no names for kinship units more than one step beyond the nuclear family. Cousins, aunts, and uncles are about as far as it typically goes. Yet even though your kin group may not be very socially important, it still exists as a "group" in that all the members share a common characteristic—they are related to you. At some point, someone may hold a family reunion, and then you may get to meet all of these people.

Clan Extended family that is typically divided into lineages based either on *patrilines* (tracing descent in the male line) or *matrilines* (tracing descent in the female line). Clans often claim descent from a single, often mythical ancestor.

Tribe Groups of clans usually linked by marriage and political ties.

In many preindustrial societies, the extended family or **clan** is very important socially. Clans are typically divided into lineages based either on patrilines (tracing descent in the male line) or matrilines (tracing descent in the female line), and clans often claim descent from a single, often mythical ancestor (van den Berghe, 1979). People in the same clan often are well acquainted with each other. In some societies, these clans make up **tribes**, and the tribe itself is an important social grouping. In many African societies today, these groupings (clans and tribes) are still important. They are particularly apparent in times of conflict, when the society often splinters along tribal lines. There was a great deal of tumult in Kenya in early 2008 after a close election, when violence broke out between the supporters of the incumbent president, President Mwai Kibaki, and the challenger, Raila Odinga. Most of President's Kibaki's supporters were from the Kikuyu tribe, whereas Raila Odinga's supporters tended to be from the Luo tribe.

Kin-based groups are found in all human societies, from the very simplest to the most complicated. Our hunter–gatherer ancestors would have lived in groups of perhaps 80–100 people, and all those people would have been closely related. There would have been other groups to which the band was more or less related that the band would have met from time to time, sometimes for the purposes of ritual, sometimes for socialization, sometimes to find marriage partners, and so on. In horticultural societies, kin groups are larger and the tribe is usually an important social entity. The leader of the tribe or the leader of the dominant tribe would have been the chief of the society. Tribes are also important social groupings in agrarian societies, such as in contemporary Iraq and other areas of the Middle East. Kin groupings throughout the world and how they are organized are discussed further in Chapter 8.

Generally, as societies become larger and more populous, kinship becomes less important as a basis of social groups, and other groups, based on class, status, region, and ethnicity, become more important. The largest agrarian societies were Alexander the Great's empire and the Roman Empire. As an example, consider the Roman Empire. It had the English, the Gauls (French), Germans, Romans, Italians, Sicilians, Greeks, and others, all held together by the Roman military and the network of roads that connected all areas of the empire to Rome (hence the expression "all roads lead to Rome"). In the Roman Empire, divisions by region and ethnicity were more important than divisions by kinship.

CLASSES AND COMPANIES

Classes

Karl Marx (1818–1883), along with Durkheim, is considered one of the founding fathers of sociology. He was the first sociologist to focus on "class" and see it as central to social life. In Marx's definition, a class is a group of people who share the same relationship to the means of production. The **means of production** are all the things having to do with the way people in that society earn their livelihoods, including equipment, technology, and materials. For example, in agrarian societies the means of production include the land, plows, horses, seed, knowledge of crop rotations, and all the tools and technology that are used in agricultural production. For Marx, a person's relationship to the means of production is determined by ownership—what he or she owns. The two primary classes in agrarian societies are consequently the owners of land (the feudal lords) and the non-owners (the peasants or farmers). There are other classes in agrarian societies, particularly the "petty bourgeoisie"—small traders or shopkeepers—but they are too small of a group to be significant. According to Marx, all this together—the agrarian means of production, along with the classes of people involved with production—make up the entire **mode of production** of an agrarian society.

Means of production All the nonsocial aspects of how people in a society earn their livelihoods, including equipment, technology, materials, and labor power.

Mode of production The means of production combined with social organization of production.

Marx thought that the ideas and values of the society simply reflect this mode of production. In fact, he thought that the ruling ideas of a society are primarily the ideas of the owning class—and that those ideas serve to justify the owning class's privileged position in the society. He also thought the politics of the society reflected the interests of the wealthy capitalist class. The ideas of a society will not change until the mode of production changes, and the mode of production will not change until technology changes. This happens slowly. Yet when technology changes enough, the mode of production changes, and the new mode of production ushers into being new classes.

Marx saw the beginning of industrial societies in these terms. The heralds of the new industrial mode of production for Marx are the "petty bourgeoisie" and they become the new elite in an industrial society. Conflict between the new elite and the old elite serves to bring down the old class system and the old power structures—and that is historically what Marx thought had happened in Europe. After the transition, Marx thought just two main classes in an industrial society remained—the owners (capitalists or bourgeoisie) and the non-owners (workers). The owners own most of the means of production—all the things that go into industrial production, including the factories, equipment, and materials—whereas the workers own nothing but their own labor. Because of their disadvantaged class position, workers can only survive by selling their labor to the capitalists.

Marx thought that most of the time classes were unrealized groupings. That is, people in the same class did not necessarily see themselves as a group. But sometimes, a class "in itself" could become a class "for itself" and unite together to bring about social change. He predicted that the class of workers in industrial societies would eventually develop "class consciousness" and unite to help bring about a new type of society—a socialist society. "Workers of the world unite," said Marx in the *Communist Manifesto*. "You have nothing to lose but your chains."

Marx's ideas had tremendous impact in the 20th century. The great experiments in socialism in the 20th century—in the Soviet Union and in China—were inspired by his writings. Yet socialism turned out not to be what the revolutionaries envisioned, and many of Marx's ideas have fallen into disfavor as a result. However, Marx's notion of **class** remains important, if in a somewhat modified form. That is, certain people who share a certain economic position in society often share many other interests in common also. As a result, they tend to socialize with each other so that rich

Class A group of people who share in common an economic position.

people tend to socialize with other rich people, middle-income people tend to socialize with other middle-income people, and so on down the economic scale.

Marx's ideas of the influence of the rich on politics have not disappeared. C. Wright Mills's book, *The Power Elite*, was one of the first to show the ties between wealthy business leaders and politicians and the tremendous influence of these groups on politics and society.

Companies

Marx did not live to see the development of a middle tier of people who were neither owners nor workers—middle managers. Nor did he see the expansion of stock ownership in most Western industrial societies. Part of the reason for this is that he did not foresee the proliferation of the company and of widespread company ownership through ownership of stocks. In fact, companies did not start to flourish until the introduction of the limited liability, joint stock company, notably with the English Joint Stock Company Act of 1862. This meant that if a company went bankrupt, those who held stock (ownership) in the company would not be fully liable for the debts of the company. This encouraged joint stock ownership of companies and made it easier for individuals to start new companies. The very popular operetta writing team of Gilbert and Sullivan included a song about this is their 1893 operetta "Utopia Limited":

If you come to grief, and creditors are craving
(For nothing that is planned by mortal head
Is certain in this Vale of Sorrow—saving
That one's Liability is Limited),—
Do you suppose that signifies perdition?
If so, you're but a monetary dunce—
You merely file a Winding-Up Petition,
And start another Company at once!
Though a Rothschild you may be
In your own capacity,
As a Company you've come to utter sorrow—
But the Liquidators say,
"Never mind—you needn't pay,"
So you start another company to-morrow!

*****

All hail, astonishing Fact!
All hail, Invention new—
The Joint Stock Company's Act—
The Act of Sixty-Two!

As a result of the Act, the number of companies in the United Kingdom soared. The legislation was widely copied, and by 1875 most U.S. states and most European countries had instituted similar laws. Increasingly more people began to own stocks as a result. Ownership of the means of production became more widespread than Marx ever dreamed, and his notion of just two classes—owners and non-owners—became obsolete. Instead, a large middle class developed. These are people who are neither owners nor complete non-owners of property. They may own small amounts of real estate and stocks. They are the people who staff the ranks of companies as middle managers, among others.

Marx also did not foresee that along with the rise of companies would be the rise of a new class of technocrats, the people who do all the technical jobs required of industry. These are the engineers, technicians, mathematicians, and others who design, build, and maintain the components of industrial production—machines, buildings, and so on. Nor did Marx see the flourishing of schools and educational institutions necessary to train these people, and all the people who would be necessary to staff these schools and institutions.

Last, Marx did not see the rise of the state as an important entity in itself and not just the "hand maiden" of the ruling class, as he termed it. The activities of the state have expanded tremendously since the time of Marx's writings. See Figure 4.2 on the expansion of federal spending as a percentage of gross domestic product from 1799 to 1997. In all industrial societies, the state is involved in education; building of roads, bridges, and other infrastructure; old age pensions; medical care; and other things.

Rise of Bureaucracy

Max Weber (1864–1920) can be considered as having a long argument with Marx. Weber, along with Marx and Durkheim, is considered one of the founders of modern sociology. One of the things that Weber was very aware of, probably because he lived after Marx, was the proliferation of compa-

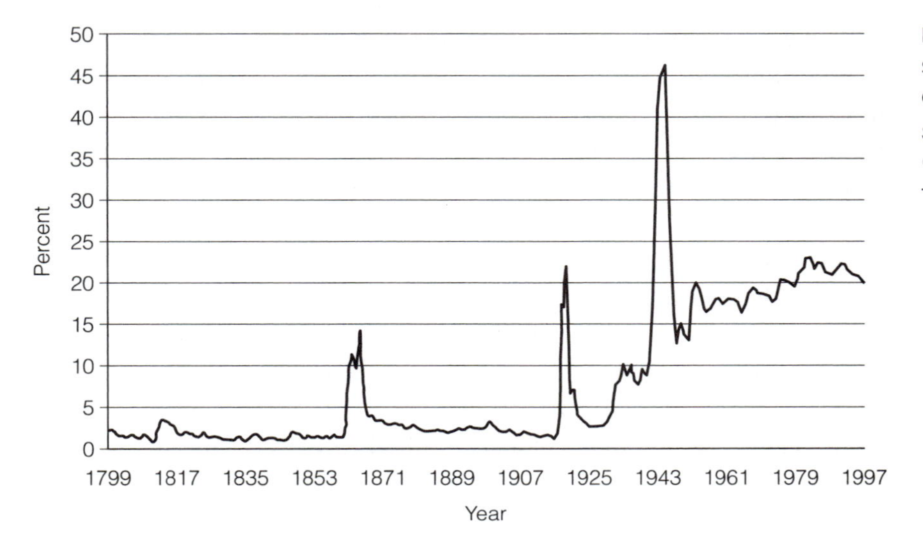

FIGURE 4.2 Federal spending as a percentage of GNP/GDP, 1799–1997.

Source: Vedder and Gallaway (1998).

nies, organizations, and large bureaucracies in industrialized societies. In fact, Weber thought that bureaucratization was a natural outcome of the increasing rationalization of economic and public life. As companies and organizations grew larger, they became bureaucracies because a bureaucracy is the most efficient way to run a very large organization that is too large to be run on a personal basis. Weber (1978 [1921], pp. 956–958) described the characteristics of bureaucracy as follows:

1. Specialization: Individuals in bureaucracies are given one specialized task.
2. Hierarchy of offices: Positions are ranked in a strict hierarchy, with those higher in the hierarchy having authority over those lower in the hierarchy. (Hence the standard phrase of the frustrated customer: "Let me speak to your supervisor.")
3. Rules and regulations: Each position in the bureaucracy is described in detail and is accompanied by rules and regulations about how the tasks of the position are to be carried out.
4. Technical competence: People to fill a position are hired on the basis of their qualifications for the job.
5. Impersonality: Rules and regulations mean that all clients of the organization are supposed to be treated in the same way.
6. Formal, written communication: Rules and regulations are written down. Everything in a bureaucracy is documented so that there is a great deal of paperwork.

As the state grew larger and became involved in more aspects of life—such as education, commerce, and roads—large state bureaucracies were created. In fact, Weber was alarmed at the increasing bureaucratization of society: He warned of what he called "the iron cage of rationality." Most of you are very well aware of the characteristics of bureaucracy and the problems with impersonality and lack of flexibility that usually accompany them.

Weber was also aware that the rise of a group of people who staffed these positions in bureaucracies in companies, organizations, and government created a new type of class—a middle class. These people were often not particularly wealthy and did not own very much, but they could have a great deal of influence over the company or organization of which they were a part. Technical advisors—engineers and scientists—became important for making these organizational decisions also. In the state, bureaucrats made increasingly more decisions that had a great impact on large numbers of people—where roads would go, where schools would be built, and so on.

STATUS

Status group A group of people who share in common a style of life.

Weber thought there were other important social groups besides classes, or groups based on wealth and ownership of property. He thought that there were what he called **status groups**—people who shared in common not an economic position but, rather, a *style of life.* We were introduced to social status in Chapter 3, in which we defined it as a person's position in a social hierarchy. A status group is not the same thing as individual status, although status groups are often ranked in a hierarchy. Status groups are found only in more populous societies, whereas individual status is found in all societies. Examples of status groups in our society are scientists and members of religious sects. Distinctions between "old money" and "new money" are status distinctions more than they are class distinctions. The Boston Brahmins, the name given to the old, upper crust New England families of Protestant (usually English) origin, are an example of a status group in the United States. The nature of the Brahmins is summarized in the doggerel "Boston Toast" by Harvard alumnus John Collins Bossidy:

> And this is good old Boston,
> The home of the bean and the cod,

BOX 4.2
WHEN CLASS MEETS STATUS

It is the late 19th century, and anti-Semitic policies are on the rise in Russia. Expulsions and pogroms (attacks involving violence and vandalism) against Jews are becoming common. In this setting, the son of a rich Jewish widow has fallen in love with the daughter of Tevye, a dairyman, and has asked for her hand in marriage. Although Tevye is also a Jew, the class difference between the two families is too wide to be bridged. Here is the widow's brother, confronting Tevye: "Either you're playing dumb," he says to me, giving me the once over, "or else you really are dumb. . . . But how could you have allowed yourself to forget who you are and who we are? Where does a sensible Jew like yourself go off thinking that a dairyman, a common cheesemonger, can marry into a family like ours?"

In this case, class meets status, and class wins.

–From *Tevye the Dairyman* by Sholem Aleichem (1987, p. 94)

Where the Lowells talk only to Cabots,
And the Cabots talk only to God.

As the rhyme suggests, people of the same status tend to socialize with each other, just as people of the same class do. In some societies, class distinctions overlap status distinctions, whereas in other societies they are more distinct.

Status groups tend to be ranked. Scientists and Boston Brahmins as groups are ranked highly in American society, even though individual scientists or Boston Brahmins may not earn very much. Members of religious sects tend not to be ranked very highly in American society even if they have a high level of income. Like members of social classes, the members of a status group may not necessarily see themselves as part of a status group.

As an example of status groups outside the United States, the groups of monks throughout Asia comprise status groups (Photo 4.1).

At its most extreme, status groups became ethnic groups—endogamous groups with their own distinctive style of life that included their own customs, culture, and even language. **Endogamous** means that people in the group only marry other people in the group.

Endogamous People in the group only marry other people in the group.

PHOTO 4.1 Saffron-robed Buddhist monks march down a street in Rangoon, Burma, with their alms bowls collecting rice. Communities of monks found in many societies throughout the world may be considered groups of people distinguished by *status* or style of life. Source: iStockphoto.

PARTY

Weber also saw the rise of a new class of people involved in politics and in state bureaucracies, and these people made up another distinct social grouping. This group is not so much distinguished by its economic posi-

PHOTO 4.2 China's top leaders stand to the national anthem during the opening ceremony of the 17th Communist Party Congress held at the Great Hall of the People in Beijing on Monday, October 15, 2007. In China, affiliation with the communist party remains important. Members of the communist party in China may be considered a group of people distinguished by *party*. Source: AP Photo/Ng Han Guan.

tion or its style of life but, rather, by its political affiliation. For Weber, **party** affiliation and status could have as much an effect on a person's life chances as class.

Party A group of people who join together for the purpose of obtaining and wielding power.

Sociologists have since noted that to some extent, the efficacy of class, status, and party depends on the society. For example, in the former Soviet Union and in contemporary communist China, this came to be especially true: One's party affiliation became vital in all aspects of life. In China today, affiliation with the ruling communist party continues to be important.

CONCLUSION

Like classes, status groups are not necessarily self-conscious groups, although they often are. Political groups (parties) are always self-conscious of what they are and what they are trying to achieve. Class, status, and party are useful analytical concepts for sociologists in that they designate people who share economic interests, status interests, or political interests. As a result, people of the same class, status, or party often do the same things and vote the same way. Furthermore, social networks often unite people of the same class, status group, or political affiliation, and through those connections the larger group can have great influence on both the individual and the society.

Much of the discussion in this chapter will be taken up again in later chapters on sociological research. Thus, for example, we revisit kin groups in Chapter 8 and class, status, and party in Chapter 9. In the next chapter, we examine the unwritten and written rules of many social groups—institutions.

REFERENCES

Aleichem, Sholem. 1987. *Tevye the Dairyman*, translated by Hillel Halkin. New York: Schocken Books.

Burt, Ronald S. 2004. "Structural Holes and Good Ideas." *American Journal of Sociology* 110(2), 349–399.

Cartwright, D., and F. Harary. 1956. "Structural Balance: A Generalization of Heider's Theory." *Psychological Review* 63, 277–292.

Dodds, Peter Sheridan, Roby Muhamad, and Duncan J. Watts. 2003. "An Experimental Study of Research in Global Social Networks." *Science* 301(5634), 827–829.

Feld, Scott L. 1991. "Why Your Friends Have More Friends Than You Do." *American Journal of Sociology* 96(6), 1464–1477.

Granovetter, Mark S. 1973. "The Strength of Weak Ties." *American Journal of Sociology* 78(6), 1360–1380.

———. 1974. *Getting a Job: A Study of Contacts and Careers*. Cambridge, MA: Harvard University Press.

Henriques, Diana B. December 19, 2008. "Madoff Scheme Kept Rippling Outward, Across Borders." *New York Times*, p. A1.

Moody, James. 1999. "The Structure of Adolescent Social Relations: Modeling Friendship in Dynamic Social Settings," Ph.D. dissertation, University of North Carolina, Chapel Hill, NC.

Rueb, Emily S. December 31, 2008. "Six Degrees of Bernard Madoff." *New York Times*.

Segal, David, and Alison Leigh Cowan. January 15, 2009. "Madoffs Shared Much; How Much Is Question." *New York Times*, p. A1.

Travers, Jeffrey, and Stanley Milgram. 1969. "An Experimental Study of the Small World Problem." *Sociometry* 32(4), 425–443.

van den Berghe, Pierre. 1979. *Human Family Systems*. Prospect Heights, IL: Waveland Press.

Vedder, Richard K., and Lowell E. Gallaway. 1998. "Government Size and Economic Growth," report prepared for the Joint Economic Committee, Jim Saxton (R-NJ), Chairman. Available at www.house.gov/jec/growth/govtsize/govtsize.pdf.

Watts, Duncan J. 2003. *Six Degrees: The Science of a Connected Age*. New York: Norton.

Weber, Max. 1978 [1921]. *Economy and Society*, Vol. 2, edited by Guenther Roth and Claus Wittich. Berkeley: University of California Press.

INSTITUTIONS
The Architecture of Society

5

INSTITUTIONS AS SYSTEMS OF RULES

Most social groups have unwritten rules. Some social groups, especially the larger ones, have written rules. Then the rules are referred to as laws. Both written and unwritten rules are part of group culture. The U.S. Constitution and the laws of the United States are the written rules of the U.S. government. As you know, the written and unwritten rules may not be the same at all. For example, the written rule is "stop at the stop light," whereas the unwritten rule (in some African cities) is "do not stop at the stop light at night or you might be carjacked." Nevertheless, it is often necessary to understand both the unwritten and the written rules of a group if we are to understand the social group. Sociologists call the unwritten and written rules of a group **institutions**. We find institutions in all the groups depicted in the pyramid given in Chapter 1, except at the level of the whole world. There are no truly worldwide institutions.

Institutions The rules and laws that govern a society; unwritten and written rules of a social group.

As noted later in this chapter, the rules of an institution must be enforced in some way; that is, people have to make sure the rules are followed. The rules can be enforced formally (e.g., by a police force) or informally (by social pressure). If they are not enforced, then we cannot call the set of rules an institution. In our society, the university is an important educational institution. It has written rules stating how a degree in a particular subject is earned. Usually this means the student has to take a particular set of courses and pass them. It has a bureaucracy to organize the teaching of courses and to ensure students follow the rules and then to reward them with a degree at the end. There are also a variety of unwritten rules, such how often one can get away with missing class, that I am sure many of you are familiar with.

GREEF: THE FIVE BASIC INSTITUTIONS

All societies have government, religious, educational, economic, and family institutions (GREEF). More complex and more populous societies have additional institutions, but the basic five are found in all societies. In simpler societies without writing, none of these institutions are based on written rules. People know the rules, regardless, and social pressure makes people abide by them. In more developed societies, the rules are written down. The Old Testament is a set of laws composed by the Hebrews between the 12th and the 2nd century BC. The oldest surviving copy of a law code is the Code of Ur-Nammu, written in the Sumerian language approximately 2100–2050 BC. In this Mesopotamian society (located in present-day southern Iraq), all members of society belonged to one of two status groups: slave or free. The law code detailed the behaviors expected of people of different statuses and the punishment for crimes, similar to the Ten Commandments listed in the Old Testament. These early law codes combined rules concerning government, religion, economics, and the family. In more complex societies and in industrial societies, there is more separation of institutions and each institution has its own set of rules. Thus, in the United States, for instance, each church follows its own set of rules, and in government, education, economics, and even the family there are often different sets of rules at the federal, state, and local level. Often, these rules are accompanied by large bureaucracies that are involved with carrying out and enforcing the rules.

Just as subsistence technology shapes a society's culture and its social groups, subsistence technology also shapes a society's institutions. Table 5.1 gives a summary of the basic institutions found in different societies classified by subsistence technology: hunting and gathering, horticulture, agrarian, and industrial societies.

In the following sections, I discuss the five primary social institutions—government, religion, education, economy, and family—found in an example of each type of society. These are by no means complete descriptions of all the institutions in each society. They are meant as brief sketches only to illustrate the nature of the main social institutions and how they vary across societies.

Hunters and Gatherers: !Kung of the Kalahari

The !Kung (Bushmen or San; Photo 5.1) of the Kalahari Desert are a small group of hunters and gatherers much studied by anthropologists as they

TABLE 5.1 Types of Institutions in Different Societies

TYPE OF INSTITUTION	TYPE OF SOCIETY			
	HUNTING/ GATHERING	HORTICULTURAL	AGRARIAN	INDUSTRIAL
Government	Headman	Chieftain	Bureaucratized state	Highly bureaucratized state
Religion	Shaman	Part-time priests	Highly bureaucratized religion	Diverse, includes highly bureaucratized religion
Education	No formal education	No formal education	Little formal education	Bureaucratized educational system
Economy	No formal economy, gift economy	Little formal economy	Formal economy, some law	Formal economy governed by law
Family	Nuclear or limitedly extended	Extended	Extended	Nuclear

continued their hunting and gathering lifestyle into the 1950s and 1960s. The following description represents their way of life when it was first studied in the 20th century.

The !Kung live in the Kalahari Desert area, a semi-desert and savannah area covering the Tropic of Capricorn in southern Africa. Band size for the !Kung varies from 8 to 61, with an average size of approximately 25–34 people depending on the local ecology. Most of the day-to-day food for people comes from the gathering that is done by women. Women gather nuts, berries, tubers, and other roots plus other edibles they can find, such as eggs and fruits. Men hunt the local wildlife with poisoned arrows and spears. The owner of the first arrow to wound the animal has first claim on the meat.

Government is by headman, and this is passed from father to son, but in practice headmen have little authority. There are no separate religious specialists. Some individuals (usually men) serve as medicine men or shaman as necessary, but this is always in addition to their usual hunting tasks. Education takes place in the family and in the group as a whole because children are taught subsistence skills by both adults and their peers. The economy is a **gift economy**, where people give each other gifts on a regular basis.

Gift economy The basis of the economy is the exchange of gifts.

Photo 5.1 Two of the !Kung (Bushmen or San) of the Kalahari Desert in Namibia.
Source: iStockphoto.

There is little or no trade of goods and services. When a large game animal is killed, the meat is distributed to all in the band along kinship lines.

Bilateral descent All lines of descent are recognized as of equal or nearly equal significance, and inheritance flows down through both the father's and mother's lines.

Bride service When the groom is obligated to give service to the parents of his bride.

The family is central to !Kung society. Descent is traced through both father and mother (**bilateral descent**). Marriage rules are loose. Incest taboos and the small size of each band ensure that most people marry outside their band, but there is no rule that they should. Although first marriages are arranged by parents, second or later marriages are by mutual consent. Few men have more than one wife at a time, and no women have more than one husband. First marriages entail a period of **bride service** for the groom, who is obligated to hunt for his parents-in-law. This period generally lasts until three children have been born to the marriage. After this period, the man is free to return to his own band and take his family if he wants to (van den Berghe, 1979, pp. 132–140).

Photo 5.2 Dani woman harvesting sweet potatoes, September 2000.
Source: Anders Ryman/Corbis.

Horticulturalists: Dani of Western New Guinea

The Dani people are a group of horticulturalists from the central highlands of western New Guinea (Photo 5.2). They are one of the most populous groups in the highlands. In the following discussion, they are described as they existed in the early 1960s, before substantial influence from the Indonesian government and other outsiders began to change Dani culture.

The Dani are known for their ritual small-scale warfare between rival villages. Men spend much of their time preparing weapons, engaging in both mock and real battle, and treating any resulting injuries. The goal of these battles is not to capture territory but, rather, to insult the enemy and wound or kill token victims.

Patrilineal The family line is traced through the males.

The family system among the Dani is **patrilineal**—the family line is traced through the males. There are two patrilineal divisions called the Wida and

Bridewealth A payment of goods and/or services by the groom to the bride's parents.

Waija. Members of each lineage are obligated to marry members of the other lineage, and this rule is strictly obeyed (Heider, 1997, pp. 84, 146). Dani men are allowed to have more than one wife, but Dani women are only allowed to have one husband. Approximately 43% of adult men have two or more wives (Heider, 1997, p. 82). There is a **bridewealth** system, in which men make payments of pigs, shells, and stone valuables in return for a wife. Payments are made over the course of the marriage and occur on various occasions—the wedding, the consummation of the marriage, the birth of a child, the initiation of a son, a daughter's marriage, and a child's death (Heider, 1997, p. 144). Women move into the huts belonging to the husband's family at marriage. Generally, the men live together with the *ab gotek* (big man or head of the lineage), whereas the women and children live in huts around the periphery.

The Dani economy is primarily a subsistence economy, with little trade and no currency. The bulk of the Dani diet is made up of crops that include sweet potato, cassava, and banana. These are grown primarily by women. Women also make salt from brine pools and tend pigs (Heider, 1997, p. 44). Pigs are the source of meat and an important aspect of wealth. These goods are exchanged among individuals, and there is some trade with outsiders of salt and pigs in exchange for shell, stone, and hardwood. Trade with outsiders is primary a male task, as is the construction and maintenance of the irrigation system and preparation of the fields for planting. These tasks do not take up much time, however. Men spend most of their time in warfare and ritual.

Decisions in the village are made by the big men. Men acquire this status by the accumulation, display, exchange, and redistribution of wealth objects, such as pigs and shell bands. It is also dependent on the number of wives a man acquires. The big men of the village organize and coordinate major public events such as rituals and warfare.

The Dani have no formal educational system other than the training in subsistence tasks children receive from adults and the rituals that children go through as they grow up. For example, all children are considered to be Wida, whatever their father's lineage. Those boys whose fathers are Waija go through a ritual process to make them Waija (the girls become Waija without this ceremony). For girls, the most important rite of passage is the wedding. Since the mid-1960s, the Indonesian government has tried to keep all Dani children in government schools from approximately age 6 to age 15 years (Heider, 1997, p. 90), but these schools are not part of Dani traditional culture.

The Dani have no formal religious institutions. They do believe in ghosts that lurk around the village at night and make it dangerous for people to move about (Heider, 1997, p. 121). Food is often set out for the ghosts in ceremonies. At funerals, some young girls who are particularly close to the person who died have their fingers chopped off to placate the ghosts (Heider, 1997, p. 133). The Dani also believe in various spirits that inhabit certain hills, rocks, and ponds, and whirlpools in streams. There are no priests or shamans; instead, the village big men organize the rituals in the village.

Agrarian Society: Japan during the Edo Period

There were four primary status groups in premodern Japan (often known as the Edo period from 1603 to 1868): the samurai, farmers, artisans, and merchants. The highest status group was the samurai, the warrior nobility, who comprised approximately 6% of the population (Photo 5.3). Only samurai were permitted to carry swords. The most numerous group was the farmer or peasant group (more than 80% of the population). Below the farmers were the craftsmen, and even below them, on the lowest level, were the merchants (Lehmann, 1982, pp. 64, 80). Institutions could vary among these groups. The institution of the family was particularly different for peasants and samurai.

Among the peasantry, the **stem family** was dominant. In a stem family, the oldest child (preferentially the oldest son) inherits the family property. If there were no sons, a son could be adopted who would marry one of the daughters (Hanley, 1997, p. 139). Marriages had to be approved by the head of the extended family, and sometimes a **dowry** (money and goods a bride brings with her at marriage) was involved. After marriage, the couple could live either with the woman's family or the man's family or by themselves. The most common pattern was for the couple to live with the man's family in an **extended family** (a **patrilocal** family rule; see Chapter 8) (Takagi, 2003). In premodern times, the extended family system was dominant among the peasantry, although there were still substantial numbers of **nuclear family** households (Koyama, 1981). Marriages were arranged by

Stem family When the oldest child (preferentially the oldest son) inherits the family property.

Dowry The money and goods a bride's family gives to her husband when she marries.

Extended family When several generations of the same family live together.

Patrilocal When a married couple lives with the man's family in an extended family.

Nuclear family Family consisting of a husband and wife and co-resident children.

Photo 5.3 Samurai with two swords in his belt. The samurai were a warrior nobility typical of elites in agrarian societies. Photo by Kimbei c.1885. Courtesy of the Tom Burton Collection.

families with little input from the couple. However, if the marriage did not work, there were no legal or religious restrictions on divorce and remarriage. In one region, the majority of the villagers' first marriages ended within 10 years (Kurosu, 2007). More than half of the divorced and widowed men and women remarried within a few years after the dissolution of their marriage. The younger a woman was when she divorced, the greater chance of her remarriage. Widows were far less likely to remarry than widowers. In some places, if the dead husband had a younger brother, it was mandatory that the younger brother marry his older brother's widow.

Samurai marriages were arranged by other samurai of the same or higher rank than those being married. Higher-ranked samurai always married women from another samurai family, whereas for lower-ranked samurai marriage with commoners was possible. There was a dowry system, in which women brought money and goods from their families to the new marriage, and the size of a prospective dowry was a key determinant in arranging a marriage (Takagi, 2003). If a samurai family had no sons, adoption was possible, but this was much less common than among the peasantry (Hanley, 1997, p. 139). A samurai could have a mistress, but her background was strictly checked by higher-ranked samurai. In many cases, this was treated like a marriage, and any sons born of the union could become samurai. A samurai could divorce his wife for a variety of reasons with approval from a superior. Unlike in the peasantry, however, for the samurai divorce was a rare event.

Like elite women in most societies, the sexuality of samurai women was strictly controlled. Samurai women blackened their teeth and shaved their eyebrows after marriage so their status was clear. (Wedding rings are a European custom introduced in Japan after the Edo period.) Chastity was important for brides and fidelity essential for wives, and any deviation from this was severely punished. In the case of the death of a samurai, the practice of marriage of the widow to the samurai's younger brother was forbidden because the older brother outranked the younger brother (Takagi, 2003).

The Edo period was a prosperous commercial period in Japan, and there was a large and sophisticated economy. There was a highly developed system of finance and nationwide trade. The construction trades flourished, along with banking facilities and merchant associations. Cities were large and populous. By the mid-18th century, Edo (Tokyo) had a population of more than 1 million, and Osaka and Kyoto each had more than 400,000 inhabitants. Rice was the base of the economy because the daimyo (landowners) collected the taxes from the peasants in the form of rice. Taxes were high—approximately 40% of the harvest. The rice was sold at the fudasashi market in Edo.

During this period, government was monarchical and aristocratic. At the top were the emperor and court nobles, together with the shogun and daimyo. Below them were the samurai, peasants, artisans, and merchants. Below them were the Eta (burakumin)and hinin—the unclean and low-status groups. Real power in the Edo period lay with the shogun, and the emperor was little more than a figurehead. There was little input from the lower classes in government.

Religion in Japan during the Edo period was either Shintoism or Buddhism or some combination of the two. Shinto was the oldest Japanese religion and was divided into many sects. In Shinto, certain places were associated with a deity or god and respected as holy. These were often scenic places such as mountaintops or areas next to water, although not always (Jinnai, 1990, p. 132). The deities in Shinto are known as kami, and there was a huge number of them. There was even a toilet god (kawaya kami):

> Since the toilet was a dark and often unpleasant place, people needed a god to protect them there. . . . At the end of the year New Year's decorations were placed in the toilet, and it was the custom in some places for family members to sit on a straw mat in front of the toilet and perform a brief ceremony to the god, each family member eating a mouthful of rice to symbolize eating something left by the god. . . . The god of the toilet was considered to be extremely beautiful, and pregnant women who wanted to have beautiful children asked the toilet god to give their babies a "high nose" and, if a girl, "dimples." (Hanley, 1997, p. 124)

Buddhism was often merged with Shintoism in premodern Japan. Buddhists follow the teachings of Buddha, although there were a variety of sects of Buddhism in Japan.

Neither Shinto nor Buddhism have elaborate priesthoods, although they do have communities of monks and religious scholars. Religious participation in both religions consists of performing rituals at various times of year, such as ceremonies honoring gods and ceremonies honoring ancestors on the day they died. Families would either have a Buddhist ancestral cabinet or a Shinto family altar where ancestors would be honored, and most religious ceremonies took place at home or at a shrine rather than at a temple (Jinnai, 1990, p. 132). The Tokugawa government required all Japanese to be registered with some recognized Buddhist sect, but for most people the temple to which they belonged was only visited on special ceremonial occasions (Photo 5.4). The major function of the Buddhist priest was as undertaker (Bellah, 1985 [1957]).

Photo 5.4 Red Shinto Shrine just outside Tokyo, Japan. Source: iStockphoto.

By the late Edo period, there was a well-developed system of education. Local schools initially were associated with Buddhist temples and were run by religious scholars; by the late Edo period, they were run by Confucianist scholars and thus were no longer tied to religion (Lehmann, 1982, p. 115). A large number of Japanese children of both peasant and upper classes attended school. Estimates vary, but perhaps 54% of boys and 19% of girls between the ages of 6 and 13 years attended school (Hanley, 1997, p. 190). All samurai men attended school and could read and write. This is also atypical of agrarian societies, in which few commoners or peasants were educated.

Industrial Society: Contemporary United States

The United States is a large, complex, post-industrial society. Men and women are free to choose their own marriage partners, although they tend to pick partners who have a similar social background. Couples exchange gifts at marriage, and typically the bride's family pays for the expenses of the wedding. Families tend to be nuclear and consist of a mother, father, and children living in a separate residence (**neolocal family** system; see Chapter 8). Extended families living in the same house are rare. Divorce is legal and common, and postdivorce children are more likely to live with their mothers than their fathers.

Neolocal family Consists of a mother, father, and children living in a separate residence.

The government of the United States is a democracy as outlined in the U.S. Constitution. It is an elected, representative government at all levels with universal rights to vote and hold office. There are no family or group rights or positions. The three branches of government at the federal level are a legislative branch made up of elected representatives (House and Senate), an executive branch made up of an elected president, and a judicial branch made up of appointed judges (the Supreme Court). In addition, each state has its own smaller version of such a government. There are also governments at the county and city level.

The economy is a large and diversified free market economy, where most people earn their livelihoods outside of agriculture. Families, and even communities, are not self-sufficient. Instead, there is a tremendous amount of specialization and interdependence that is facilitated by institutions such as money and civil law (Photo 5.5).

Religion is formally organized, often on a national or international scale. Religions are diverse and range from large hierarchical churches to small sects. Most of the population is Christian, with smaller groups of other religions including Judaism and Islam. Weddings and funerals typically take

Photo 5.5 The New York Stock Exchange. Source: iStockphoto.

place in a church or religious house of some kind, although there are also civil weddings that take place in courthouses (Photo 5.6).

The education system is universal and formal, with formal credentials awarded. From 6 to 18 years of age most people attend school. A large percentage of the population also attend school after age 18. Much of this schooling is training for the types of jobs that exist in an advanced industrial society. There are three levels of schooling: primary or elementary, secondary, and tertiary. Attendance at school through the secondary level is required by law, although some people can arrange to teach their children at home. At each level, there are many different types of schools both public and private, some affiliated with a religion and some not. Continuation to the next level of education is dependent on completing previous levels of school. Attendance at high school is free; after high school, colleges and universities charge large fees.

Photo 5.6 St. Patrick's Cathedral, New York City. Source: iStockphoto.

EFFECTS OF INSTITUTIONS

Different systems of rules can have different effects on society. The U.S. Constitution has often been admired for its separation of powers of executive, legislative, and judicial branches, and these institutions have been credited with making the United States a prosperous society. Written rules are neither necessary nor sufficient for a successful government, however. Many countries have duplicated the U.S. Constitution without reproducing U.S. government. English society is based on unwritten (common) law, yet it has been home to a successful democratic government for centuries. What is essential with rules is that they are enforced and that they mesh with local cultures—the unwritten rules of society.

WHERE DO INSTITUTIONS COME FROM?

History

The U.S. Constitution owes a great deal to English common law (the unwritten rules of English government) because many of the first settlers in the United States were English. Similarly, institutions throughout the world often take the form they do based on history. For example, law codes in Mexico resemble the Napoleonic codes used in Spain because the Spanish settled Mexico and brought their law codes with them.

Power

It also matters who has power in the society. Adolf Hitler was voted into office in Germany under a democratic system of government, but he then proceeded to dismantle the democratic system of government and installed himself as dictator. At the end of the Edo period, the Meiji lords in Japan were able to break the power of the Shogunate, reinstall the emperor, and usher in a new period of oligarchic and militaristic rule.

CONCLUSION

In analyzing social groups, it is important to understand the rules of the group (both written and unwritten). When analyzing an entire society, it is important to understand the rules of the five basic institutions—government, religion, education, economy, and family. We discuss the forms of these institutions in more detail in the chapters on political sociology, sociology of religion, sociology of education, economic sociology, and the sociology of the family.

REFERENCES

Bellah, Robert. 1985 [1957]. *Tokugawa Religion.* New York: Free Press.

Hanley, Susan B. 1997. *Everyday Things in Premodern Japan.* Berkeley: University of California Press.

Heider, Karl. 1997. *Grand Valley Dani. Peaceful Warriors*, 3rd ed. Fort Worth, Texas: Harcourt Brace.

Jinnai, Hidenobu. 1990. "The Spatial Structure of Edo." Pp. 124–146 in *Tokugawa Japan: The Social and Economic Antecedents of Modern Japan*, edited by Chie Nakane and Shinzabur Oishi; translation edited by Conrad Totman. Tokyo: University of Tokyo Press.

Koyama, Takashi. 1981. "The Pre-Modern Peasant Family and Its Life Cycle Pattern." *Journal of Comparative Family Studies* 12(3), 293–304.

Kurosu, Satomi. 2007. "Remarriage in a Stem Family System in Early Modern Japan." *Continuity and Change* 22(3), 429–458.

Lehmann, Jean-Pierre. 1982. *The Roots of Modern Japan.* New York: St. Martin's Press.

Takagi, Tadashi. 2003. "Marriage and Divorce in the Edo Period." *Japan Echo* 30, 5.

van den Berghe, Pierre. 1979. *Human Family Systems.* Prospect Heights, IL: Waveland Press.

DEMOGRAPHY

6

AS MENTIONED IN CHAPTER 2, essential to understanding any group or society is an understanding of its demography—that is, its population and its distribution among age, sex, and other subgroups. How large is the society? Are its members primarily young or old? Are many babies born or only a few? Can people expect to live a long time? What do people tend to die of? In sociology, the specialty area of demography answers these questions.

The largest group of study (or unit of analysis) for sociologists is the whole world, so we start with a brief history of the population of the world. Then we discuss contemporary demography and its characteristics in modern industrialized societies (e.g., the United States) and in premodern societies (e.g., Africa). Last, we examine the effects of the demographic composition of a group on group dynamics.

POPULATION TRENDS IN HISTORY

For most of world history, the population was stable at ten million people or so. Then in approximately 1650, the population of the world started to increase (Figure 6.1). Beginning in approximately 1900, the world population began to skyrocket. From approximately 500 million in 1650, it has increased to nearly 7 billion today. What happened? Before 1650, life expectancy was low. If a person survived childhood, he or she could expect to live to 50 or 60 years of age. However, that was a big "if," and infant mortality (the proportion of babies dying) was extremely high. The major change after 1650 was that people, especially babies, stopped dying as much. This happened in a number of places throughout the world but most notably in northwestern Europe. So what went on in northwestern

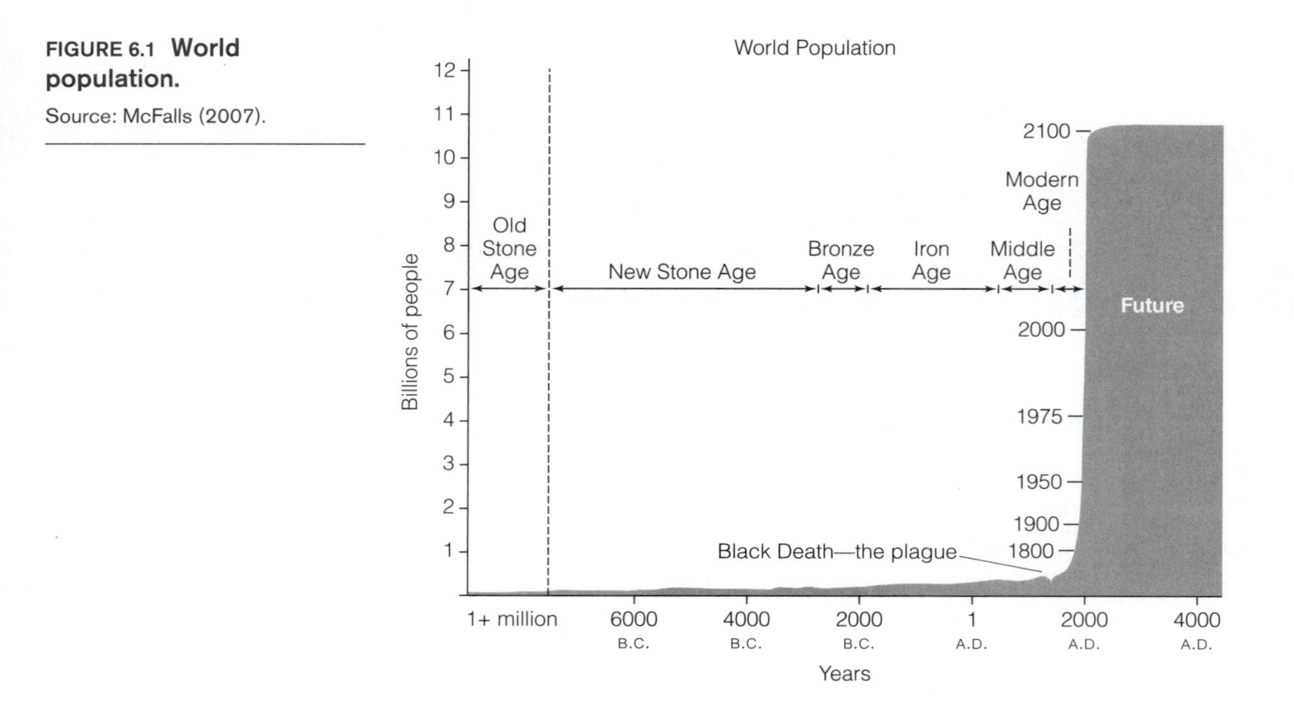

FIGURE 6.1 World population.
Source: McFalls (2007).

Europe? If you have ever been there, then you know that it is not a particularly attractive place. The weather is lousy much of the time—gray, overcast, and rainy—and the winters are cold. Much of the childhood and adult mortality there had been from communicable diseases, such as typhoid fever, diphtheria, scarlet fever, typhus, gastrointestinal diseases, and tuberculosis. Most of these diseases are spread by contaminated water, bugs such as ticks and fleas, or close contact with infected people.

Improvements in Public Health

One of the major changes that helped lower the incidence of disease was that cities in northwestern Europe, which had been hotbeds of disease, started to clean up their act. Public sewers were installed, and the water supply was monitored to ensure that sewerage did not get into the water. This meant that people were less likely to get sick from contaminated water. Swamps and water-laden pastures were drained to remove breeding grounds for mosquitoes and other bugs that spread disease (Razzel, 1974). Food production was cleaned up and became more hygienic.

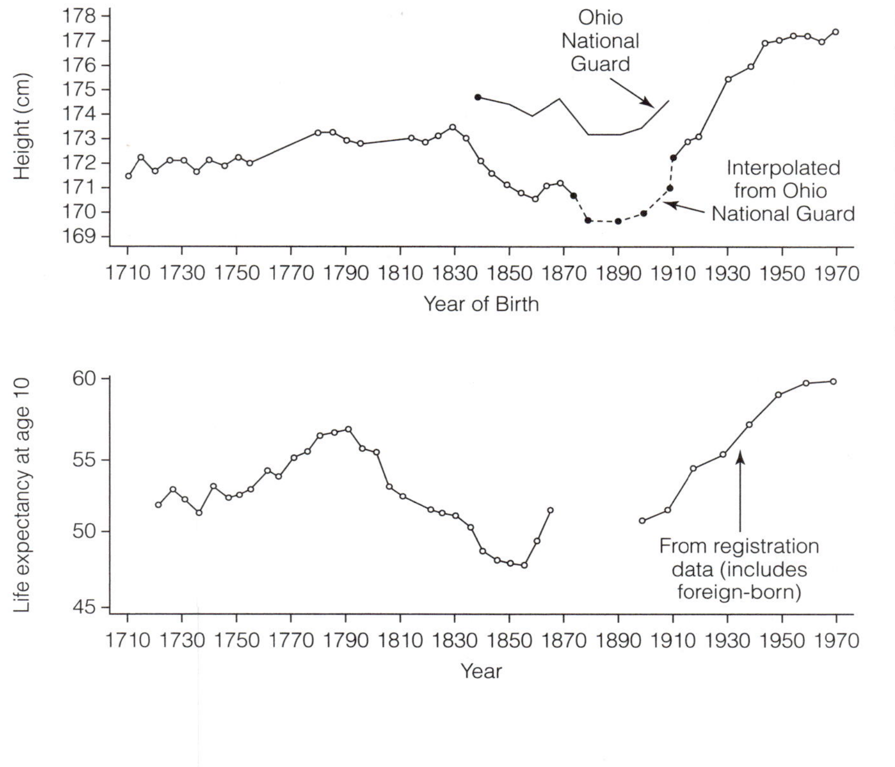

FIGURE 6.2 Trend in mean final height of native-born, white U.S. males and trend in their life expectancy at age 10 years. Note that height is by birth cohort and life expectancy at age 10 years by period.

Source: Fogel and Costa (1997).

Better Nutrition

Not only was food production cleaned up but also the amount of food produced increased (McKeown, Brown, and Record, 1972). Agricultural production increased in western Europe after 1650, which meant more food for people and for livestock. More livestock meant people began to eat more meat, so people had more protein in their diets. Governments started to do things such as stockpile grain for use during years of bad harvests, so people were less likely to starve in lean years. More food, more meat, and consistent supplies of food meant better nutrition. Better nutrition meant that body size began to increase, and people became more robust and more resistant to disease. In the United States since 1700, body size (height and weight) has increased by 50% and average longevity has increased more than 100% (Fogel and Costa, 1997; Figure 6.2).

Advances in Health-Related Knowledge

People started realizing that little things, such as washing hands before eating, made a difference regarding whether or not they got sick (Mokyr, 1993). People also started washing their clothes more often. This was helped by the introduction of cotton. Before cotton, clothes were made of wool, which was difficult to clean and, as a result, clothes were infrequently washed and became home to bugs and bacteria. Cotton was easier to wash, and thus it was washed more frequently.

As a result of all these changes, by 1900 the population of the world had reached approximately 1.7 billion. That means the population was approximately three and a half times larger than what it had been 250 years before—an increase previously unheard of in the history of the world.

Fertility Decline

Crude birth rate The number of babies born per 1000 people in a given year.

Replacement fertility Just enough babies are born to replace those people who die each year.

Then something happened that was even more unusual. In the late 1800s, the number of babies born in Europe began to decline. The **crude birth rate** decreased from approximately 30–40 babies born per 1,000 people per year to approximately 27.6 in 1900 (data for England and Wales; Andorka, 1978, p. 114). Today in Europe and the United States, the birth rate is approximately 14.1 births per 1000 people. Europe, the United States, and other similar countries are now considered to have **replacement fertility**—just enough babies are born to replace those people who die each year.

Why did the change occur? Increased industrialization in northwestern Europe was important. This meant that there was less demand for lots of children. On a farm, children are helpful—more children mean more workers for the farm. When people start working outside of agriculture, more children are not necessarily helpful to the family's bottom line. This is particularly so if jobs require being able to read and write. This means children have to be sent to school, and the time they are in school is costly for the family because it is time they are unable to contribute to the family economy. Thus, the costs of having children increased.

Also important was the decline in child mortality, because this meant that families could be sure that the children they had would survive to adulthood (Sanderson, 2001). This is important considering the evolved nature of people discussed in Chapter 2: People can be expected to want

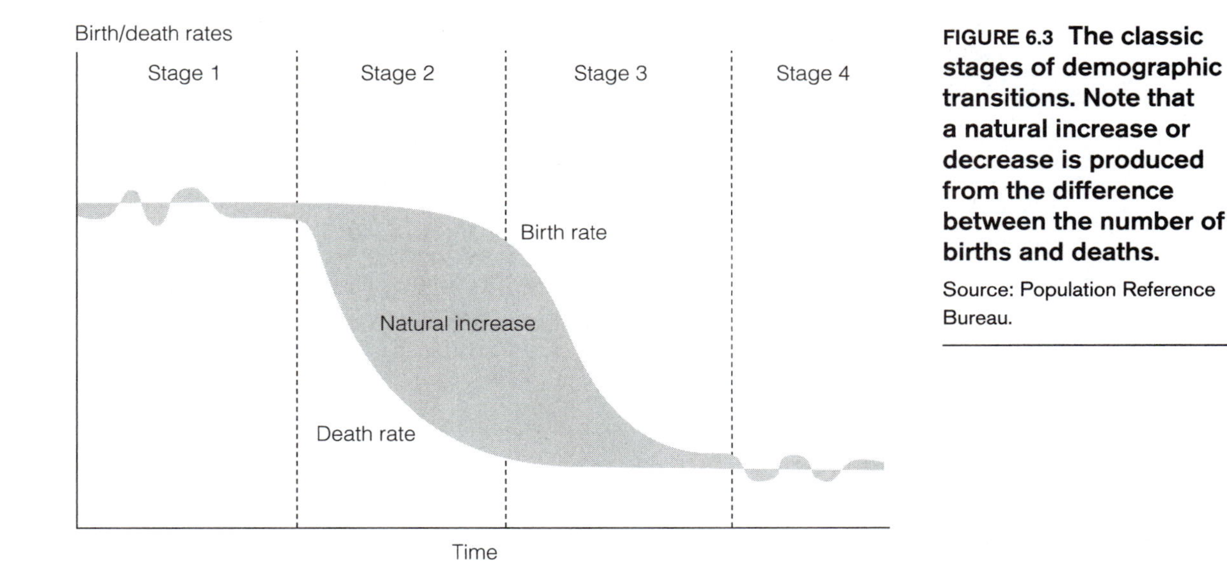

FIGURE 6.3 The classic stages of demographic transitions. Note that a natural increase or decrease is produced from the difference between the number of births and deaths.

Source: Population Reference Bureau.

their children to survive and thrive and give them grandchildren. When infant mortality rates were high, families would have to have many children just to ensure that a few survived.

Cultural change was also important. It became the norm to have a smaller family, and larger families became the butt of jokes. The transition away from patriarchal family structures to a more egalitarian family structure meant women were less under the control of a dominant husband and were more able to control how many children they had.

The Demographic Transition

This change from high **crude death rates** to low death rates and the subsequent change from high birth rates to low birth rates together are referred to as the **demographic transition**. Demographers have found that once the death rate in a society begins to fall, the fall in the birth rate follows eventually (Figure 6.3).

Death rates began to fall in the less developed countries of the world in the late 1940s. Many of the same changes that promoted mortality decline in Europe, including improvements in public health and improved agricultural production, have been important in bringing this about. Developing

Crude death rate The number of deaths per 1,000 people in a given year.

Demographic transition Change from high death rates to low death rates, and the subsequent change from high birth rates to low birth rates.

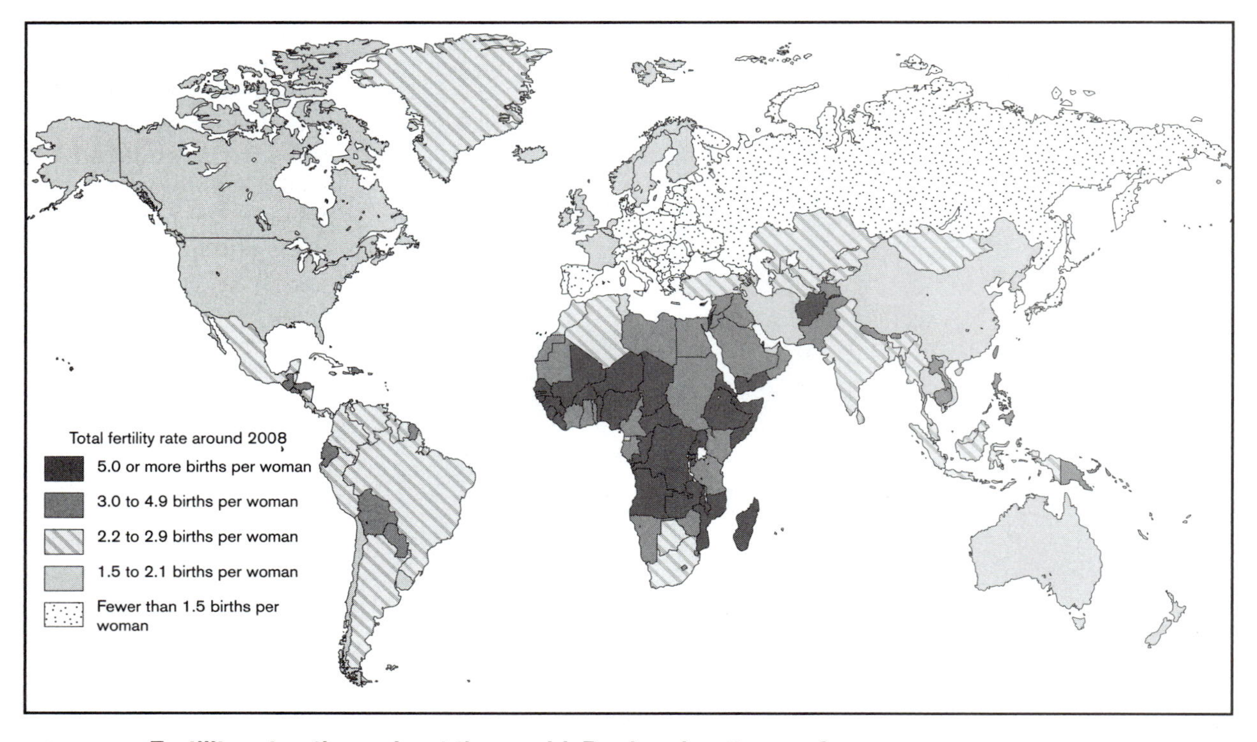

FIGURE 6.4 **Fertility rates throughout the world. Regional patterns of fertility support continued world population growth. Total fertility rate is the average number of children a woman would have assuming that current age-specific birth rates remain constant throughout her childbearing years (usually considered to be ages 15–49 years).**

Source: Adapted from C. Haub and M. M. Kent, *2008 World Population Data Sheet.*

countries also have had the benefit of being able to import medical technology from developed countries (e.g., antibiotics), which helped to rapidly lower death rates.

Since the 1960s, following the stages of the demographic transition, fertility has also begun to decline in the less developed world. The demographic transition has begun throughout most of the world, the most conspicuous exception being Africa. As in Europe, declines in fertility have been accompanied by economic development, industrialization, and urbanization (Mauldin and Berelson, 1978; Sanderson, 2001). Some countries have instituted family planning programs that have helped speed the decline.

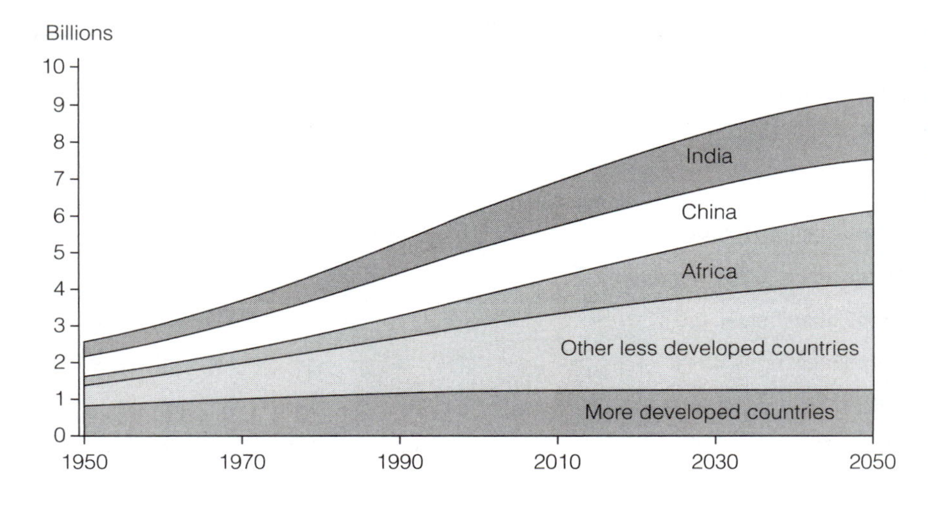

FIGURE 6.5 Africa and other developing regions make up an increasing share of world population.

Source: United Nations Population Division (2007).

CONTEMPORARY DEMOGRAPHY

Fertility is now quite low throughout the world except in a few places—in much of Africa and in areas of Southeast Asia and South America. Figure 6.4 shows the pattern of fertility rates throughout the world in approximately 2008.

This pattern of fertility means that the less developed countries of the world add more to world population than do the developed countries of the world, and this will continue into the foreseeable future (Figure 6.5).

The Rich and Poor World Divide

In 2009, in poor countries men can expect to live until they are 63.5 years of age, women can expect to live until they are 67.5. Of every 1,000 infants born, 44.6 are expected to die within their first year. In rich countries, in contrast, **life expectancy at birth** is at least 10 years longer. Men can expect to live until age 73.5 and women until age 80.5. Infant mortality is a fraction of that in poor countries. For every 1,000 infants born, 6.5 can be expected to die within their first year. People in poor countries are most likely to die of infectious diseases, whereas people in the rich world are most likely to die of diseases of old age such as heart disease or cancer. Life expectancy is increasing in all countries of the world, but it is increasing fastest in the rich

Life expectancy at birth The number of years a person can expect to live when he or she is born.

TABLE 6.1 Demographic Divide between Italy and the Democratic Republic of the Congo

	ITALY	CONGO, DEM. REP.
Population mid-2008	59.9 million	66.5 million
Population 2025 (projected)	62.0 million	109.7 million
Population below age 15	8.4 million	31.3 million
Population ages 65+	11.9 million	1.7 million
Lifetime births per woman	1.3	6.5
Annual births	568,120	2.9 million
Annual deaths	575,300	0.8 million
Life expectancy at birth	81 years	53 years
Percentage of population undernourished	<2.5	74

Source: C. Haub and M. M. Kent, *2008 World Population Data Sheet.*

world (Crimmins et al., 1997). In rich countries, people not only are living longer but also are living without disability longer than ever before.

The birth rate in less developed countries averages 21.9 births per 1,000 people per year, whereas in developed countries the birth rate averages 10.9 births per 1,000 people per year. In less developed countries, the death rate averages 7.7 deaths per 1,000 people per year, whereas in developed countries it averages 10.5 deaths per 1,000 people per year. Death rates are often lower in less developed countries because they have such young populations. Thus, the death rate is higher in Sweden than in Nigeria, even though Sweden has a healthier environment and better medical services. The demographic divide is illustrated with data from Italy and the Democratic Republic of the Congo, shown in Table 6.1.

Population Pyramids

High fertility rates also mean that less developed societies are younger than more developed societies. Demographers depict the number of people in different age and sex groups using a population pyramid. A population pyr-

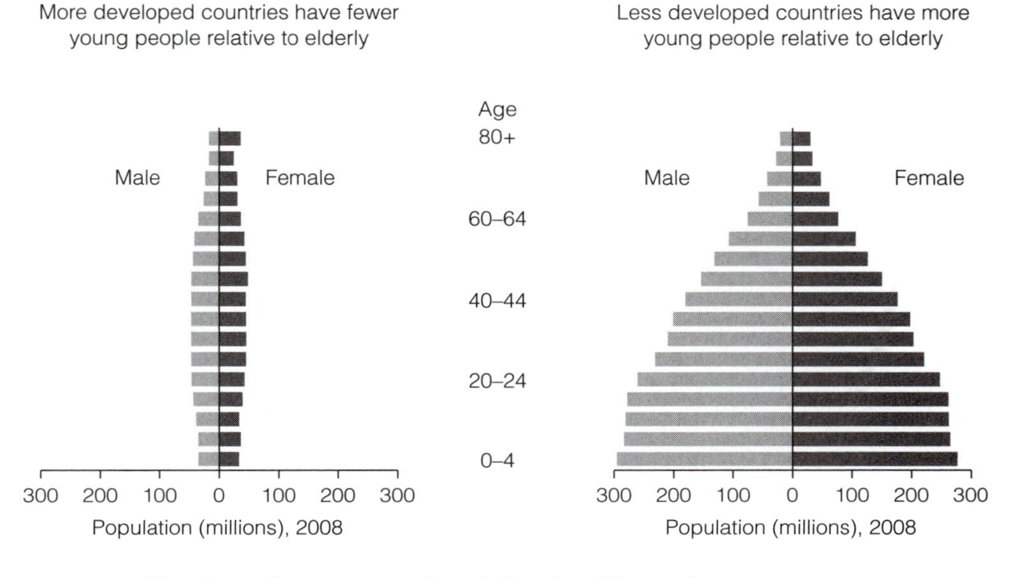

FIGURE 6.6 Number of young people relative to old people.
Source: United Nations Population Division (2007).

amid resembles two bar graphs (one for men and one for women) turned on their sides with their bases put together. The height of each bar represents the number of people in the population (in millions) in that age and sex category. In less developed countries, the **age and sex structure** looks like a pyramid. There are many children and few people in the older age groups. In developed countries, because of low birth rates, the age and sex structures look less like a pyramid and more like a column (Figure 6.6).

Age and sex structure The distribution of people across different age and sex groups in a population.

IMPLICATIONS OF DEMOGRAPHY FOR SOCIETY

Age Structure

There are different implications for a society with many older people compared to a society with many younger people. Lots of young people means there are many jobs for educators—teachers and professors—and many jobs for all the other people who work for educational institutions. More young people also means more crime because most crime is committed by young people. It also means that those industries that often cater to the young, such as the music industry, often boom. For example, in the United States

FIGURE 6.7 U.S. population pyramids, 1950 and 1980, showing the baby boom generation as a "spare tire."

Source: U.S. Census Bureau, *International Data Base.*

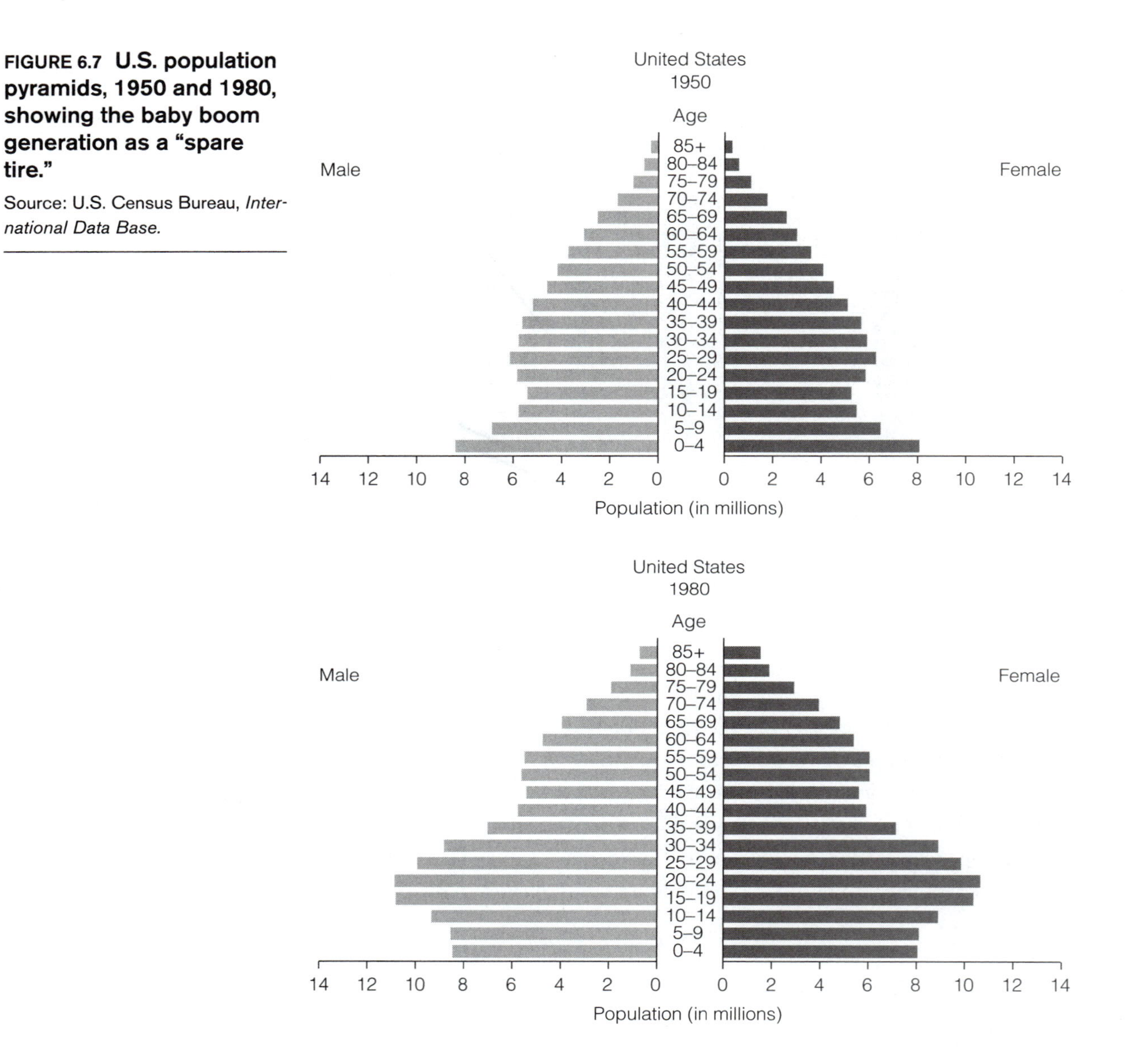

Baby boom generation
These were children born between approximately 1945 and 1965 in the United States and elsewhere.

and Europe (and other developed countries), the rise of rock-and-roll music in the 1950s and 1960s was due in part to the large size of the **baby boom generation** (Peterson, 1990). These were children born between approximately 1945 and 1965, a time when fertility rates increased in the United States (and elsewhere) and a large number of children were born. The baby boom can be seen in the age pyramid shown in Figure 6.7.

PHOTO 6.1 Some of the nearly 19,000 Beatles fans, most of them young girls, scream their enthusiastic approval as their idols appear in the Convention Hall, Atlantic City, August 31, 1964. Source: Associated Press photo.

Many of these young people were drawn to music that was different from anything their parents had listened to, and they were able to listen to it because they had access to small transistor radios. Thus, rock-and-roll became a commercial (and cultural) phenomenon (Photo 6.1).

When there are more older people, there is less crime but more costs for old age pensions and medical care for the elderly. There are also many jobs catering to the elderly—in medical facilities and in retirement leisure activities such as golf and travel. The economy of regions where there are many old people tends to be more stable because they receive pensions and health care payments that are less subject to economic upheaval than other sources of income (*The Economist*, 2009). In a society in which there are comparatively more older people and younger people than middle-aged people, there is more stress on the people in the middle, who pay for their children's care and also, through their taxes, pay for the care of retired people.

Like most advanced industrial societies, the United States currently has an aging population and, as a result, the costs of medical care and social security are becoming a great concern. The baby boom generation will begin retiring in approximately 2010, and it is unclear whether the U.S. Social Security fund and Medicare, the health care plan for the elderly, will be able to absorb the costs of the retirement of all these people.

The age structure of a population influences social trends (e.g., the rise of rock-and-roll music) and market trends (e.g., an increase in the demand for teachers or nurses). For a social scientist, it is important to keep the age structure of a population in mind when analyzing social and market trends. What may seem like a dramatic social change may simply reflect the age composition of the population. For example, many observers of the United States in the 1960s thought the world was going mad but it wasn't—it was just full of young people, who sometimes are difficult for older people to understand.

Urbanization and Population Density

It is not just the size and age structure of a population that matters but also how densely people are packed into a country. The United States has a density of 31 people per kilometer squared, compared to the world's most densely populated place, Monaco, with 16,754 people per kilometer squared and the world's least densely populated place, Greenland, with 0.026 people per kilometer squared (source: http://en.wikipedia.org/wiki/List_of_countries_by_population_density). The most densely populated countries tend to be the most urbanized countries. Monaco, although technically a sovereign principality, is basically one large city, which accounts for its high **population density**. Greenland's largest city (Nuuk) has only 14,501 people—hardly a city at all.

Population density The number of people per unit of land area (square mile or square kilometer).

People who live in less densely populated countries enjoy larger homes and yards than people who live in more densely populated countries. There tend to be fewer problems with pollution and environmental degradation in less densely populated countries simply because there are fewer people.

Population density can have important effects on the society's culture and institutions. Settler societies on large, sparsely populated landmasses such as Australia, Canada, and the United States as well as societies in sparsely populated mountainous regions are typically known for their individualism, whereas more densely populated societies are often known for their collectivist or group-oriented cultures (e.g., Japan).

Age and Sex Structure in Smaller Groups

The age structure of any social group influences group dynamics. Consider a sports team. Generally, if the team is full of older players, it will be full of wiser and more experienced players, whereas if the team is full of younger players the players will be less experienced but will be stronger and faster. A family with many very young children operates very differently from a family in which the children are teenagers. A business staffed with many young people will be very different from a business full of older people. Consider the culture at Google compared to that at IBM. Google is a young business staffed with young people where the office environment is very relaxed and people dress very casually. IBM is an old, established business staffed with many older people where the office environment tends to be more formal and people do not dress casually.

The sex structure of a group also influences group dynamics. The culture in a men's dormitory is very different from that in a women's dormitory. Whether a work group is primarily composed of men or women will make a difference in the way that work group operates. Research suggests that men are more comfortable with a clear hierarchy in a group, whereas women prefer a more egalitarian, democratic structure.

How Many People Can the World Bear?

Despite the fact that many countries have undergone the demographic transition, world population continues to grow. This is because some countries still have very high fertility. In addition, some of those countries with close to replacement fertility continue to grow in size because of **population momentum**. That is, if there is a disproportionately large number of women in their childbearing years, the population will continue to grow

Population momentum A large number of women of childbearing age means that the population continues to grow even when women only have two children each.

even if each of those women has only two children. Large numbers of people accompanied by industrialization in less developed countries results in great stress on the environment (see Chapter 17).

Immigration

Immigration tends to bring people from poor countries into rich countries, where they fill low-level jobs that nobody else wants to do. In that these jobs are filled and immigrants pay taxes (that support, among other things, old age pension programs), immigration has good effects on the recipient society. Sometimes, however, the presence of culturally and often ethnically distinct groups can fuel ethnic tensions within the society. Anti-immigration sentiment is the result. This is especially likely in economic downturns, when jobs are scarce and immigrants are more likely to be seen as taking jobs from natives.

Societies with many immigrants (e.g., the United States) look very different from societies with very few immigrants (e.g., Japan). Societies without immigrants are culturally homogeneous (everyone shares the same culture), whereas societies with many immigrants are culturally heterogeneous (there are many cultures). In U.S. cities, the presence of Little Italys and Chinatowns stands as testament to past groups of immigrants. Such places do not exist in Japanese cities.

Demography and the Democratic Process

In economic downturns, people often elect officials who promise more restrictive immigration policies. This is just one way that demography influences the democratic process in democratic countries because the majority group generally votes for policies that are in its interests. For example, large numbers of retired people in a population mean more votes for politicians who promise policies and programs that benefit the aged and fewer votes for things such as school bond initiatives and spending on higher education (Button, 1992).

Internationally, much of the belligerent talk that comes from leaders of Middle Eastern countries such as Iran can be attributed to the fact that politicians are trying to appeal to a disproportionately young and hence less pragmatic population, for whom denouncing the United States (and other Western countries) is a popular pastime (Figure 6.8).

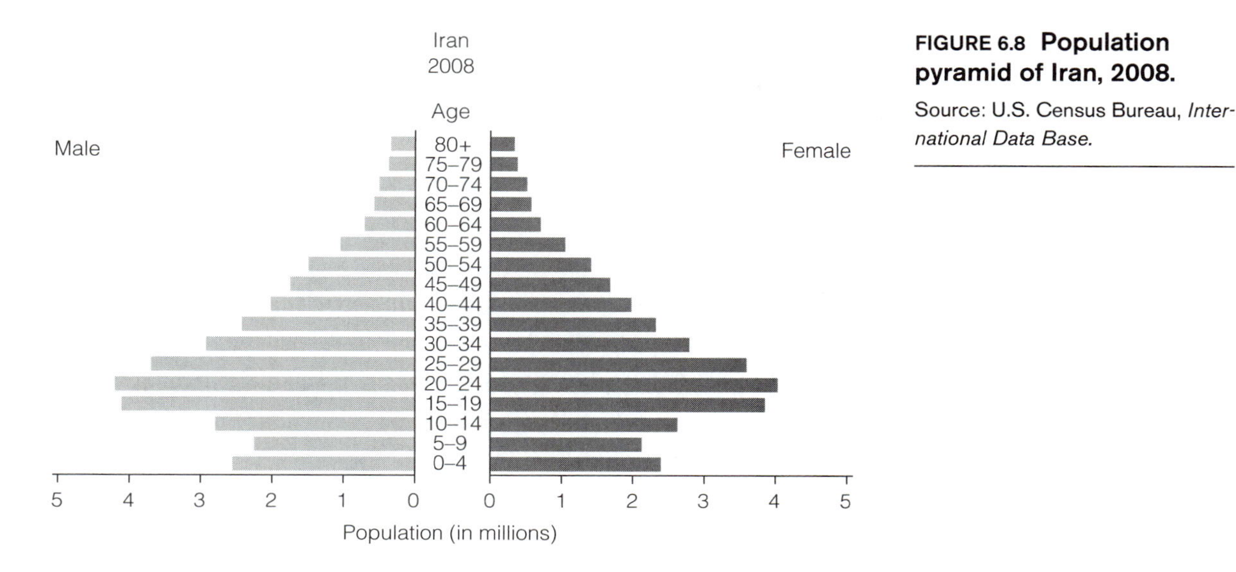

FIGURE 6.8 Population pyramid of Iran, 2008.

Source: U.S. Census Bureau, *International Data Base.*

CONCLUSION

The demography of any group makes a difference in the way that group functions. Any analysis of a social group must consider its demography—is the group old or young, mostly male or female, ethnically homogeneous or ethnically heterogeneous? The demography of a society has implications for its culture and, in a democracy, for the democratic process.

REFERENCES

Andorka, Rudolph. 1978. *Determinants of Fertility in Advanced Societies.* New York: Free Press.

Button, T. 1992. "A Sign of Generational Conflict: The Impact of Florida's Aging Voters on Local School and Tax Referenda." *Social Science Quarterly* 73, 786–798.

Crimmins, Eileen, et al. 1997. "Trends in Disability-Free Life Expectancy in the United States, 1970–90." *Population and Development Review* 23, 555–572.

The Economist. 2009. "Gilded Age: Age and Californian cities," p. 33.

Fogel, Robert W., and Dora Costa. 1997. "A Theory of Technophysical Evolution, with Some Implications for Forecasting Population, Health Care Costs and Pension Costs." *Demography* 34(1), 49–66.

Haub, Carl, and Mary Mederios Kent. 2008. *2008 World Population Data Sheet.* Washington, DC: Population Reference Bureau.

Mauldin, W. Parker, and Bernard Berelson. 1978. "Conditions of Fertility Decline in Developing Countries, 1965–75." *Studies in Family Planning* 9, 89–147.

McFalls, Joseph A. Jr. 2007. "Population: A Lively Introduction, 5th Edition." *Population Bulletin*, Vol. 62, no. 1. Washington, DC: Population Reference Bureau.

McKeown, Thomas, R. G. Brown, and R. G. Record. 1972. "An Interpretation of the Modern Rise of Population in Europe." *Population Studies* 26(3), 345–382.

Mokyr, Joel. 1993. "Technological Progress and the Decline of European Mortality." *American Economic Review* 83, 324–329.

Peterson, Richard A. 1990. "Why 1955? Explaining the advent of rock music." *Popular Music* 9, 97–116.

Population Reference Bureau. 2007. "Population: A Lively Introduction." *Population Bulletin* 62(1).

Razzel, P. M. 1974. "An Interpretation of the Modern Rise of Population in Europe, a Critique." *Population Studies* 28(1), 5–17.

Sanderson, Stephen K. 2001. "An Evolutionary Interpretation of Fertility Decline: New Evidence." *Population and Environment* 22(6), 555–563.

United Nations Population Division. 2007. *World Population Prospects: The 2006 Revision, Medium Variant.* New York: United Nations Population Division.

United States Census Bureau. 2009. *International Data Base.* Available at http://www.census.gov/ipc/www/idb/country.php.

TOPICS IN SOCIOLOGY

7 MICROSOCIOLOGY*

AS THE WORD SUGGESTS, *microsociology* is sociology that concerns small-scale social processes. Specifically, it is about social effects on *individuals*, interaction between *pairs* of individuals, or interaction in *small groups* (e.g., up to 12 people) and how this interaction creates social effects. It is a two-way street. There are social effects on individuals and groups, and individuals and groups also produce social effects. Two common synonyms for microsociology are *social psychology* and *group processes*.

Microsociology is interesting and worth studying for at least two reasons. First, the majority of us spend much of our time in small groups and most of our social concerns are with small group processes. Our family, the set of friends we regularly spend time with, and the people we work with on a day-to-day basis typically are small groups. If we understand how such groups affect their members and how such groups generally operate, we thereby understand a great deal about people's everyday lives.

Second, many of the important events and decisions that affect society at large in fact are produced in small group settings and, therefore, are at least partly the result of small group processes. The actions of major corporations—such as launching a new product, buying another company, and issuing stock—typically result from decisions taken by one or a few people after discussions within a small group. The same holds for many political decisions. The president will decide how to respond to a crisis often primarily through discussion with a few close advisors. The Federal Reserve Board and the U.S. Supreme Court are small groups that make decisions with wide-ranging consequences. This means that processes of microsociology can have macrosociological effects.

---

*This chapter is co-authored with Joseph M. Whitmeyer.

Microsociology straddles the disciplines of sociology, concerned with social phenomena, and psychology, concerned with individuals. There is a subarea of psychology called social psychology, which overlaps with social psychology in sociology. The principal difference is that psychological social psychology tends to concentrate on social effects on individuals, whereas microsociology tends to focus on how individuals create social effects. Understanding social effects on individuals is important for sociology, however, if only because social effects on individuals often affect social processes as well. For example, individuals in a group are less likely to help others in need than are individuals by themselves. This, then, makes it appear that people in mass social environments such as cities are apathetic and selfish.

The first area of research we consider, therefore, is that of important social effects on individuals, although many of the key findings are due to psychologists. The three subsequent sections each focus on one important kind of social process for which microsociologists have made considerable progress in understanding.

Because the processes of microsociology involve only a small number of people, researchers in this area have research techniques available to them that are generally not possible for other sociologists. Specifically, researchers often can and do conduct experiments, either to test hypotheses derived from theories or to search for effects of some cause. Some research in microsociology does employ surveys, but researchers usually prefer experiments and use them where possible. The advantage to experimental studies is that the researcher can vary, often precisely, the independent variables (causal factors) of interest and can eliminate or control the effects of variables that he or she is not interested in. This is often practicable because a few people can be brought into a laboratory or engaged in a natural setting and what happens to them can be precisely controlled, at least for a short period of time. Often, this is sufficient to test the hypotheses or probe the effects of interest. Most of the results that we discuss in this chapter were discovered or tested through experiments. Students are typically the subjects of these experiments, and students are not representative of all people in society. However, most microsociologists assume that any individual will respond to a social situation in a similar way, and that all small groups function in more or less similar ways, so these processes can be studied using small groups of students.

SOCIAL EFFECTS ON INDIVIDUALS

Many of the early and most interesting findings concerning social effects on individuals stemmed from questions provoked by serious and often shocking antisocial behavior that social scientists observed in the world. In World War II, for example, a large number of people in Nazi Germany obeyed orders and thereby committed or assisted in the commission of heinous crimes. In the 1960s, a woman named Kitty Genovese was murdered outside her apartment building in New York City; despite her screams over a considerable period of time, no one in the building did anything to help her, not even to the extent of calling the police. Rather than simply attributing the events to Germans being an especially obedient nation or New Yorkers being especially callous, social psychologists endeavored to find out to what extent people in general would perform similar behaviors, and especially how their circumstances would affect people's commission of these behaviors.

Milgram's Obedience Studies

One of the earliest studies was an obedience study carried out by Stanley Milgram (the investigator who conducted the small world experiment discussed previously). Milgram wanted to find out how far people would go in carrying out orders from an authority even when it involved inflicting pain. He also wanted to find out what conditions affected people's obedience.

Milgram conducted a series of experimental studies. The basic experiment involved three people—the experimenter and the teacher in one room and the learner in another. The situation was presented to each participant in the study as follows: The participant was the teacher and her goal was to get the other person, the learner, to learn something. If the learner got an answer to a question wrong, the teacher was to punish him by administering an electric shock at an intensity specified by the experimenter. In the course of the experiment, the experimenter would raise the shock levels increasingly higher and, correspondingly, the learner would give evidence of increasing suffering, for example, through grunts, screams, and pleas to end the experiment. As you probably suspect, the learner was, in fact, a confederate of the experimenter and received no shock or pain at all. However, the participant, the teacher, did not know this.

The basic study found surprisingly high levels of obedience from the participants (who were college undergraduates). A majority of participants continued to raise shock levels as ordered even when audible groans and sounds of pain came from the learner. Various modifications to the basic experiment lowered the amount of obedience fairly predictably: Obedience was less if the learner was in the same room as the teacher, was even less if the teacher had to physically hold the learner's hand on the shocking device, and was least when an assistant to the experimenter in the room challenged the experimenter's orders.

It is tempting, when confronted with disturbing results from old laboratory studies, to suppose that nowadays people are different—that we are more sophisticated and know better. Social psychologists disagree and believe that the old studies would produce the same results in the modern world. When old studies are replicated, this is, in fact, what researchers generally find. For example, the basic Milgram obedience study was run again at Santa Clara University (Burger, 2009), and the results were essentially the same as those obtained 50 years earlier. Even undergraduates in modern California appear to be surprisingly obedient to authority.

Asch's Conformity Studies

Another famous set of studies from the 1950s were carried out by Solomon Asch on the phenomenon of conformity. In the basic study, a group of people seated at a table were shown two cards, the first of which showed three vertical lines of obviously different lengths, and the other was a reference card with one straight line (Figure 7.1). Proceeding around the table, each person said which of the three vertical lines on the first card he or she thought was the same as the line on the reference card. After a few correct identifications by everyone, the people began to identify a line that clearly was not the same length as the line on the reference card. Everyone at the table, in fact, except the last person, was a confederate of the experimenter. The question was to what extent would the last person conform to the plainly wrong answer of the others. Asch found that approximately two-thirds of the participants conformed at least once and that overall there was conformity to the wrong answers on approximately one-third of the slides. Asch ran other studies varying some of the conditions and found, for

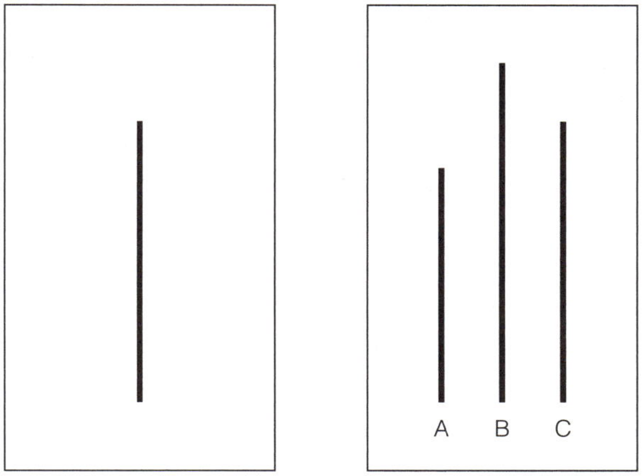

A B C

FIGURE 7.1 One of the pairs of cards used in the Asch experiment. The card on the left has the reference line, and the one on the right shows the three comparison lines.

Source: Wikipedia.

example, that even if only one other person said the correct answer, then the participant always gave the correct answer and never conformed to the majority.

Studies of Helping Behavior

Sociologists have always been interested in prosocial or cooperative behavior and what makes it more or less likely. This is a key element of many large-scale social phenomena: the formation and success of social movements such as the civil rights movement; participation in environmentally friendly activities such as recycling; cooperative responses to disasters such as earthquakes, floods, and terrorist acts; and even ordinary behaviors such as honestly paying taxes.

In the 1960s and 1970s in particular, social psychologists investigated smaller-scale forms of cooperation: When an individual apparently needs help, what variables affect whether another individual comes to his or her aid. Two of the most important determinants in fact have importance in macro areas as well. One is uncertainty or lack of information. When people are unsure of the situation, especially of possible risks to them from helping or whether the need for help is legitimate, they are reluctant to leap in and often look to see how others respond. If everyone does this, of course, no one sees anyone else take action and so no one takes action.

Free rider problem Where no one in a group performs some necessary but costly or unpleasant activity because they think some other member of the group will do so.

The other determinant has been labeled "diffusion of responsibility" by social psychologists but is known in other contexts as the **free rider problem**. This is simple and well known: A person is more likely to perform some costly or unpleasant activity that needs to be done if she believes she is the only one who can do it than if she thinks that others can do it and that if she does not then probably someone else will. This is often a problem in group projects because some members of the group may shirk in the belief that others will pick up the slack. For example, think of the potluck dinner in which everyone brings something easy and cheap (bags of chips, store-bought cookies, etc.) and no one brings a home-prepared meat dish, as everybody was hoping that someone else would take the time and spend the money to bring a nutritious main dish.

With regard to helping behavior, studies have shown, for example, that a person who believes he is the only one who knows of an emergency, such as another person undergoing an epileptic seizure, is more likely to take action such as calling for help than if he thinks others know about it too. Indeed, in many cases a group of people collectively respond less, on average, than a single individual. Other studies have shown, for example, that people asked to scream as loud as they can or to pull in a tug-of-war as hard as they can still scream less loudly and pull with less force when they are part of a group than when they are acting alone.

Conclusion

One general conclusion to draw from these and other findings about social effects on individuals is that in explaining social behavior, the characteristics of the situation are more important than we generally think, whereas the characteristics of the individual, such as personality, beliefs, and attitudes, are less important than we generally think. Another way of looking at this research is that it shows that there are behavioral tendencies common to all humans that produce similar responses to situations. These common behavioral tendencies often are more important than differences between people, whether inherited or acquired, in determining their responses. When you think about it, this is what we would expect given that we all share the same basic evolved, biological human nature, as described in Chapter 3.

SYMBOLIC INTERACTIONISM

When people interact with each other, what matters is frequently not what they actually do or say but some underlying message of their deeds or words. In other words, actions and utterances are important, often most important, as symbols. Suppose we meet an acquaintance—a fellow student or a co-worker. What do we do? We smile and raise our eyebrows, say some greeting word and perhaps a question such as "How are you doing?" and perhaps wave. These are all symbols that tell the other person that we recognize and respect him or her. Usually, for example, we do not really want to know how the other person is doing. If she is a close friend then, yes, we may want to know details and she may want to tell us. But if she is just someone whose last name we do not even know, it would be strange if she were to launch into a detailed account of a recent calamity or triumph of hers.

Also, suppose when we meet an acquaintance, smile, and say hello, he looks at us without expression and walks past. We would take that as a symbol too. Is he so disdainful of us that he does not need to acknowledge us? Is he angry at us? Is he terribly upset or preoccupied with something so that despite appearances he does not really notice us?

This in-depth analysis of what we normally might think of as a minor social event is characteristic of **symbolic interactionism**. It describes and explains people's social behavior and the social phenomena they produce in terms of the meanings these behaviors have for the people involved. Often, a symbolic interactionist analysis gives us the sense of pulling the wool from our eyes, of solving a mystery by showing how all the confusing clues make a coherent whole, or of polishing some gem of social life that we normally would pass over without noticing.

Symbolic interactionism
An area of sociological study that describes and explains people's social behaviors and the social phenomena they produce in terms of the meanings these behaviors have for the people involved.

Most sociologists consider George Herbert Mead (1863–1931) to be the principal founder of symbolic interactionism, which makes it the earliest of the microsociological perspectives. Mead is best known for emphasizing how our regard for how others see us affects our own sense of self and our own behavior, as discussed in Chapter 3. Mead (1934) noted that as we grow up, we develop the practice of seeing ourselves through others' eyes. Those others, first, are particular people important to us, such as our mother, other family members, and perhaps teachers or caregivers. Later, those others become people in general. To see his point, notice that small children do not get embarrassed, but older children and adults do.

According to Mead, this is because the older children and adults imagine how they appear to other, even anonymous people.

Mead suggested that how others see us becomes a key part of the self, how we see ourselves. Symbolic interactionists see the self and identity, in turn, as being primary determinants of behavior, including social behavior. Thus, for example, suppose Boris sees himself as rough, tough, independent, straightforward, and all-American. It may affect the clothes he wears—never jackets or ties, or even khakis—and the car he drives (an American-made pickup). It may affect his interactions with his wife or at least the spin he puts on them. He may insist on driving, for example, when he is with her. He may put off doing chores his wife mentions until he can safely interpret his behavior as being his choice rather than following an order. Also, if he does cooking or cleaning, he may tell himself and others not that he is cooking or cleaning but that he is helping his wife.

The self is also central to Erving Goffman, whom we have discussed already. The chief interest of Goffman and many subsequent symbolic interactionists, however, is impression management. In other words, what matters about your self and identity is not how *you* see them but how *others* see them. From this standpoint, much of our social behavior is aimed at giving impressions strategically, getting others to see us the way we want them to see us.

Beryl, for example, entering a classroom the first day of class has to choose where to sit. This could be a difficult decision. Sitting in the front row will probably give a favorable impression to the teacher, at least compared with sitting in the back row. Unfortunately, it may give a correspondingly unfavorable impression to her acquaintances and friends in the class, to whom she does not want to appear too serious about school. Also, she may want to meet some guy she spots when she walks in, but sitting next to him might give him (and others) the impression of being too eager or desperate. Thus, perhaps she should sit two seats away—close enough that he will notice her but still giving the impression that being close might be an accident and that she is not necessarily interested.

Stepping back, we can see that there are two somewhat different perspectives within symbolic interaction. One is that how we see our self and identity is an important determinant of our social behavior, and the other is that what matters is how we want others to see our self and identity. The implication of both, nevertheless, is that even ordinary social behavior and social life is rich in symbolic meaning. Also, we can step back even further and note that this is probably biologically inevitable: Our brains have evolved to work on a symbolic level (Deacon, 1997), and where those symbols are most important to us is, naturally, in our social lives. The close link of these processes with emotions is explicitly laid out in affect control theory (Heise, 1977). Emotions are physiological processes and, hence, are good indicators of innate tendencies, so it is likely that our concern with symbols and their meanings is an evolved trait.

EXCHANGE PROCESSES

Much of human social interaction can be looked at as exchange, an idea that is at the heart of **exchange theory** (Coleman, 1990; Homans, 1974). Individuals give something to others and expect something in return. Most people do reciprocate, following the Golden Rule (discussed in Chapter 2) that is universal in all cultures. This exchange relation is obvious with economic relations: Your boss gives you money and you do work for her. It is also obvious with quasi-economic relations: You do what your professor wants—namely come to class, turn in work, and learn things—and your professor gives you credits. But it is also true for more social relationships: A couple provide things to each other that they are looking for and tolerate eccentricities and annoyances from each other. A friend provides company, perhaps fun, perhaps a listening ear in difficult times in return for similar benefits.

Exchange theory A sociological theory that considers much social behavior as based on exchanges (of things, time, friendship, etc.) between people.

One way to see that this is true is to note what happens if one side does not hold up its end of the exchange. If a couple exchange fidelity, for example, and one party strays, then that puts severe, perhaps fatal, stress on the relationship. In a friendship, if one friend believes he is always accommodating the other—for example, going along with the activity, the time, the other people, and so forth while getting little in return—he may lower his involvement in the friendship or even end it.

The observation that much social interaction is exchange has been very useful because it allows general principles to be stated that then apply to any exchange relationship, regardless of what is being exchanged. One of the most basic of these is the power-dependence principle.

The Power-Dependence Principle

The **power-dependence principle** (Emerson, 1962) states that in an exchange relationship between two people, the person who is least dependent

Power-dependence principle The principle in exchange theory that the person who is least dependent on a relationship has the most power in that relationship.

has the most power. Suppose Chris and Pat are friends, and Pat is more dependent on Chris than Chris is on Pat. One possible reason could be that Pat has no other close friends, whereas Chris does. Then Chris has more power than Pat, which means that Pat is likely to have more say-so over what they do and when they do it or will be able to indulge herself more when they are together.

The power-dependence principle has been tested and supported in laboratory experiments. It has had many applications as well. Applying it to marriage, sociologists have hypothesized—and supported with survey research (Blumstein and Schwartz, 1983)—that power between spouses will be more equal if they both are full-time in the labor force than if one of them earns no income. It also applies to more economic situations: When workers have many attractive alternatives to their current jobs, they are less dependent on their employers and therefore more able to get concessions and tolerance for practices such as coming in late and taking time off. When times are tougher and workers consider themselves fortunate to have a job and have few opportunities elsewhere, then the workers are more dependent on their employers. The employers, correspondingly, have more power and are able to be more strict and demanding with their employees.

The Prisoner's Dilemma

Two students, Sam and Tracy, decide to study together for a difficult test. They get together as arranged one evening and discover that neither of them have reviewed the material, both counting on the other person to help them out during the review session. As a result, they can accomplish little during the review, and when they leave both are somewhat unhappy.

This is an instance of the common exchange predicament known as the "prisoner's dilemma." Two people have something to offer each other and decide to enter into an exchange. Each person, however, is tempted to cheat—to not fully uphold his end of the deal. That way, he benefits from what the other person is doing for him and can keep his own resources, whether money, effort, time, or something else. Unfortunately, if both parties cheat then they end up with a mutually unsatisfactory outcome, as in the Sam and Tracy story—an outcome that is worse for both of them than if they had both cooperated.

The prisoner's dilemma is important because it characterizes many, perhaps most, social exchange situations. When two people live together, whether roommates, spouses, or some other arrangement, often there is a division of labor of some sort. This is an exchange: "I'll cook today and you cook tomorrow" (or "you clean up"). "You clean the bathroom this week and I'll clean the bathroom next week." With the exchange comes the temptation to cheat a little—to cook the easy meal and let the other person cook a more difficult one or to do just a rough job on the bathroom because the other person will do it thoroughly the next week. But if both people are playing this strategy, the food is usually dissatisfactory and the bathroom gets increasingly grungier.

With the married couple, another exchange could be fidelity: I'll be faithful to you, expecting you to be faithful to me. Sometimes there can be temptation, however, to cheat on the spouse while counting on the spouse to remain faithful to you. A restaurant may be tempted to cheat a customer by serving lower-quality food than promised, and a customer may be tempted to cheat the server by stinting on the tip. A babysitter is perhaps tempted to cheat her charge by ignoring him and doing something she would prefer; the charge may be tempted to behave badly and refuse to cooperate with his babysitter.

Solutions to the Prisoner's Dilemma

If all we could do were to identify a prisoner's dilemma, when and where it occurs and lament its existence, we would not get far. Social scientists, however, have made the prisoner's dilemma a useful concept by identifying solutions to it and using those solutions to deduce implications for social life. There are at least three ways of dealing with a prisoner's dilemma. One is to construct the exchange formally and have external parties enforce that its conditions are met. The exchanging parties can publicly agree to a legal contract—for example, such that cheating constitutes a breach of contract that will be punished through the judicial system. This is a common method of reducing prisoner's dilemma elements in the employer–employee relationship.

A formal agreement, however, cannot cover all elements of exchange. Also, in many situations, such as between friends, a formal agreement is obviously inappropriate. Of the remaining two solutions, the inferior one, although it may do some good, is communication. Before Sam and Tracy have their study session, they can talk to each other to make sure they are both preparing adequately. They may even divvy up the different topics between them to be efficient and to ensure that free riding on a topic will not occur. If it is Sam's topic and Sam shirks and does not prepare, there will be no falling back on Tracy. The weakness in the communication solution, however, is that it does not eliminate a strong temptation for each party to cheat. Tracy can divide the topics with Sam and then repeatedly assure Sam, "Oh, yes, I'm preparing my topics. I've pretty much got them down. I can show you anything." But when they meet, Sam may find that Tracy, in fact, never got around to doing much preparation and that Tracy has nothing to provide in return for Sam's help.

The last solution, therefore, is repetition. If the two parties in an exchange believe that the exchange is likely to be repeated if it goes well, then they have a strong incentive not to cheat or free ride. If Sam and Tracy anticipate that there will be other times in the future when studying with each other might be possible and useful, they may not want to torpedo those chances by free riding in their first attempt. A married person tempted to be unfaithful may decide against it because of the potential loss of the long-term marital relationship. When a babysitter takes care of a child regularly, both of them are likely to treat the other better so they get treated better themselves.

This has immense importance for understanding social processes because it explains the importance of long-term relationships to humans and, therefore, why long-term relationships are such a key element of humans' lives. In a nutshell, because it benefits them, humans exchange with each other; this in turn creates the danger of the prisoner's dilemma, so to thwart this humans often enter into long-term relationships.

It appears, moreover, that the utility of long-term relationships has become incorporated into basic human nature. People often want to be in long-term exchange relationships—with a friend, a romantic partner, or even a business and a university (their "alma mater"). Loyalty—commitment to a long-term relationship—can be created easily in exchange relationships (Lawler and Yoon, 1996, 1998) and is valued. Long-term relationships evoke emotions such as pleasure and joy in the nurturing of such a relationship and anger and sadness when one ends.

Trust and Reputation

Because of the risk of being cheated, entering an exchange relationship means placing trust in your partner. This is especially true when there is a time lag between when one party fulfills its side of the exchange and when the other side does so. This is often the case with social exchange. A person may pursue a career with a particular employer, for example, in the expectation that the employer will treat him well in the future—promote him, not lay him off arbitrarily, maintain his pension, and so forth. A woman may have children with a man in the expectation that the man will remain with her and help her support and raise them.

The need to place trust leads to a concern with reputation. When we speak of a person's reputation—or, for that matter, a business's reputation—we usually are concerned with the person's or business's trustworthiness in some area. We want to know others' reputations to know whether we can place trust in them (Milinski, Semmann, and Krambeck, 2002; Rapoport, Diekmann, and Franzen, 1995; Raub and Weesie, 1990). The much maligned activity called gossip is a social process devoted to spreading social information, including information about trustworthiness. This is one reason we gossip—to find out what those around us are doing in key areas of social life where placing trust is important, such as friendships and alliances, striving for status, sexual behavior, and work behavior (Burt and Knez, 1996). A desire to gossip and to pay attention to gossip is probably an evolved human predisposition (Runciman, 2000).

Knowing how important reputation is, we are also concerned to establish, maintain, or shore up our own reputations, because that will affect whether others trust us and, therefore, whether they are willing to enter into exchanges with us. We try to show others that we can keep secrets, can use resources that we are given productively, can score when we are given the ball, or can be entertaining and fun to be with if someone risks spending an evening with us. Note that a concern with our exchange reputation is apparently automatic with us and that problems with our reputation are accompanied by emotions (Frank, 1988; Trivers, 1971).

The matter of reputation leads us back to symbolic interaction. Our reputation is likely to be a key part of our self and identity. The impressions we try to give others are often precisely that we are trustworthy in some area and our goal may be to establish a reputation for this trustworthiness. Suppose Boris, for example, is in the early days of a potential romantic relationship. He may try to do and say things to give the impression of being kind and considerate—hold the door for his date, ask for her input on decisions, ask about her life with appropriate empathy, and so forth. He may try to give the impression of being a good partner in terms of resources—show that he works hard, he has plans and ambitions, and also that he is willing to share the fruits of his work. He may explain his history of relationships, both to convey that he is honest and trusting and to remove any doubts about his trustworthiness that his past may have created. His potential partner is likely to act similarly.

It is true, as well, that in addition to trying to give impressions to show we are trustworthy, we are trying to make sense of the impressions other people are giving us, to try to answer the question of whether *they* are trustworthy. We can end up in a back-and-forth game (also noted by Goffman [1959]): We realize they are trying to create an impression of trustworthiness that may not be true, so we look for impressions they unintentionally give off that may tell us whether they are truly trustworthy. However, they suspect we are doing the same, so they try to make the signs that they are trustworthy appear unintentional. But we suspect they are doing *that* . . . and so on.

STATUS PROCESSES

Status processes How hierarchies form and operate in small groups.

The last major topic in microsociology that we consider is **status processes**. You will see that there are again connections to both exchange processes and symbolic interaction. Also, human nature plays a role in status processes just as it did in symbolic interaction and in exchange processes.

Suppose you and a few others are selected for a work group. None of you know each other, but now you have to work together on some task. For sociologists, an interesting question is how the group will organize itself and how its members will work together. One answer that experimental research has discovered is that a hierarchy will form in the group, and usually this happens astonishingly quickly, most often within 10 minutes (as noted in Chapter 2). Specifically, there will be a leader of the group, obvious even to outsiders because she is the person who talks the most, who makes the most declarative statements, and who usually addresses statements to the group as a whole rather than to specific individuals. The others say less, are more tentative, and tend to address themselves to just one other person, often the leader. When researchers survey group members after the work is done, the group members almost always rate the contributions of the leader to the project as the highest and also rate the leader's abilities the highest. The hierarchy, although it forms quickly, is surprisingly resilient. It takes a lot, usually an event or events that strongly discredit the leader or other high-status individuals, for the status order to change.

This strong tendency for humans in groups to form a hierarchy is not surprising. It was noted in Chapters 2 and 3 that status is very important for all humans. Animals that live together in groups, including chimpanzees and other apes, almost always form hierarchies (de Waal, 1996; Wilson, 1975). It is likely, therefore, that creating and adhering to a hierarchy is human nature.

Sociologists have been especially interested in how people's place in the hierarchy or "status structure," as sociologists often term it, is determined (Berger et al., 1977). Three kinds of determinants seem to be key. One is where people stand with regard to particular characteristics. Among key characteristics that matter generally are gender, age, race, ethnicity, and level of education. Older people, for example, are likely to get higher status than younger people. These general characteristics are called **diffuse status characteristics**. There may also be some interdependency between the characteristics. Young women tend to be given lower status than young men, but this difference is not found for older women and men (Hopcroft, 2006). Some characteristics are less general in that they have effects only in particular settings. Military rank matters only within the armed services, rank in a corporation matters only within the corporation, and so forth.

Diffuse status characteristic A characteristic that generally matters in all social interaction, such as gender, age, and race.

Note that the preceding characteristics need not have any obvious connection to whatever activity the group is doing. As you might expect, however, some characteristics that affect status relate directly to the group activity. If you and a bunch of people are accidentally stranded in the middle of a forest—perhaps your tour bus broke down—and one member of your group is a park ranger by profession, the group is likely to choose her to be the leader. For a group with a particular task, these more directly relevant characteristics tend to have more influence on status than the general ones. These characteristics are called **specific status characteristics**.

Specific status characteristic A characteristic that relates directly to the group activity.

In addition to all the characteristics people bring with them to their groups, people's behavior in the group also helps determine their status, as you might imagine. Talking a lot, phrasing your contributions as statements rather than questions, as well as a variety of nonverbal behaviors will help you to obtain high status. These behaviors have to be performed very early in the existence of the group, however, because the hierarchy is likely to set up quickly and be permanent, as noted previously. If you try high-status behaviors—for example, being vocal and assertive—too late, you will just draw the irritation and then the censure of the other group members.

You might wonder how all these elements, the different characteristics and behaviors, work together to produce a hierarchy. Researchers have discovered that they basically just add up. All your characteristics and behaviors that boost your status go together, albeit with diminishing effect; all your characteristics and behaviors that lower your status go together, with diminishing effect. Then the total positive effect and the total negative effect together—perhaps net positive, perhaps net negative, or perhaps net no effect—give you the total effect. One belief that crops up occasionally among people is that there is some "master status," that some particular characteristic is far more important than any other in determining a person's place in the hierarchy. Gender, race, and a physical condition such as disability, beauty, or height are sometimes suggested. Careful experimental research, however, has suggested that no characteristic trumps the others.

Finally, note that status processes are connected with the other microsociological processes we have discussed. With regard to symbolic interaction, your status in various groups is likely to be part of your self and identity, as noted in Chapter 3. Moreover, the impressions you give to other group members, whether intentionally or not, are part of the process by which your position in the hierarchy is determined. These could be both status-affecting behaviors and status characteristics. Indeed, people often lie or stretch the truth about attributes such as credentials in order to garner a higher status. Status is also relevant to exchange processes because people tend to suppose that higher-status people have more to offer, such as better leadership, better ideas, and better skills. Research has shown, for example, that people tend to give better deals to higher-status people than to lower-status people (Ball and Eckel, 1998; Ball et al., 2001).

CONCLUSION

In this chapter, we examined microsociology, the smallest-scale social processes, and focused on four subareas: social effects on individuals, symbolic interaction, exchange processes, and status processes. These aspects of social processes, however, are inevitably intertwined. It is part of our evolved human nature to be concerned with exchange (Smith, 1977 [1776]) and status (Veblen, 1918 [1899]), to operate at a symbolic level (Deacon,

1997), and to condition our behavior on our social surroundings (Mead, 1934). Naturally, we do these things simultaneously.

Despite the ordinariness of most microsociological processes, they are connected to many of the most important subjects of more macrosociology. Status processes in small groups, for example, are a small-scale example of stratification. Much of the stratification we see in society at large, for example, related to gender, race, and age, is probably linked to these small-scale status processes. Many aspects of the culture of a society—clothes, the arts, and leisure activities, for example—concern symbols that are both provided and used by small-scale symbolic interaction. Also, as emphasized more than a century ago by Durkheim (1997 [1893]), exchange processes, by leading people to be interdependent, create the solidarity of modern societies. In the next chapter, we examine sociological research on one real-life small group that is found in all societies—the family.

REFERENCES

Ball, Sheryl B., and Catherine C. Eckel. 1998. "The Economic Value of Status." *Journal of Socio-Economics* 27, 495–514.

Ball, Sheryl B., Catherine C. Eckel, Philip J. Grossman, and W. Zame. 2001. "Status in Markets." *Quarterly Journal of Economics* 116, 161–188.

Berger, Joseph, M. Hamit Fisek, Robert Z. Norman, and Morris Zelditch, Jr. 1977. *Status Characteristics and Social Interaction: An Expectation States Approach.* New York: Elsevier.

Blumstein, Phillip, and Pepper Schwartz. 1983. *American Couples: Money, Work, Sex.* New York: Morrow.

Burger, Jerry M. 2009. "Replicating Milgram: Would People Still Obey Today?" *American Psychologist* 64, 1.

Burt, Ronald S., and Marc Knez. 1996. "Trust and Third-Party Gossip." Pp. 68–89 in *Trust in Organizations: Frontiers of Theory and Research*, edited by Roderick M. Kramer and Tom R. Tyler. Thousand Oaks, CA: Sage.

Coleman, James S. 1990. *Foundations of Social Theory*. Cambridge, MA: Harvard University Press.

Deacon, Terrence. 1997. *The Symbolic Species: The Co-Evolution of Language and the Brain.* New York: Norton.

de Waal, Frans. 1996. *Good Natured: The Origins of Right and Wrong in Humans and Other Animals.* Cambridge, MA: Harvard University Press.

Durkheim, Emile. 1997 [1893]. *The Division of Labor in Society.* New York: Free Press.

Emerson, Richard M. 1962. "Power-Dependence Relations." *American Sociological Review* 27, 31–41.

Frank, Robert H. 1988. *Passions within Reason: The Strategic Role of the Emotions.* New York: Norton.

Goffman, Erving. 1959. *The Presentation of Self in Everyday Life.* Garden City, NY: Doubleday.

Heise, David R. 1977. "Social Action as the Control of Affect." *Behavioral Science* 22, 163–177.

Homans, George C. 1974. *Social Behavior: Its Elementary Forms.* New York: Harcourt Brace Jovanovich.

Hopcroft, Rosemary L. 2006. "Status Characteristics among Older Individuals: The Diminished Significance of Gender." *Sociological Quarterly* 47, 361–374.

Lawler, Edward J., and Jeongkoo Yoon. 1996. "Commitment in Exchange Relations: Test of a Theory of Relational Cohesion." *American Sociological Review* 61, 89–108.

———. 1998. "Network Structure and Emotion in Exchange Relations." *American Sociological Review* 63, 871–894.

Mead, George Herbert. 1934. *Mind, Self, and Society*, edited by Charles W. Morris. Chicago: University of Chicago Press.

Milinski, Manfred, Dirk Semmann, and Hans-Jürgen Krambeck. 2002. "Reputation Helps Solve the 'Tragedy of the Commons.'" *Nature* 415, 424–426.

Rapoport, Anatol, Andreas Diekmann, and Axel Franzen. 1995. "Experiments with Social Traps IV: Reputation Effects in the Evolution of Cooperation." *Rationality and Society* 7, 431–441.

Raub, Werner, and Jeroen Weesie. 1990. "Reputation and Efficiency in Social Interactions: An Example of Network Effects." *American Journal of Sociology* 96, 626–654.

Runciman, W. G. 2000. *The Social Animal.* Ann Arbor: University of Michigan Press.

Smith, Adam. 1977 [1776]. *An Inquiry into the Nature and Causes of the Wealth of Nations.* Chicago: University of Chicago Press.

Trivers, Robert. 1971. "The Evolution of Reciprocal Altruism." *Quarterly Review of Biology* 27, 1–32.

Veblen, Thorstein. 1918 [1899]. *The Theory of the Leisure Class.* New York: Viking.

Wilson, Edward O. 1975. *Sociobiology: The New Synthesis.* Cambridge, MA: Belknap.

SOCIOLOGY OF THE FAMILY

8

IN CHAPTER 2, WE DISCUSSED the human predisposition toward kin-based altruism that explains why the family is an important social group in all societies. In all societies, groups of related people help each other out on a day-to-day basis. Because of gender-based asymmetry in parenting, men and women tend to play somewhat different roles in the family and look for somewhat different characteristics in a long-term partner.

Yet despite these universals, there are a great many differences in families from society to society. Kinship may be more or less central to the society as a whole, and different types of kinship groups may form. Marriages are formed somewhat differently from society to society, and families also operate differently. In this chapter, we examine these differences and similarities in families in societies throughout the world, both past and present.

PREINDUSTRIAL MARRIAGE PATTERNS

Some form of official marriage is found in all human societies. Marriage is not always between one man and one woman as it is in U.S. society. Marriages may be between one man and one woman (**monogamy**), between one man and multiple women (**polygyny**), or between one woman and multiple men (**polyandry**). Polyandry is rare in human societies, whereas monogamy and polygyny are more common. Of 853 societies listed in George P. Murdock's (1967) *Ethnographic Atlas*, 83.5% permit or prefer polygyny, whereas only 0.5% permit polyandry. In many Islamic countries, a man is permitted to have up to four wives.

Monogamy Marriage between one man and one woman.

Polygyny Marriage between one man and multiple women.

Polyandry Marriage between one woman and multiple men.

Given the male predisposition toward sexual jealousy discussed in Chapter 2, you might wonder how polyandry could possibly work, given that several men share one woman. In fact, polyandry is rare because it usually does not work well. Polyandry often involves brothers sharing the same wife, and this serves to diminish the sexual jealousy that inevitably emerges. Even so, polyandry involving pairs of brothers succeeds better than polyandry involving larger groups of brothers (Levine and Silk, 1997).

In hunting and gathering societies, men typically have one or, at most, two wives. In horticultural societies in which the primary subsistence activity is gardening, more than one wife is common among headmen or prominent men in the community. In large-scale, agrarian societies, it is common for very high-status men to have numerous wives. Many emperors and monarchs had harems, mostly filled with young and attractive women from all over the realm. For example, in imperial China, by the end of the Chou dynasty (approximately 771 BC), emperors kept 1 queen, 3 consorts, 9 wives of the second rank, 27 wives of the third rank, and 81 concubines (van Gulick, 1974, p. 17). In South America, Incan rulers kept thousands of women in houses of virgins, who were brought to the king on demand (Cieza de Leon, 1959, p. 41). In modern democracies, such exotic practices are rare, and most societies have laws confining men (and women) to one spouse at a time (monogamy).

Hypergamy Marrying a partner with more resources and status than one has.

In most cases, men marry somewhat younger women, as they do to this day. On average, across societies men are 3 years older than their wives (Buss, 1989). Women are more likely to marry up in status and wealth (**hypergamy**) than men. This has created problems with women at the top of the hierarchy, who do not have anyone higher in status to marry. In preindustrial Europe, this problem was solved by sending elite women into nunneries. In 19th-century India, among the richest and most powerful castes, the marriage prospects for very high-status girls were considered so poor that daughters were routinely killed at birth. Sarah Hrdy (1999) describes this as follows:

> Selective elimination of daughters first attracted attention in the West during the years of the British Raj. Nineteenth century travelers visiting Rajasthan and Uttar Pradesh in northern India remarked on the rarity of seeing girls among any of the elite clans. It was assumed that as part of purdah the daughters of these proud descendants of warrior kings were kept in seclusion. "I have been nearly four years in India and never beheld any women but those in attendance as servants in European families, the low caste wives of petty shopkeepers and [dancing] women," wrote Fanny Parks in her 1850s travelogue through northern India. It did not occur to the observer that *there were no daughters.*

> Bit by bit, the light dawned. One British official stumbled on the phenomenon of missing daughters while engaged in negotiations with local landowners. He mistakenly referred to one of these mustachioed men as the son-in-law of the other, evoking sarcastic laughter. This was scarcely possible, they told him. The birth of a daughter would be such a calamity to families of their rank that she would never survive. It was unthinkable that any of their daughters would reach marriageable age. Among the most elite clans such as the Jhareja Rajputs and the Bedi Sikhs, known locally as the *Kuri Mar*, or "daughter destroyers," censuses confirmed the near total absence of daughters; lesser elites killed only later born daughters. Overall, including lower ranking clans that kept some or all daughters, sex ratios in the region were as high as 400 little boys surviving for every 100 girls. (p. 326)

This discussion also shows how reproductive interests (the difficulty of finding a marriage partner for a high-status daughter) and culture can override the natural predisposition to love one's children, described in Chapter 2.

The common practice of hypergamy for women has also been problematic for men at the bottom of the social hierarchy because women in their own status group have often married higher-status men. As a result, low-status men have often had trouble marrying. The Mukogodo of east Africa illustrate this. The Mukogodo are an impoverished group of pastoralists (cattle herders). Whereas young Mukogodo women typically marry men from wealthy neighboring groups, the Mukogodo men often find difficulty in securing bridewealth payments necessary for marriage and either delay marriage or do not get married at all (Cronk, 1989).

Groups tend to intermarry with other groups that share a similar position in the class and status hierarchy. In most preindustrial societies, a person is expected to marry out of their own group (**exogamy**), but typically there is also a specific group or groups into which one is expected to marry (**endogamy**). Thus, for example, I may be born into group X but am expected to marry someone from group Y. The group into which the individual is expected to marry is typically a member of the larger tribe or the same ethnic group. For example, President Barack Obama's father was from Kenya, and his ethnic group was Luo. As a Luo, Barack Obama Senior was expected to marry another Luo, which he did in 1954 (his first wife Kezia). Later, he traveled to the United States, where he met Barack Obama's mother.

Exogamy Marrying out of one's group.

Endogamy Marrying within one's group.

In some small societies, there were specific rules that one had to marry a "cross cousin." That is, men were expected to marry either their father's sister's daughter or their mother's brother's daughter. If no such person was available, then individuals were expected to marry their second or even third cousins. Such preferences helped preserve the economic and political position of family members but also meant that most preindustrial human populations were somewhat inbred. However, all human societies prohibit marriage and/or sexual relations between siblings and between parents and offspring. These incest taboos have limited the more deleterious effects of inbreeding.

Bridewealth versus Dowry

Bridewealth A payment of goods and/or services by the groom to the bride's parents.

Across most human societies, when a couple marries there is some sort of exchange of goods or money between the families of the bride and groom. **Bridewealth** is a payment of goods and/or services by the groom to the bride's parents. Bridewealth societies tend to be horticultural societies, where much of the agricultural work is done by women, although they may be agrarian societies such as contemporary Afghanistan.

Approximately two-thirds of the societies in Murdock's *Ethnographic Atlas* (1967) had some form of bridewealth or bride price payments (van den Berghe, 1979). In Afghanistan in 2002, bridewealth payments were approximately $5,000, more than most men could earn in 10 years of work (Stewart, 2004).

Dowry The money and goods a bride's family gives to her husband when she marries.

In highly stratified societies, dowry is common. A **dowry** is a large sum of money or goods that goes with the bride to her new home when she marries. These tend to be agrarian societies, in which land and the heavy labor necessary for plow agriculture are largely supplied by men. In Murdock's data, this was approximately 3% of all societies. In societies in which both men and women contribute to the family economy, gift exchange is most common. Our society has remnants of a dowry system. Brides can have trousseaux and/or "hope chests"—smaller versions of dowries consisting of things a bride has collected for her wedding—and traditionally the bride's family pays for the wedding.

Rules of Descent and Marital Residence

All human societies have rules of descent, which specify that certain lines of descent of the individual are traced and not others. The four patterns of descent common in human societies are bilateral, patrilineal, matrilineal, and double descent. In **bilateral descent**, all lines of descent are recognized as of equal or nearly equal significance. In **patrilineal** descent, the only line recognized is the male line and wealth flows down from father to son. In **matrilineal descent**, the only line recognized is the female line. Inheritance of wealth and resources is mostly between males but through the female line—that is, mother's brother to sister's son. Most preindustrial societies are patrilineal: In fact, patrilineal societies outnumber matrilineal societies three to one. **Double descent** means that both a matrilineage and a patrilineage are recognized, typically with different functions (van den Berghe, 1979).Our modern society is bilateral, but there are remnants of a patrilineal past. Surnames, for instance, traditionally trace down through the father's line.

In most societies, people live together after they are married. Where they live is determined by customs of the group. In most preindustrial societies, the couple either lives with the man's parents after marriage (*virilocality* or **patrilocality**) or lives with the woman's parents (*uxorilocality* or **matrilocality**). Sometimes, couples have a choice as to whose family they want to live with (**bilocal**). **Avunculocality** is also practiced, in which a couple settles in proximity to the groom's mother's brother. With **neolocality**, typical in modern industrial societies, the couple takes up a separate residence. This is comparatively rare because it is only in modern societies that new couples can routinely afford to set up a residence on their own. According to Murdock's (1967) *Ethnographic Atlas*, the most common pattern of residence is patrilocal, followed by matrilocal (Table 8.1). Rules of residence follow closely from rules of descent. Patrilineal societies tend to be patrilocal, whereas matrilineal societies tend to be matrilocal.

CONTROL OF WOMEN'S SEXUALITY

As discussed in Chapter 2, in all human societies males are often concerned about whether their partner's children are in fact their own. This is particularly the case in patrilineal societies, in which wealth flows down through the male line. Given that fathers bequeath their wealth to their sons, they are, not surprisingly, concerned that they are investing in their own children. This is less likely the case in matrilineal societies, in which wealth flows from mother's brother to sister's son. The relative lack of concern with paternity reflects the fact that a man can be sure his sister's son is his biological nephew.

Bilateral descent All lines of descent are recognized as of equal or nearly equal significance, and inheritance flows down through both the father's and mother's lines.

Patrilineal descent Descent is traced through the male line and wealth flows from father to son.

Matrilineal descent Descent is traced through the female line and wealth flows down the female line, generally from the mother's brother to the sister's son.

Double descent Both a matrilineage and a patrilineage are recognized, typically with different functions.

Patrilocal (virilocal) residence Couple typically lives with the man's parents.

Matrilocal (or uxorilocal) residence Couple typically lives with the woman's parents.

Bilocal residence Couples have a choice as to whose family they want to live with.

Avunculocal residence A couple settles in proximity to the groom's mother's brother.

Neolocal residence Typical in modern industrial societies; where the couple takes up a separate residence.

TABLE 8.1 Rules of Descent and of Residence (as Presented in van den Berghe, 1979)

RULE OF RESIDENCE	RULE OF DESCENT: PATRILINEAL		MATRILINEAL		DOUBLE DESCENT		BILATERAL		TOTAL	
	N	%	N	%	N	%	N	%	N	%
Patrilocal	384	96.2	18	14.8	25	92.6	161	52.0	588	68.6
Matrilocal	0	0.0	44	36.0	0	0.0	67	21.7	111	13.0
Avunculocal	0	0.0	36	29.5	1	3.7	0	0.0	37	4.3
Bilocal	5	1.3	14	11.5	1	3.7	53	17.2	73	8.5
Neolocal	6	1.5	6	4.9	0	0.0	28	9.1	40	4.7
Duolocal	4	1.0	4	3.3	0	0.0	0	0.0	8	0.9
Total	399	100.0	122	100.0	27	100.0	309	100.0	857	100.0
% of grand total	46.5		14.2		3.2		36.1		100.0	

Source: Murdock (1967).

As a result of such concerns, in most patrilineal societies adultery by wives is severely punished. Nathaniel Hawthorne's novel *The Scarlet Letter* spoke of the ostracism and shaming of Hester Prynne, a woman who committed adultery in colonial America. Hester was forced to wear a large scarlet "A" branding her as an adulteress, and she was ostracized from society. Such punishments for adulterous wives are common in preindustrial societies, and in fact Hester's punishment was mild compared to some. The traditional penalty for adultery for women in some Muslim societies is death by stoning. In some countries, the woman's family is duty bound to kill the offending woman.

In most societies, to guard against any impropriety women are carefully supervised both before and after marriage. In Muslim societies, this involves veiling and wearing clothing that entirely covers the body and head. Women are only allowed in public places when accompanied by a male relative. They are typically forbidden from working outside of the home, driving, or participating in public life. In most patrilineal societies, residence of the couple is with the husband's family, who are vigilant in monitoring the behavior of the wife.

Women at the top of the social status hierarchy are most likely to have their virginity closely guarded before marriage. This is because it is most important that they be chaste before marriage to secure the highest-status husband, which their class and rank demand. The story of Rapunzel reflects the reality that in preindustrial Europe many upper-class women were literally kept prisoners in their own homes, by their own parents, to protect their virtue.

Other methods of controlling women in agrarian societies have included practices such as foot binding in imperial China. Although ostensibly a beautifying practice (it being considered ladylike to have small feet), foot binding meant that women's mobility was severely curtailed because many of these women could barely walk. They literally could not go anywhere by themselves if they tried! This effectively controlled their behavior, including their sexual behavior. In the Middle Ages in Europe, men sometimes left their wives locked up in chastity belts so as to ensure their wives did not stray in their absence.

Other indirect methods of controlling the behavior of women include restricting the freedom of women to go and do as they please. In many agrarian societies, and in Western societies until very recently, women are legally the property of men and are required to obey the wishes of related men (fathers, brothers, and husbands). The law codes of ancient Babylon are the first known to describe women as the possessions of men (Lerner, 1986). Women are typically restricted in their ability to gain an education or work outside of the home.

Usually, these indirect methods have the effect of controlling the sexuality of women. Sometimes, this is made explicit. For example, Rory Stewart (2004, p. 53) reports of a regional governor in contemporary Afghanistan who ordered that women who were found to have met men to whom they were not related were to be taken to the hospital to undergo forced examination to determine whether they had recently had sex.

Infibulation and Clitoridectomy

In contemporary Africa, interest in controlling women's sexuality has extended to the practices of infibulation and clitoridectomy. **Infibulation** is the sewing up of the vagina to prevent intercourse. **Clitoridectomy** is the cutting out of the clitoris so that sexual activity is not pleasurable for

Infibulation Sewing up of a woman's vagina to prevent sexual intercourse.

Clitoridectomy The cutting out of the clitoris so that sexual activity is not pleasurable for the woman.

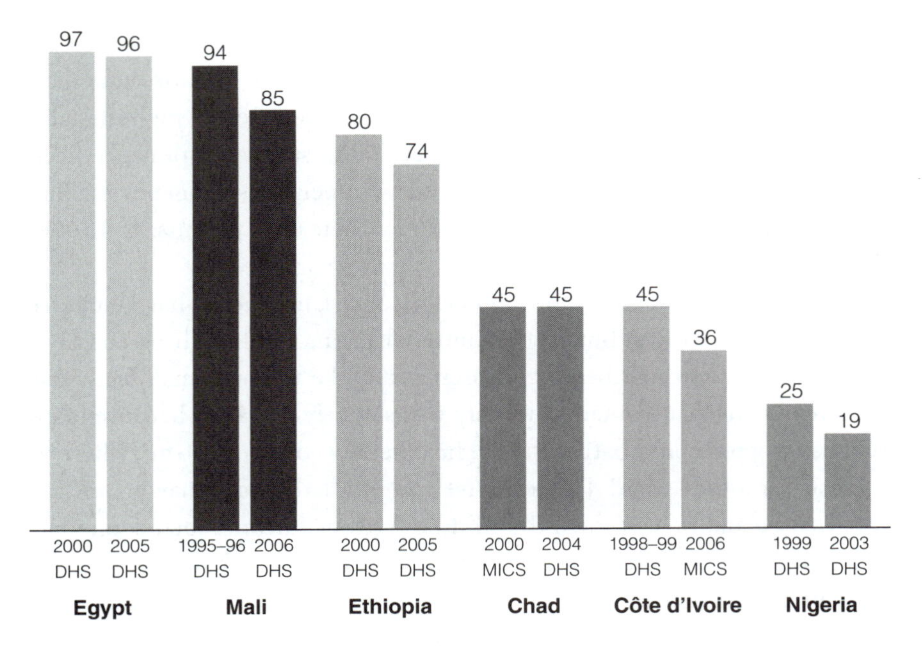

FIGURE 8.1 Trends in female genital mutilation/cutting (FGM/C). During the past decade, a downward trend in the percentage of women cut in some countries indicates that abandonment of FGM/C seems to be occurring, although in other countries there is still little or no apparent change.

Source: Feldman-Jacobs and Clifton (2008).

the woman. These practices generally are performed on young girls, generally at the behest of their mothers. In 2008, an estimated 100–140 million girls and women worldwide had undergone female genital mutilation (cutting) (Figure 8.1; Feldman-Jacobs and Clifton, 2008). The practice reflects the reality of impoverished populations, where few men are wealthy and hence desirable as husbands. Parents are afraid that if their daughters do not undergo the practices, they will be less attractive on the marriage market and will not find a desirable (wealthy) husband. Hence, they are willing participants in forcing their young girls to undergo what is a highly painful and often dangerous operation.

Menstrual Taboos

Many societies have menstruation taboos, whereby women are expected to live in special houses during their menstrual period. This is likely because it advertises to all in the community the reproductive status of women—that is, whether they are cycling and not pregnant or not cycling and pregnant. Making this private information public knowledge is an indirect method of controlling female sexuality by giving everyone in the community knowledge of when a woman is pregnant or not. This is especially the case in a preindustrial society, in which women do not menstruate very often because in such groups women spend a lot of the time pregnant and then nurse for several years after babies are born. Nursing babies in a subsistence-level society leads to postpartum amenorrhea or lack of ovulation and hence lack of menstruation. According to Beverly Strassmann's (1992) study of the Dogon of Mali (an ethnic group in West Africa), women aged 20–34 spent only 15% of the time cycling (whereas 29% of the time they were pregnant and 56% of the time in postpartum amenorrhea).

Sex and the Double Standard

Marriage includes sex, but most societies are tolerant of some forms of nonmarital sex for men, particularly premarital sex. Typically, there is a sexual double standard, whereby it is considered acceptable for men to experiment sexually but not acceptable for women. This of course poses a problem: Some women are going to of necessity be involved. As a result, "loose" women are found in all societies but are generally looked down upon. Prostitution is also found in most human societies, and the vast majority of prostitutes have men as their customers (even male prostitutes, who cater to homosexual men).

FAMILIES AND CHILDREN

In hunting and gathering societies, children are well spaced because of lengthy periods of breast-feeding (approximately 4 years) and associated postpartum amenorrhea or lack of ovulation. This means that family sizes are small, probably each woman has four or five children in her lifetime, and not all of them survive to adulthood. In agrarian societies, family sizes are larger because shorter periods of breast-feeding mean less time between children for a woman. The milk of domestic animals such as cows can be substituted for breast milk, so children can be weaned earlier. In addition, children are social and economic assets in farming societies. More children means more workers for the farm, and a large family is therefore a sign of both health and wealth. Families can be very large as a result, although many children do not survive to adulthood. In most preindustrial societies today, a large family is on the decline (as noted in Chapter 6) as the demographic transition has begun.

Within the preindustrial family, the typical pattern is one of patriarchy, with the father dominant over the family and the mother dominant over the children. In patrilocal societies, the authority of the wife in the home is often second to the authority of the husband's mother over the wife and children within the residence of the extended family. Needless to say, this often causes great misery for the wife, whose only consolation is that she, one day, will be a mother-in-law. In matrilocal, matrilineal societies, the authority of the father is generally second to that of the mother's brother, who often is the father figure to his sister's children.

MODERNIZATION AND CHANGE IN MARRIAGE PATTERNS

At first, the shift toward an industrial economy in the 19th century in Europe and North America only involved men and unmarried women as workers in factories and businesses. Married women, particularly middle- and upper-class women, were either legally prohibited from working or there were strong norms that women would quit their jobs when they married. Higher education was usually unavailable to women, and they were generally forbidden from the professions. This began to change in the 20th century.

Other changes followed the entry of women into the labor force. Women first won the right to vote in New Zealand in 1893. The United States followed in 1920. World War II (1939–1945) stimulated the entry of women into the workforce because women were needed to take over the civilian jobs left vacant by men when they went to war. After the GIs returned, women returned to the home, but the experience that women were able to do men's jobs as well as men had long-term effects. Although feminists had been drawing attention to the status of women for some time, in the late 1950s and early 1960s the feminist revolution gathered pace. In 1963, Betty Friedan published *The Feminine Mystique*, a book that documented the unease of educated women with domestic lives and that is often credited with beginning the feminist movement. At the same time, the introduction of the birth control pill helped free women from unwanted pregnancies. The late 1960s saw the full scope of the women's movement and more rolling back of practices that had kept women from working outside of the

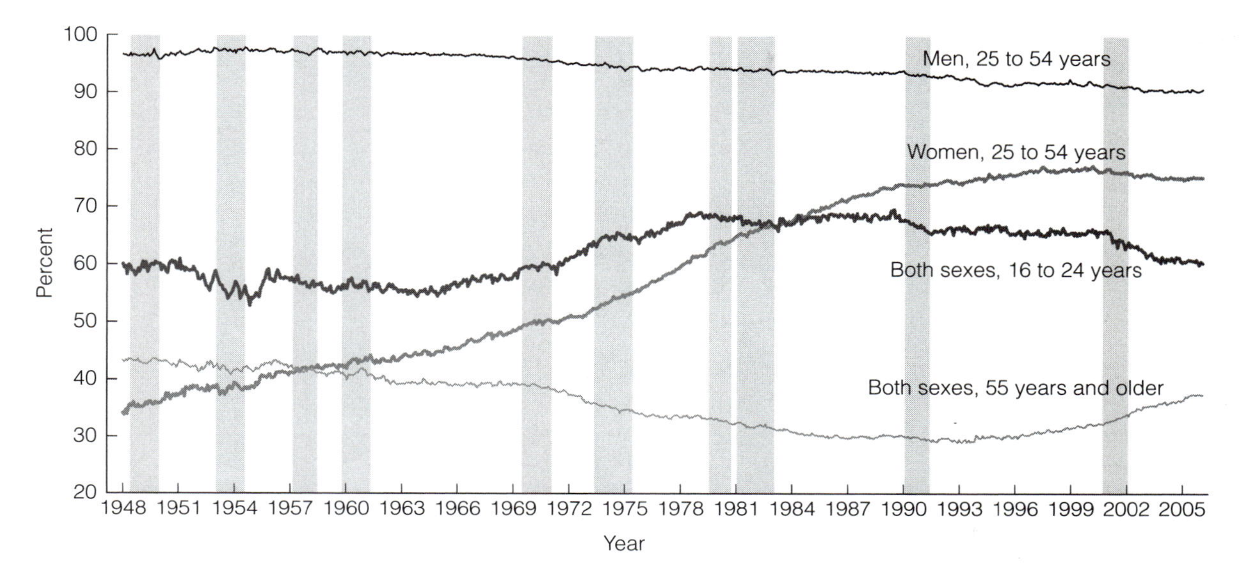

FIGURE 8.2 Labor force participation rates for major age–sex groups, seasonally adjusted, 1948–2006. Shaded areas represent recessions.

Source: Mosisa and Hipple (2006).

home. By the 1980s, women comprised 50% of the workforce in the United States, and they comprised similarly large proportions of the paid workforce in other advanced industrial societies (Figure 8.2).

The Divorce Revolution

Accompanying the feminist revolution was the divorce revolution. In the United States, notably beginning in the late 1960s, the number of divorces mushroomed (Figure 8.3). Today, approximately half of all new marriages end in divorce. This does not mean that all couples have a 50% chance of being divorced, because people who are repeatedly married and divorced disproportionately contribute to divorce statistics.

To some extent, the divorce rate follows the marriage rate, which increased during the Depression (1930s) and peaked after World War II.

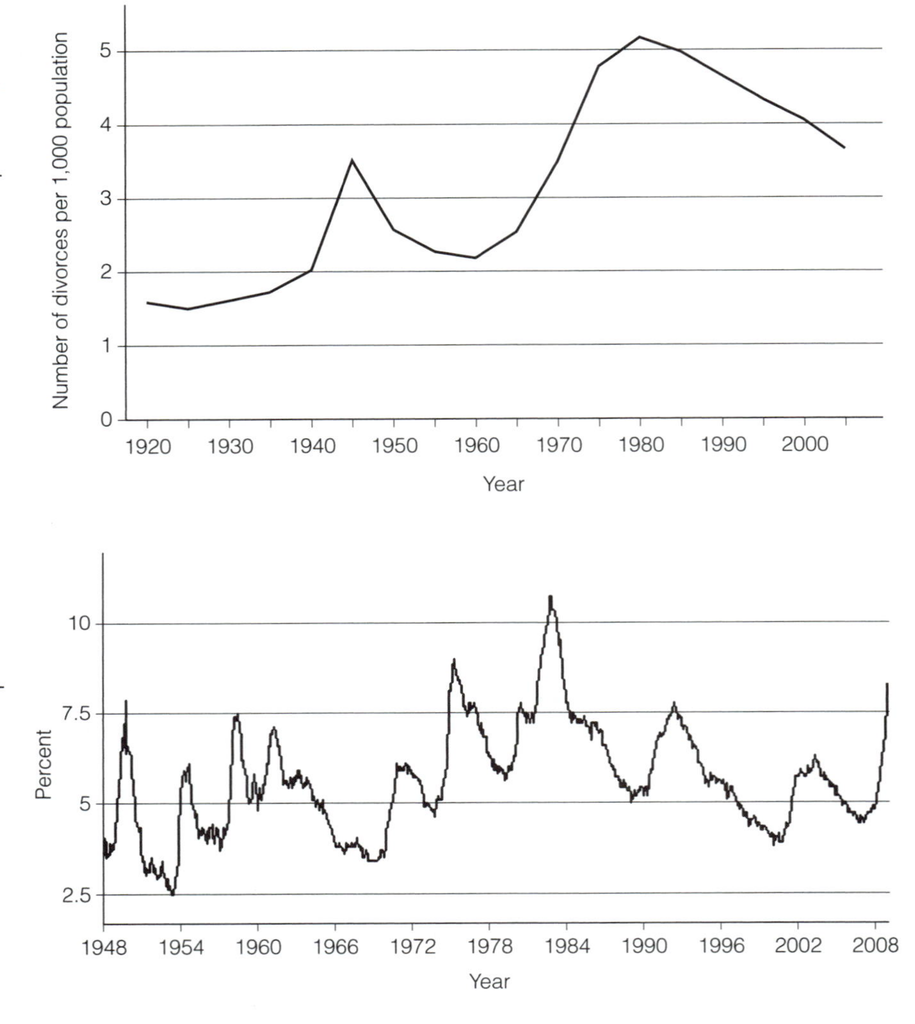

FIGURE 8.3 Divorces per 1,000 population for the United States, 1920–2004.

Source: National Center for Health Statistics.

FIGURE 8.4 Unemployment rate—16 years and older.

Source: Labor force statistics from the Current Population Survey.

It is also instructive to note that the unemployment rate follows a similar pattern, peaking at approximately the same time the divorce rate peaks (late 1940s and again in approximately 1980) (Figure 8.4).

Demography also plays a role. People are less likely to divorce when they are older than age 40 years, and now most of the largest demographic group (the baby boom group born after World War II) are older than 40 years.

These two revolutions—the feminist revolution and the divorce revolution—have had tremendous influence on marriage and the family in the United States and most countries of the developed, industrialized world.

TABLE 8.2 Estimated Median Age at First Marriage by Sex, 1890 to Present

YEAR	MEN	WOMEN
2003	27.1	25.3
2000	26.8	25.1
1990	26.1	23.9
1980	24.7	22.0
1970	23.2	20.8
1960	22.8	20.3
1950	22.8	20.3
1940	24.3	21.5
1930	24.3	21.3
1920	24.6	21.2
1910	25.1	21.6
1900	25.9	21.9
1890	26.1	22.0

Source: U.S. Bureau of the Census.

Women (and men) who can work to support themselves and live on their own are far less likely to heed parental pressures about when and whom they should marry. They are also more likely to delay marriage. As a result, there is very little prescription of who should marry whom, and thus the age at first marriage has increased and continues to increase. Average age at first marriage for women in the United States is now 25.3 years, and for men it is 27.1 years (Table 8.2). The female preference for an older husband, and the male preference for a younger wife, is still apparent, although the average age difference between bride and groom in the United States has been decreasing over time.

Modern Love

So why do people decide to get married? One reason is that people fall in love (although there are other reasons, of course). Being in love is a biochemical state characterized by increased levels of the neurotransmitters dopamine and norepinephrine—a chemical derived from dopamine (Fisher, 2004). Brain scans show greater blood flow to the caudate nucleus, a part of the brain that is part of the primitive, reptilian brain. It is part of the reward system of the brain. The more passionate the love, the more activity in this part of the brain. Although people in all societies experience romantic love, it is only in recent societies that it has become the most important factor in marriage.

Romantic love is entwined with lust. Romance triggers lust, but lust can also trigger romantic love because sexual activity can raise levels of dopamine and norepinephrine. Attachment is different from romantic love, and biochemically it is associated with the "satisfaction hormones" rather than the "reward hormones." In males, these satisfaction hormones include vasopressin, and in females they include oxytocin. High levels of vasopressin and oxytocin tend to lower levels of dopamine and norepinephrine, so the chemistry of attachment can quell the chemistry of romance. Romantic love usually lasts approximately 12–18 months, whereas attachment can last a lifetime.

Contemporary Marriage

Despite the greater involvement of romantic love in marriage formation, modern marriages do not appear to be much different from marriages in preindustrial societies. People still tend to marry people from the same class and social backgrounds as themselves (Table 8.3). This may be simply a result of *propinquity*, or nearness in terms of place, because people are more likely to meet people of the same class and social backgrounds as themselves in school and in the workplace. In the United States, people also tend to marry those with similar education and earning potential. Highly educated, high-earning men tend to marry highly educated, high-earning women, and vice versa, and this has become increasingly the case in recent years (Sweeney and Cancian, 2004; Schoen and Cheng, 2006). This trend is more true of the United States than other advanced industrial societies (Kalmijn, 1998).

Yet consistent with the principle of gender asymmetry in parenting, women tend to have slightly different criteria in picking a long-term mate than men. Women in the United States are still more likely to prefer mates who offer resources and status than are men, and men are still compara-

TABLE 8.3 Family Organization across Societies

	TYPE OF SOCIETY			
TYPE OF INSTITUTION	HUNTING/ GATHERING	HORTICULTURAL	AGRARIAN	INDUSTRIAL
Rule of residence	Flexible	Patrilocal, less commonly matrilocal	Patrilocal	Neolocal
Rule of descent	Bilateral or patrilineal	Unilineal–patri- or matrilineal	Patrilineal or bilateral	Bilateral
Marriage type	Limited polygyny	Extensive polygyny	Upper class polygyny, peasant monogamy	Monogamy
Marriage rules	Few and flexible	Prescriptive exogamy, often with cross cousins	Prescriptive exogamy, status group endogamy	Few prescriptions, preferential class isogamy
Exchange of goods and services at marriage	Gift exchange	Bridewealth	Gift exchange and/or dowry	Gift exchange

tively more interested in youth and beauty (Buss, 1989). Marriage timing in the United States is still determined by the economic position of men, not women (Oppenheimer, 2000). Even women who earn a great deal of money usually say they are interested in men who earn at least as much as they do. Role reversal is not expected or desired. When wives earn substantially more than their husbands, the risk of divorce is increased (Sayer and Bianchi, 2000). The absence of female earnings does not have the same effect, on average, on marital stability.

Men prefer younger mates, and women prefer mates who are the same age or older. Age preferences of men and women are one reason why unmarried households in the United States are much more likely to be female headed than male headed, because divorced men are more likely to remarry than divorced women. Women's chances of remarriage decline quickly as they age (Bumpass, Sweet, and Castro, 1990). Marriage and divorce patterns resemble a recycling of marriageable men, where high-earning men go on to remarry more often than comparable women (Blumstein and Schwartz, 1983; Oh, 1986).

Of course, all these trends are about the average, and any individual's experience may not reflect these trends. You probably know individuals who are not like the average at all. But if you think about it, you probably also know many people who fit the trends.

The Contemporary Family in the United States

Within the family, sex roles have become more egalitarian. However, although dual-income families are typical, husbands are still disproportionately major economic providers for the family (Raley, Mattingly, and Bianchi, 2006), and fathers on average still spend more hours in paid work than mothers (Nomaguchi, Milkie, and Bianchi, 2005).

Women still tend to more of the housework and child care. This is the case even in Sweden, where traditional marriage has become uncommon and cohabitation the rule (Evertsson and Nermo, 2004). Women also tend to be the more committed parents. It is mothers who typically end up with custody of the children after separation or divorce. In the case of a disabled child, it is mothers who are the most likely to be the primary caregiver. Judith Seltzer (1994, p. 235) stated it as follows: "Women provide for children's needs, whether or not the women are married to their children's fathers. For men, marriage defines responsibilities to children. At divorce, men typically disengage from their biological children."

It is likely that given the smaller families of today, children receive more individual attention than did children in the past. They certainly receive massive investments. It has been estimated that the average cost of raising a child to the age of 18 years is approximately $250,000 in the contemporary United States. Despite their cost, children in general tend to create stability in the family. This is expected given kin-based altruism because children create shared genetic interests in the family since both father and mother have an equal genetic stake in their children. This encourages cooperation between parents and joint investment in children. The stabilizing effect of children on a couple's relationship occurs with or without legal marriage (Manning, 2004). It is also possible that people are more likely to choose to leave a relationship when no children are born.

Divorce (and/or separation) disrupts this joint investment in children and tends to have negative effects on children. Remarriage generally does not ameliorate problems. Children brought up in other arrangements receive less education and have lower occupational achievement than children raised by their biological parents or even their mother alone (Biblarz and Raftery 1999; Case, Lin, and McLanahan 2001; Cherlin and Furstenberg, 1994; Furstenberg et al., 1995). Negative effects of divorce even extend across generations (Amato and Cheadle, 2005). Divorce lessens the flow of inheritance from parents to children (Furstenberg et al., 1995).

Despite high rates of divorce, marriage at least in the United States remains popular. One reason may be that cooperation and altruism within the family unit are good for people. Studies show that in the United States, married people live longer, healthier lives, and they are less likely to suffer mental illness. Married people are also more likely to report that they are very happy (Waite, 2000). This may not be solely a result of being married because it is likely that people who marry are healthier and happier to begin with than people who do not get married.

Nonbiological Families

In many industrial societies, alternative family forms have arisen. These remain a minority of family forms. Families in which children are adopted are most common. Families that adopt tend to be above average in income and education, and as a result adopted children receive, on average, more investment than the typical biological child. When comparing families that are similar in income and education, studies suggest that adopted children receive approximately the same amount of investment as biological children (Hamilton, Cheng, and Powell, 2007).

Stepchildren tend to receive less investment than adopted children. Studies suggest that blended families with stepchildren often are more problematic than other families. The divorce rate is higher in remarriages than in first marriages. White and Booth (1985) found that "a comparison of parents with stepchildren and those without shows a strong and consistent pattern: Parents with stepchildren would more often enjoy living away from their children, perceive their children as causing them problems, are dissatisfied with their spouse's relationship to their children, think their marriage has a negative effect on their relationship with their own children, and wish they had never remarried." Biblarz, Raftery, and Bucur (1997) found that biological parents do better at promoting the occupational upward mobility of their children. Next best were single mothers and then stepfamilies.

Apparently, the demands of several sets of genetic interests in one family are too much for many individuals to handle. Homosexual couples also adopt children, but there is too little evidence to determine how children raised in these families fare in later life.

Late-Life Families and Fertility

Delay in childbearing has led to an increasing number of women seeking medical help with conception. The fertility industry has become a lucrative one. Currently, approximately 1% of all babies are born using assisted reproduction technologies (Gazzaniga, 2008, p. 377). One consequence of the increased use of these technologies is an increase in multiple births, and this has adverse health consequences for mothers and babies. Babies who are part of multiple births tend to have more health problems than singletons. At the same time, these techniques do not always work, and so there has also been an increase in (involuntary) childlessness among women. Other unanticipated problems include the problem of what to do with the embryos that are created during fertility treatments but end up not being used. Many families are in a quandary as to what to do with these surplus embryos. They are often reluctant to destroy them but at the same time reluctant to give them to others. So they remain in freezers in clinics throughout the country (nearly half a million by current estimates) (*New York Times*, 2008).

Currently, embryos created through *in vitro* fertilization can be tested for certain genetic diseases and discarded if problematic. That in itself poses ethical dilemmas. In the future, it seems very likely that not only will embryos be tested for disease but also problematic genes will be replaced with nonproblematic genes. Genetic engineering of humans (adjusting embryos to meet certain specifications) is technologically not too far distant—a thought that makes many people uncomfortable.

VIOLENCE IN THE FAMILY

Although family life is a happy experience for most people, it can also be a place of conflict and trauma, even homicide. Male sexual jealousy fuels some of this violence because men who fear they are losing their partner react in a controlling and sometimes violent way. For the woman, the most

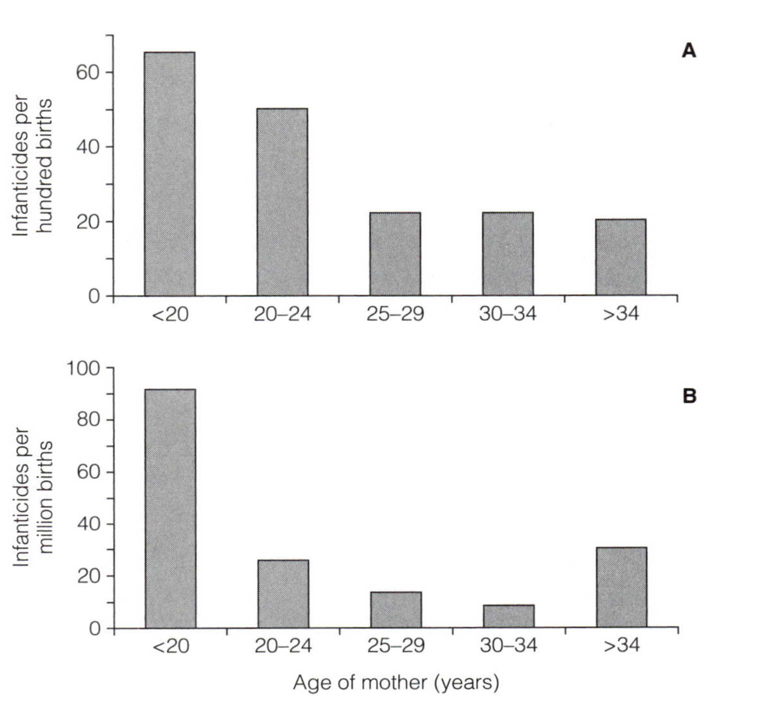

FIGURE 8.5 Rates of infanticide by mothers as a function of maternal age among (A) Ayoreo Indians of South America ($n = 54$ victims) and (B) Canadians ($n = 87$ victims), 1974–1983.

From Daly and Wilson (1988).

dangerous time can be when she actually leaves the relationship. Daly and Wilson (1988) have shown that this is the most common time for uxoricide, or wife killing, to occur. For this reason, the locations of battered women's shelters in most cities are kept secret.

Child Abuse

The vast majority of parents are loving and helpful to their children. However, child abuse does occur and can even result in the death of a child. Mothers kill or abandon their children for a variety of reasons—for example, they are too young to deal with parenthood and have too little in the way of money and social support. Young mothers are particularly likely to kill or abandon their newborns. Older mothers are much less likely to do this: They often are better established financially and socially and can take on the demands of parenthood. There is also the point that young mothers have much more time in which to have more children, whereas older mothers do not have this option (Figure 8.5). Figure 8.5 shows that among two very different cultural groups, the Ayoreo Indians of South America and

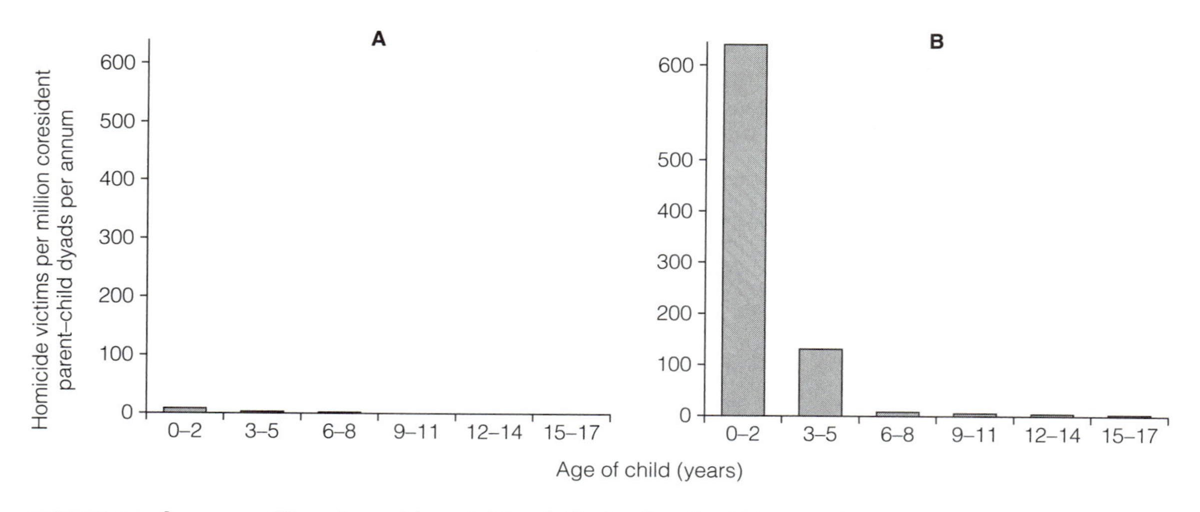

FIGURE 8.6 Age-specific rates of homicide victimization by (A) genetic parents ($n = 341$ victims) or (B) stepparents ($n = 67$ victims), Canada, 1974–1983.

From Daly and Wilson (1988).

Canadians, between 1974 and 1983, most infanticides were committed by teenage mothers. Married women of all ages are much less likely to kill or abandon their children.

The chances of a biological parent (either father or mother) killing his or her biological children are dwarfed by the chances of a nonbiological guardian killing a child (Figure 8.6). A nonbiological caregiver (typically, but not always, the mother's boyfriend or new husband) is approximately 40 times more likely to kill a child than is a biological parent. Adoptive parents, however, are not more likely to harm their children. Figure 8.6 shows the age-specific rates of homicide victimization using Canadian data from 1974 to 1983. Given that most children live with their natural parents, the rates given in Figure 8.6 control for the greater number of children living with natural parents as opposed to stepparents.

CONCLUSION

Marriage and the family are found in all human societies. Family systems vary greatly from society to society, but there are constant themes. Older men tend to marry younger women, and marriage celebrations are marked by some sort of gift exchange. Women face more restrictions on their sexual behavior than do men. Women are typically more committed to children than are men and take a greater role in child care. Kinship or blood ties bind within the family, and altruism tends to follow those ties. Although families are a source of much human happiness, they can also be places of conflict between both husbands and wives and parents and children. This can escalate into violence and homicide. These constancies echo human biology, but there are important differences by society depending on its level of economic development and its own particular cultural heritage.

REFERENCES

Amato, Paul R., and Jacob Cheadle. 2005. "The Long Reach of Divorce: Divorce and Child Well-Being across Three Generations." *Journal of Marriage and the Family* 67(1), 191–206.

Biblarz, Timothy J., and Adrian E. Raftery. 1999. "Family Structure, Educational Attainment, and Socioeconomic Success: Rethinking the 'Pathology of Matriarchy.'" *American Journal of Sociology* 105(2), 321–365.

Biblarz, Timothy J., Adrian E. Raftery, and A. Bucur. 1997. "Family Structure and Social Mobility." *Social Forces* 75, 1319–1341.

Blumstein, Phillip, and Pepper Schwartz. 1983. *American Couples: Money, Work, Sex*. New York: Morrow.

Bumpass, Larry, James Sweet, and Teresa Castro. 1990. "Changing Patterns of Remarriage." *Journal of Marriage and the Family* 52(3), 747–756.

Buss, David M.1989. "Sex Differences in Human Mate Preferences: Evolutionary Hypotheses Tested in 37 Cultures." *Behavioral and Brain Sciences* 12, 1–49.

Case, Ann, I-Fen Lin, and Sara McLanahan. 2001. "Educational Attainment of Siblings in Stepfamilies." *Evolution and Human Behavior* 22(4), 269–289.

Cherlin, Andrew J., and Frank F. Furstenberg, Jr. 1994. "Stepfamilies in the United States: A Reconsideration." *Annual Review of Sociology* 20, 359–381.

Cieza de Leon, P. 1959. *The Incas*. Norman: University of Oklahoma Press.

Cronk, Lee. 1989. "Low Socioeconomic Status and Female-Biased Parental Investment: The Mukogodo Example." *American Anthropologist* 91(2), 414–429.

Daly, Martin, and Margo Wilson. 1988. "Evolutionary Social Psychology and Family Homicide." *Science* 242, 519–524.

Evertsson, Marie, and Magnus Nermo. 2004. "Dependence within Families and the Division of Labor: Comparing Sweden and the United States." *Journal of Marriage and the Family* 66(5), 1272–1286.

Feldman-Jacobs, Charlotte, and Donna Clifton. 2008. "Female Genital Mutilation/Cutting: Data and Trends." *Population Data Sheet*. Washington, DC: Population Reference Bureau.

Fisher, Helen. 2004. *Why We Love*. New York: Holt.

Furstenberg, Frank, et al. 1995. "The Effects of Divorce on Intergenerational Transfers: New Evidence." *Demography* 32, 319–333.

Gazzaniga, Michael S. 2008. *Human. The Science behind What Makes Us Unique*. New York: HarperCollins.

Hamilton, Laura, Simon Cheng, and Brian Powell. 2007. "Adoptive Parents, Adaptive Parents: Evaluating the Importance of Biological Ties for Parental Investment." *American Sociological Review* 72(1), 95–116.

Hrdy, Sarah. 1999. *Mother Nature*. New York: Ballantine.

Kalmijn, Matthijs. 1998."Marriage and Homogamy: Causes, Patterns, Trends." *Annual Review of Sociology* 24, 395–421.

Lerner, Gerda. 1986. *The Creation of Patriarchy*. New York: Oxford University Press.

Levine, Nancy E., and Joan B. Silk. 1997. "Why Polyandry Fails: Sources of Instability in Polyandrous Marriages." *Current Anthropology* 38(3), 375–398.

Manning, Wendy D. 2004. "Children and the Stability of Cohabiting Couples." *Journal of Marriage and the Family* 66(3), 674–689.

Mosisa, Abraham, and Steven Hipple. October 2006. "Trends in Labor Force Participation in the United States." *Monthly Labor Review*. Washington, DC: U.S. Bureau of Labor Statistics.

Murdock, George P. 1967. *Ethnographic Atlas.* Pittsburgh, PA: University of Pittsburgh Press.

New York Times. December 4, 2008. "Parents Torn over Extra Frozen Embryos from Fertility Procedures," p. A22.

Nomaguchi, Kei M., Melissa A. Milkie, and Suzanne M. Bianchi. 2005. "Time Strains and Psychological Well-Being: Do Dual-Earner Mothers and Fathers Differ?" *Journal of Family Issues* 26(6), 756–792.

Oh, Sunjoo. 1986. "Remarried Men and Remarried Women: How Are They Different?" *Journal of Divorce* 9(4), 107–113.

Oppenheimer, Valerie Kincade. 2000. "The Continuing Importance of Men's Economic Position in Marriage Formation." Pp. 283–301 in *The Ties That Bind: Perspectives on Marriage and Cohabitation*, edited by Linda J. Waite et al. New York: Aldine de Gruyter.

Raley, Sara B., Marybeth J. Mattingly, and Suzanne M. Bianchi. 2006. "How Dual Are Dual-Income Couples? Documenting Change from 1970 to 2001." *Journal of Marriage and the Family* 68(1), 11–28.

Sayer, Liana C., and Suzanne M. Bianchi. 2000. "Women's Economic Independence and the Probability of Divorce." *Journal of Family Issues* 21(7), 906–943.

Schoen, Robert, and Yen-hsin Alice Cheng. 2006. "Partner Choice and the Differential Retreat from Marriage." *Journal of Marriage and the Family* 68(1), 1–10.

Seltzer, Judith. 1994. "Consequences of Marital Dissolution for Children." *Annual Review of Sociology* 20, 235–266.

Stewart, Rory. 2004. *The Places in Between.* Orlando, FL: Harcourt.

Strassmann, Beverly I. 1992. "The Function of Menstrual Taboos among the Dogon: Defense against Cuckoldry?" *Human Nature* 3, 89–131.

Sweeney, Megan M., and Maria Cancian. 2004. "The Changing Importance of White Women's Economic Prospects for Assortative Mating." *Journal of Marriage and the Family* 66, 1015–1028.

van den Berghe, Pierre. 1979. *Human Family Systems.* Prospect Heights, IL: Waveland Press.

van Gulick, R. H. 1974. *Sexual Life in Ancient China.* London: Brill.

Waite, Linda J. (Ed.). 2000. *The Ties That Bind: Perspectives on Marriage and Cohabitation.* New York: Aldine de Gruyter.

White, Lynn K., and Alan Booth. 1985. "The Quality and Stability of Remarriages: The Role of Stepchildren." *American Sociological Review* 55, 235–242.

SOCIAL STRATIFICATION

9

ONE OF THE FOUNDERS of sociology, Karl Marx, was greatly concerned with social stratification, or the differences in the economic position of people in society. At the time Marx was writing, during the early days of industrialization in the 19th century, the difference between the haves and have-nots in society was only too apparent. To give you an idea of what work in those early English factories was like, here is an extract of some testimony on child labor in the textile industry, given before a parliamentary committee in 1832:

> Mr. Matthew Crabtree, called in; and Examined.
>
> What age are you? — Twenty-two.
>
> What is your occupation? — A blanket manufacturer.
>
> Have you ever been employed in a factory? — Yes.
>
> At what age did you first go to work in one? — Eight.
>
> How long did you continue in that occupation? — Four years.
>
> Will you state the hours of labour at the period when you first went to the factory, in ordinary times? — From 6 in the morning to 8 at night.
>
> Fourteen hours? — Yes.
>
> With what intervals for refreshment and rest? — An hour at noon.
>
> When trade was brisk what were your hours? — From 5 in the morning to 9 in the evening.
>
> Sixteen hours? — Yes.
>
> With what intervals at dinner? — An hour.
>
> How far did you live from the mill? — About two miles.
>
> Was there any time allowed for you to get your breakfast in the mill? — No.
>
> Did you take it before you left your home? — Generally.
>
> During those long hours of labour could you be punctual; how did you awake? — I seldom did awake spontaneously; I was most generally awoke or lifted out of bed, sometimes asleep, by my parents.
>
> Were you always in time? — No.

What was the consequence if you had been too late? — I was most commonly beaten.

Severely? — Very severely, I thought.

In those mills is chastisement towards the latter part of the day going on perpetually? — Perpetually.

So that you can hardly be in a mill without hearing constant crying? — Never an hour, I believe.

—Evidence Given before the Sadler Committee
[Parliamentary Papers, 1831–1832, vol. XV, pp. 44, 95–97, 115, 195, 197, 339, 341–342. Reprinted in Scott and Baltzly (1930)]

The children of the well to do, of course, never worked in the textile factories. These inequalities continue to exist, if not in so extreme a form, and they have continued to be a central interest of sociologists. In this chapter, we examine the type and amount of social stratification in preindustrial societies, and then we examine social stratification in contemporary U.S. society and other industrial societies.

STRATIFICATION IN PREINDUSTRIAL SOCIETIES

There is little stratification among hunters and gatherers. No one owns very much other than their own clothes and hunting or gathering equipment. Houses are temporary huts that are quickly taken down and put up again in a new campsite. Life is lived on a day-to-day basis, and there is no means for preserving and storing food for any length of time. Women gather according to their own skill and capabilities, and with this they feed their families. Men hunt for themselves and their families, but a large kill is almost always shared among all. There is typically a headman in such a group, but his privileges are few and responsibilities are many. The headman usually has no way of enforcing his authority and has to rely on his own ability to convince people to go along with his decisions. Some bands have no headman at all.

Prestige The social honor (status) accorded individuals.

There are differences in **prestige**, or the social honor accorded individuals. Older people, good hunters, people with skill or expertise in various tasks, those who are kind and generous, good talkers, and storytellers are afforded prestige in the group. Men tend to have a little more prestige and authority than women in the group, but this difference is slight.

There is more social stratification in horticultural societies. Horticultural societies can be either tribes or chiefdoms. A **tribe** is like a collection of bands linked by ties of kinship. A **chiefdom** is a tribe with a single, permanent leader. Tribes have a little more social stratification than hunting and gathering bands. The increased productivity of gardening, and the fact that horticulturalists stay put in the same village for long periods of time, meant that people could accumulate more material possessions, and this becomes the basis of some social inequality. Material possessions include objects of utilitarian value such as tools, weapons, clothes, pottery, baskets, and the like, but also less utilitarian objects such as masks, jewelry, musical instruments, and artistic creations, as well as status symbols such as skulls and trophies. Wives are also an important manifestation of inequality because some men can afford to keep more than one wife and some men cannot.

Tribe Groups of clans usually linked by marriage and political ties.

Chiefdom A tribe with a single, permanent leader.

Tribes are often characterized by prominent men, often referred to as "big men." Big men are found, for example, in Melanesia, such as among the Dani of New Guinea (Heider, 1997; Photo 9.1). The typical aspiring big man begins his career by cultivating a larger garden than everyone else and raising a larger pig herd than others, and he thereby accumulates a hoard of desirable foodstuffs and goods. He often draws on the help of his close relatives, so it helps if the aspiring big man is from a large family. Eventually, the big man has enough foodstuffs and other goods to hold a large feast to which everyone in the village is invited. During the feast, the big man gives away all the extra food and goods he has accumulated. The man who succeeds in holding the biggest and most frequent feasts becomes the village "big man." He is given considerable prestige and has disproportionate influence over the village. He also tends to grow relatively wealthy and tends to have several wives. There are limits on his wealth, however. If the big man hoards too much, then the community may take revenge and kill him.

In chiefdoms, social inequality becomes even more pronounced. First, the position of leader becomes hereditary—the chief passes on his position to his son. In hunting and gathering bands and tribes, the position of leader is usually temporary. Second, the chief's family and relatives become a permanent "aristocracy" in the society with special privileges, and these are also hereditary. Usually people are required to give a certain proportion of their crop or the game they catch to the chief and the aristocracy. There are also prestige differences between aristocrats and commoners, mostly based

PHOTO 9.1 Yali Mabel, Big Man of the Dani, Indonesia, November 14, 2008. Source: © Javarman/Dreamstime.com.

on rules of behavior and dress codes. These rules of behavior typically involve food, ritual practices, and duties. Dress codes are often so elaborate that they are a physical handicap for the aristocrats who are required to follow them. For example, look at the dress of the Zulu warrior in Photo 9.2. The different behavior and dress of aristocrats and commoners mean that there are true "status groups," as Weber defined them, in chiefdoms.

There are limits on material inequality in chiefdoms, however. Chiefs are expected to share their wealth in feasts much as big men do. Also, if a chief refuses to redistribute his wealth or if the tribe becomes unhappy with him for some reason, he can be deposed and often killed.

Social inequality is most pronounced in agrarian societies. Different status groups are fully defined in agrarian societies, and there are vast differ-

PHOTO 9.2 Zulu warrior, Utimuni, nephew of Chaka the late Zulu king, 1849. Source: The Stapleton Collection, Art Resource, New York.

ences between the lifestyles of those in the top-ranked groups and those in the bottom. Membership in each class or group is hereditary. Mobility between groups is possible but rare.

At the top, there is typically a monarch or king, who is hugely wealthy. Along with the monarch is a large aristocratic or ruling class, and the ruling group and the king take the vast majority of the wealth of the society. Below the aristocracy is a retainer class, made up of officials, professional soldiers, and household servants to the aristocracy. These people have the task of making sure that the king's orders are obeyed and that the lower groups do not get out of line. There is also a priestly class that can be very extensive.

Below these upper classes are the farmers or peasants—the vast majority of people who work the land. In contrast to the aristocracy, whose lifestyle is lavish, these people live close to subsistence. The peasantry have enough

PHOTO 9.3 Leatherworkers (tanners) in Japan, 1873. They are Burakumin, members of an unclean or degraded class in premodern Japan. Source: Courtesy of the Tom Burton Collection.

food to eat (although not that much) and a few possessions, and that is it. Below the peasantry are groups of slaves, craftsmen and artisans, an unclean or degraded class, as well as a group of beggars and petty criminals—the expendable class. The *eta* or *Burakumin* of premodern Japan are examples of an unclean or degraded class (Photo 9.3). The *hinin* of premodern Japan are an example of an expendable class.

The Caste System of India

This system of ranked groups of people in agrarian societies reaches its most rigid form in the Indian caste system. Each caste is an endogamous, hereditary group. At the top are the Brahmins, or priestly class. After the Brahmins are the rulers and aristocrats, the Kshatria. Next are the landlords and businessmen, or Vaisia. After them in the hierarchy are the Sudra, the peasantry and those who work in nonpolluting jobs. Below these castes are the outcasts, who are untouchable and who work in unclean jobs such as tanning and garbage collection. The first three castes have social and economic rights that the Sudra and the untouchables do not have. Interaction between the castes is strictly regulated, and there are penalties for people who do not follow the rules.

STRATIFICATION IN AN ADVANCED INDUSTRIAL SOCIETY: THE UNITED STATES

Compared to agrarian societies, there is less inequality in advanced industrial societies. More important, people in the bottom ranks of an advanced industrial society have a much higher standard of living than people in the bottom ranks of an agrarian society. There is still substantial inequality, however, and that varies depending on the society. How much inequality exists also depends on whether we are considering money or status inequality. Let's look at money inequality in the United States first. Money can be **income**, which means the wages and payments people receive from a job or investments, or money can be **wealth**, which means assets in the form of real estate, capital assets, stocks, bonds, and savings. Income inequality is easily measured in the United States because the Internal Revenue Service collects information on income from everyone every year.

Income The wages and payments people receive from a job or investments.

Wealth Assets in the form of real estate, stocks, bonds, and savings.

Income Inequality

Let's discuss the distribution of income first. Table 9.1 shows the split of household income by quintiles (fifths of the population). Equivalence-adjusted income takes into consideration the number of people living in the household and how these people share resources and take advantage of economies of scale. For example, the household income–based distribution treats income of $30,000 for a single-person household and a family household similarly, whereas the equivalence-adjusted income of $30,000 for a single-person household would be more than twice the equivalence-adjusted income of $30,000 for a family household with two adults and two children. You can see that the highest quintile (top fifth) of households earned nearly half of all income in 2007.

What areas in the United States have the highest levels of income inequality? Figure 9.1 shows income inequality throughout the United States in

TABLE 9.1 Income Distribution Measures Using Money Income and Equivalence-Adjusted Income, 2006 and 2007

	2006				2007			
	MONEY INCOME		EQUIVALENCE-ADJUSTED INCOME		MONEY INCOME		EQUIVALENCE-ADJUSTED INCOME	
MEASURE	ESTIMATE	90% CONFIDENCE INTERVAL (±)[a]	ESTIMATE	90% CONFIDENCE INTERVAL (±)[a]	ESTIMATE	90% CONFIDENCE INTERVAL (±)[a]	ESTIMATE	90% CONFIDENCE INTERVAL (±)[a]
Shares of aggregate income by percentile								
Lowest quintile	3.4	0.04	3.7	0.03	3.4	0.04	3.7	0.03
Second quintile	8.6	0.10	9.4	0.07	8.7	0.10	9.6	0.07
Middle quintile	14.5	0.16	15.0	0.11	14.8	0.16	15.3	0.12
Fourth quintile	22.9	0.25	22.5	0.17	23.4	0.25	22.9	0.17
Highest quintile	50.5	0.56	49.4	0.36	49.7	0.54	48.5	0.35
Top 5%	22.3	0.51	22.2	0.33	21.2	0.48	21.1	0.31
Summary measures								
Gini index of income inequality	0.470	0.0047	0.454	0.0029	0.463	0.0039	0.279	0.0027

[a]A 90% confidence interval is a measure of an estimate's variability. The larger the confidence interval in relation to the size of the estimate, the less reliable the estimate.

Source: DeNavas-Walt, Proctor, and Smith (2008).

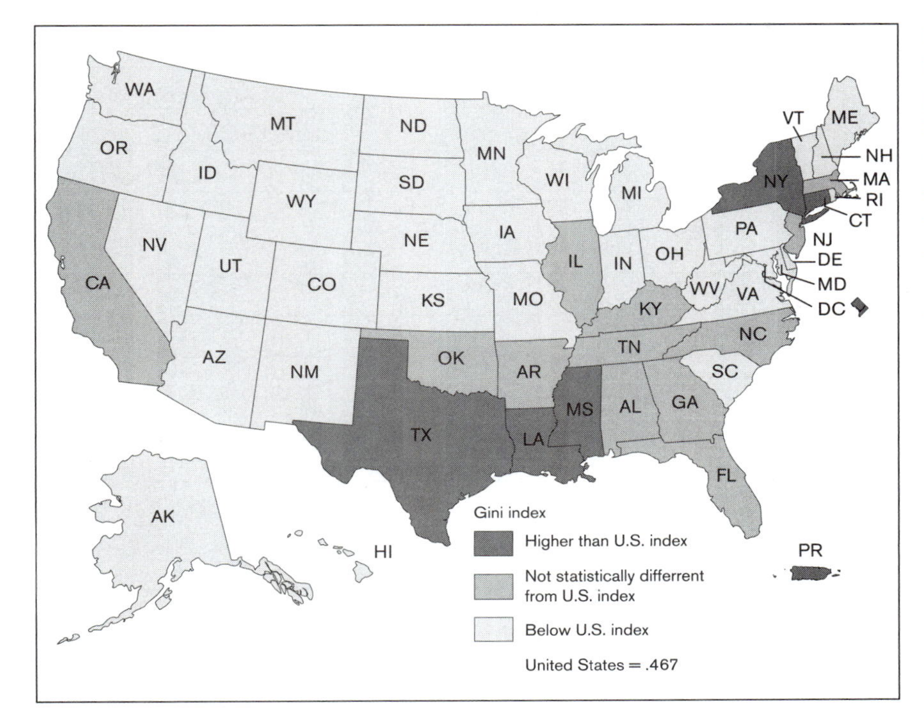

FIGURE 9.1 Gini index of income inequality in the past 12 months by state, 2007.

***Washington, DC, is represented at 4.5 times the scale of other continental states.**

Source: Bishaw and Semega (2008).

2007 measured using a Gini index, a measure of inequality. The areas that have above-average measures of inequality include some you might guess—New York, for example—and some you might not realize, including Texas, Louisiana, and Mississippi.

Is income inequality in the United States increasing or decreasing? Figure 9.2 shows that since 1967, income inequality has increased.

What Is the Median Income?

So what is the average income in the United States? In general, when we talk about the average income we talk about the **median income**—that is, the income that is in the middle of all incomes ranged from high to low. The reason for this is because there are some people with extremely high incomes, and these high incomes push up the value of the arithmetical average so it does not reflect what an ordinary person actually earns. Real median household income was $50,233 in 2007, according to the U.S. Census Bureau.

Median income The income that is in the middle of all incomes ranged from high to low.

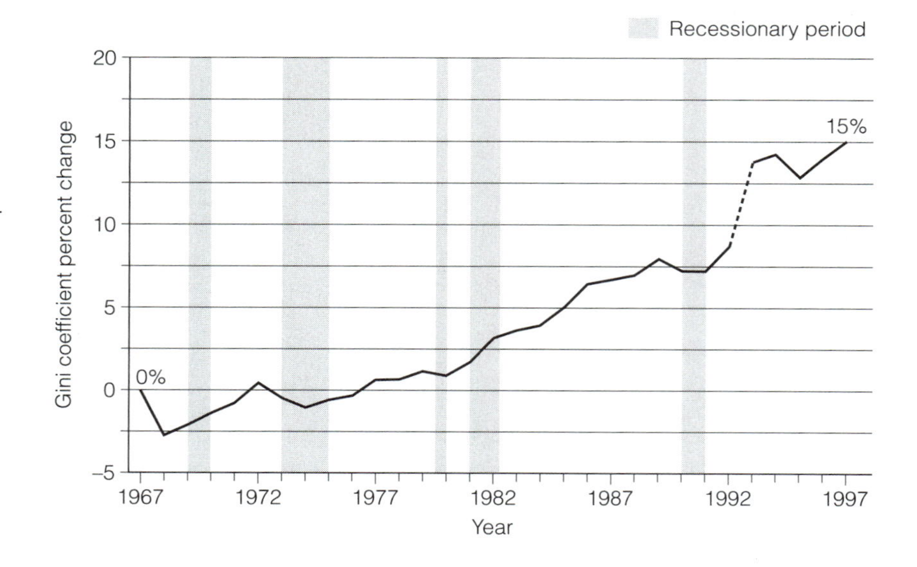

FIGURE 9.2 Household income inequality has shown a steady increase.

Source: U.S. Census Bureau, March Current Population Survey, 1967–1997.

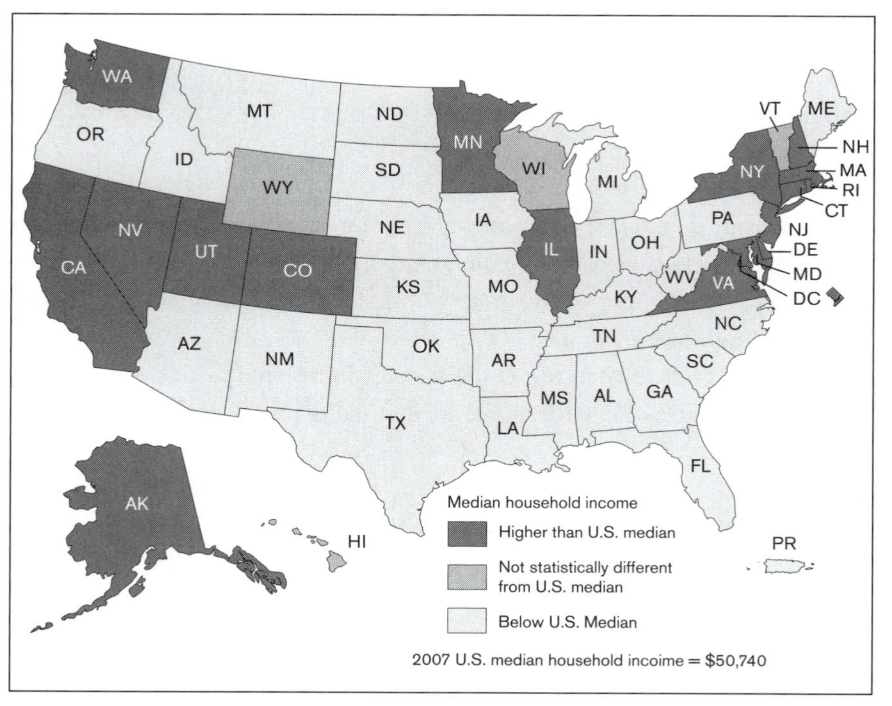

FIGURE 9.3 Median household income in the past 12 months by state, 2007 (in 2007 inflation-adjusted dollars).

***Washington, DC, is represented at 4.5 times the scale of other continental states.**

Source: Bishaw and Semega (2008).

Where do people earn the most? The usual suspects, New York and California, are included, but so are some other places you might not guess (e.g., Minnesota). See Figure 9.3.

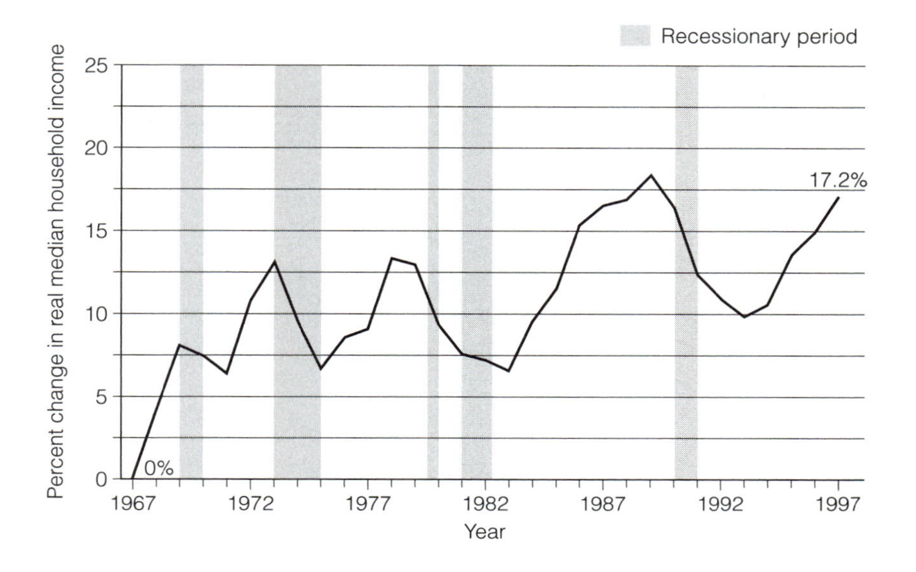

FIGURE 9.4 Median household income displays a cyclical pattern.

Source: U.S. Bureau of the Census, March Current Population Survey, 1967–1997.

How has average income changed over time? Figure 9.4 shows that although it has had its ups and downs, median household income has been rising in the United States since 1967.

You might be wondering whether this is because more women have gone to work. It is true that more women have joined the workforce since the 1960s. It is also true that women working helps account for some of the increase in the median household income. Figure 9.5 shows that the median income of families in which the wife is in the labor force is consistently higher than the median income of families in which the wife is not in the paid labor force. The figure also shows that families in which the wife is not in the paid labor force have seen their incomes stagnate and even fall, at least since approximately 1970.

How Many People Live in Poverty?

We have seen that inequality has risen during the last part of the 20th century, but at the same time median income has also risen (partly because of women going to work). How about poverty? Is that getting better or worse? Figure 9.6 shows that the nation's official poverty rate in 2007 was 12.5%, which is not statistically different from that in 2006. There were 37.3 million people in poverty in 2007, up from 36.5 million in 2006. Most of those

FIGURE 9.5 Married couple median family income grows as wives enter the labor force.

Source: U.S. Bureau of the Census, March Current Population Survey, 1947–1997.

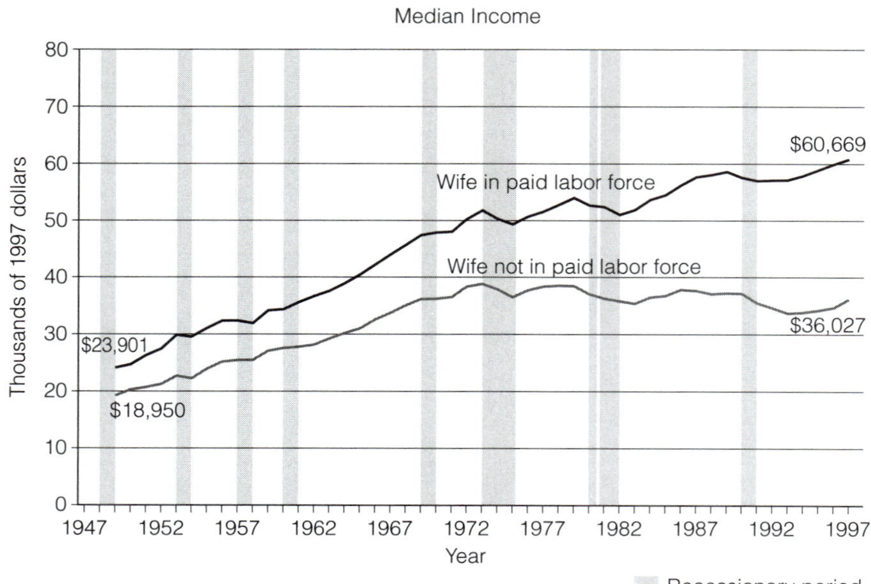

FIGURE 9.6 Percentage of people in poverty in the past 12 months by state, 2007.

***Washington, DC, is represented at 4.5 times the scale of other continental states.**

Source: U.S. Census Bureau, 2007 American Community Survey and 2007 Puerto Rico Community Survey.

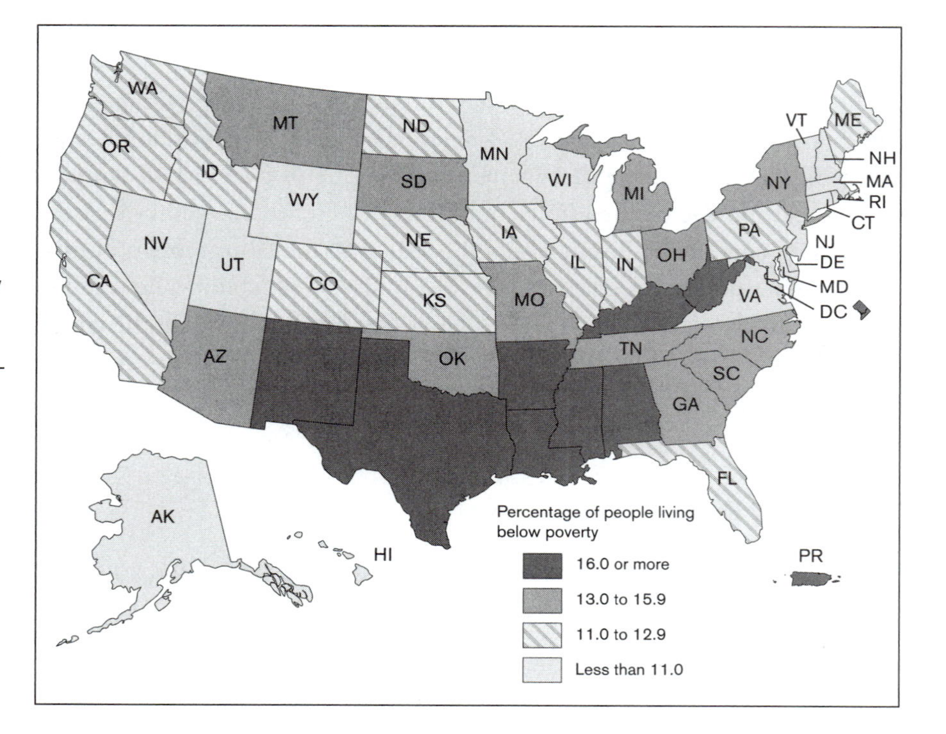

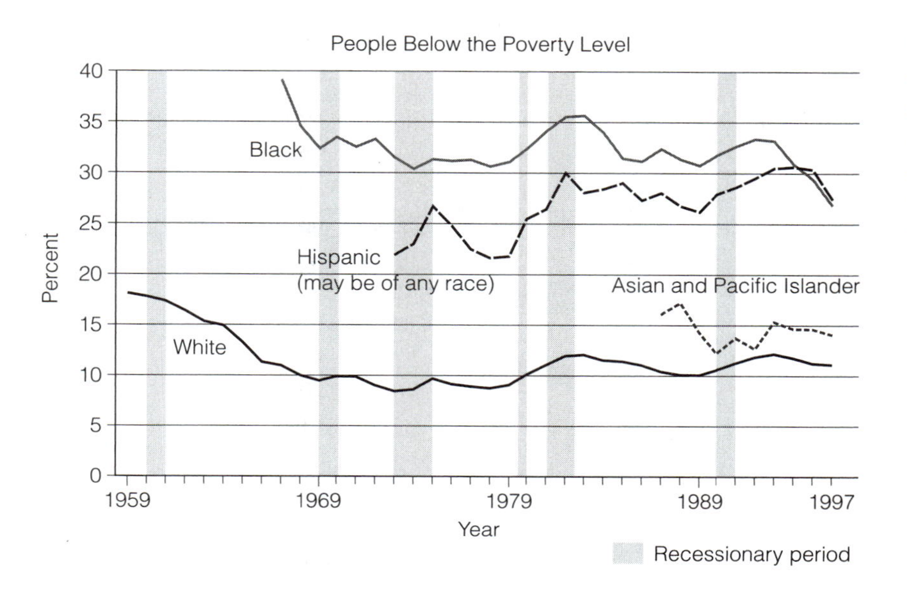

FIGURE 9.7 Poverty for most races has declined since 1959.

Source: U.S. Bureau of the Census, March Current Population Survey, 1959–1997.

people lived in the South. Because the difference in number in poverty in 2006 and 2007 is not statistically different, this means that the difference in number is likely due to measurement error or chance.

So is poverty getting better or worse? The good news is that poverty has declined since 1959 (Figure 9.7), and it has declined for most groups.

Wealth Inequality

The United States is also characterized by inequality of wealth. Wealth, unlike income, is often directly inherited. Wealth transfers from parents to children even before the death of the parents can be quite extensive (McGarry and Schoeni, 1995). Such transfers from parents to children can influence children's educational attainment, ability to own a business, and financial security, and in many ways they promote the economic well-being of children (Spilerman, 2000).

Figure 9.8 shows the distribution of median net worth across income quintiles or fifths. Net worth is equity in home, stocks and bonds, IRAs and 401k accounts, savings, equity in vehicles, etc. Median net worth is the net worth of those in the middle of all wealth owners ranked from high wealth to low wealth. The figure shows that in 2002, households in the highest

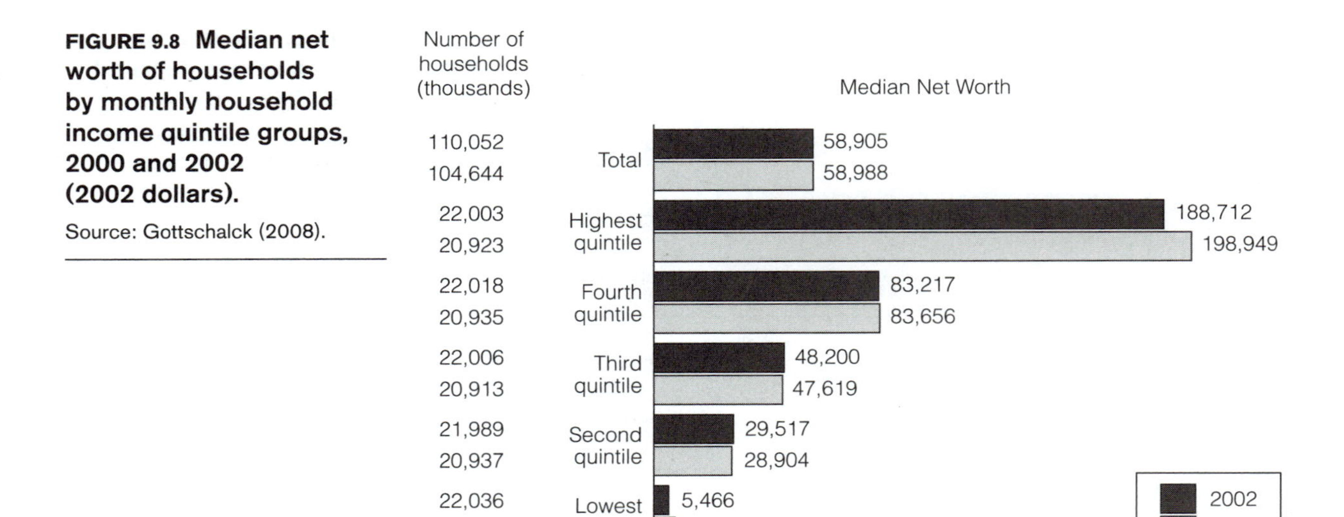

FIGURE 9.8 Median net worth of households by monthly household income quintile groups, 2000 and 2002 (2002 dollars).

Source: Gottschalck (2008).

fifth of income earners had substantially higher median net worth than anyone else.

How has the distribution of wealth changed over time? Figure 9.9 shows that the median net worth of everyone has increased since 1984. This figure also shows that median net worth tracks the ups and downs of the economy (see line in Figure 9.9). When the economy is doing well, everybody's net worth tends to increase.

Status Inequality in the United States

Weber referred to status as "style of life," and there are status groups in American society that may be defined by their style of life. For example, on January 30, 2009, the reality TV show *Wife Swap* featured Gayla Long, a Missouri wife and mother of four whose family loves fast food, all-terrain vehicles (ATVs), and paintball. Gayla swapped lives with life coach and weight-loss hypnotherapist Renee Stephens, who lives in San Francisco, spends $40,000 a year to send her two young children to a French bilingual private school, and, along with her husband, is die-hard about environmental issues and staying healthy. This swap did not work out very well, partly because the two families had such different ways of life (see Box 9.1). Renee

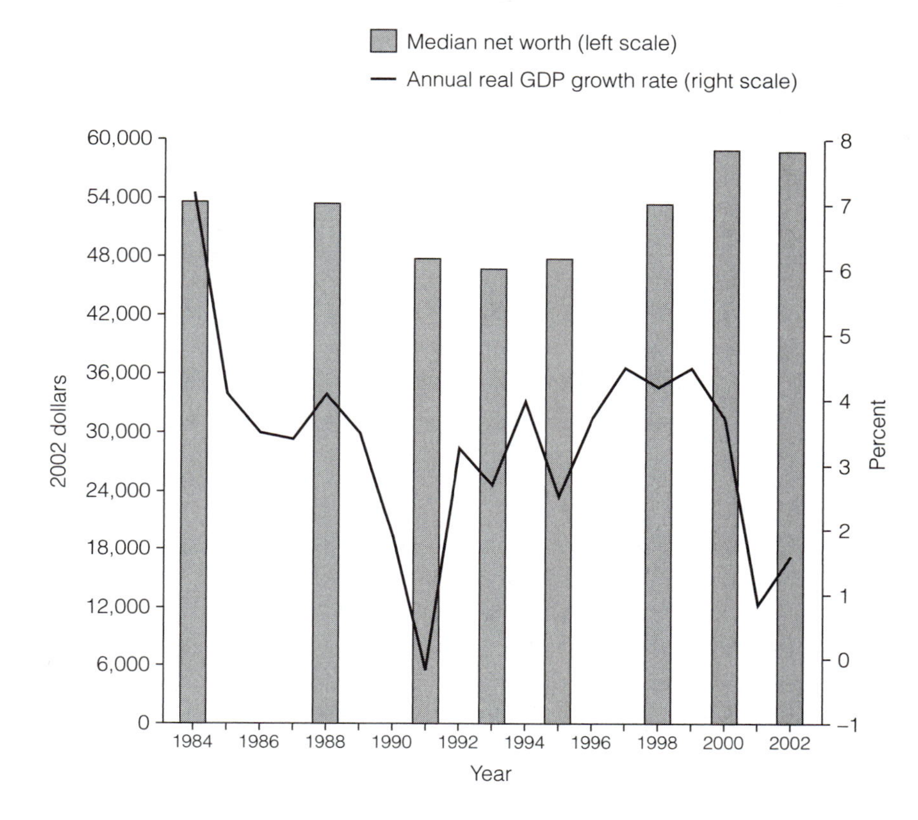

FIGURE 9.9 Median net worth and annual real gross domestic product (GDP) growth rate, 1984–2002.

Source: U.S. Census Bureau, Survey of Income and Program Participation; Bureau of Economic Analysis.

Stephen's husband (Stephen Fowler) was verbally abusive to Gayla Long, suggesting that she came from a "po-dunk" town and saying things such as he didn't know she could read. Needless to say, many people were very offended by his actions.

The ranking of a status group often corresponds to its income and wealth ranking, but not always. Except at the very top and the very bottom, where people tend not to have any occupation at all, status groupings correspond most closely to occupational groupings, because a person's occupation greatly influences the way he or she lives. Certain occupations have more prestige than others, and generally people agree on the prestige of any given occupation. People in high-prestige jobs are often accorded more respect than people in low-prestige jobs. This in turn affects their style of life, and hence their status group. Fussell (1983) describes status groups in American society as follows:

BOX 9.1 WIFE SWAP

The Long Family from Missouri

The Longs from Missouri are a patriotic, all-American family who live for paintball. Wife Gayla (37) is just one of the boys on the paintball field, but at home she is happy to take care of all the household chores, which husband Alan has deemed "skirt work." When Alan (38) is not wreaking havoc with his four wild and crazy boys–Cody (15), Coltan (10), Clayton (8), and Cameron (4)–he serves as the mayor of their 55-person town. The Longs are proud of their Midwestern roots and consider their lifestyle the "American way." Corn dogs and fast food are staples in their home, and their exercise comes from riding ATVs. Alan and Gayla want their kids to have fun; education and the environment can take a backseat.

The Stephens-Fowler Family from California

The Stephens-Fowler family from Northern California consider themselves "citizens of the world." They strive for excellence in both mind and body. Life coach and certified weight-loss hypnotherapist Renee (43) and British-born environmental entrepreneur Stephen (49) raise their children, Juliette (11) and James (8), to be both health and environmentally conscious. With a diet of strictly organic food and weekends spent doing "family fitness activities," the kids admit they can't remember the last time they had a French fry. Domestics are taken care of by a housekeeper, as that is regarded as a necessity in the Stephens-Fowler set. In order to ensure acceptance to an Ivy League school, they push their kids to excel in highbrow activities such as music, fencing, and speaking foreign languages. Both children attend a bilingual school and have already visited over 12 countries.

The top out-of-sight group: This group lives entirely on inherited capital. This is most prestigious if it is at least three or four generations old (e.g., Rockefellers). You can never see their houses from the street or road. They like to hide away in the hills or off on Greek or Caribbean islands, safe from envy and taxation.

The upper: This group inherits much of its money but earns a lot too, "usually from some attractive, if slight work, without which they would feel bored or even ashamed." This work might be controlling banks or older corporations, think tanks, or foundations. This group also likes to busy itself with the older universities (e.g., Harvard, Princeton, and Yale) or the Council on Foreign Relations. These people have streets named after them. You may be a houseguest at the home of an upper-class person because these people have many houseguests. There is often much devotion to horses in this group.

Upper middle: This group may have as much money as the upper group, but it earned it from law, medicine, finance, oil, shipping, real estate, or the more honorific kinds of trade such as art. Their houses tend to have too many rooms, and their clothes tend to be unisex. This is the most gender-neutral class. If you are in this group, it is best to be from New York. This group likes to appear in old clothes made of natural materials.

Middle: The middle is the most earnest and insecure group. Middle-class people are very concerned about what people think of them and often obsessed with doing everything right. Middle-class people have jobs in the middle ranks of companies. They tend to live in the suburbs. They strive for good taste in furniture and housing. Middle-class people tend to be optimists and convinced of the likelihood of self-improvement with hard work. They like to wear clothing with symbols of famous brand names or other status symbols on it. Snobs (e.g., Stephen Fowler) are found in the middle class.

High proletarian: This group is made up mostly of blue-collar workers, people who are skilled workers and craftspeople. People in this group are proud of their work and are tempted to call what they do a profession. They make games and sports central to their lives. They can be highly relaxed and un-self-conscious and will typically do, say, and wear anything they like without feelings of shame. They like to spend money on elaborate TVs and tricky refrigerators, and they do not care about seeming "tacky." Gender roles are very pronounced in this group—men are men and women are women. People in this group like to wear clothing with words on it. The Longs fit into this status group.

Mid proletarian: This group is composed of operators such as bus drivers, truck drivers, and heavy equipment operators. They tend to have more supervision in their jobs than the high proletarians. They often retreat into private pursuits (home workshops) or they hunt, fish, camp, and watch sports. Members of this group also like to wear clothing with words on it.

Low proletarian: These people have uncertain employment such as seasonal jobs. They are highly supervised on the job and often prefer social isolation outside of work.

Destitute: These people never have even seasonal work but live wholly on welfare.

Bottom out-of-sight: The homeless and those in charitable or correctional institutions.

Social Mobility

Perhaps less important than actual inequality is the amount of mobility there is from generation to generation. Can children do better or worse than their parents? Is there immobility—that is, do children tend to inherit their economic and social position from their parents? The literature on social mobility shows that there has been considerable upward occupational mobility in the past century. Most of this research examines occupational mobility from fathers to sons because women have only joined the paid labor force in large proportions in relatively recent years. However, much of this upward mobility is due to changes in the nature of available jobs. As the economy has developed, there have been more white-collar jobs created (in services such as education, finance, law, and medicine), and many of the old blue-collar jobs in manufacturing industries have disappeared. This means that blue-collar fathers are likely to have a son in a white-collar job. However, this is because of structural changes in the economy and not because society is becoming more fluid. Researchers document that, in fact, if you adjust rates of mobility for mobility due to changes in the available jobs, then in fact rates of mobility have not changed since data collection began (Breen and Jonsson, 2005; Erikson and Goldthorpe, 1992).

Research shows that people get into white-collar occupations by going to school, and that the family is very important in helping to ensure their children get the education they need to get a good job (Entwistle, Alexander, and Olson, 2005). This is what we might expect, given the predisposition toward helping kin, especially children, that we discussed in Chapter 2. Families strive to help children do at least as well as their parents, if not better. Consistent with the principle of gender asymmetry in parenting, mothers appear to be highly important in this process: "The farther alternative family structures take sons away from their mothers, the more the intergenerational transmission process breaks down" (Biblarz, Raftery, and Bucur, 1997, p. 1319).

INCOME AND WEALTH INEQUALITY IN COMPARATIVE PERSPECTIVE

Table 9.2 shows that the United States is by far the richest nation compared to the rich nations of Western Europe and Canada, with a gross domestic product per capita of $34,100 in 2000 (Smeeding, 2005). The next richest

TABLE 9.2 Average Standard of Living, Unemployment, and Social Expenditures across Eight Developed Countries, 2005

NATION (YEAR)	AVERAGE STANDARD OF LIVING GDP/CAPITA (IN 2000 U.S. DOLLARS)[a]	INDEX	OECD STANDARDIZED UNEMPLOYMENT RATE	OECD SOCIAL EXPENDITURES ON NONELDERLY[b]
United States (00)	34,106	100	4.0	2.8
The Netherlands (99)	26,517	78	3.2	10.5
Sweden (00)	25,363	74	5.6	12.6
Germany (00)	25,329	74	7.8	8.9
Canada (97)	25,044	73	9.1	6.0
Finland (00)	24,530	72	9.8	12.1
United Kingdom (99)	23,723	70	5.9	6.4
Belgium (97)	23,541	69	9.2	8.9

[a]Using 2000 purchasing power parities, price adjusted in each nation to correct year.

[b]Countries with data year 2000 are given the most recent (1999) values available from the Organisation for Economic Co-operation and Development (OECD).

Source: Smeeding (2005). Data from U.S. Bureau of Labor Statistics and OECD.

country is The Netherlands, with a gross domestic product per capita of $26,517 in 1999. Part of the reason for this is that Americans work hard: They work long hours each day and more weeks of the year than people in other countries. Europeans often take a month off in the summer, for example, which is unusual in the United States. It is also because unemployment tends to be low. In families, a higher proportion of U.S. couples are dual earner than in other countries (Jacobs and Gornick, 2002).

At the same time, the United States has the highest level of real income inequality among rich countries (Smeeding, 2005). Figure 9.10 shows the difference between the disposable income of high- and low-earning households (in this table the household income is converted into an individual equivalence income). Only in Russia and Mexico is inequality higher, and they are both considered developing countries by many.

As in the United States, in many areas of Europe inequality has increased in recent years (Figure 9.11). However, the overall level of inequality is still

	P10 (Low Income)	Length of bars represents the gap between high and low income individuals	P90 (High Income)	P90/P10 (Decile Ratio)	Gini Coefficient[1]
Luxembourg 2000	66		215	3.24	0.260
Czech Republic 1996	60		179	3.01	0.259
Sweden 2000	57		168	2.96	0.252
Norway 2000	57		159	2.80	0.251
Finland 2000	57		164	2.90	0.247
Slovak Republic 1996	56		162	2.88	0.241
Netherlands 1999	56		167	2.98	0.248
Austria 2000	55		173	3.17	0.260
Germany 2000	54		173	3.18	0.252
Denmark 1992	54		155	2.85	0.236
Hungary 1999	54		194	3.57	0.295
France 1994	54		191	3.54	0.288
Romania 1997	53		180	3.38	0.277
Slovenia 1999	53		167	3.15	0.249
Belgium 2000	53		174	3.31	0.277
Poland 1999	52		188	3.59	0.293
Switzerland 1992	52		188	3.62	0.307
Taiwan 2000	51		196	3.81	0.296
Spain 1990	50		197	3.96	0.303
Canada 2000	48		188	3.95	0.302
United Kingdom 1999	47		215	4.58	0.345
Estonia 2000	46		234	5.08	0.361
Japan 1992[2]	46		192	4.17	0.315
Australia 1994	45		195	4.33	0.311
Italy 2000	44		199	4.48	0.333
Israel 2001	43		216	5.01	0.346
Ireland 2000	41		189	4.57	0.323
United States 2000	39		210	5.45	0.368
Russia 2000	33		276	8.37	0.434
Mexico 2002	33		309	9.36	0.471
		0 50 100 150 200 250 300 350			
Average[3]	50		194	4.04	0.300

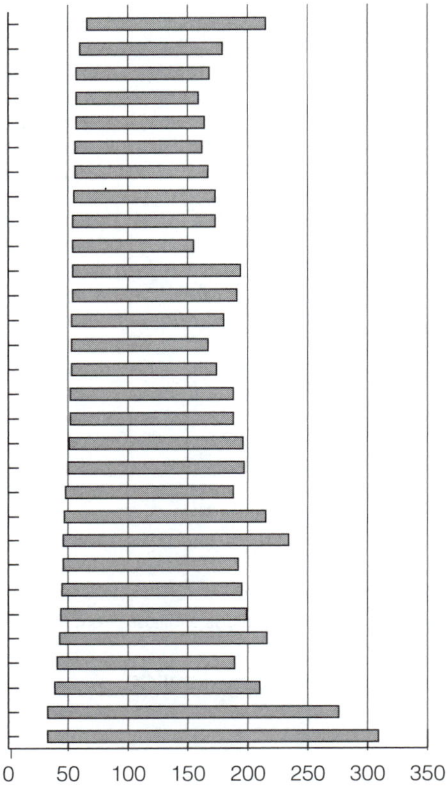

[1]Gini coefficients are based on incomes, which are bottom coded at 1 percent of disposable income and top coded at 10 times the median disposable income.

[2]Japanese Gini coefficient as calculated in Gottschalk and Smeeding (2000) from Japanese Survey of Income Redistribution.

[3]Simple average.

FIGURE 9.10 Income inequality in thirty nations for various years around the turn of the century.

Source: Smeeding (2005).

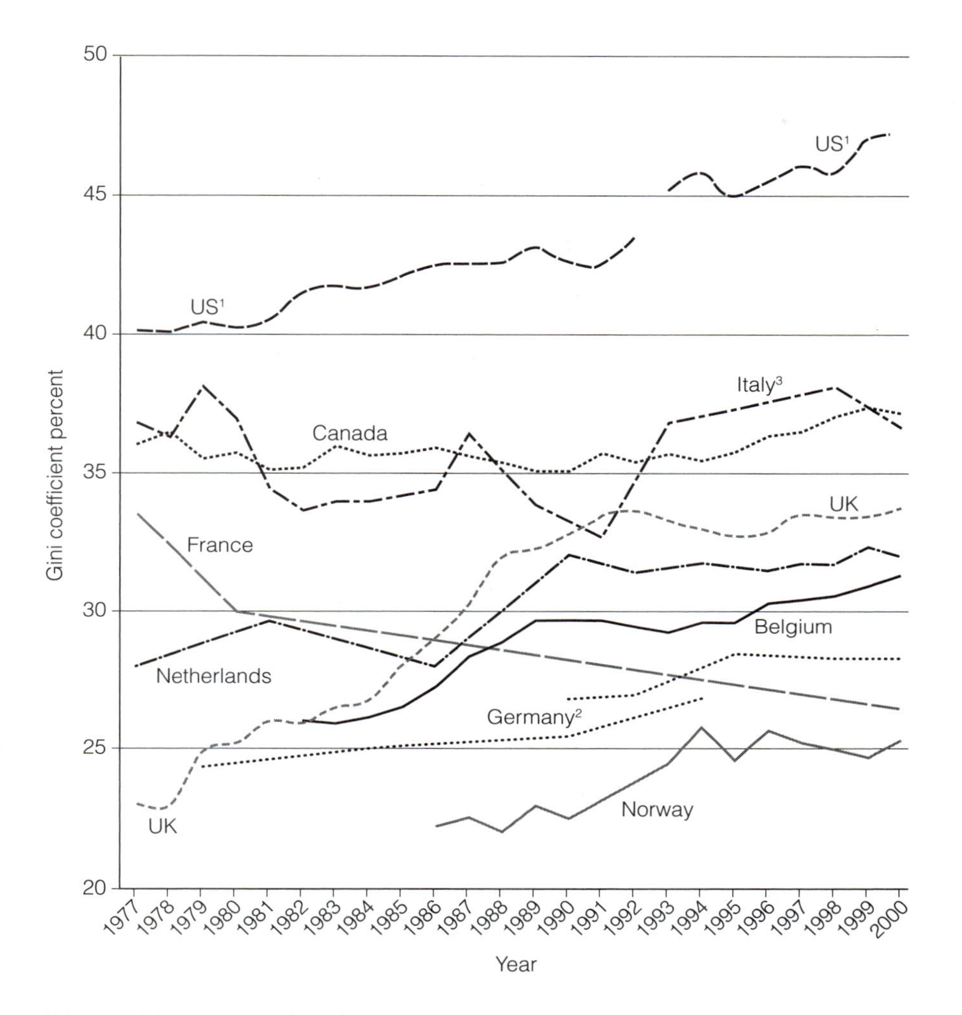

[1]Major revisions in series (1993).

[2]German trends come from two time series, the government income and expenditure series until 1995 and the German Socio Economic Panel after. Germany includes the eastern states, as well as the western, after 1989.

[3]Italian series are from Brandolini (2002, 2004) and are for household disposable income excluding imputed rents, interest, and dividends.

FIGURE 9.11 Visual representation of inequality trends in select OECD countries.

Source: Smeeding (2005).

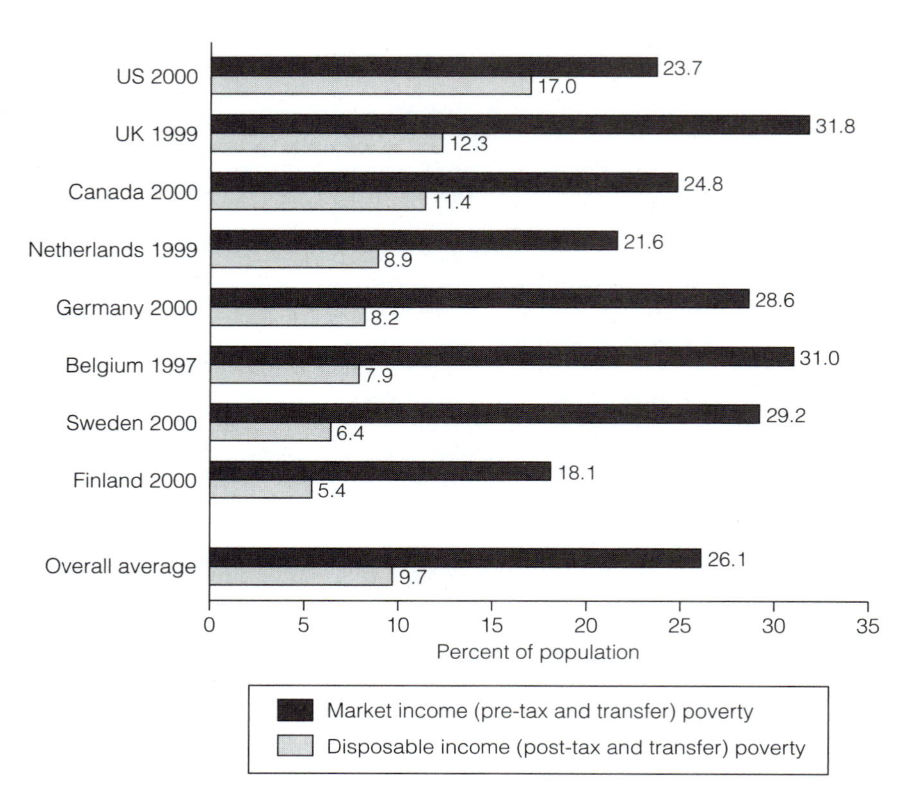

FIGURE 9.12 Relative poverty rates and anitpoverty effects in eight rich nations at the turn of the century (percentage of people with market income and disposable income less than half of adjusted national disposable median income).

Source: Smeeding (2005).

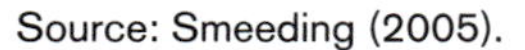

much higher in the United States (Moran, 2006; Smeeding, 2005). The United States also has a higher percentage of people in poverty than do rich European countries (Figure 9.12).

Why the differences? One reason is that other industrialized societies have a much larger social welfare "safety net" than the United States. The other reason is that the wages of low wage earners tend to be lower in the United States than in other developed countries. It is not because there is more occupational mobility in other countries. If you consider rates of occupational mobility minus the mobility due to change in the nature of available jobs, they are fairly similar across advanced industrialized countries and have actually become more so recently (Breen and Jonsson, 2005).

CONCLUSION

The history of inequality takes the shape of a hill—lowest in hunting and gathering societies, highest in agrarian societies, and lower again in advanced industrial societies. In the United States, levels of inequality have been increasing since the middle of the last century. The good news is that median household income has increased also and poverty has decreased. There are differences in levels of inequality among rich countries, with the United States having the highest levels of inequality and poverty. At the same time, the United States is the world's richest country. The greatest inequality, however, is between the countries of the developed or industrialized world and countries of the less developed world. It is to this we now turn.

REFERENCES

Biblarz, Timothy J., Adrian E. Raftery, and A. Bucur. 1997. "Family Structure and Social Mobility." *Social Forces* 75, 1319–1341.

Bishaw, Alemayehu, and Jessica Semega. 2008. *Income, Earnings, and Poverty Data from the 2007 American Community Survey*, U.S. Census Bureau, American Community Survey Reports, ACS-09. Washington, DC: Government Printing Office.

Breen, Richard, and Jan O. Jonsson. 2005. "Inequality of Opportunity in Comparative Perspective: Recent Research on Educational Attainment and Social Mobility." *Annual Review of Sociology* 31, 223–243.

DeNavas-Walt, Carmen, Bernadette D. Proctor, and Jessica C. Smith. 2008. *Income, Poverty, and Health Insurance Coverage in the United States: 2007*, U.S. Census Bureau, Current Population Reports, P60-235. Washington, DC: Government Printing Office.

Entwistle, Doris R., Karl L. Alexander, and Linda Steffel Olson. 2005. "First Grade and Educational Attainment by Age 22: A New Story." *American Journal of Sociology* 110(5), 1458–1502.

Erikson, Robert, and John H. Goldthorpe. 1992. *The Constant Flux: A Study of Class Mobility in Industrial Societies*. New York: Oxford University Press.

Fussell, Paul. 1983. *Class: A Guide through the American Status System*. New York: Summit Books.

Gottschalck, Alfred O. 2008. *Net Worth and Asset Ownership of Households: 2002*, U.S. Census Bureau, Current Population Reports, P70-115. Washington, DC: Government Printing Office.

Heider, Karl. 1997. *Grand Valley Dani: Peaceful Warriors*, 3rd edn. Fort Worth, TX: Harcourt Brace.

Jacobs, Jerry A., and Janet C. Gornick. 2002. "Hours of Paid Work in Dual-Earner Couples: The United States in Cross-National Perspective." *Sociological Focus* 35(2), 169–187.

McGarry, K., and R. Schoeni. 1995. "Transfer Behavior in the Health and Retirement Study." *Journal of Human Resources* 30, S184–S225.

Moran, Timothy Patrick. 2006. "Statistical Inference and Patterns of Inequality in the Global North." *Social Forces* 84(3), 1799–1818.

Scott, Jonathan F., and Alexander Baltzly (Eds.) 1930. *Readings in European History Since 1814*. New York: Appleton-Century-Crofts.

Smeeding, Timothy M. 2005. "Public Policy, Economic Inequality, and Poverty: The United States in Comparative Perspective." *Social Science Quarterly* 86(Suppl. 1), 955–983.

Spilerman, Seymour. 2000. "Wealth and Stratification Processes." *Annual Review of Sociology* 26, 497–524.

GLOBAL INEQUALITY

10

THE NATURE OF GLOBAL INEQUALITY

The movie *Slumdog Millionaire* showed the rich world some of the inequalities found in places such as Mumbai, India, where the movie was set—notably the extremes of rich and poor and the lives of street children (Photo 10.1).

India is one place where people's lives are generally getting better, as incomes have risen rapidly. Yet within India, there are huge differences between those involved in the new high-tech industries centered around places such as Bangalore and the vast majority of people who live in poor rural areas.

PHOTO 10.1 Scene from the movie *Slumdog Millionaire*, 2008. Source: Film 4/Celador Films/Pathe International/The Kobal Collection.

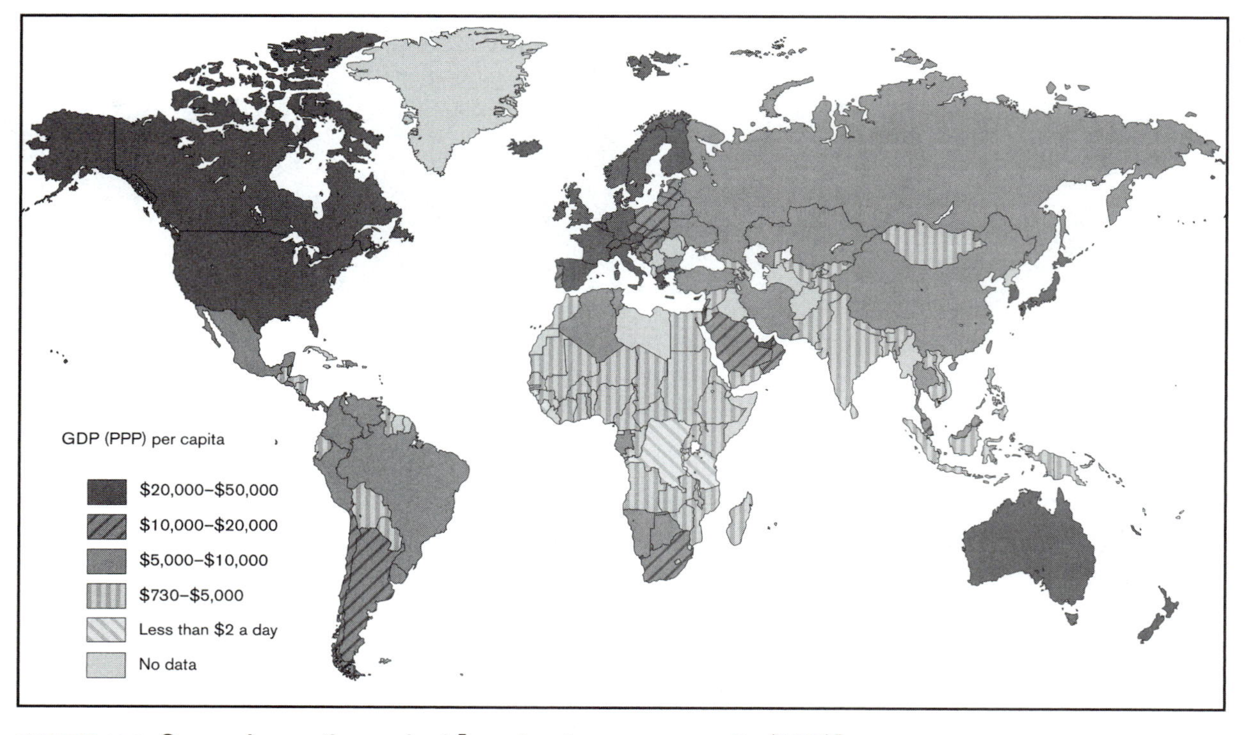

FIGURE 10.1 Gross domestic product [purchasing power parity (PPP)] per capita, 2004.

Source: University of California Atlas of Global Inequality (http://ucatlas.ucsc.edu/income.php).

In the world today, the richest 25% of the population receives 75% of the world income (Milanovic, 1999). Where do they live? Figure 10.1 gives gross domestic product (GDP) per capita in 2004. The GDP per capita gives the amount of goods and products produced per person. It is a rough estimate of average national productivity, and it is a good measure of the wealth of a country. The figure shows that the richest people of the world today live in Europe, North America, and Australia, whereas the poorest people of the world today live in Africa and India and in regions in China, Southeast Asia, and South and Central America.

People in poor countries of the world have little in the way of possessions. Many do not even possess shoes. Gadgets such as TVs, radios, and cell phones are few and far between. Most people who need glasses cannot afford them. Houses are often shacks, and beds are often a few bedclothes on the floor. Very few people can afford cars. The typical way people get

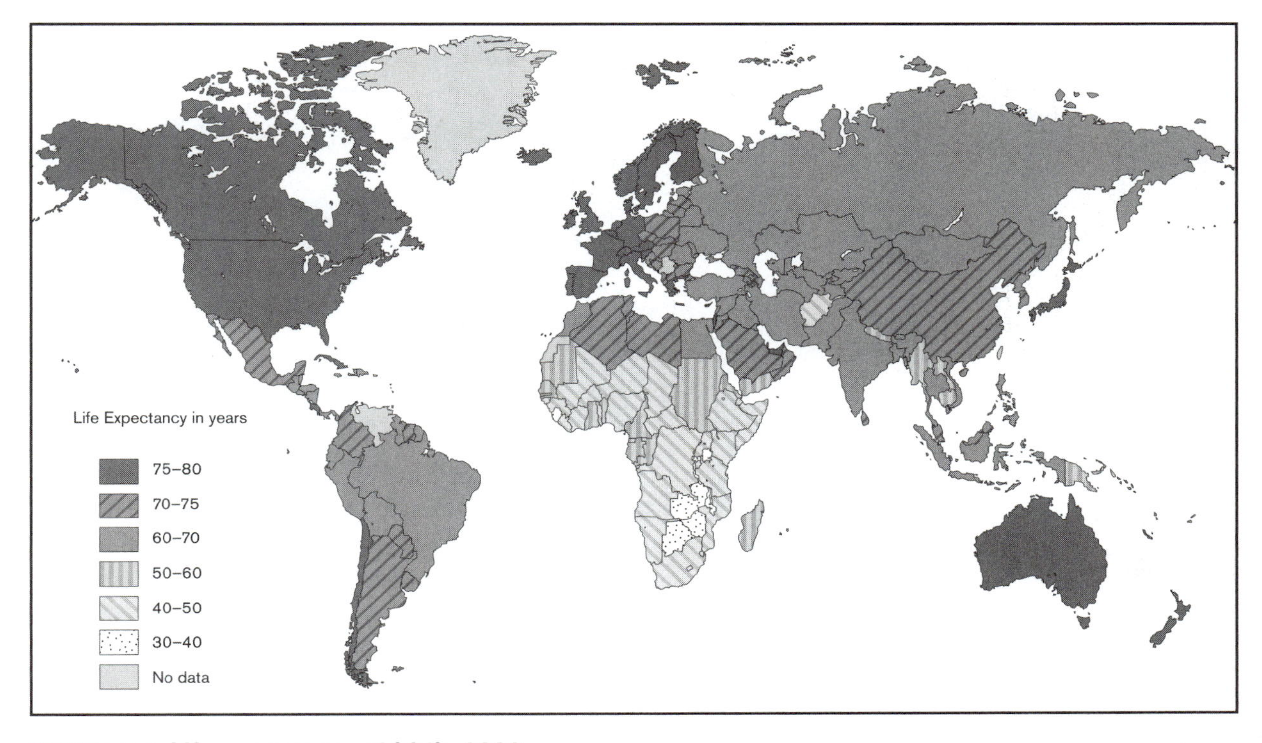

FIGURE 10.2 **Life expectancy at birth, 2000.**

Source: University of California Atlas of Global Inequality (http://ucatlas.ucsc.edu/life_new/life_index.html).

around is by walking. Children, particularly girls, often do not attend school. Medical care is limited and often very costly. Unemployment and underemployment are common in the poor countries of the world. Hyperinflation and other economic problems are not uncommon. Violence and war occur more regularly and affect more people's lives.

People's diets are inadequate and consist mostly of starch such as rice or maize, with little meat or animal protein. Fresh fruits and vegetables are rare. Going to the toilet often means squatting in a field or using an outdoor lavatory; sewage systems are rare and usually inadequate. The water supply is typically suspect and often a source of disease. Disease—cholera, measles, malaria, AIDS, and dysentery—is ever present. As a result, people in poor countries die at young ages, and many children do not live to see their first birthdays (Figures 10.2 and 10.3).

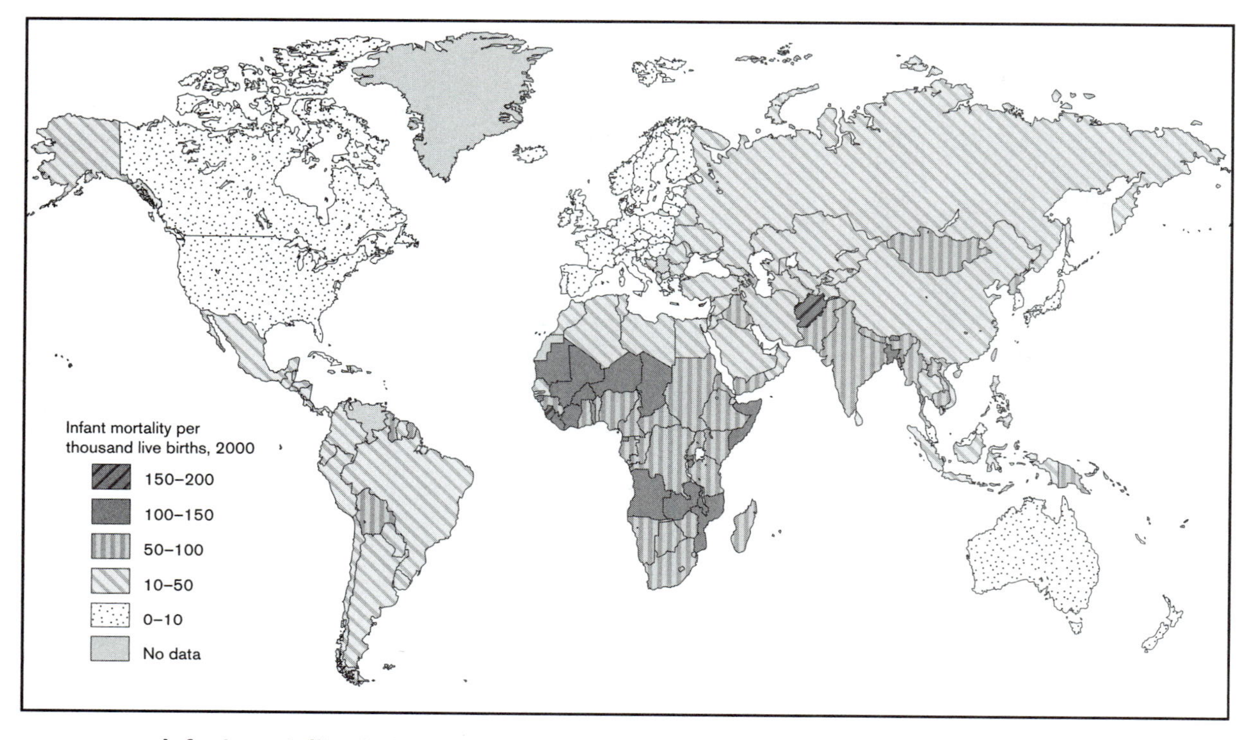

FIGURE 10.3 Infant mortality, 2000.

Source: University of California Atlas of Global Inequality (http://ucatlas.ucsc.edu/life/infant.html).

Rural Poverty

Figure 10.4 shows that the poorest people in poor countries live in rural areas.

In most of the poor countries and regions of the world, agriculture is still the dominant economic activity, and more than half of the population is engaged in agriculture. Agricultural productivity is often not very high, and despite large numbers of people in agriculture, there are often scarcities of food. The reasons for this are complicated. Growing populations, poor government policies, and traditional farming techniques lead to overuse of land, deforestation, erosion, and low yields. Government policies in poor countries typically favor urban populations, where governments are

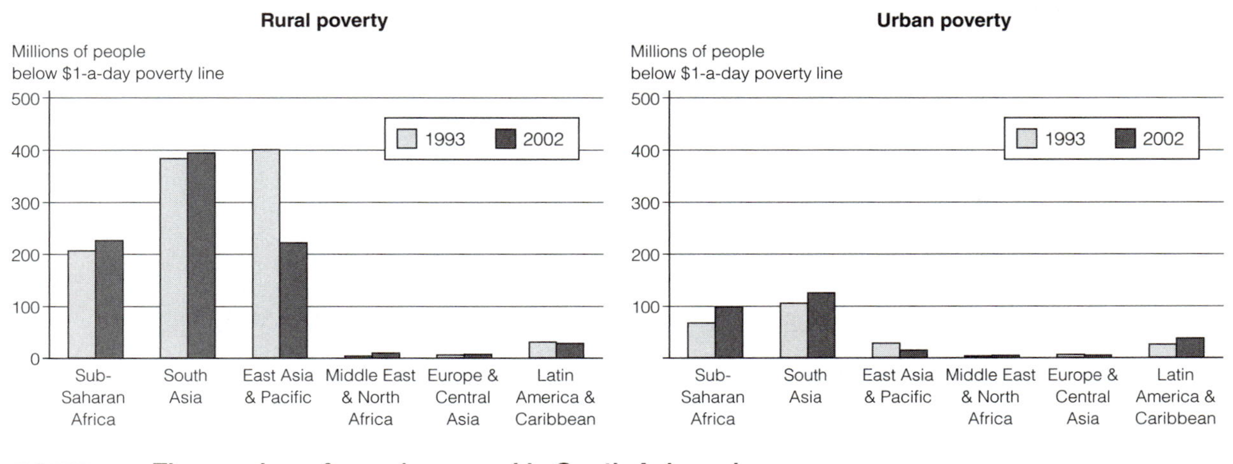

FIGURE 10.4 The number of poor increased in South Asia and Sub-Saharan Africa from 1993 to 2002 ($1-a-day poverty line).

Source: The World Bank, World Development Report 2008.

located. Often, these policies involve caps on the prices of basic commodities such as grain because these policies are popular with urban populations that must buy all their food. Low prices for grain mean the farmers who could produce more grain have little reason to do so. Government policies in rich countries are also to blame. Many rich world governments protect the agricultural products of their own countries from the competition from lower priced imports. This means that people in poor countries are unable to sell their low-cost food to rich countries, and people in rich countries pay more for food.

Is Global Inequality Getting Better or Worse?

Whether global inequality is getting better or worse depends largely on how it is measured (Milanovic, 2005). If you use GDP per capita for all countries, and the Gini measure of inequality measuring inequality among all countries, then global inequality is increasing. If you use GDP per capita for all countries, but weight countries by their population so that large and populous countries such as China and India count for more, then the Gini measures of inequality show that global inequality is decreasing. This is because those populous countries, China and India, have been rapidly developing in recent years and their GDP per capita has been rising quickly. Given that they each have a disproportionate share of the world's population, this means that more people in the world are seeing their standard of living increase. Thus, whereas global inequality by country is increasing, global inequality for individuals is actually decreasing.

THEORIES OF GLOBAL INEQUALITY

Modernization Theory

Modernization theory originated with Rostow (1960). He thought development of the poor countries of the world and rising standards of living were inevitable. He posited four stages of development:

1. The traditional society
2. The preconditions for takeoff
3. The drive to maturity
4. The age of high mass consumption

Problems that could hinder progress through these stages include the following:

1. No capital for investment
2. Lack of modern techniques of marketing, accounting, finance, and so on
3. Customs and traditions that hinder change, and lack of the kind of rational outlook necessary for development
4. No spirit of entrepreneurship
5. Political structures that encourage corruption in government and the economy

However, Rostow thought that eventually, by copying the developed countries, the poor countries of the world would develop.

Modernization theory has been criticized for being overly optimistic: 50 years later, many countries throughout the world have not developed and seem unlikely to develop in the near future. It also places most of the blame for a failure to develop within the poor countries, and it ignores the actions of rich world countries (e.g., import quotas on agricultural and other goods) that help prevent poor countries from developing.

Dependency Theory

Dependency theory has its origins in the work of Andre Gunder Frank (1967, 1979) and Samir Amin (1974). These authors suggested that the reason why poor countries did not develop is that they were forcibly dependent on rich countries. According to dependency theory, poor countries fell into the trap of providing raw materials for the industries of the rich world—rubber, cotton, oil, etc. Often, this led to overdependence on one crop or commodity, with drastic consequences when the demand for that particular commodity declined. Also, because all the processing of the materials was done in the rich countries, this meant that factories were never built in the poor countries and most of the profits of manufacturing stayed in the rich countries. As a result, there was no capital in poor countries to build manufacturing industries. Dependency theorists suggested there was elite complicity in all this—elites in poor countries cooperated with international companies to provide raw materials and received kickbacks and payoffs for their cooperation. These elites then spent all their money on foreign goods, so even this source of wealth did little to benefit the poor country.

Immanuel Wallerstein's world system theory incorporated many of the ideas of dependency theory. Wallerstein further sorted countries into rich countries (core), poor countries (periphery) that are economically dependent on rich countries, and countries that are not fully part of the world economic system (semi-periphery). He believed that the world economic system was the product of history, and he described the emergence of the modern world system in his book of the same name (Wallerstein, 1974).

There have been many criticisms of both dependency and world system theories. Dependency theory has difficulty accounting for the success of many of the settler nations throughout the world, including Canada, Australia, and even the United States, which were originally and often still are primary producers of basic agricultural commodities but have managed to build their own industries. Dependency and world system theories have difficulty explaining the recent emergence of China and India. Until recently, these were densely populated, poverty-stricken regions. Yet they used their greatest asset—people—and their low-cost labor to develop export-oriented manufacturing industries, and as a result in recent years they have seen extremely high economic growth rates.

CONCLUSION

The greatest inequality in the world today is between the citizens of the developed countries and the citizens of the less developed countries. People in poor countries live shorter, less comfortable lives than people in rich countries. There is debate about whether this inequality in the world is increasing or decreasing. Like many things, it depends how you measure it. On a country-by-country basis, inequality is increasing, but for the people of the world, inequality is decreasing.

REFERENCES

Amin, Samir. 1974. *Accumulation on a World Scale: A Critique of the Theory of Underdevelopment*, translated by Brian Pearce. New York: Monthly Review Press.

Frank, Andre Gunder. 1967. *Capitalism and Underdevelopment in Latin America; Historical Studies of Chile and Brazil.* New York: Monthly Review Press.

———. 1979. *Dependent Accumulation and Underdevelopment.* New York: Monthly Review Press.

Milanovic, Branko. 1999. "True World Income Distribution, 1988 and 1993: First Calculation Based on Household Surveys Alone." Washington, DC: World Bank.

———. 2005. *Worlds Apart: Measuring International and Global Inequality.* Princeton, NJ: Princeton University Press.

Rostow, W. W. 1960. *The Stages of Economic Growth: A Non-Communist Manifesto.* Cambridge, UK: Cambridge University Press.

Wallerstein, Immanuel. 1974. *The Modern World System.* New York: Academic Press.

CONTEMPORARY GENDER INEQUALITY

11

COMPARATIVE GENDER INEQUALITY

There are no—and to the best of anyone's knowledge there have never been—societies in which women have more power and authority than men. There have been egalitarian societies, and there have been extremely gender stratified societies, but there have been no female-*dominated* societies. Even today, men have the most political power in even the most gender egalitarian societies such as Sweden. Figure 11.1 shows the proportion of seats in state legislatures around the world held by women.

How much gender inequality there is depends in part on the amount of overall stratification, because gender inequality tracks the amount of stratification in a society. Just as hunting and gathering societies have the least stratification, they also have the least gender inequality. Just as agrarian

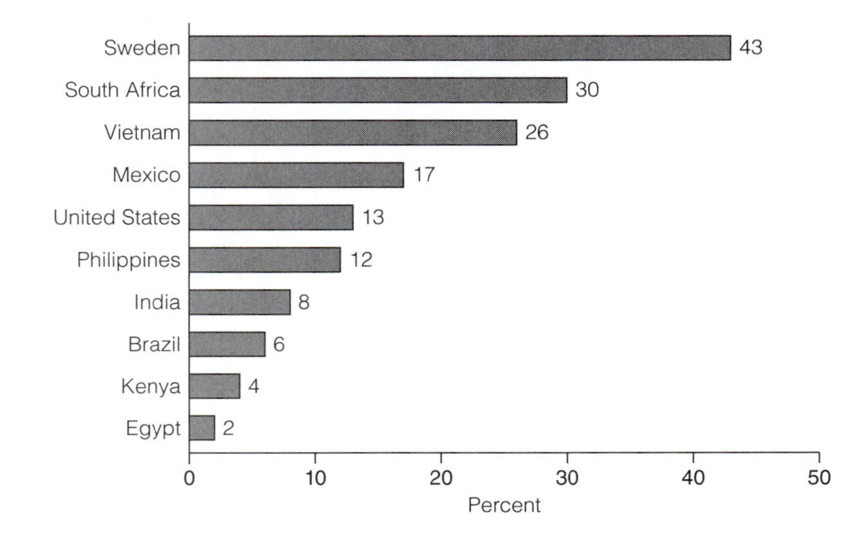

FIGURE 11.1 Legislative seats held by women, selected countries, 1999.

Source: United Nations, *The World's Women 2000: Trends and Statistics* (2000).

societies have the most stratification, they also have the most gender inequality (Blumberg, 1988; Chafetz, 2004).

The most gender inequality today is found in the developing, formerly horticultural and agrarian societies of Africa, Asia, and the Middle East. In many of these societies, discrimination against women is built into the culture, and sometimes into government policies and laws. In Africa and the Middle East, for example, to varying degrees throughout the region family law codes place women under the guardianship of their fathers, husbands, or another male relative. These family laws are typically drawn from **Sharia**, or Islamic, law. Under Sharia law, women need their guardians' consent to marry and have limited rights regarding divorce, child custody, and inheritance.

Sharia law Islamic law.

These countries are by no means the only ones that are inegalitarian. As we have seen, concern about controlling young women's sexuality is found in most societies, and different societies have different ways of doing this. Especially in poor countries, there are a variety of rules (both formal and informal) that restrict the freedom of women to do as they please: customs of veiling and **purdah** (seclusion), constant supervision, rules against the education of girls, rules preventing women from taking paid jobs or even earning a decent amount of money for a job, and informal norms that promote the toleration of wife beating.

Purdah Seclusion of women in the home.

Table 11.1 shows that in the 1990s, in less developed countries girls were less likely than boys to go to secondary school (although the sex gap in school attendance has narrowed since the 1980s). The biggest sex difference is in south central Asia (countries such as India and Bangladesh).

Table 11.2 shows that throughout the world, women are much less likely to work for pay than are men. Especially in poor countries, when women do work for pay, they get paid much less than men do for similar jobs. See Figure 11.2 for the sex difference in wages in manufacturing industries.

In poor countries, women are often beaten by their husbands (Figure 11.3). Not only are women subject to violence at the hands of their husbands but they often suffer most during civil wars and military confrontations. *The Economist* newsmagazine put it as follows: "Girls, their mothers and grandmothers (and sometimes male relatives too) raped at knife or gunpoint, the weapons then used to inflict mutilation. Women hauled off to camps or just tied to trees and gang-raped. . . . In eastern Congo, the UN says that between June 2007 and June 2008, in Ituri province alone, 6,766

TABLE 11.1 Secondary School Enrollment by Sex in World Regions, 1980 and 1990s

	% ENROLLED[a]			
	1980		1990s	
REGION	BOYS	GIRLS	BOYS	GIRLS
More developed countries	88	89	99	102
Less developed countries	43	30	57	48
Northern Africa	47	29	63	57
Sub-Saharan Africa	19	10	29	23
Western Asia	49	31	63	48
South-central Asia	38	20	55	37
Southeast Asia	40	35	53	49
East Asia	59	45	77	70
Central America	46	42	56	57
Caribbean	–	–	49	55
South America	38	42	–	–

–, not available.

[a]The percentage enrolled is the ratio of the total number enrolled in secondary school (regardless of age) to the number of secondary school–age children, or the gross enrollment ratio. Data from the 1990s are the latest available, generally between 1990 and 1996.

Source: Boyd, Haub, and Cornelius (2000), based on national data from UNESCO, Statistical Yearbook 1999.

cases of rape were reported, with 43% involving children; and for each rape reported, it is likely that 10–20 go unreported" (*The Economist*, 2009, p. 61). Women who are raped are disproportionately likely to be infected with HIV. Young girls who are raped and become pregnant are also much more likely to develop a condition called a fistula—when the baby is too big for the birth canal and tears a hole that lets urine stream out constantly through the vagina. Sometimes the rectum is damaged and stool leaks out. The result is often the death of both the baby and the mother. If the mother lives, she is afflicted with a condition that often causes her family and friends to reject her and send her out in the street. Fistulas currently afflict approximately

TABLE 11.2 Women's Share of the Labor Force, 1980 and 1997

REGION	WOMEN AS PERCENTAGE OF LABOR FORCE	
	1980	1997
Africa		
Northern Africa	20	26
Sub-Saharan Africa	42	43
Latin America and Caribbean		
Caribbean	38	43
Central America	27	33
South America	27	38
Asia		
East Asia	40	43
Southeast Asia	41	43
Southern Asia	31	33
Central Asia	47	46
Western Asia	23	27
More developed regions		
Eastern Europe	45	45
Western Europe	36	42
Other more developed regions	39	44

Source: United Nations, *The World's Women 2000: Trends and Statistics* (2000, p. 110).

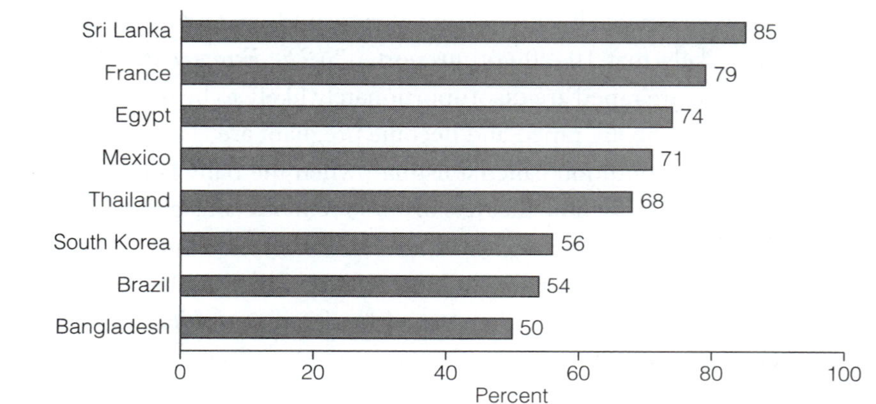

FIGURE 11.2 Women's wages as a percentage of men's wages, in manufacturing, selected countries, 1992–1997.

Source: United Nations, *The World's Women 2000: Trends and Statistics* (2000).

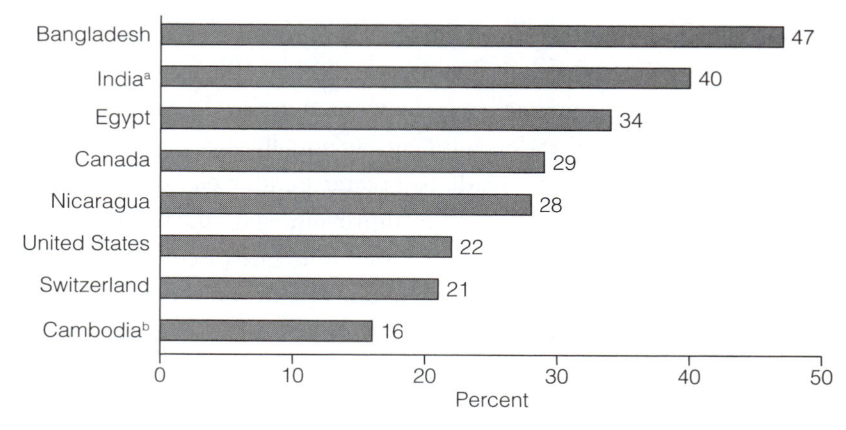

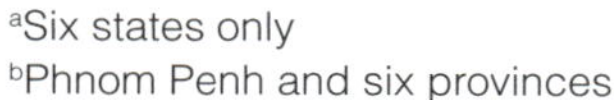

FIGURE 11.3 Women reporting physical assault by male partner, selected studies, 1990s.

Source: Heise, Ellsberg, and Gottemoeller (1999).

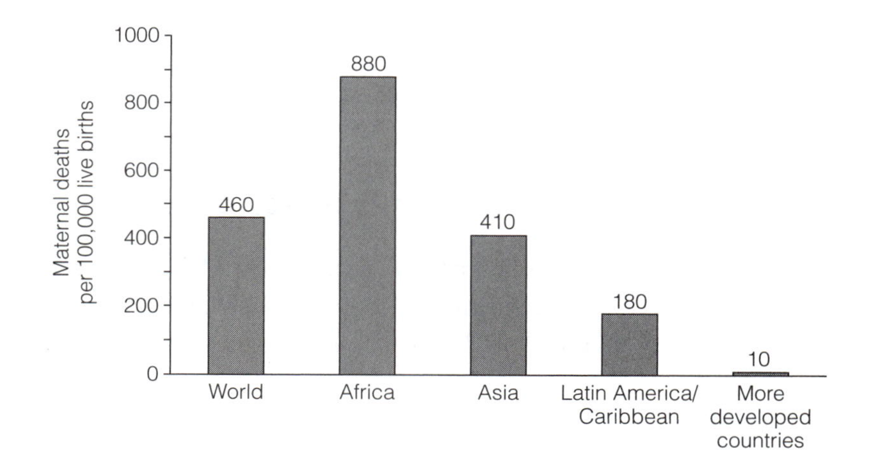

FIGURE 11.4 Maternal mortality ratios in world regions, early 1990s.

Source: Parikh and Shane (1998), based on data from the World Health Organization, UNICEF, and the United Nations.

2 million women, most in Sub-Saharan Africa and Asia (Grady, 2009). Women are deprived of medical care that could save their lives during childbirth and treat problems such as HIV and fistula. High rates of maternal death during childbirth are one result (Figure 11.4).

What Causes Improvements in Women's Position in Society?

Women's position in society typically improves with economic development. Modernization theories suggest that this happens immediately. Development can open work opportunities in factories and export industries for women (Villarreal and Yu, 2007), and the more women participate in the paid labor force, the better their position tends to be (Seguino, 2007).

Another theoretical perspective is the women in development approach. This approach suggests that development can initially widen gender inequality and then only eventually leads to greater gender equality (Hannum, 2005). This is because initial economic improvements at the household level can lead to greater investment in boys rather than girls. Economic development can also stimulate conservative reactions that promote restrictions on the freedom of women.

In addition to development, government policies regarding the education of boys and girls are important. The type of educational system is also important (Brinton, 1988). Policies and laws about women, such as the legality of abortion and the availability of family leave, also influence gender stratification (Wernet, 2008). Particularly important are beliefs about women's place in politics, education, and the labor force (Paxton and Kunovich, 2003). Religious beliefs also play a role, as is the case in the Middle East.

GENDER INEQUALITY IN THE UNITED STATES

As a developed, advanced industrial nation, the United States has a comparatively low level of gender inequality. Since 1967, women have joined the paid labor force in the United States in ever larger numbers (Figures 11.5 and 11.6).

Women have experienced increases in income at all educational levels and have also experienced rising income relative to that of men (Figures 11.7 and 11.8). Yet there are still differences in the earnings of men and women: The median income of women is still much lower than the median income of men.

In 2007, the median income for men was $45,100, whereas for women it was $35,100 (full-time, year-round workers only). This means that women make approximately 78% of what men do. Women often make less than men even when they work in the same industries.

In families, women are better off economically if they are married. Married women do better than single women (Figure 11.9). One result of this is that female-headed families are most likely to be in poverty (Figure 11.10). This is because women earn less, on average, than men but are most likely to

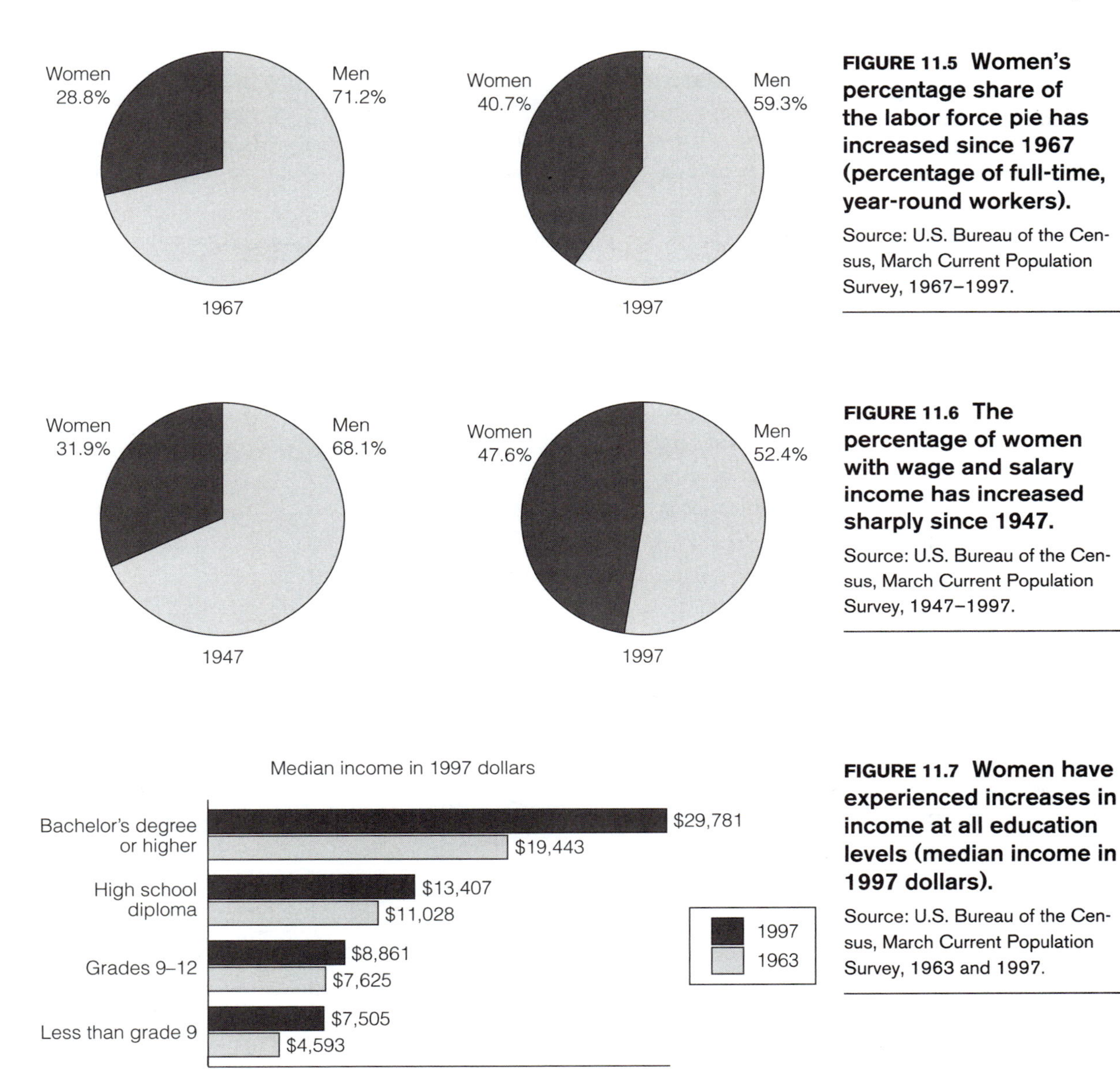

FIGURE 11.5 Women's percentage share of the labor force pie has increased since 1967 (percentage of full-time, year-round workers).

Source: U.S. Bureau of the Census, March Current Population Survey, 1967–1997.

FIGURE 11.6 The percentage of women with wage and salary income has increased sharply since 1947.

Source: U.S. Bureau of the Census, March Current Population Survey, 1947–1997.

FIGURE 11.7 Women have experienced increases in income at all education levels (median income in 1997 dollars).

Source: U.S. Bureau of the Census, March Current Population Survey, 1963 and 1997.

have greater responsibility for children in the case of separation or divorce. It is also because the poor are less likely to marry in the first place and are more likely to be divorced. This creates the phenomenon often referred to as the **feminization of poverty** (Brady and Kall, 2008).

Feminization of poverty
The tendency for households headed by women to be poor.

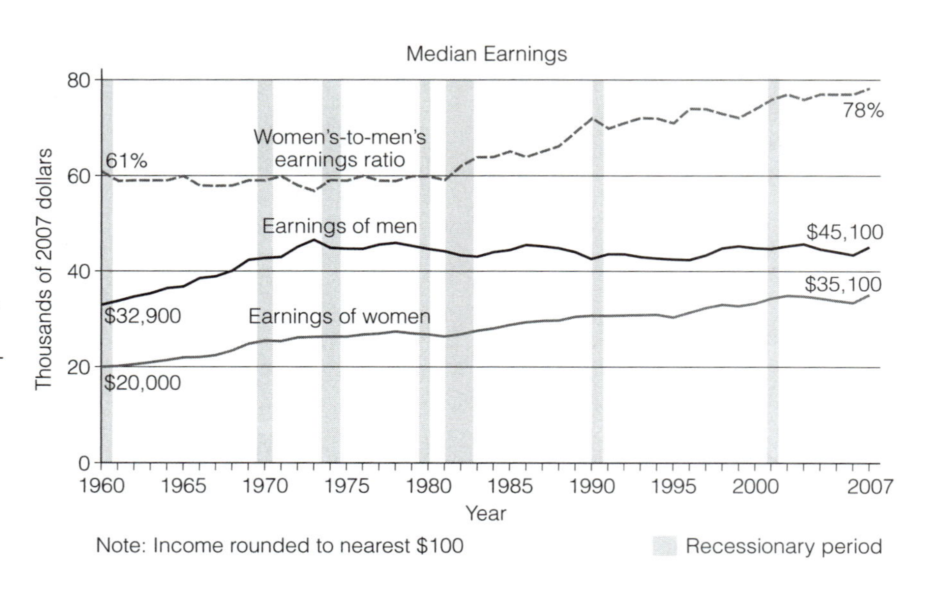

FIGURE 11.8 Women's to men's median earnings ratio and real median earning, 1960–2007 (full-time, year-round workers only).

Source: U.S. Census Bureau, Current Population Survey, 1961 to 2008 Annual Social and Economic Supplements.

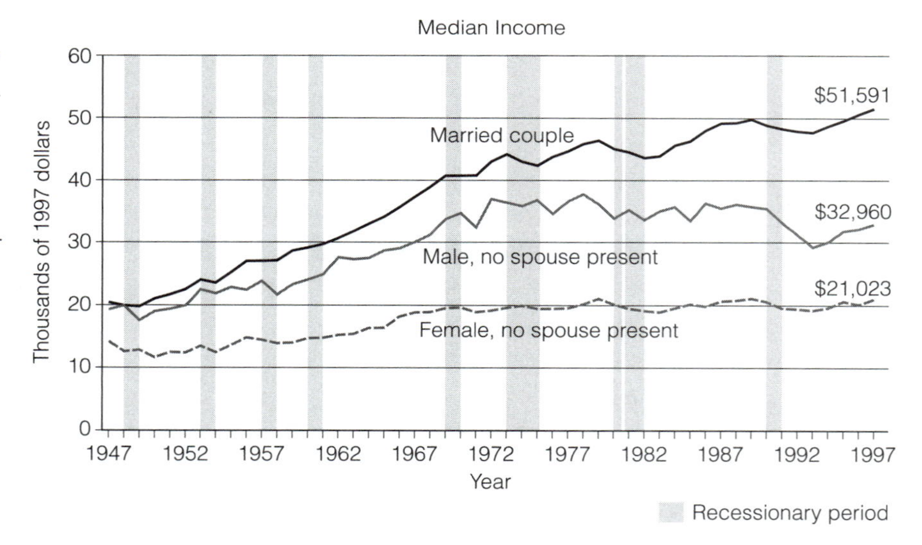

FIGURE 11.9 Married-couple families fare better economically than their single counterparts.

Source: U.S. Bureau of the Census, March Current Population Survey, 1947–1997.

Why the Gender Difference in Income?

Women are in different jobs than men are, and the types of jobs women have tend to pay less than the types of jobs men have. Even for jobs in which women are a majority of workers, men are more likely to have the high-level, better-paid positions. Women are much less likely than men to be in senior management positions in *Fortune* 500 companies, even though

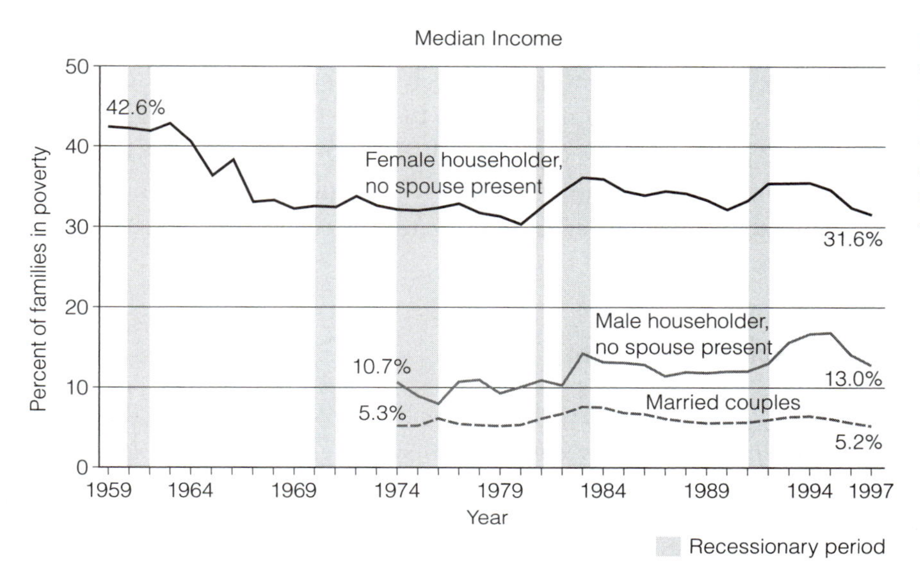

FIGURE 11.10 Single-parent families have the highest poverty rate.

Source: U.S. Bureau of the Census, March Current Population Survey, 1959–1997.

they comprise approximately half of all managers (Dencker, 2008). Men are less likely than women to be the "trailing spouse"—that is, a person who follows his or her spouse when the spouse moves to take a better-paying job (Bielby and Bielby, 1992). Women are more likely to adjust their careers to fit childbearing and family demands and are more likely to work part-time.

Yet some sociologists suggest that women's jobs are devalued simply because they are held by women (England, Allison, and Wu, 2007). Furthermore, there is evidence that discrimination still keeps women from climbing as far up the corporate ladder as men (the glass ceiling). One reason for this is the traditional ideas of what men and women are supposed to do. Another reason may be that unconscious cognitive biases (that are probably evolved; see Chapter 2) mean that women are less likely than men to move into positions of authority (Reskin, 2003; Ridgeway, 1997) and hence less likely to move into the most lucrative senior management jobs.

DO EVOLVED SEX DIFFERENCES INFLUENCE WORK BEHAVIOR?

In Chapter 2, we discussed sex differences between men and women. It is reasonable to ask if these sex differences influence women's workplace behavior.

Given their higher commitment to children, women are more likely than men to have competing demands on their time because of child care considerations. Some women may choose to work fewer hours, take on less demanding jobs, or be less career-oriented as a result. This may influence their earning ability and career trajectory. Yet evolved sex differences influence more than just time demands and career orientation.

Workplace Harassment

Evolved sex differences also influence patterns of harassment in the workplace. Given their lesser investment in prospective offspring, males are likely to be less discriminating in potential mates than females. This promotes a greater interest in any prospective mate—that is, any young healthy female. There is evidence that males are more likely to read a sexual subtext in an interaction than females. That is, in experimental scenarios, men are more likely than women to interpret sexual intent on the part of the woman in the scenario. Given these misinterpretations of intent, this promotes a situation in which sexual harassment of women by men can occur.

Leadership Style

For males, the limiting resource on reproduction is females. Hence, those males who in the environment of evolution were able to attract as many females as possible were more likely to leave more descendants. Because females are interested in males who are both willing and able to invest, committed, and resource rich, high-status mates were more desirable than others. Hence, males are likely to have an evolved predisposition to be interested in, and conscious of, their social status relative to other males.

There is evidence that males are very conscious of their position in a hierarchy, and that even small boys naturally form hierarchies with clear leaders during playtime. As a result, we would expect men to be more comfortable in hierarchical social situations, and there is evidence that this is the case.

For females in the environment of evolution, status attainment would have less of an effect on the number of descendants they left. Girls, therefore, are likely to be predisposed to have less of an interest in status and status acquisition. There is evidence that groups of women are based more on equality of members than status, and that women are less comfortable in a hierarchical situation in the workplace.

These differences suggest that males and females are likely to have different leadership styles, on average. Males are more likely to prefer to have a clear chain of command. Women are more likely to prefer a more collegial and consensus-based form of decision making.

Language Use

The male interest in status and status acquisition influences their use of language. Linguist Deborah Tannen (1991) described how status is key to understanding male conversation. According to Tannen, all male conversation may be seen as a negotiation over status—who has it and who does not. For females, however, the key to understanding women's conversation is to understand it as a negotiation for intimacy or closeness. Such sex differences in conversational style can lead to misunderstandings between men and women. Men may interpret a desire for consensus on the part of women as indecisiveness. Women may interpret male decision-making style as egotistical and selfish.

Deference Behaviors

There is much evidence from experiments that women are more likely to defer in mixed-sex interactions, be less influential, receive lower evaluations of their performance, and receive fewer rewards (Wagner and Berger, 1997). As discussed in Chapter 2, these predispositions toward deference behaviors may be evolved.

Such an evolved trait—deference by young women to men and lack of deference by men to young women—may influence interactions between genders in the contemporary workplace. For example, a predisposition not to defer to young women by men may make it more difficult for a young woman to occupy a position of authority over men than vice versa. In negotiations, a male predisposition not to defer to young women may make it more difficult for women to gain the upper hand in negotiations with men.

In addition, young women may be somewhat inhibited in their negotiations with men.

Similarly, a tendency not to defer to women may promote devaluation of women's competence and worth by male supervisors. There is evidence that women are more likely to be promoted when they have powerful male mentors. This may be because the judgment of the male mentor is unlikely to be questioned, and he can vouch for his protégé's competence (Burt, 1998).

HOW DOES THE UNITED STATES COMPARE TO OTHER DEVELOPED SOCIETIES?

In terms of the ratio of male to female income (all workers both full-time and part-time), the United States ranks ninth behind Sweden, Norway, Denmark, Australia, Finland, New Zealand, Canada, and Iceland (Table 11.3). When full-time workers alone are considered, Australia has the lowest gender gap in wages (Christopher et al., 2002).

The feminization of poverty is similar in all countries. Female-headed families are disproportionately likely to be poor in all countries (Christopher et al., 2002).

In terms of authority in the workplace, in most countries women have less authority on the job than do men (Rosenfeld, Van Buren, and Kalleberg, 1998). Rosenfeld et al. found that Australia and the United States have high levels of gender equality in authority, whereas Sweden and Japan are at the lower end of gender equality in authority. Again, this is consistent with the idea of universal cognitive biases that promote differences in deference behavior by gender. However, these universal biases manifest themselves to a different extent in different cultures.

CONCLUSION

Although gender inequality is pervasive, some countries are more egalitarian than others. In today's world, these are typically the richer countries. However, rich countries are by no means gender egalitarian. Female-headed families are disproportionately poor, and women still face obstacles moving into the best jobs with the most lucrative salaries.

TABLE 11.3 Ratio of Estimated Female to Male Earned Income

COUNTRY	RATIO OF FEMALE TO MALE INCOME
Sweden	0.83
Norway	0.74
Denmark	0.72
Australia	0.71
Finland	0.70
New Zealand	0.69
Canada	0.63
Iceland	0.63
United States	0.62
United Kingdom	0.60
France	0.59
The Netherlands	0.53
Germany	0.52
Belgium	0.50
Switzerland	0.50
Japan	0.46
Italy	0.45
Spain	0.44
Ireland	0.40
Luxembourg	0.38
Austria	0.36

Source: United Nations Development Programme, Human Development Report 2004.

REFERENCES

Bielby, William T., and Denise D. Bielby. 1992. "I Will Follow Him: Family Ties, Gender-Role Beliefs, and Reluctance to Relocate for a Better Job." *American Journal of Sociology* 97(5), 1241–1267.

Blumberg, Rae Lesser. 1988. "Income under Female versus Male Control. Hypotheses from a Theory of Gender Stratification and Data from the Third World." *Journal of Family Issues* 9(1), 51–84.

Boyd, A., C. Haub, and D. Cornelius. 2000. *The World's Youth 2000.* Washington, DC: Population Reference Bureau.

Brady, David, and Denise Kall. 2008. "Nearly Universal, But Somewhat Distinct: The Feminization of Poverty in Affluent Western Democracies 1969–2000." *Social Science Research* 37(3), 976–1007.

Brinton, Mary C. 1988. "The Social-Institutional Bases of Gender Stratification: Japan as an Illustrative Case." *American Journal of Sociology* 94(2), 300–334.

Burt, Ronald S. 1998. "The Gender of Social Capital." *Rationality and Society* 10(1), 5–46.

Chafetz, Janet Saltzman. 2004. "Gendered Power and Privilege: Taking Lenski One Step Further." *Sociological Theory* 22(2), 269–277.

Christopher, Karen, Paula England, Timothy M. Smeeding, and Katherin Ross Phillips. 2002. "The Gender Gap in Poverty in Modern Nations: Single Motherhood, the Market, and the State." *Sociological Perspectives* 45(3), 219–242.

Dencker, John C. 2008. "Corporate Restructuring and Sex Differences in Managerial Promotion." *American Sociological Review* 73(3), 455–476.

The Economist. February 21, 2009. "Women and Children Worst," p. 61.

England, Paula, Paul Allison, and Yuxiao Wu. 2007. "Does Bad Pay Cause Occupations to Feminize, Does Feminization Reduce Pay, and How Can We Tell with Longitudinal Data? *Social Science Research* 36(3), 1237–1256.

Fairfield, Hannah. February 28, 2009. "Why Is Her Paycheck Smaller?" *New York Times.*

Grady, Denise. February 24, 2009. "After a Devastating Birth Injury, Hope." *New York Times*, p. D1.

Hannum, Emily. 2005. "Market Transition, Educational Disparities, and Family Strategies in Rural China: New Evidence on Gender Stratification and Development." *Demography* 42(2), 275–299.

Heise, L., M. Ellsberg, and M. Gottemoeller. 1999. "Ending Violence against Women." *Population Reports,* Series L, No. 11. Baltimore,

MD: Population Information Program, Johns Hopkins University School of Public Health.

Parikh, L., and B. Shane. 1998. *Women of Our World*. Washington, DC: Population Reference Bureau.

Paxton, Pamela, and Sheri Kunovich. 2003. "Women's Political Representation: The Importance of Ideology." *Social Forces* 82(1), 87–114.

Reskin, Barbara F. 2003. "Including Mechanisms in Our Models of Ascriptive Inequality." *American Sociological Review* 68(1), 1–21.

Ridgeway, Cecilia. 1997. "Interaction and the Conservation of Gender Inequality." *American Sociological Review* 62, 218–235.

Rosenfeld, Rachel A., Mark E. Van Buren, and Arne L. Kalleberg. 1998. "Gender Differences in Supervisory Authority: Variation among Advanced Industrialized Democracies." *Social Science Research* 27(1), 23.

Seguino, Stephanie. 2007. "PlusCa Change? Evidence on Global Trends in Gender Norms and Stereotypes." *Feminist Economics* 13(2), 1–28.

Tannen, Deborah. 1991. *You Just Don't Understand: Women and Men in Conversation*. New York: Ballantine.

Villarreal, Andres, and Wei-hsin Yu. 2007. "Economic Globalization and Women's Employment: The Case of Manufacturing in Mexico." *American Sociological Review* 72(3), 365–389.

Wagner, David G., and Joseph Berger. 1997. "Gender and Interpersonal Task Behaviors: Status Expectation Accounts." *Sociological Perspectives* 40(1), 1–32.

Wernet, Christine A. 2008. "An Index of Pro-Woman Nation-States. A Comparative Analysis of 39 Countries." *International Journal of Comparative Sociology* 49(1), 60–80.

RACE AND ETHNICITY

12

THE AFRICAN DIASPORA AND THE EMERGENCE OF HUMAN PHENOTYPES

Race

As discussed in Chapter 2, all humans originated in East Africa and spread out of Africa into all the other continents of the world approximately 50,000 years ago. Since that time, there has been small-scale evolution in traits such as skin color, hair color, hair texture, and so on. It is these differences that give rise to the phenomenon most people refer to as "race." It is true that people whose ancestors come from a certain part of the world often share in common certain features. The genes that give rise to these different features are inherited and do cluster in groups corresponding to what we call races, but they are a tiny fraction of the entire human genotype. People of all races share the vast majority of their genetic material, and scientists have long known that there is more genetic variety *within* races than *between* races. Nevertheless, the differences in features have a *social* reality, and for social scientists it is this social reality that is most salient. People who are deemed to be of another race are often treated differently. They are frequently subject to prejudice and discrimination. Sometimes they have been enslaved and their humanity has been denied. A case in point is the enslavement of black Africans for use in plantations in the Americas, but there have been many other similar cases. Nor is it always lighter skinned people enslaving darker skinned people. The darker skinned Romans in classical times enslaved the lighter skinned Britons (natives of England at that time).

Ethnicity

Ethnic group A group that shares a common language and culture. Ethnic groups are typically endogamous; that is, they preferentially marry people from within the same ethnic group.

Race or racial group Group of people who share certain phenotypical features and are deemed by others to constitute a "race."

People who come from the same part of the world not only often look alike but also they are likely to share customs and culture. When they move to new places, they often find they are more comfortable with people who share the same customs and culture that they do, so they form an **ethnic group**. An ethnic group may or may not be considered a **racial group**, but all people in the group share a common language and culture. Ethnic groups are typically endogamous—that is, they preferentially marry people from within the same ethnic group. Like racial groups, members of ethnic groups have been subject to prejudice and discrimination. Also like racial groups, members of ethnic groups have been enslaved and mistreated.

CONTEMPORARY RACE AND ETHNIC RELATIONS THROUGHOUT THE WORLD

Racial and Ethnic Conflict

Genocide Systematic killings of members of one group by the members of another group.

Racial and ethnic tensions fuel conflicts throughout the world. One well-known case is the Rwandan genocide of 1994. **Genocide** is the systematic killing of one group (typically an ethnic or racial group) by another group. On April 6, 1994, a jet carrying the president of Rwanda (a member of the Hutu ethnic group) and the president of Burundi was shot down. Later that day, militiamen in Kigali, the capital of Rwanda, started going house to house pulling people out and killing them. The gunmen were members of the Hutu ethnic group, and their victims were mostly ethnic Tutsis. The genocide continued until the Tutsi-led rebel group, the Rwandan Patriotic Front, overthrew the Hutu government in mid-July and took power (Photo 12.1). In total, perhaps half a million people were killed, many hacked to death with machetes (*The Economist*, 2009). Conflicts between ethnic and/or religious groups have fueled mass killings in Cambodia, Bosnia, and Darfur. The best known genocide is the systematic killing of 6 million European Jews by Nazis during World War II.

Economic Divergence

Throughout the world, ethnic and racial group membership often has consequences for a person's economic situation. For example, in Latin

PHOTO 12.1 Children who fled the fighting in Rwanda rest in the Ndosha camp of the United Nations Assistance Mission in Goma, July 1994. Many of the children had witnessed the killings of their parents and were crying for their mothers. Source: UN Photo/John Isaac.

America, members of the indigenous groups (the natives of South America who were there before the Spanish conquest) are most likely to be poor (Figure 12.1). The dominant group in Latin America is the Spanish- or

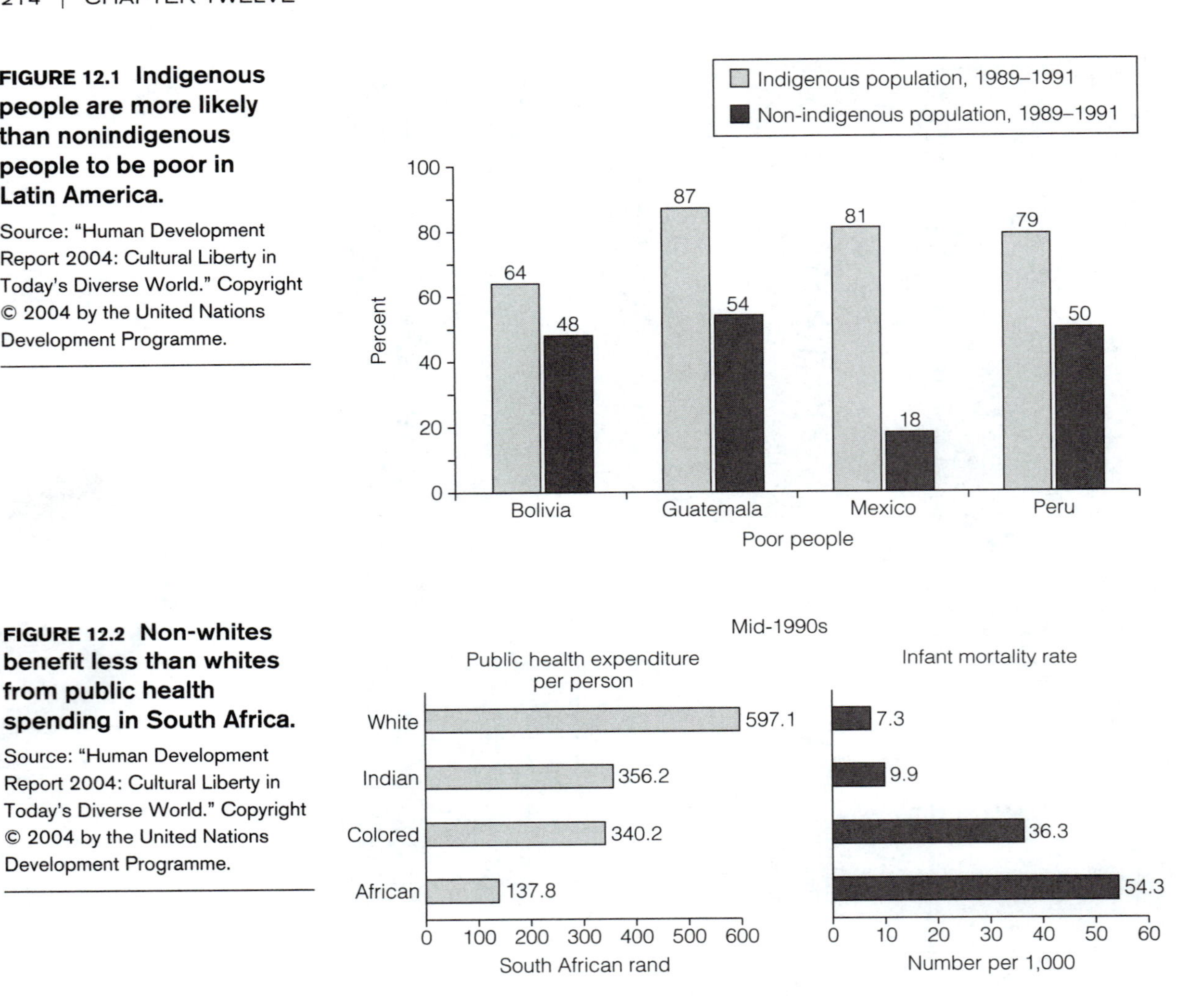

FIGURE 12.1 Indigenous people are more likely than nonindigenous people to be poor in Latin America.

Source: "Human Development Report 2004: Cultural Liberty in Today's Diverse World." Copyright © 2004 by the United Nations Development Programme.

FIGURE 12.2 Non-whites benefit less than whites from public health spending in South Africa.

Source: "Human Development Report 2004: Cultural Liberty in Today's Diverse World." Copyright © 2004 by the United Nations Development Programme.

Portuguese-speaking, mixed-raced descendants of the European colonists. In South Africa, the divide is between white (people of European ancestry) and black (people of African ancestry) (Figure 12.2).

The Role of Immigration

In many countries, immigration brings racial and ethnic groups together in the same place. Table 12.1 shows the countries that receive the most immigrants as a proportion of the whole population. The areas that currently

TABLE 12.1 Top 10 Countries by Share of Migrant Population, 2000

COUNTRY	%
United Arab Emirates	68
Kuwait	49
Jordan	39
Israel	37
Singapore	34
Oman	26
Switzerland	25
Australia	25
Saudi Arabia	24
New Zealand	22

Source: United Nations (2003).

receive the most immigrants are the oil-producing states of the Middle East (United Arab Emirates, Jordan, Kuwait, Oman, and Saudi Arabia); the settler societies of Israel, Australia, and New Zealand; and the rich countries of Europe (e.g., Switzerland). In rich countries, immigrants often take on the jobs that nobody else wants. For example, in the oil-producing countries of the Middle East, foreigners fill a wide array of domestic service jobs, such as drivers, caregivers, butchers, or retail workers, as well as more skilled jobs in the private sector. Foreigners filled more than 90% of private-sector jobs in Kuwait and Qatar in the early 2000s. Nationals opted for public-sector jobs with more security, higher salaries, and better benefits (Roudi-Fahimi and Kent, 2007).

Immigrant groups are typically ethnically (and/or racially) different from the dominant group, and this can pose problems. An example is the headscarf dilemma in France (Box 12.1).

RACE AND ETHNIC RELATIONS IN THE UNITED STATES

More so than any other advanced industrial society, the United States is home to a great many ethnic and racial groups. Some of these people are descendants of the people who were here before white settlement (Native

BOX 12.1
THE HEADSCARF DILEMMA IN FRANCE

The controversy over headscarves in French schools began in 1989 when a secondary school expelled three young women who wore headscarves to school on the grounds that this violated French principles of secularism. "Secularism" is the principle that state institutions have no religious affiliation. This began a public debate on whether the secondary school did the right thing or not and whether the girls should have been allowed to wear headscarves to school. The Council of State declared that it was permissible to wear religious tokens to school (e.g., headscarves) if they did not have an "ostentatious" or "militant" character. The controversy quieted down until 2002, when another girl was banned from school for wearing a headscarf. Some teachers threatened to go on strike if the girl was allowed to wear the headscarf in school.

In 2003, a law was passed banning the wearing of any obvious religious symbols in schools, including headscarves. A poll in 2004 showed that the majority of French people (69%) were against the wearing of headscarves in school, including 49% of all Muslim women. Those who defend the ban say it is a defense of freedom: freedom of religion and freedom of women from subordination (headscarves being seen as a token of subordination). Those who are against the ban also say their position is a defense of freedom: freedom against discrimination on the basis of religion and unequal opportunities.

Source: Adapted from United Nations Development Programme, Human Development Report 2004.

Americans), some are descendants of people who were brought forcefully as slaves (African Americans), and some are descendants of the many immigrants who have come to America to find a better life for themselves and their families. Here, we discuss the history of the incorporation of each of these groups into the United States, in part because a group's history influences the situation of the group today.

Native Americans

When the first Europeans came to America, they found the eastern United States to be heavily populated. These groups of Native Americans were horticulturalists who were skilled in farming, hunting, gathering, and fishing. They had no domesticated animals except dogs, no wheeled vehicles, and no written languages, but they lived in well-laid-out villages of comfortable wigwams. Native Americans were organized as tribes that sometimes had permanent leaders, sometimes not. It was a fairly loose social structure. Private rights to land were rare or nonexistent because most land was considered to belong to the community as a whole (Dinnerstein, Nichols, and Reimers, 1990, pp. 6–8).

Early Contacts

The early settlers had contradictory views of the natives. On the one hand, they hoped to meet with friendly tribesmen who would be a help to them in the new land. On the other hand, they were afraid of them and feared Indian attacks (Dinnerstein et al., 1990, p. 5). For a while, the Native Americans had a commodity that the whites wanted—furs. The fur trade formed the basis of Indian-white relations for many years. However, contact with whites and the goods bought by the proceeds of the fur trade—guns, alcohol, and other items—helped promote both war and cultural breakdown among the Indians. Indians used the guns to fight their ancient enemies—the members of other Indian tribes. The use of guns meant that the death toll from intertribal conflicts was higher than it ever had been before. White settlers further encouraged this tribal warfare by offering other guns and goods in exchange for Indian prisoners captured in battle. These prisoners were then enslaved. However, Indian slaves were problematic. They tried to escape, made trouble for their owners, or died, and thus the slave trade in Indian prisoners did not last long (Dinnerstein et al., 1990, pp. 9–10).

Alcohol also served to break down native cultures. The natives were not used to the alcohol and often became quickly addicted to it. This addiction in turn encouraged laziness and vice among a once proud people. Adoption of guns, the use of European goods, and the copying of European culture further served to break down the Native American culture and community. New diseases brought by the immigrants took a further deadly toll on the Native Americans. Native Americans had no natural immunity to diseases Europeans brought with them such as small pox, and so these new diseases proved deadly to them.

The coming of the white man thus brought warfare, cultural erosion, disease, and population decline to the Native American Indians. Gradually, as the Native American Indians left their own ways and adopted those of the incoming white settlers, as they became more dependent on the goods the whites had to offer, they lost their independence and strength relative to the white man.

Besides furs, Indians had only one other resource that white settlers wanted—land. At first, there were so few white settlers that their land demands were small and usually easily accommodated by the Native Americans. However, the new European farmers wanted laborers for their farms. Because attempts to enslave the Indians had failed, white settlers brought in more Europeans to fill their labor needs. Thus, the numbers of land-hungry settlers grew, whereas the numbers of Indians became ever fewer. The situation was ripe for conflict, and conflict soon came. In their weakened state, the American Indians were inevitably the losers in the land deals and conflicts with the new settlers. The early 17th century was marked by repeated conflicts between white settlers and Native Americans. Generally, Native Americans were defeated and forced to flee from their ancestral lands.

For example, in 1622, conflicts with settlers in the Virginia colony led to a full-scale effort by the local Indians to drive the colonists out. However, although they inflicted great casualties on the whites, they were not able to eradicate the new colony. At the end, the English signed a treaty with the Indians around Jamestown that in effect began the reservation system. This treaty guaranteed to the indigenous people a sanctuary from white land hunger and aggression. This pattern was repeated in land conflicts between Indians and whites for many years to come. As a rule, major land conflicts were ended through the signing of a treaty that assured the Indians certain reserved lands. After a while, however, white settlers invariably ignored the treaty, settled on Indian lands, and eventually evicted the Native Americans.

In addition, tribal land was often purchased with liquor and goods from individuals who had no real right to sell the land because the land was owned communally. This contributed to the loss of land. The liquor and goods obtained in return simply degraded the culture of the Indians. Large segments of proud and dignified tribes became demoralized in drunkenness and disease, and they became further willing to give up their land for a few European goods and alcohol.

Throughout the East, conflicts between settlers and Indians continued in the 17th and 18th centuries. During the years preceding the War of Independence, British authorities had tried to satisfy the new settlers' demand for land by concluding treaties with the Indians in New York, Pennsylvania, and Kentucky.

During the War of Independence, some Indians in the North sided with the British, convinced that this was their last hope for protecting their lands from the intrusions of settlers. The British loss did not enhance their position in the new country.

After the War of Independence, the U.S. Congress decided to follow the policies established by the English. More treaties were signed and once again were widely violated. Some Indian leaders protested the taking of land by the white settlers and the selling of land to the new settlers by some of the Indians. They called for a revival of Indian culture and mode of life. However, such protests were to little avail. The systematic destruction of the Native American way of life, culture, and population continued in the face of the influx of Europeans.

Indian Removal and the Trail of Tears (1838)

When the Indians could not be driven off their land or could not be persuaded to sell it, they were removed. The federal government decided to pursue a new policy of removal of all Indians east of the Mississippi River to the lands west of the river. This program was announced in 1825 by James Monroe. In his first inaugural address, Andrew Jackson announced his intention to push the Indians beyond the Mississippi. The Indian Removal Act was passed in 1830 (Dinnerstein et al., 1990, p. 41).

This policy simply made formal what had actually been happening informally for many years—that is, the pushing of the Indian tribes westward. It was seen as a way of quickly ending conflicts between white settlers and Indians. It also freed up more land for white settlers. The removal policy applied to tribes in the North and the Midwest as well as those in the South.

A notable case was that of the Cherokee of North Carolina, Tennessee, and north Georgia. They had responded well to the federal government's attempts to encourage assimilation of the Native Americans into mainstream, Anglo-American culture. The Cherokee nation accepted missionary-sponsored schools and benefited from the education. They developed a Cherokee syllabary that enabled them to read their own language for the first time. The Cherokee also accepted the federal government's help with buying seed, livestock, and new tools, and they were willing to learn the more intensive agricultural techniques of the Europeans.

Other Cherokee learned skills such as blacksmithing and mechanics. By the mid-1820s, the Cherokee owned at least 22,000 cattle, approximately 1,300 slaves, 31 grist mills, 10 saw mills, and 8 cotton gins (Dinnerstein et al., 1990, p. 39). The tribe also operated 18 schools and published the *Cherokee Phoenix*, a bilingual Cherokee–English newspaper. The Cherokee in particular hoped to use their adaptation to European ways as a reason for retaining their lands. The tribal leaders met during the summer of 1827, drafted a constitution, and formed the Cherokee republic. However, the constitution prohibited the creation of a new state within an existing state without its permission, and Georgia refused to give this permission. The government of Georgia instead insisted that the federal government force the Indians to vacate their lands.

When the Indian Removal Act was passed in 1830, the Cherokee appealed to the U.S. Supreme Court. The Court ruled in the Indians' favor, but it was unable to enforce the ruling. President Andrew Jackson is said to have stated about the ruling, "John Marshall has made his decision. Now let him enforce it" (Dinnerstein et al., 1990, p. 42). Thus, the Cherokee, like the others, were forcibly moved west. During the 1830s, approximately 73,800 Indians were moved west (p. 41). Usually, the federal government appointed a special agent to gather, organize, supply, and lead the Indians. Civilians supervised the removal of cooperative Indians, and the military supervised the removal of those who were unwilling to go. Local businessmen provided food, clothing, and transportation, which were paid for by federal agents. However, these agents often bought spoiled meat and flour to feed the Indians and pocketed the difference. The federal agents also rented the cheapest and most unreliable boats and transportation. Of the Cherokee, historians estimate that nearly 4,000 of the 15,000 tribesmen who started the trip west died either on the trip or during the first months in Oklahoma. Thus, the trek has been aptly named the "Trail of Tears."

Slavery and Race in North America

The first Africans were brought to Virginia as indentured servants in approximately 1619. Indentured servants were people who, in exchange for bed and board and passage to America, had agreed to serve a certain length of time as servants. At this time, they were not slaves because the law in the colony did not recognize slavery (Dinnerstein et al., 1990, p. 15). In the late 17th century, however, things changed. The demand for labor led to the importation of African workers en masse. As the numbers of black Africans in the colonies increased, the states of Virginia and Maryland began to recognize slavery and passed the first slave codes in the 1660s. In Africa, Africans were either captured by slave traders in West Africa or were prisoners captured in battle by other African tribes and sold to the slave traders. Most of these slaves went to South America, and only a small proportion went to North America. In North America, slaves were sent to the states with the tobacco, cotton, and rice plantations on which they were to work—Maryland, Virginia, and South Carolina. By 1770, they accounted for 40% of the population in those states (p. 17). In contrast to the South, very few black slaves were brought to the North. By the late 18th century, they only accounted for approximately 5% of the population in the North (p. 20).

Because of the threat of slave revolt, however, white southerners tried to control slaves in several ways. First, they restricted the ratio of slaves to whites to try to ensure that slaves did not greatly outnumber whites. They also tried to reduce the chances of slaves organizing and rebelling against whites. They separated members of tribes when the Africans were first brought to America. Slaves were not allowed to speak in their native tongues or retain their African names. They were only permitted to travel very short distances. White slave patrols were used to police the activities of slaves. It was illegal for a slave to learn to read or write or for anyone to teach a slave those skills. Slaves were restricted in the property they could own, they were not entitled to a jury trial, nor could they testify against whites (Dinnerstein et al., 1990, p. 53). Last, it was illegal to free a slave because it was feared that freed slaves would be able to organize the others and thus bring about a revolt. Slaves in the North fared better than slaves in the South. For example, in New England slaves were given more protection as persons than were southern slaves. Although they could still be bought and sold, they were entitled to a jury trial and could testify against whites in some cases, and they were also able to own property.

During the 18th century, there was much antislavery agitation, especially in the North. Eventually, slavery was abolished in the North in 1787, in what was to become Ohio, Indiana, Illinois, Michigan, and Wisconsin. The slave trade was officially ended in 1808 (Dinnerstein et al., 1990, p. 70). However, even after Congress prohibited the trade, smuggling continued for several more decades.

In the South, only a few whites owned a large number of slaves. Approximately 25% of white families owned slaves, and only 12% of these owners had more than 20 slaves. Most slaves lived on plantations that had 20 or more slaves (Dinnerstein et al., 1990, pp. 50–51). These were usually the large cotton plantations in Alabama, Mississippi, and other cotton-growing regions, rice plantations in South Carolina, and sugar plantations in Louisiana. The "peculiar institution" (as it was called) of slavery only came to an end after the Civil War, with the Thirteenth Amendment to the Constitution in 1865. In the South, however, Jim Crow laws kept those of African descent as an impoverished group of second-class citizens until the civil rights movement of the 1960s.

History of Immigration and Immigration Law in the United States

From the beginning, the demand for labor in the new colonies had brought European settlers and indentured servants to America. Immigration from Europe increased in the 19th and 20th centuries, with three great immigrant streams—1820–1889, 1890–1924, and after 1965 (McLemore, Romo, and Baker, 2001, p. 78). The first great immigrant stream to America began in approximately 1820 and brought people escaping poverty and famine from Ireland, Germany, the United Kingdom, France, and Scandinavia. On the West Coast, many Chinese immigrants arrived. The 1840s saw the arrival of approximately 1.7 million people, whereas the 1850s saw the arrival of approximately 2.6 million people (p. 77). Most of the immigrants were Irish and German, with the Germans being the larger group (and the largest single group of immigrants to the United States). Whereas the Irish tended to concentrate in the large eastern cities, the Germans became more dispersed over the entire country, although mostly in the North and Midwest.

The influx of culturally different newcomers promoted a movement against immigrants and immigration. Much of this was anti-Catholic because the Irish in particular were predominantly Catholic. The Irish were seen by many Americans as drunken, slovenly, and lazy. On the West Coast, people agitated against the arrival of Chinese immigrants. They were blamed for taking away jobs that "belonged" to white Americans and for driving wages down to a substandard level. Anti-immigrant feelings promoted the emergence of a political party—the "Know-Nothing" party. They were called

Know-Nothings because, when questioned about their party and its goals, they would reply "I know nothing." This group advocated "America for Americans." Know-Nothings on the East Coast particularly wished to abolish Catholic immigration, and Know-Nothings on the West Coast wished to abolish Chinese immigration. Although they were not successful on the federal level, on the local level the Know-Nothings were often able to create state laws that were aimed at certain ethnic groups. For example, California adopted licensing statutes for foreign miners and fishermen—laws that were enforced against the Chinese only. However, in the 1850s the Know-Nothing party dissolved, mostly because of the rising attention to the dispute over slavery (Dinnerstein et al., 1990, pp. 122–123).

On the West Coast, even with the demise of the Know-Nothings, anti-Chinese agitation continued. Newspapers joined in blaming the Chinese for the economic plight of the working class. In California, Chinese people, Chinese businesses, and Chinese institutions were all attacked. Finally, Congress responded by passing the Chinese Exclusion Act of 1882. That act suspended immigration of Chinese laborers for 10 years, except for those who were already in the country on November 17, 1880. Others who were not lawfully in the United States were to be deported. Chinese immigrants were also prohibited from obtaining U.S. citizenship after the effective date of the act. This 1882 act was amended in 1884 to cover all subjects of China and Chinese who resided in any other country as well. The Chinese exclusion law was extended in 1892 and 1902, and in 1904 it was extended indefinitely.

The second great stream of immigration to America occurred from 1890 to 1924 and contained significant numbers of Italians, Jews, Bohemians, Bulgarians, Croatians, Greeks, Lithuanians, Moravians, Poles, Serbs, Slovaks, and Slovenes (McLemore et al., 2001, p. 88). These new southern, central, and eastern Europeans seemed even more foreign to Americans than had the Irish and Germans. Their appearance, manner, and foods were more alien. These immigrants flooded into eastern cities. Their main jobs were as unskilled laborers on the railroads or in factories, and they became the main source of workers for nearly all segments of industrial production. The years 1901–1910 saw a surge of immigration to the United States. A total of nearly 9 million people immigrated in those years (McLemore et al., 2001, p. 88). Of these people, more than 6 million were from southern and eastern Europe. Large numbers of immigrants kept coming to the United States during the period 1911–1920 (Photo 12.2).

PHOTO 12.2 Immigrants waiting to be transferred, Ellis Island, October 30, 1912.
Source: Library of Congress.

Once again, this influx of newcomers promoted anti-immigration sentiment. In 1917, Congress made literacy a condition of immigrating to the United States—a direct attempt to keep many of the south, central, and eastern Europeans out because many of these people were illiterate. Finally, in 1921, Congress created a temporary quota law that limited the number of aliens of any nationality who could immigrate to 3% of the U.S. residents of that nationality already living in the country in 1910 (Dinnerstein et al., 1990, p. 246). The total annual immigration allowable in any one year was set at 350,000. The (intended) effect of the quota law was to limit immigration to people of western and northern European stock, because by far the majority of U.S. residents of non-U.S. nationality came from western and northern Europe in 1910. This temporary quota became a permanent one with the enactment of the 1924 National Origins Act. Now all new immigrants had to obtain a visa before coming to the country and had to have a sponsor within the United States. The 1924 act also served to discriminate against admitting people of African ancestry in general and against those from the West Indies in particular.

Immigration from any Asian country was prohibited in the Immigration Act of 1917. This act created an Asia-Pacific Triangle, an Asiatic barred zone, designed to exclude all Asians from immigration to the United States.

PHOTO 12.3 Members of the Mochida family awaiting evacuation bus, May 8, 1942. Identification tags were used to aid in keeping a family unit intact during all phases of evacuation. Mochida operated a nursery and five greenhouses on a two-acre site in Eden Township, California. Source: National Archives and Records Administration, Records of the War Relocation Authority.

The only exemptions from this zone were from an area that included Persia (present-day Iran) and areas of Afghanistan and Russia. All of this legislation effectively closed the golden door, and immigration tapered off.

Japanese American Internment during World War II

Japanese people, like other Asians, were effectively barred from immigration to the United States by the legislation of 1917. Nevertheless, there were substantial numbers of Japanese already in the United States by this time, with most in the western United States, particularly California. By the time of World War II, Japanese Americans included the children and grandchildren of these early immigrants, and they were American citizens by right of birth. Nevertheless, during World War II, Japanese Americans in western states were forced to leave their homes and businesses and were sent to internment camps for the duration of the war (Photo 12.3). Ostensibly, this was for their own protection because anti-Japanese sentiment was running high in the United States. Yet anti-German sentiment was also acute, and none of the descendants of the many German immigrants to the United States were put into camps. At the time, the United States was fighting both the Japanese in the Pacific and the Germans in Europe. Approximately 110,000 Americans of Japanese descent were rounded up and sent to the camps, where they were kept from 1942 to 1945. The losses to these individuals of their homes, jobs, and businesses were never fully compensated, although in the 1970s the surviving Japanese Americans who had been interned were compensated approximately $20,000 each (Dinnerstein et al., 1990, p. 254).

The 1965 Amendments

Immigration to the United States did not increase again until 1965, when there was a complete revision of U.S. immigration law. The 1965 amendments of the immigration law broke with older laws that had systematically favored Europeans over non-Europeans. These amendments established a new system of preferences for immigration. These preferences were as follows (McLemore et al., 2001, p. 99):

1. Reunite families
2. Permit certain skilled workers to enter the country
3. Provide asylum for political refugees

These new laws led to a dramatic increase in the numbers of immigrants to the United States, although relative to the size of the population, the influx of immigrants has been smaller than the previous immigrant streams. The result of these 1965 laws was to dramatically increase the numbers of immigrants of non-European descent. Between 1961 and 1970, the number of European immigrants declined to 34% of the total of all immigrants—the lowest it has ever been. In the period 1981–1990, Asia contributed approximately 37% of the total number of immigrants, whereas Mexico and Latin America contributed approximately 50%. Most of these new immigrants came searching for jobs, although some were political refugees from communist takeovers in Cuba and Southeast Asia. Unlike previous groups, this third stream also contained a sizable group of well-educated and skilled people, who came to the United States not to avoid poverty but to improve

TABLE 12.2 Median Household Income in the Past 12 Months by Race and Hispanic Origin, 2007[a]

RACE AND HISPANIC ORIGIN	MEDIAN HOUSEHOLD INCOME (DOLLARS)	
	ESTIMATE	MARGIN OF ERROR (±)[b]
All households	50,740	75
White alone	53,714	109
White alone, not Hispanic	55,096	106
Black alone	34,001	208
American Indian and Alaska Native alone	35,343	714
Asian alone	66,935	465
Native Hawaiian and other Pacific Islander alone	55,273	2660
Some other race alone	40,755	270
Two or more races	44,626	610
Hispanic (any race)	40,766	182

[a]In 2007 inflation-adjusted dollars. Data are limited to the household population and exclude the population living in institutions, college dormitories, and other group quarters. For information on confidentiality protection, sampling error, nonsampling error, and definitions, see www.census.gov/acs/www.

[b]Data are based on a sample and are subject to sampling variability. A margin of error is a measure of an estimate's variability. The larger the margin of error in relation to the size of the estimate, the less reliable the estimate. When added to and subtracted from the estimate, the margin of error forms the 90% confidence interval.

Source: U.S. Census Bureau, 2007 American Community Survey.

their careers. The Asians in particular tended to be better educated than immigrants from Latin America.

Status of Race and Ethnic Groups in the United States Today

By 2000, the descendants of the Irish, Italians, Germans, and all the other European groups that came in the 19th and early 20th centuries were assimilated into white American society and culture. The children, grandchildren, and great-grandchildren of poor, often illiterate, European peasants are now doctors, lawyers, bankers, professors, and so on. The descendants of Asians and new Asian immigrants have done particularly well. Asians had the highest median income of any group in 2007 (Table 12.2).

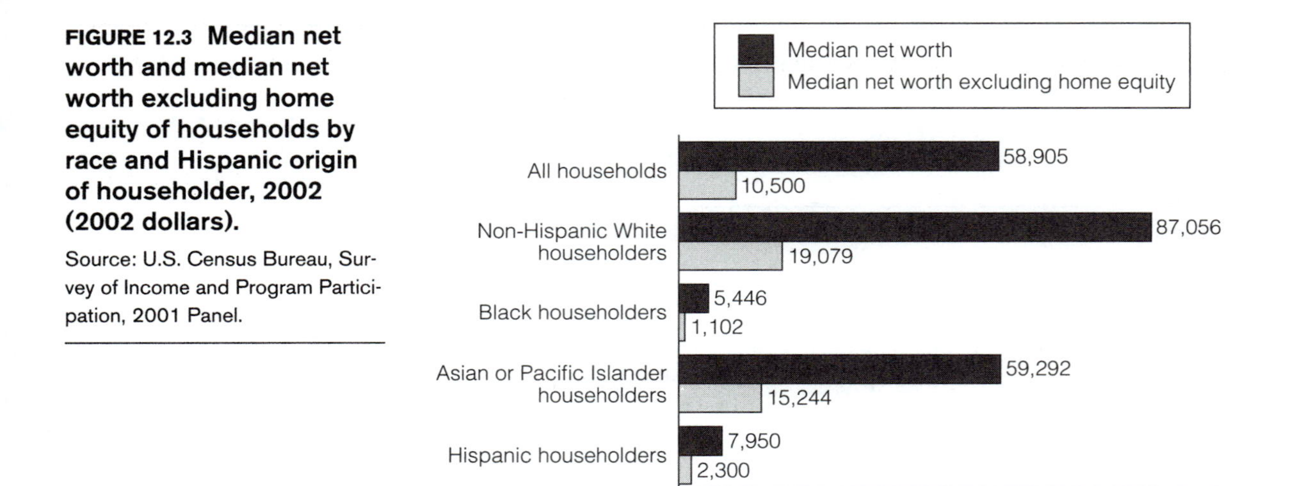

FIGURE 12.3 Median net worth and median net worth excluding home equity of households by race and Hispanic origin of householder, 2002 (2002 dollars).

Source: U.S. Census Bureau, Survey of Income and Program Participation, 2001 Panel.

In terms of wealth, the wealthiest group is the descendants of European immigrants (non-Hispanic whites; Figure 12.3). Other groups have not fared so well. In 2007, Native Americans and African Americans had the lowest median incomes of any group. In 2007, median household income for whites was $53,714, whereas for African Americans it was $34,001 and for Native Americans it was $35,343. The wealth disparities between white and African American households are even greater. In 2002, the median net worth of whites (including equity in homes) was $87,056, whereas for African Americans it was $5,446. One reason for this is that wealth is often built up in families over time. As a family achieves middle-class status, it is able to bequeath money and property to the next generation. There have been few African Americans in the middle class until recently.

African Americans are also more likely to be in poverty than are whites (see Table 12.3). Whereas approximately 10% of whites lived in poverty in 2007, nearly 25% of African Americans did. This is despite the fact that since the 1960s and greater incorporation into American economic and civil life, the economic prospects of African Americans have been steadily improving. Between 1967 and 1997, African American median household income increased 31%, whereas during the same period white household income increased by only 18% (Figure 12.4).

TABLE 12.3 Number and Percentage of People in Poverty in the Past 12 Months by Race and Hispanic Origin, 2007

RACE AND HISPANIC ORIGIN	ALL PEOPLE FOR WHOM POVERTY STATUS IS DETERMINED[a]	BELOW POVERTY			
		NO.	MARGIN OF ERROR (±)[b]	%	MARGIN OF ERROR (±)[b]
All races	293,744	38,052	233	13.0	0.1
White alone	217,751	22,284	166	10.2	0.1
White alone, not Hispanic	193,759	17,404	142	9.0	0.1
Black alone	35,681	8,807	77	24.7	0.2
American Indian and Alaska Native alone	2,278	576	19	25.3	0.8
Asian alone	13,000	1,376	35	10.6	0.3
Native Hawaiian and other Pacific Islander alone	422	66	7	15.7	1.5
Some other race alone	18,330	3,890	63	21.2	0.3
Two or more races	6,283	1,054	23	16.8	0.4
Hispanic (any race)	44,471	9,219	89	20.7	0.2

[a]Poverty status is determined for individuals in housing units and noninstitutional group quarters except people living in college dormitories or military barracks. Unrelated individuals younger than 15 years are also excluded from the poverty universe.

[b]Data are based on a sample and are subject to sampling variability. A margin of error is a measure of an estimate's variability. The larger the margin of error in relation to the size of the estimate, the less reliable the estimate. When added to and subtracted from the estimate, the margin of error forms the 90% confidence interval.

Source: U.S. Census Bureau, 2007 American Community Survey.

PREJUDICE AND DISCRIMINATION

Why were Americans, whose Constitution reads that "all men are created equal," so willing to enslave Africans and deprive the Native Americans of land they had occupied for generations? Why did it take so long for African Americans to realize their full civil rights (right to vote, etc.)? Why was anti-Chinese sentiment so virulent in California? Why were people willing to

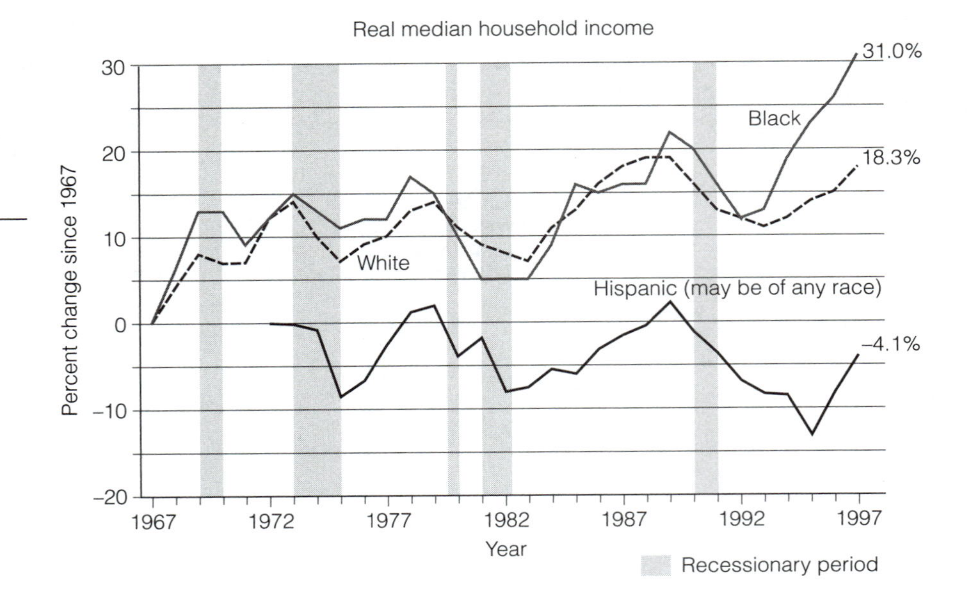

FIGURE 12.4 Black household income has increased noticeably.

Source: U.S. Bureau of the Census, March Current Population Survey, 1967–1997.

commit the genocidal atrocities in Rwanda, Bosnia, and Cambodia? Why did the Nazis systematically kill 6 million Jews? Prejudice, hatred, and discrimination against out-groups seem only too common across all human societies. Social scientists usually distinguish between **prejudice** and hatred, which are beliefs or feelings, and **discrimination**, which is putting those beliefs and feelings into action.

Prejudice An unfavorable attitude toward people because they are members of a particular racial or ethnic group.

Discrimination An unfavorable action toward people because they are members of a particular racial or ethnic group.

Us and Them

Researchers have found it very easy to create mutually antagonistic in-groups and out-groups. One famous example is the Robbers Cave experiment (Sherif et al., 1954/1961). In this study, the experimental subjects were 22 stable, middle-class white Protestant boys from the fifth and sixth grades, selected from 22 different schools in Oklahoma City. All of them were doing well in school, and their median IQ was 112. They were as well-adjusted and as similar to each other as the researchers could manage. The 22 boys were divided into two groups of 11 campers, and each group was taken to a separate area of the Robbers Cave State Park in Oklahoma. At first, the groups were unaware of each other. Each group developed its own swimming hole and hideouts, and group members cooperated in activities such as pitching tents, preparing meals, and hiking. During this stage, each group spontaneously developed its own rules, status hierarchy, and identity. They even adopted names: One group became the "Rattlers" and the other group became the "Eagles." When they became aware of each other, hostility between the two groups quickly emerged. They began hurling insults at each other. Each group became very possessive when the other group infringed on spaces it considered its own, such as a campground or baseball diamond. The researchers purposefully fueled friction between the groups by hosting competitive sports games. Tensions between the two groups became so bad that the researchers had to end this part of the experiment early. In the last stage of the experiment, the researchers tried to reduce friction between the two groups. Mere contact (being present without any contest) did not reduce friction between the two groups. Attending pleasant events together, such as a Fourth of July picnic with fireworks, did not reduce friction; instead, it developed into a food fight. Finally, the boys were informed that there might be a water shortage in the whole camp due to mysterious trouble with the water system—possibly due to vandals. The two groups had to cooperate to solve the problem. A few more common tasks, requiring cooperation from both groups (e.g., restarting a stalled truck) did the job. In the end, the boys wanted to ride back home together on the same bus.

Why Prejudice?

The ease with which hostility develops between in-groups and out-groups, as demonstrated in the Robbers Cave experiment, suggests that such a tendency may have a basis in human nature, as discussed in Chapter 2. Nevertheless, some groups are more prejudiced and discriminate more against outsiders than do other groups. What causes this variation from group to group?

Some theories of prejudice suggest that children learn prejudice the same way they learn a language and other aspects of a particular culture. Shared beliefs about out-group members we often call "stereotypes." That is, we can define a stereotype as a shared belief about the characteristics of out-group members. Stereotypes may or may not have some basis in reality. Early studies of dominant group members in the 1930s in America found that stereotyping was very strong in American culture. For example, the Princeton study by Katz and Braly (1933) found that more than half of the Princeton college students in their sample agreed that Germans are scientific and industrious, Italians are artistic, the English are sportsmanlike, Jews are shrewd, and blacks are superstitious and lazy. Recently, there has been a decline in the willingness of people to admit to holding stereotypes about particular groups. However, this does not mean that people no longer stereotype; it just means they have learned that it is not considered socially appropriate to do so. Stereotypes reflect popular perceptions of reality, and they change as popular perceptions change. Thus, in the 1933 study, Italians were viewed as artistic, but by 1951 this was no longer the case. Soon after World War II, the Japanese were viewed as being "treacherous" and "nationalistic," whereas later they were seen as being "intelligent" and "progressive." Regardless of how true or not true they may be, negative stereotypes about a certain ethnic group are likely to lead to prejudice against that ethnic group.

The second aspect of culture that is important in determining prejudice is the nature of its shared beliefs about how distant or apart it is best to be from out-group members. This is called *social distance* (Bogardus, 1933). If a person from one group is willing to marry a person from an ethnic group, then that group is low in social distance from the first group. If a person from one group would try to exclude members from another ethnic group from the country, then that group is high on social distance from the first group. In general, in American society people from the British Isles and from northern and western Europe have low social distance, whereas racial minorities such as African Americans have high social distance.

Critics suggest that the major problem with cultural theories of prejudice is that within a single culture there are variations in the levels of prejudice that individuals hold. Even members of the same family may disagree about stereotypes or the desired social distance of a group. There are a variety of theories to explain the variation in prejudice across individuals.

One hypothesis is the *frustration-aggression hypothesis*. That is, individuals become prejudiced when they are frustrated in their own lives, and they vent their frustration by hostility and name-calling of ethnic group members (Dollard et al., 1939). Thus, the theory is that ethnic group members are used as scapegoats. However, this is not the whole story. People who scapegoat on an innocent person may feel guilty about doing so. Alternatively, they may be frightened that the innocent person will retaliate. This in turn increases their frustration, and they may react by being more prejudiced and aggressive toward the ethnic group members. This creates a vicious cycle of frustration and aggression.

Cognitive dissonance may also serve to increase prejudice, if the ethnic group is being used as a scapegoat. Cognitive dissonance theory (Festinger, 1957) states that human beings are uncomfortable when their attitudes and beliefs are not consistent with each other. Thus, if a person scapegoats an ethnic group member but knows that person to be innocent, he or she may try to avoid cognitive dissonance by imagining the person is not innocent. That is, the person was in some way deserving of the bad treatment he or she received. Thus, the person who scapegoats may accept negative stereotypes of the ethnic group members and be prejudiced against them.

Why Discrimination?

Prejudiced people may or may not discriminate against the object of their prejudice. This was shown in a study conducted by LaPiere in the 1930s (LaPiere, 1934). He and a Chinese couple traveled approximately 10,000 miles across the United States, stopping at 67 hotels along the way and eating at approximately 184 restaurants. At this time in the United States, anti-Chinese sentiment was exceptionally strong. Yet in all 251 cases, the couple and the researcher were refused service only once at one hotel.

After the trip was over, LaPiere mailed a questionnaire to all the places they had stayed or eaten. He asked all of them whether they would serve "members of the Chinese race" at their establishments. Of those who answered the questionnaire, the overwhelming majority (92% of the hotel proprietors and 93% of the restaurant proprietors) said they would not. That is, the majority claimed they would discriminate against Chinese customers even though they had already accepted the Chinese couple as customers. Clearly, what they said they would do and what they actually did in the situation were different. That is, knowing the proprietors' prejudices did not predict their actions—whether or not they were going to discriminate.

Why didn't people discriminate against the Chinese couple when they said they would? First, the couple did not fit the prevailing negative stereotype of Chinese people: They were well dressed, and they were accompanied by a distinguished-looking white man. Given this situation, proprietors were reluctant to discriminate against the Chinese couple, despite their strong prejudices. It would have been very embarrassing for a proprietor to have refused service to the Chinese couple because then he or she would have had to refuse service to the distinguished-looking white man as well.

Then the proprietor would be treating as low status a person who in this society is usually afforded high status, and other customers, for example, may not have approved of this. If the white man had not been there, the same proprietors may have had no qualms about discriminating against the same Chinese couple. This study demonstrated that discriminatory actions often depend on the situation.

Fundamental attribution error When judging the behavior of others, people tend to attribute more causal weight to the person's personality and less causal weight to the situation. When judging their own behavior, people tend to attribute less causal weight to their own personality and more causal weight to the situation.

It is true that many people overlook the importance of the situation in determining individual behavior, although they do not overlook this importance when evaluating their own behavior. This is called the **fundamental attribution error**. When judging others' behavior, people tend to attribute more causal weight to the person's personality and less causal weight to the situation. In judging their own behavior, people tend to attribute less causal weight to their own personality and more causal weight to the situation. (People often say "I had no choice," which is a common expression of this). Situational pressure theories of discrimination suggest that each individual case of discrimination is a product of the social pressures present in any given situation.

Other theories of discrimination suggest that it is a result of group strategies for achieving some desired end, such as property, prestige, or power. That is, people discriminate because it is in the interests of themselves and the social group to which they belong—their class, status group, or other group. For example, the *split labor market theory* of discrimination suggests that discrimination serves the interests of higher-priced labor because it is a method they can use to protect their jobs from competition by lower-priced migrant workers (Bonacich, 1972). There is some evidence from the 1960s, for instance, that urban white Americans did benefit in terms of jobs and wages by the subordination of African Americans (Glenn, 1966). That is, the better jobs with better wages were effectively "reserved" for whites. These effects were greater in southern cities, as you might expect, because the proportion of blacks was greater there than in northern cities. This supports the split labor market theory of discrimination. Moreover, it suggests that there will be more discrimination where the ethnic or racial minority is more numerous, and the group presents more of a competitive threat in the job market. There is much evidence to bear this out.

Economic considerations suggest that there are problems with group gains theories such as the split labor market theory. This is because employers who do not discriminate—that is, they hire ethnic and minority group members—should save money on labor costs. For example, consider a certain well-paid job typically reserved for whites. Now a qualified black candidate for the job, facing discrimination, will be prepared to work for lower wages than a similarly qualified white. The employer who hires the black will end up saving money on labor costs. Such savings will give all such nondiscriminating employers a competitive edge because they will be able to price their products more competitively than others. Faced with such competition, eventually discriminating employers will be forced out of business. Thus, the competitive market should favor employers who do not discriminate on the basis of ethnic or racial group membership.

However, one kind of discrimination can survive highly competitive markets. This is **statistical discrimination**, which is discrimination that occurs when an individual is judged on the basis of the average characteristics of the group to which he or she belongs rather than his or her own characteristics. For instance, consider the case of young men and car insurance rates. Young men often pay higher car insurance premiums because, regardless of the individual's own driving record, young men as a group have more accidents than other groups. Charging all young men a higher premium is an economically rational strategy for insurance companies because it saves them the time and effort of finding out about every young man's individual driving record. Similarly, if minorities are unlikely to have a certain qualification, then employers may find it easier to simply exclude all minorities from the pool of possible people to hire rather than spend the time and money researching each individual job applicant's particular background to find out if he or she actually does have the necessary qualification. Thus, if the minority group is less likely to have the necessary qualifications, then statistical discrimination may actually be cost-effective for the employer when hiring people for a job, just as it is for insurance companies when charging insurance premiums. Such statistical discrimination can serve to reserve certain jobs for white workers as well as to allow higher-paid workers to exclude minority workers from employment, as the split labor market theory suggests.

Statistical discrimination Discrimination against individuals because of average characteristics of the group to which they belong.

CONCLUSION

Throughout the world, conflicts often erupt between groups differentiated by race or ethnicity. Ethnic or racial prejudice and discrimination seem only too common in the world today. Usually, it is the least powerful and least resource-rich group who receives the worst of it. The history of race and ethnic relations in America shows the same dynamic—repeated conflicts between groups differentiated by race and ethnicity, with the least powerful group bearing the worst treatment (Native Americans, African slaves, and, later, recent European immigrants). In the United States, time and laws reinforcing the rights of minority groups have helped create a comparatively peaceful, multiethnic society. However, group inequalities continue, partly because of historic continuity and partly because of continued prejudice and discrimination. Although it is likely innate for people to discriminate against members of out-groups, in this chapter we also tried to answer the question of why people vary in how much they are prejudiced and how often they discriminate.

REFERENCES

Bogardus, Emory S. 1933. "A Social Distance Scale." *Sociology and Social Research* 17, 265–271.

Bonacich, Edna. 1972. "A Theory of Ethnic Antagonism: The Split Labor Market." *American Sociological Review* 37, 547–559.

Dinnerstein, Leonard, Roger L. Nichols, and David M. Reimers. 1990. *Natives and Strangers: Blacks, Indians and Immigrants in America*, 2nd ed. New York: Oxford University Press.

Dollard, John, Leonard Doob, Neal Miller, O. H. Mowrer, and R. R. Sears. 1939. *Frustration and Aggression*. New Haven, CT: Yale University Press.

The Economist. February 19, 2009. "Alison Des Forges, a Witness to Genocide, Died on February 12th, Aged 66."

Festinger, Leon. 1957. *A Theory of Cognitive Dissonance*. Stanford, CA: Stanford University Press.

Glenn, Norval D. 1966. "White Gains from Negro Subordination." *Social Problems* 14, 159–178.

Katz, Daniel, and Kenneth W. Braly. 1933. "Ethnic Stereotypes of One Hundred College Students." *Journal of Abnormal and Social Psychology* 28, 280–290.

LaPiere, Richard T. 1934. "Attitudes vs. Actions." *Social Forces* 13, 230–237.

McLemore, Dale S., Harriett D. Romo, and Susan Gonzalez Baker. 2001. *Racial and Ethnic Relations in America*, 6th edn. Boston: Allyn & Bacon.

Roudi-Fahimi, Farzaneh, and Mary Mederios Kent. 2007. "Challenges and Opportunities—The Population of the Middle East and North Africa." In *Population Bulletin*, Vol. 62, No. 2. Washington, DC: Population Reference Bureau.

Sherif, M., O. J. Harvey, B. J. White, W. R. Hood, and C. W. Sherif. 1954/1961. *Study of Positive and Negative Intergroup Attitudes between Experimentally Produced Groups: Robbers Cave Study*. Norman: University of Oklahoma.

United Nations. 2003. *World Population Prospects 1950–2050: The 2002 Revision Population Database*. New York: United Nations Population Division, Department of Economic and Social Affairs.

SOCIOLOGY OF RELIGION

13

RELIGIOUS UNIVERSALS

People throughout the world have beliefs in supernatural beings of some sort, whether they are the spirits of ancestors, ghosts, or spirits of trees or animals. In simple societies such as hunting and gathering societies and horticultural societies, there are usually a great many of these supernatural beings; these tend to be **polytheistic religions**. In agrarian societies, there is often just one primary being featured; these are **monotheistic religions**. The three great religions of the world—Islam, Judaism, and Christianity—are products of agrarian societies, and they are all monotheistic: They propose just one primary supernatural being or God. However, this is just a tendency and as with all tendencies there are exceptions. As discussed in Chapter 4, preindustrial Japan was an agrarian society and the religion was Shinto-Buddhism, a religion with multiple supernatural beings (spirits and ancestors) as well as beliefs in the Buddha.

Polytheistic religions Religions characterized by belief in multiple gods.

Monotheistic religions Religions characterized by belief in one god.

Another tendency is that in the more complex societies, religion is more institutionalized and often bureaucratized. In agrarian societies, beliefs in one God are associated with places of worship (churches, temples, or shrines) and groups of full-time religious leaders, such as monks or priests. In industrial societies, religious beliefs are associated with churches and a professional ministry or priesthood.

Most religions have characteristics that follow the four "M's": magic, membership, morality, and mysticism (Collins, 2008). Magic and mysticism are related to beliefs in spirits and gods. Magic is using spiritual means to achieve practical ends. Mysticism is immediate contact with the divine. Membership and morality are related to the social organization of religion. One must be a member of the religion and participate in the religious rituals and also be a moral person. To be moral is to accept religious taboos (e.g., not to work on the Sabbath) and follow certain rules of social conduct (e.g., thou shalt not kill) and asceticism (e.g., doing without certain things or striving for perfection). Religions in different societies stress the components of the four M's to a different degree, although they are present to a certain extent in all religions.

Churches, Sects, and Cults

Sociologists often distinguish among three different types of religious organizations: churches, sects, and cults. *Churches* are the established religious organizations of society. They tend to be the most formal and are most likely to intellectualize religious teachings. *Sects* are more informal religious organizations that stress the emotional content of religion, and they tend toward fundamentalism in their teachings (Photo 13.1). Sects are often based on a rejection of materialism, a denial of this world, and a focus on the next world. Sects often appeal to people low in the socioeconomic scale who have little in the world. Niebuhr (1929) suggests that sects begin to appeal to the middle and upper classes only when they shift their emphasis to more worldly affairs. As a result, they typically become more formalized, less emotional, and eventually turn into churches. Churches appeal to the middle and upper classes because they are not interested in rejecting a world that has served them well. According to Niebuhr, all successful religious organizations eventually shift their emphasis toward this world and away from the next world and hence develop from sects to churches.

Cults are new religious movements, whereas churches and sects represent the already established religion(s) of the society. Although new cults appear constantly in all societies, most of them fail (Stark and Bainbridge, 1985). Often they fail because of internal problems. Frequently, cult members are looked down upon by others in the society and they often suffer discrimination, harassment, and even persecution. Some cults do succeed and become established as sects or churches. The major successes in history have of course been the major world religions—Christianity, Islam, Judaism, Hinduism, and Buddhism. For example, Christianity began as a small sect of Judaism in the area of the world that is now Israel. Later, it became a cult among elite Romans (particularly elite Roman women) in a society in which the established religion was based on beliefs in a large

PHOTO 13.1 Members of the polygamist sect Fundamentalist Church of Jesus Christ of Latter Day Saints (FLDS) leave a courthouse in San Angelo, Texas, May 22, 2008. These women were residents of the Yearning for Zion Ranch in Eldorado County, Texas. Source: Associated Press photo/LM Otero.

number of Roman/Greek gods (Stark 1996). At first, the early Christians were persecuted by the Romans and others. As Christianity grew, it began to appeal to increasingly wider sections of society. Eventually, the Roman Emperor himself became Christian. Thus, Christianity moved from being a sect to a cult and to a church. Eventually it split into a large number of different churches (including the Catholic, Protestant, Greek Orthodox, Russian Orthodox, and Church of Latter Day Saints).

RELIGION IN THE WORLD TODAY

Secularization hypothesis
As societies industrialize and modernize, religion diminishes in importance to people in the society.

Early sociologists of religion hypothesized that as societies industrialized and became more complex, religion would diminish in importance (Gorski, 2000). This is called the **secularization hypothesis,** and it appears to be true, at least somewhat. Table 13.1 shows the percentages of people in the population reporting that they attended religious services at least once a month. In 1998, in industrialized countries the percentage of the population reporting that they attended church services at least once a month ranged from 9% in East Germany to 38% in Spain. In developing countries, many more people attend church at least once a month (percentages range from a low of 41% in Argentina to a high of 87% in Nigeria).

As in many things, however, the United States is something of an exception. Table 13.1 shows that in 1998, 55% of Americans reported attending religious services at least once a month. That is higher than any other single developed nation. Furthermore, in the United States today, the vast majority of the population self-identifies as religious. The American Religion Identification Survey conducted by the Program on Public Values at Trinity College in Hartford, Connecticut, surveyed a representative sample of 54,461 adults from February through November of 2008. The results are presented in Table 13.2.

Table 13.2 shows that nearly 80% of Americans self-identify as religious. Most Americans are Christian (76%), with only small minorities espousing other religions (approximately 4%). Catholics are the largest religious group, with 25% of Americans (57 million) saying they belong to the church.

In the United States, however, there are distinct regional differences in religious propensity. In 2008, northern New England was the least religious region, with Vermont reporting the highest share of those claiming no religion at 34% (Figure 13.1). The Pacific Northwest is the next least religious area of the United States. Generally, the South and the Midwest are the most religious areas of the United States.

In the United States, the number of people claiming that they have no religion is increasing. The 2008 American Religion survey found that the number of people claiming no religion has increased from 8.2% of the population in 1990 to 15% in 2008. However, this is still far below similar percentages in other rich nations.

TABLE 13.1 Percentage Attending Religious Services at Least Once a Month, by Country and Year

COUNTRY	1981	1990–1991	1995–1998	NET CHANGE
Advanced Industrial Democracies[a]				
Australia	40	–	25	−15
Belgium	38	35	–	−3
Canada	45	40	–	−5
Finland	13	13	11	−2
France	17	17	–	0
East Germany	–	20	9	−11
West Germany	35	33	25	−10
Great Britain	23	25	–	+2
Iceland	10	9	–	−1
Ireland	88	88	–	0
Northern Ireland	67	69	–	+2
South Korea	29	60	27	−2
Italy	48	47	–	−1
Japan	12	14	11	−1
Netherlands	40	31	–	−9
Norway	14	13	13	−1
Spain	53	40	38	−15
Sweden	14	10	11	−3
Switzerland	–	43	25	−18
United States	60	59	55	−5
Ex-Communist Societies[b]				
Belarus	–	6	14	+8
Bulgaria	–	9	15	+6
Hungary	16	34	–	+18
Latvia	–	9	16	+7
Poland	–	85	74	−11
Russia	–	6	8	+2
Slovenia	–	35	33	−2
Developing and Low-Income Societies[c]				
Argentina	56	55	41	−15
Brazil	–	50	54	+4
Chile	–	47	44	−3
India	–	71	54	−17
Mexico	74	63	65	−9
Nigeria	–	88	87	−1
South Africa	61	–	70	+9
Turkey	–	38	44	+6

[a]Sixteen of 20 advanced industrial democracies declined; mean change = −5.

[b]Of ex-Communist societies, 5 of 7 increased; mean change = +4.

[c]Of developing and low-income societies, 5 of 8 declined; mean change = −4.

Source: Inglehart and Baker (2000).

TABLE 13.2 Religious Self-Identification of the U.S. Adult Population, 1990, 2001, and 2008

	1990		2001		2008	
	ESTIMATED NUMBER OF PEOPLE	%	ESTIMATED NUMBER OF PEOPLE	%	ESTIMATED NUMBER OF PEOPLE	%
Catholic	46,004,000	26.2	50,873,000	24.5	57,199,000	25.1
Other Christian	105,221,000	60.0	108,641,000	52.2	116,203,000	50.9
Total Christians	151,225,000	86.2	159,514,000	76.7	173,402,000	76.0
Other Religions	5,853,000	3.3	7,740,000	3.7	8,796,000	3.9
Nones	14,331,000	8.2	29,481,000	14.2	34,169,000	15.0
DK/Refused	4,031,000	2.3	11,246,000	5.4	11,815,000	5.2
Total	175,440,000	100.0	207,983,000	100.0	228,182,000	100.0

Source: Barry A. Kosmin and Ariela Keysar, American Religious Identification Survey (ARIS 2008) Summary Report, Trinity College, Hartford, CT (March 2009).

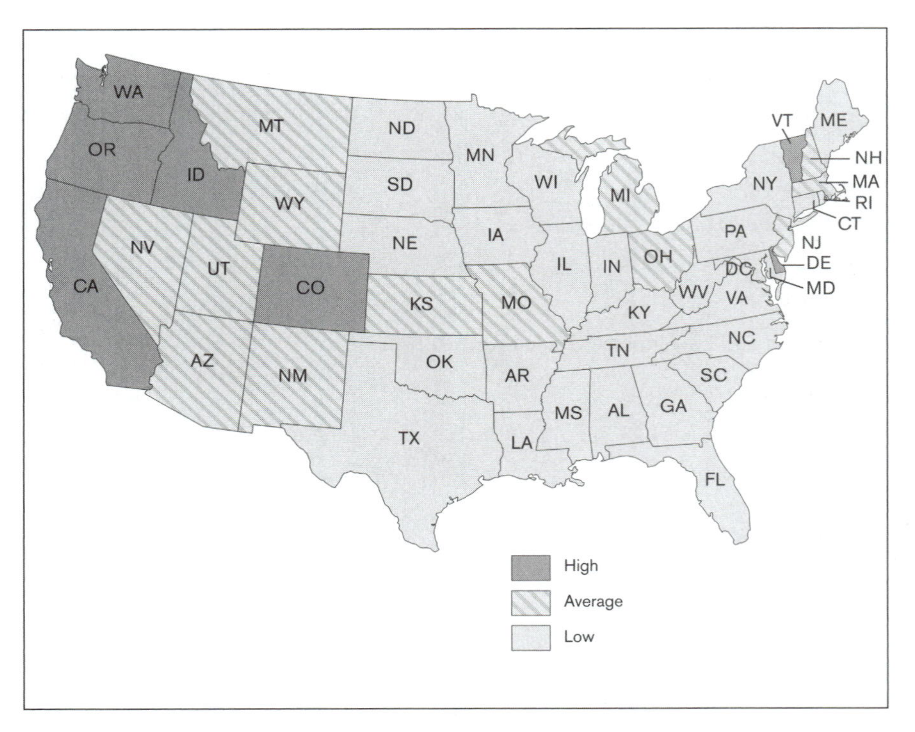

FIGURE 13.1 No religion population by state, 2001.

Source: Barry A. Kosmin and Ariela Keysar, with Ryan Cragun and Juhem Navarro-Rivera, "American Nones: The Profile of the No Religion Population," a report based on ARIS 2008, Trinity College, Hartford, CT (September 2009).

Why Is the United States So Religious in Comparison to Other Developed Societies?

Why is America different? Sociologists of religion have tackled this question. Those from the **religious economies** theoretical perspective (Finke and Stark, 1988) suggest that it is because the United States has always been home to a multitude of different religions and there is no state-sponsored religion. Many European countries have a government-sponsored religion, such as the Church of England in Britain. According to the religious economies perspective, a state-sponsored religion has a monopoly on the provision of spiritual services. Like many monopolistic companies, they are not faced with competition from other religious groups and hence have no incentive to appeal to the consumers of their services—the believers. As a result, the church stops offering what people want. Hence, people become disenchanted with the church and drift away. In societies such as America, many religious groups compete to offer spiritual services; as a result, people are more likely to find a religious group that meets their particular spiritual needs. Thus, people remain religious in the United States. Like many theories at the aggregate level, there is debate about whether pluralism (many religions) increases or decreases how religious people are (Chaves and Gorski, 2001). Others argue that state religions can foster widespread religiosity and point to the success of Islam (and Islamicist parties) in the Middle East.

Religious economies theory
The theory that the religions are stronger when they have to compete with each other.

Sex Differences

Throughout the world, women are more likely to follow religious practices or espouse religious beliefs. This is the case even in places where people overall are not very religious, such as western Europe (Miller, 2000). It is also true in the United States (Table 13.3).

There are a variety of theories of why this is so. Miller and Hoffmann (1995) suggest that men, more than women, are more willing to take risks. In general, people who are willing to take risks are less likely to be religious than people who are not willing to take risks. So this is one reason for the sex difference: Men are more willing to take risks and therefore are more likely to be nonreligious (Miller and Hoffmann, 1995).

What is the risk? It may be the risk of hell or damnation in the afterlife; however, the sex difference exists even in religions that do not have a strong

TABLE 13.3 Gender Composition of the Religious Traditions, 2008

	% MALE	% FEMALE
Catholic	46	54
Baptist	43	57
Mainline Christian	44	56
Christian generic	48	52
Pentecostal/Charismatic	42	58
Protestant denominations	45	55
Mormon/LDS	45	55
Jewish	49	51
Eastern religions	53	47
Muslim	52	48
NRM & other religions	52	48
Nones	60	40

sense of heaven and hell (Miller, 2000). Miller (p. 15) notes that "a society's religious tradition defines the degree to which not conforming to traditional religious norms constitutes risk-taking behavior." The issue may not be risk, therefore, but simply facing life unaided by a higher power. Men, it seems, are more willing to do this than are women.

WHY DO PEOPLE JOIN A RELIGION?

A common belief is that people join a religion because the religious doctrine appeals to them. Sociological research indicates otherwise, suggesting that people join a religion for social reasons: Either they were raised in a particular religion or their friends and family had already joined a particular religion.

Religious Capital

Most commonly, people continue with the religion they learned from their parents. In addition, people often marry others of the same religion. The longer people participate in a religion, the longer they are likely to continue to participate in that religion. Iannaccone (1990) suggests that this is because of what he refers to as **religious capital**. People who have been raised in a religion or have been participating in a religion for a long time therefore have a large store of "religious capital." Religious capital is familiarity with a religion's doctrines, rituals, traditions, and members. As religious capital grows, people are more likely to continue to participate in the religion.

Religious capital This is familiarity with a religion's doctrines, rituals, traditions, and members.

Social Networks

Sociological research has shown that the primary way people join any religious group or sect, or cult, is through social networks. That is, people join because their friends do. In the early 1960s, John Lofland and Rodney Stark studied the followers of the religious movement founded by Sun Myung Moon, a Korean electrical engineer. This movement was called the Unification Church (later referred to as the Moonies). They found that all of the members of the church were united by close friendship ties that predated their contact with the Moonies. The first converts to the Unification Church were the couple who rented an apartment to Dr. Kim, the Unification Church's first missionary to the United States. The next converts were two housewives who lived next door, and the next convert was a friend of the couple from the husband's work. Other people with existing ties to this group eventually joined. Other efforts to recruit members through talks to various groups, press releases, radio slots, and public meetings yielded no new members. Eventually, Lofland and Stark (1965) realized that an individual was only likely to join a new religious group if the number of social ties the individual had to members of the new religion outweighed the number of ties he or she had to nonmembers. This has been found time and again with data from other religious groups in other places. Stark and Bainbridge (1985) also found that new converts to religions are overwhelmingly from relatively *irreligious* backgrounds—that is, they lack religious capital and they do not have social ties drawing them to other religious groups. These people are not poor and uneducated. In fact, Stark and Bainbridge found that converts to new religions such as the Unification Church tend to be well educated with excellent career prospects.

EFFECTS OF RELIGION

The Protestant Ethic and the Spirit of Capitalism

Max Weber, one of the early founders of sociology who we discussed in Chapter 4, wrote a famous essay titled *The Protestant Ethic and the Spirit of Capitalism*. In this essay, he argued that the early Protestant sects promoted behaviors that facilitated the emergence of a capitalist market economy. These behaviors include hard work, thrift, honesty, and the avoidance of luxury. Weber contrasted these behaviors with the behaviors he thought typical of economic traditionalism: only working as much as necessary, the avoidance of undue effort, and the full enjoyment of the fruits of one's labors.

Weber particularly pointed to Calvinism as an example of the kind of Protestant religion he was talking about. Calvinists believe that certain people have already been chosen to go to heaven (the elect) but there is no way anyone can know if they are one of the elect. However, hard work and the display of virtuous characteristics coupled with worldly success are characteristics of the elect. Hence, Calvinists were eager to behave in those ways, to display evidence that they were themselves "elect." These behaviors helped capitalism because they ensured that people worked hard and saved, and these accumulated savings became available for investment. Hard work and honest dealings further greased the wheels of commerce.

Does Religion Make You Happier?

The evidence is that religious people in the United States are happier than nonreligious people (Stark and Maier, 2008). The same is true in other countries, if less strongly so (Snoep, 2008). This is consistent with the idea (presented in Chapter 2) that all people are predisposed to religious beliefs. If spiritual needs of some sort are a part of human nature, then those who have these needs met are happier than others who do not.

Does Religion Make You Healthier?

The evidence suggests that religious people are also healthier than nonreligious people and get well sooner after an illness. Idler and Kasl (1992) found that religious group membership protected Christians and Jews against mortality in the month before their respective religious holidays. Koch (2008) found that the health benefits of religion were particularly evident for poorer people. Critics of this research note that being religious is typically associated with other behaviors that are likely to extend one's life, such as having an orderly life.

Religion and Violence

Throughout history, people have committed violence in the name of religion. There were the Christian campaigns against Muslims in the Middle Ages; the fighting of Catholics and Protestants during the Reformation and, more recently, in Northern Ireland; and, today, the violence perpetrated by terrorists espousing radical Islam. It is easy, therefore, to think that religion promotes violence. Does it? The answer is there has been violence in the name of religion, but there has been a great deal of violence for nonreligious reasons, too.

Religious leaders (especially the founders of new religions) are often blessed with personal charisma: They are very attractive to many people (Wallis, 1982). Max Weber used the word "charisma" to describe people who are able to inspire faith in others and get others to believe their message. Not all charismatic leaders are religious leaders, but many are. Most of the founders of the world religions were charismatic individuals, including Mohammed, the Buddha, and Jesus Christ.

Some religious and nonreligious leaders use their charisma to lead their followers into war. For example, Richard I of England (Richard the Lionheart) used his personal charisma to lead the Third Crusade to the Holy Land (1187–1192). Similarly, Osama bin Laden has used his personal charisma to inspire religious jihad (holy war) against the capitalist societies of the West. These leaders can only succeed when there are people willing to hear their message. In bin Laden's case, it is millions of young, poor Islamic men in many areas of the world. The poverty of their countries means there are few avenues of upward mobility, yet they are aware of the wealth of the West. Awareness of such inequality fuels resentment against the West and means there are many young people only too happy to answer bin Laden's call for holy warriors.

CONCLUSION

Religion is a human universal, although the type of religion and extent of religious commitment and participation vary from society to society. Generally, more developed societies are less religious than less developed societies, but there are important exceptions (notably the United States). Social ties are the most important reason why people join and participate in a particular religion. Participation in religion in turn has effects on individuals (they are generally healthier and happier), and it also influences the nature of the society as a whole.

REFERENCES

Chaves, Mark, and Philip S. Gorski. 2001. "Religious Pluralism and Religious Participation." *Annual Review of Sociology* 27, 261–281.

Collins, Randall. 2008. "The Four M's of Religion: Magic, Membership, Morality and Mysticism." *Review of Religious Research* 50(1), 5–15.

Finke, Roger, and Rodney Stark. 1988. "Religious Economies and Sacred Canopies: Religious Mobilization in American Cities, 1906." *American Sociological Review* 53, 41–49.

Gorski, Philip S. 2000. "Historicizing the Secularization Debate: Church, State, and Society in Late Medieval and Early Modern Europe, ca. 1300 to 1700." *American Sociological Review* 65(1), 138–167.

Iannaccone, Laurence R. 1990. "Religious Practice: A Human Capital Approach." *Journal for the Scientific Study of Religion* 29(3), 297–314.

Idler, Ellen L., and Stanislav V. Kasl. 1992. "Religion, Disability, Depression, and the Timing of Death." *American Journal of Sociology* 97(4), 1052–1079.

Inglehart, Ronald, and Wayne E. Baker. 2000. "Modernization, Cultural Change and the Persistence of Traditional Values." *American Sociological Review* 65, 19–51.

Koch, Jerome R. 2008. "Is Religion a Health Resource for the Poor?" *Social Science Journal* 45(3), 497–503.

Lofland, John, and Rodney Stark. 1965. "Becoming a World-Saver: A Theory of Conversion to a Deviant Perspective." *American Sociological Review* 30, 862–875.

Miller, Alan S. 2000. "Going to Hell in Asia: The Relationship between Risk and Religion in a Cross Cultural Setting." *Review of Religious Research* 42(1), 5–18.

Miller, Alan S., and John P. Hoffmann. 1995. "Risk and Religion: An Explanation of Gender Differences in Religiosity." *Journal for the Scientific Study of Religion* 34(1), 63–75.

Niebuhr, H. Richard. 1929. *The Social Sources of Denominationalism*. New York: Henry Holt.

Snoep, Liesbeth. 2008. "Religiousness and Happiness in Three Nations: A Research Note." *Journal of Happiness Studies* 9(2), 207–211.

Stark, Rodney. 1996. *The Rise of Christianity: A Sociologist Reconsiders History*. Princeton, NJ: Princeton University Press.

Stark, Rodney, and William Sims Bainbridge. 1985. *The Future of Religion: Secularization, Revival, and Cult Formation*. Berkeley: University of California Press.

Stark, Rodney, and Jared Maier. 2008. "Faith and Happiness." *Review of Religious Research* 50(1), 120–125.

Wallis, Roy. 1982. *Millennialism and Charisma*. Belfast, Northern Ireland: The Queen's University.

CRIME AND VIOLENCE

14

CRIME AND VIOLENCE ACROSS HUMAN SOCIETIES

Which Societies Have the Most Crime?

All societies have some crime and violence, but some societies have much more than others. With regard to premodern societies such as hunting and gathering societies or horticultural societies, it is difficult to know how much crime and violence occurred because there are no good records. Studies of contemporary horticultural and hunting and gathering societies show much variation in levels of violence, but they can be very high. For example, the Yanomamo of the Amazon rainforest are known to be violent and warlike, with high rates of homicide (Chagnon, 1988). The Eskimo of the central Canadian Arctic lack group warfare, yet homicide rates were estimated by one authority at 1 person per 1,000 per year, which is more than 10 times the contemporary U.S. rate (Gat, 2000). Richard Lee reports that among the !Kung of the Kalahari (1979, p. 398; 1982, p. 44) in his study area in the period 1963–1969, there were 22 cases of homicide; 19 of the victims were males, as were all of the 25 killers. This amounts to a homicide rate of 0.29 persons per 1,000 per year—approximately four times the contemporary U.S. rate. Before the introduction of state authority, the homicide rate among the !Kung had been 0.42 persons per 1,000 per year—approximately six times higher than the contemporary U.S. rate.

In the modern era, crime and violence are easier to document because governments keep records. Homicide is always the easiest crime to document because it is almost always reported to authorities. Other crimes, such as robbery, theft, and many others, are less likely to be reported to authorities. For example, Table 14.1 shows homicide rates per 100,000 population (averaged over years given) from 44 different countries (Lafree and Tseloni,

TABLE 14.1 **Descriptive Statistics for Homicide Rates**

COUNTRY	TOTAL YEARS	YEARS		HOMICIDE RATE[a]			
		FIRST	LAST	MEAN	SD[b]	MIN	MAX
Australia	50	1950	1999	1.70	0.26	1.04	2.39
Austria	51	1950	2000	1.23	0.23	0.84	1.77
Belgium	43	1954	1996	1.19	0.46	0.57	2.15
Bulgaria	41	1960	2000	2.95	0.99	0.80	5.07
Canada	49	1950	1998	1.80	0.52	0.99	2.70
Chile	44	1954	1999	3.32	1.23	1.75	6.60
Colombia	28	1951	1994	37.36	22.15	14.45	89.50
Costa Rica	46	1955	2000	4.28	1.15	2.39	8.35
Czechoslovakia	48	1953	2000	1.35	0.32	0.88	2.27
Denmark	49	1950	1998	0.89	0.32	0.39	1.45
Dominican Republic	25	1956	1985	5.05	1.64	2.08	9.38
El Salvador	24	1950	1993	33.86	6.63	24.31	51.53
Estonia	8	1991	1998	20.11	5.44	10.79	28.22
Finland	51	1950	2000	2.81	0.43	1.82	3.63
France	44	1950	1999	0.95	0.16	0.70	1.32
Germany	50	1950	1999	1.12	0.13	0.86	1.39
Greece	43	1956	1998	1.06	0.43	0.51	2.74
Hungary	45	1955	2000	2.54	0.70	1.56	4.09
Iceland	48	1950	1997	0.79	0.76	0.00	3.31
Ireland	50	1950	1999	0.60	0.32	0.18	2.00
Israel	40	1954	1998	1.27	0.60	0.12	2.43
Italy	50	1950	1999	1.49	0.45	0.81	2.84
Japan	50	1950	1999	1.28	0.55	0.55	2.37
Luxembourg	33	1967	2000	1.36	0.72	0.25	2.91
Mauritius	33	1968	2000	2.05	1.05	0.61	6.10
Mexico	39	1958	2000	18.88	4.97	9.78	32.28
Netherlands	50	1950	1999	0.74	0.34	0.21	1.36
New Zealand	50	1950	1999	1.28	0.54	0.00	2.40
Norway	50	1950	1999	0.78	0.34	0.26	1.56
Panama	34	1954	1987	4.14	1.63	1.73	7.24
Paraguay	18	1969	1987	11.71	3.56	6.54	16.60
Philippines	20	1957	1981	6.20	5.59	0.38	17.40
Poland	41	1955	2000	1.55	0.65	0.83	2.94
Portugal	48	1950	2000	1.29	0.29	0.73	1.88
Singapore	42	1959	2000	1.76	0.53	0.57	3.02
Spain	49	1950	1999	0.62	0.34	0.06	1.18
Sweden	50	1950	1999	1.01	0.28	0.56	1.50
Switzerland	50	1950	1999	1.04	0.38	0.54	2.84
Thailand	33	1955	1994	15.39	5.73	6.71	28.77
Trinidad and Tobago	30	1962	1994	6.09	2.30	2.10	11.43
United Kingdom	51	1950	2000	0.84	0.25	0.51	1.52
United States	50	1950	1999	7.51	2.12	4.50	10.55
Uruguay	32	1955	1990	3.81	1.00	1.99	5.68
Venezuela	47	1950	2000	9.75	3.62	5.02	26.35
All countries	51	1950	2000	3.91	7.40	0.00	89.50

[a]Homicide rates per 100,000 residents.

[b]Standard deviation.

Source: Lafree and Tseloni (2006).

2006). You can see that less developed societies, such as Colombia and El Salvador, have much higher homicide rates than developed societies such as the United States. The countries that have high rates of homicide tend to also have high rates of theft and nonlethal violence (van Wilsem, 2004). Thus, in general there tends to be more crime and deviance in less developed societies than in developed societies.

Again, however, the United States stands out from other developed countries as having a comparatively high rate of homicide. The U.S. homicide rate averages 7.51 per 100,000 residents, the highest in the developed world. Once again we are faced with the case of American exceptionalism. We last saw this with religiosity: The United States has comparatively high rates of religiosity compared to other developed countries. Perhaps ironically, those regions in the south and west of the United States that have the highest rates of religiosity also tend to have the highest rates of violent crime.

Why is this? There are a variety of explanations. Pampel and Gartner (1995) suggest that collectivist institutions in many developed countries and particularly a large social welfare net—full-employment policies, unemployment benefits, and general access to public support—tend to suppress crime. A more individualistic ethos and fewer social welfare benefits in the United States may promote individualized means of attaining status and resources, including criminal means. Pratt and Godsey (2002) found that, as measured by percent of the nation's GDP spent on health care and education, social support was inversely related to homicide rates. Greater racial heterogeneity in the United States and a greater gap between the haves and have-nots compared to other advanced industrial societies may also promote crime (including homicide) (Blau and Blau, 1982; Pratt and Godsey, 2002).

Who Is Most Likely to Commit Crime?

Although homicide rates vary, one phenomenon that does not vary is that in all societies, the vast majority of homicides and other violent crimes are committed by men. Table 14.2 shows sex differences in same-sex homicide (men assaulting men and women assaulting women). Although homicide rates vary widely from culture to culture, the proportion of these homicides committed by men against men is always very high. In most of these studies, more than 90% of the same-sex homicides were committed by males.

TABLE 14.2 Numbers of Same-Sex Homicides in Which Victim and Killer Were Unrelated: Various Studies[a]

LOCATION/SOCIETY	PERIOD OF STUDY	MALE	FEMALE
Chicago	1965–1981	7439	195
Detroit	1972	316	11
Miami	1980	358	0
Canada	1974–1983	2387	59
England and Wales	1977–1986	2195	95
Scotland	1953–1974	143	5
Iceland	1946–1970	7	0
A Mayan village (Mexico)	1938–1965	15	0
Bison-Horn Maria (India)	1920–1941	36	1
Munda (India)		34	0
Oraon (India)		26	0
Bhil (India)	1971–1975	50	1
Tiv (Nigeria)	1931–1949	74	1
BaSoga (Uganda)	1952–1954	38	0
Gisu (Uganda)	1948–1954	44	2
BaLuyia (Kenya)	1949–1954	65	3
Banyoro (Uganda)	1936–1955	9	1
JoLuo (Kenya)	1949	22	2
Alur (Uganda)	1945–1954	33	1
!Kung San (Botswana)	1920–1955	12	0

[a]Data are from a 1990 publication by Daly and Wilson, who included both original tabulations and every published study that they were able to find meeting the following criteria: (1) that the data set comprise all homicides known to have occurred in a given jurisdiction rather than a selected subset and (2) that same-sex, nonrelative cases be identifiable. Victim and killer were unrelated co-wives of a polygynous man in the single female–female case in each of the Maria, Bhil, Banyoro, and Alur data sets, as well as in one BaLuyia case and one JoLuo case; co-wives were not deemed marital "relatives" because their relationship is analogous to that of unrelated male rivals and hence they were included.

Source: Daly and Wilson (1997).

In the United States, most victims and perpetrators in homicides are male (Table 14.3 and Figure 14.1). Table 14.4 shows that women are more likely than men to be killed by an intimate or family member; men are more likely to be killed by an acquaintance or stranger. Table 14.5 shows that other crimes are also disproportionately perpetrated by men.

TABLE 14.3 U.S. Homicides, 2008

OFFENDER/VICTIM	%
Male offender/male victim	65.3
Male offender/female victim	22.7
Female offender/male victim	9.6
Female offender/female victim	2.4
Total	100.0

TABLE 14.4 Victim/Offender Relationship by Victim Gender, 1976–2005

	% OF HOMICIDE VICTIMS BY GENDER	
VICTIM/OFFENDER RELATIONSHIP	MALE	FEMALE
Intimate	5.0	30.0
Spouse	3.0	18.3
Ex-spouse	0.2	1.4
Boyfriend/girlfriend	1.8	10.4
Other family	6.8	11.8
Parent	1.3	2.8
Child	2.1	5.4
Sibling	1.2	0.9
Other family	2.2	2.8
Acquaintance/known	35.3	21.8
Neighbor	1.1	1.3
Employee/er	0.1	0.1
Friend/acquaintance	29.4	17.0
Other known	4.6	3.4
Stranger	15.5	8.7
Undetermined	37.4	27.6
Total	100.0	100.0

Source: Federal Bureau of Investigation, Supplementary Homicide Reports, 1976–2005.

TABLE 14.5 Percentage Distribution of Single-Offender Victimizations, by Type of Crime and Perceived Gender of Offender, 2006

		% OF SINGLE-OFFENDER VICTIMIZATIONS			
			PERCEIVED GENDER OF OFFENDER		
TYPE OF CRIME	NO. OF SINGLE-OFFENDER VICTIMIZATIONS	TOTAL	MALE	FEMALE	NOT KNOWN AND NOT AVAILABLE
Crimes of violence	4,734,310	100	78.3	19.7	1.9
Completed violence	1,439,840	100.0	78.4	20.5	1.1[b]
Attempted/threatened violence	3,294,460	100.0	78.3	19.4	2.3
Rape/sexual assault[c]	222,400	100.0	95.4	2.9[b]	1.8[b]
Robbery	356,860	100.0	82.6	15.4	2.0[b]
Completed/property taken	215,380	100.0	82.0	16.0[b]	2.0[b]
With injury	73,360	100.0	80.9	19.1[b]	0.0[b]
Without injury	142,020	100.0	82.5	14.4[b]	3.1[b]
Attempted to take property	141,470	100.0	83.6	14.5[b]	2.0[b]
With injury	36,060[b]	100.0[b]	67.5[b]	32.5[b]	0.0[b]
Without injury	105,410	100.0	89.1	8.3[b]	2.6[b]
Assault	4,155,030	100.0	77.0	21.0	1.9
Aggravated	1,025,560	100.0	79.9	17.6	2.5[b]
Simple	3,129,470	100.0	76.1	22.1	1.7

Detail may not add to total shown because of rounding.

[b]Estimate is based on 10 or fewer sample cases.

[c]Includes verbal threats of rape and threats of sexual assault.

The Young Male Syndrome

Young male syndrome The disproportionate tendency for young males aged 15–24 years to be involved in crime.

In particular, it is young men aged 15–24 years who are most likely to perpetrate crimes (Figure 14.2). This is often referred to as the **young male syndrome**. At age 20 years, men are approximately six times more likely than females to be the victims of homicide. From the mid-20s on, males are less likely to become victims of homicide. Males aged 15–24 years in this

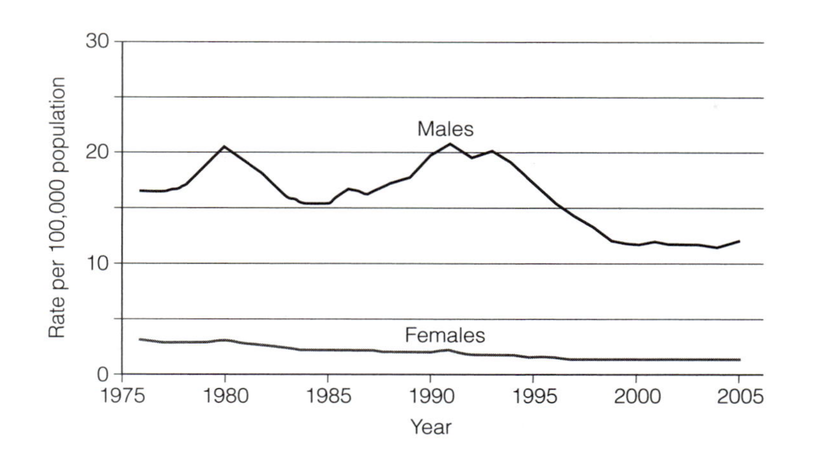

FIGURE 14.1 Homicide offending by gender, 1976–2005.

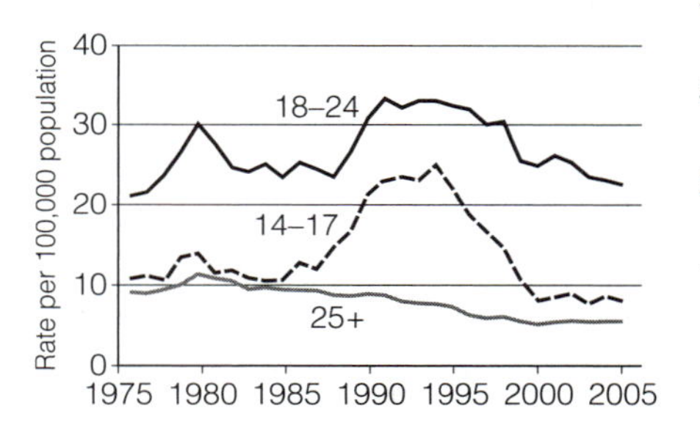

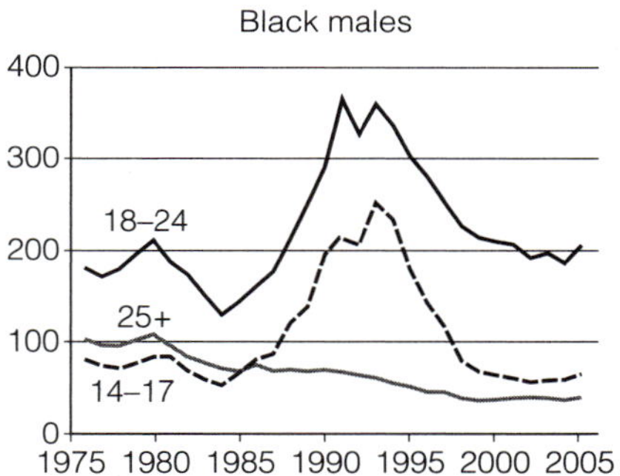

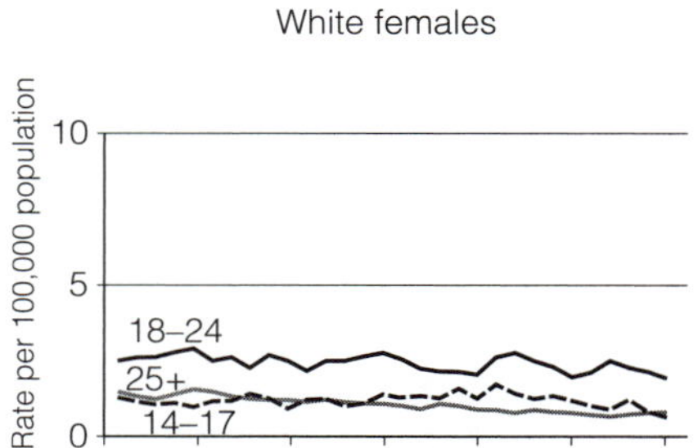

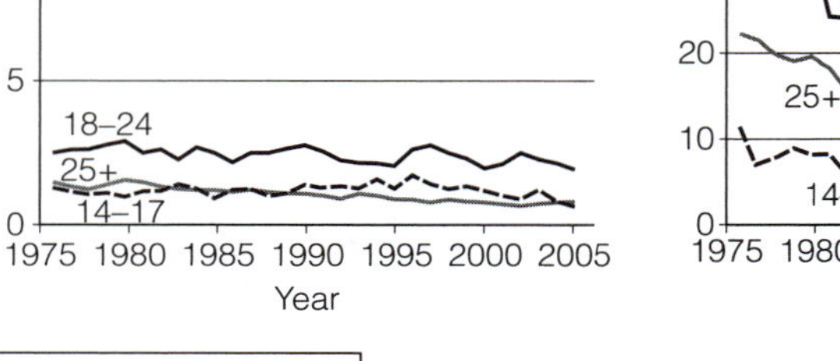

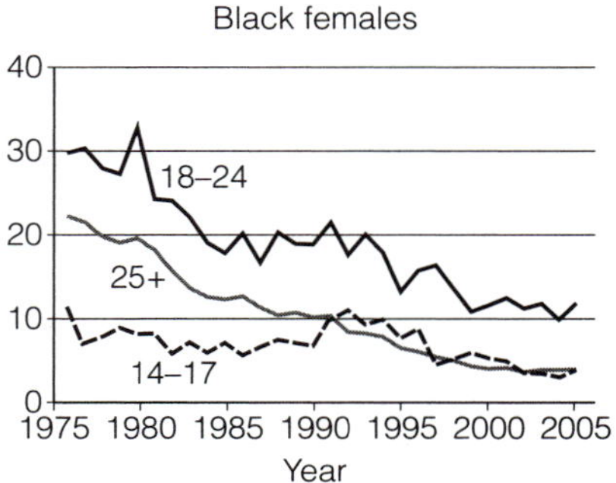

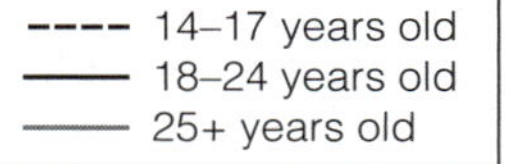

FIGURE 14.2 Homicide offending by age, gender, and race, 1976–2005.

Source: Bureau of Justice Statistics (http://www.ojp.usdoj.gov/bjs/homicide/ageracesex.htm).

age group are also likely to be the perpetrators of homicide, as shown in Figure 14.2. In fact, the higher the percentage of males in this group in any society, the higher the levels of violent aggression. One of the reasons why violent crime has declined in the United States in recent years is because of the decline in the proportion of young men in the population. Young men are also responsible for many nonviolent crimes.

The high involvement of young men in violence and crime is shown by incarceration rates. Men are much more likely than women to have spent time in prison, and men in age groups 25–34 and 35–44 years have the highest probability of having spent time in state or federal prison. Table 14.6 shows that in the United States in 2001, 6.5% of men aged 35–44 years had spent time in prison, compared to only 0.9% of women that age.

Why are young men disproportionately involved in crime? Evolutionary theorists explain that this early peak of male aggression occurs because in the ancestral environment this was the period when there was most intense competition among young males (Daly and Wilson, 1997). This was the time when a young man seeking a wife had to display formidable physical prowess in hunting, tribal raids, tribal defense, and defense of his interests. Men who did not show prowess in these areas were unlikely to obtain a wife. In a modern environment, men no longer have to show prowess at hunting and warfare, but they do have to earn money and status. For some men, particularly those without recourse to legitimate methods of earning money and status, crime and violent behavior can be a way to earn those things.

What Keeps Young Men on the Straight and Narrow?

Men who are employed full-time are less likely to commit any kind of crime than men who are unemployed or underemployed. Men who are married are less likely to be involved in crime (Gottfredson and Hirschi, 1990). For young men, the presence of a biological father while growing up seems to be particularly important for avoiding crime. Harper and McLanahan (2004) used survey data to follow a group of 2,846 young men aged 14–17 years to determine which teens had the greatest risk of ending up in prison. They found that whereas having a poorly educated mother who was in her teens when she first had children, being African American, and living in poverty all contributed to the likelihood of incarceration, the presence of a biologi-

TABLE 14.6 Percentage of Adult Population Ever Incarcerated in a State or Federal Prison, by Gender, Race, Hispanic Origin, and Age, 2001[a]

	% OF ADULT POPULATION EVER INCARCERATED IN A STATE OR FEDERAL PRISON, BY AGE					
	18–24	25–34	35–44	45–54	55–64	65 OR OLDER
Gender						
Male	2.7	6.0	6.5	5.3	4.0	3.1
Female	0.2	0.7	0.9	0.6	0.3	0.2
Race/Hispanic origin						
White[b]	0.6	1.6	2.0	1.7	1.4	1.1
Male	1.1	2.8	3.5	3.1	2.5	2.0
Female	0.1	0.3	0.5	0.3	0.2	0.2
Black[b]	4.4	10.9	12.1	9.5	6.7	5.9
Male	8.5	20.4	22.0	17.7	13.0	11.6
Female	0.4	2.1	2.8	1.9	1.1	0.9
Hispanic	2.2	5.1	5.8	5.2	3.6	2.2
Male	4.0	9.0	10.0	9.5	6.6	4.1
Female	0.3	0.8	1.1	0.9	0.6	0.3

[a]Percentages are based on intercensal resident population estimates from the U.S. Census Bureau.

[b]Excludes persons of Hispanic origin.

Source: Bureau of Justice Statistics, Special Report: Prevalence of Imprisonment in the U.S. Population, 1974–2001.

cal father strongly reduced the likelihood that a young man would be put in jail. The adolescents who faced the highest incarceration risks were those in stepparent families, including father–stepmother families. Similarly, Mackey and Mackey (2003) found that father absence, rather than poverty, was a strong predictor of young men's violent behavior.

CONTEMPORARY PATTERNS OF CRIME IN THE UNITED STATES

Both violent crime and property crime have declined recently (see Figures 14.3 and 14.4).

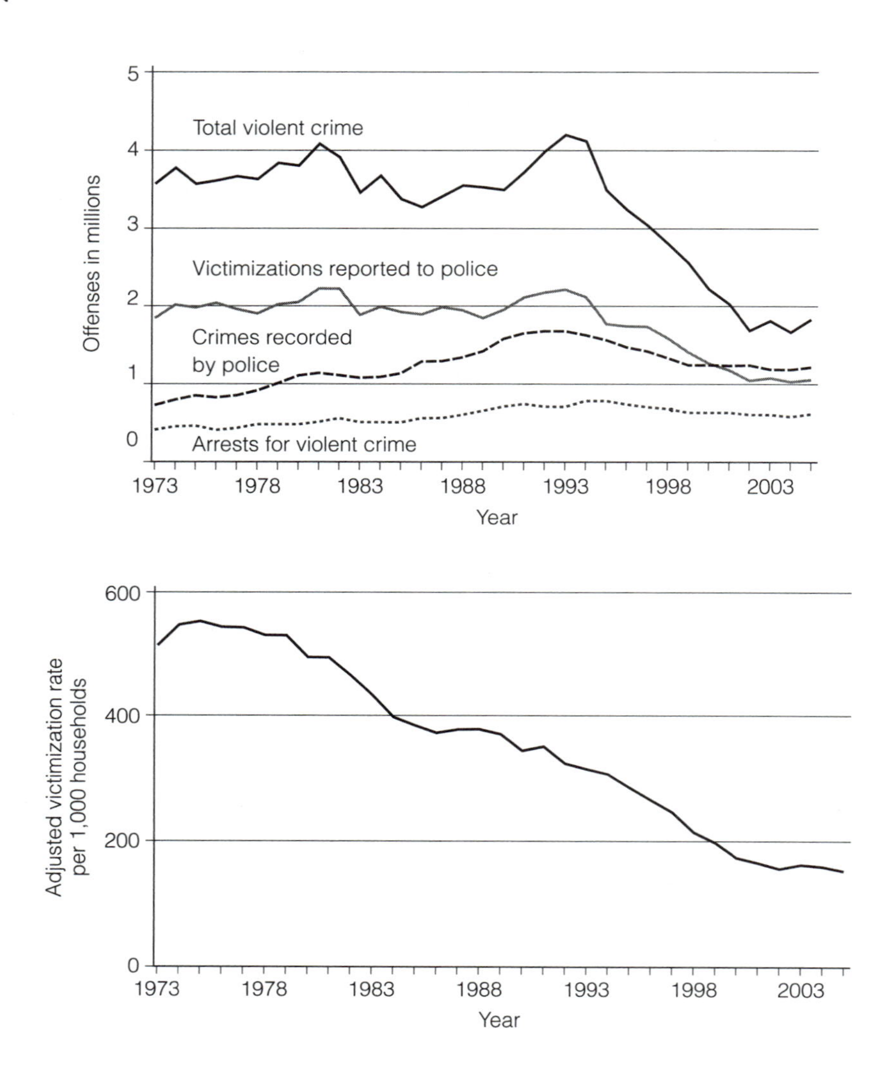

FIGURE 14.3 Four measures of serious violent crime.

Source: Bureau of Justice Statistics (http://www.ojp.usdoj.gov/bjs/glance/cv2.htm).

FIGURE 14.4 Property crime rates.

Source: Bureau of Justice Statistics, The National Crime Victimization Survey.

Why Has Crime Decreased Recently?

Explanations of the recent decrease in crime abound. They include better policing, economic growth, and changing demography and a decline in the proportion of people in high-crime ages (Pampel and Gartner, 1995). Perhaps the most controversial explanation is that of Levitt and Dubner (2005), who suggest that the legalization of abortion in the early 1970s resulted in fewer poor men from single-parent families in the 1990s. Given that this group has the highest risk of being involved in crime, fewer people in this group means less crime.

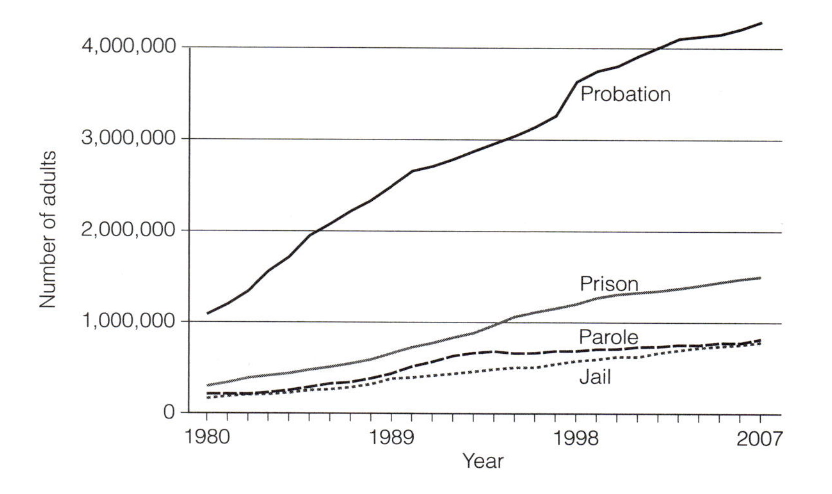

FIGURE 14.5 Adult correctional populations, 1980–2007.

Source: Bureau of Justice Statistics correctional surveys (the Annual Probation Survey, National Prisoner Statistics Program, Annual Survey of Jails, and Annual Parole Survey) as presented in Correctional Populations in the United States, Annual, Prisoners in 2007 and Probation and Parole in the United States, 2007–Statistical Tables.

Another explanation is that because incarceration rates have increased, there are fewer cases of former criminals committing new crimes. This is important because of high rates of *recidivism*—the tendency of people who have committed a crime once to commit crimes again. Incarceration rates have increased greatly in the United States since 1980 (Figure 14.5).

Figure 14.5 shows that in the United States in 2007, more than 7.3 million people were under some form of correctional supervision, including probation, prison, parole, and jail. In the figure, *probation* refers to court-ordered community supervision of convicted offenders by a probation agency. In many instances, the supervision requires adherence to specific rules of conduct while in the community. *Prison* means confinement in a state or federal correctional facility to serve a sentence of more than 1 year. *Jail* means confinement in a local jail while pending trial, awaiting sentencing, serving a sentence that is usually less than 1 year, or awaiting transfer to other facilities after conviction. *Parole* refers to community supervision after a period of time spent in prison.

How Does the United States Compare to Other Countries?

The United States has the highest prison incarceration rate in the world at 756 per 100,000 of the national population. It is followed by Russia (629 per 100,000), Rwanda (604 per 100,000), St. Kitts & Nevis (588 per 100,000), and Cuba (approximately 531 per 100,000) (Walmsley, 2009).

Throughout the world, more than 9.8 million people are held in penal institutions, mostly as pretrial detainees (remand prisoners) or as sentenced prisoners. Almost half of these are in the United States (2.29 million), Russia (0.89 million), or China (1.57 million sentenced prisoners). A further 850,000 are held in "administrative detention" in China; if these are included, the overall Chinese total is more than 2.4 million and the world total is more than 10.65 million.

WHY DO PEOPLE COMMIT CRIME?

Sociologists have found that whether or not you commit crime is greatly influenced by where you live, who you hang out with, and what you have to lose if you commit crimes.

Where You Live: Social Disorganization

According to social disorganization theory, poor neighborhoods with high rates of people moving in and out, many different ethnic groups, and high rates of family disruption have the highest crime and delinquency rates (Lowenkamp, Cullen, and Pratt, 2003; Sampson and Groves, 1989). Part of the reason for this is that there are many opportunities for crime in such neighborhoods (Cohen and Felson, 1979). Because people are not home during the day and people do not know each other, homes and property are left unattended and unwatched. Family disruption means that young people are often not adequately supervised by parents (Unnever, Cullen, and Pratt, 2003)

Who You Hang Out With

Edwin Sutherland (1883–1950) suggested that individuals get into trouble because of who their friends are. If your friends encourage criminal behaviors, then you are more likely to become involved in criminal behavior. For example, the majority of delinquent acts are performed by groups of youths (Erickson, 1971). In addition, there is evidence that crime runs in families—that people who are involved in crime are more likely than others to have family members who are involved in crime (West and Farrington, 1977). This theory is referred to as **differential association theory**.

Differential association theory Theory that who you associate with influences whether you become involved in criminal activity.

What Do You Have to Lose?

Emile Durkheim first suggested that the real question should be not why people commit crime but, rather, why they do not. This line of thought has been best developed by Travis Hirschi (1969) and is usually referred to as **control theory**. According to this theory, people do not commit crimes when they have too much to lose by doing so. This is one of the reasons why crime rates are lower for people in older age groups—as people get older, they often have much more to lose. What people have to lose is based on their *attachments*, *investments*, *involvements*, and *beliefs*. If we have strong attachments to people who expect us to live up to certain standards, we are unlikely to do things that would jeopardize those attachments. Likewise, if we have a great deal invested in a home, a career, a family, or a lifestyle, we are likely to be unwilling to do things that jeopardize those investments. If we are involved in many legitimate activities, we are unlikely to have the time for criminal acts. Last, if we strongly believe that we should act in certain ways, and not in others, then we are less likely to engage in criminal acts.

Control theory Theory that people do not commit crime because they have too much to lose based on their attachments, investments, involvements, and beliefs.

CONCLUSION

All societies have crime, but generally more developed countries have less crime than less developed countries. Regardless of the level of development, however, in all countries the vast majority of all crime is committed by young men. The United States stands out among developed countries as having a comparatively high crime rate, although crime rates have declined recently in the United States. The reasons for this are varied, including changing demography and a smaller proportions of people in the crime-prone ages.

REFERENCES

Blau, Judith R., and Peter M. Blau. 1982. "The Cost of Inequality: Metropolitan Structure and Violent Crime." *American Sociological Review* 47(1), 114–129.

Chagnon, Napoleon. 1988. "Life Histories, Blood Revenge, and Warfare in a Tribal Population." *Science* 239, 985–992.

Cohen, Lawrence E., and Marcus Felson. 1979. "Social Change and Crime Rate Trends: A Routine Activity Approach." *American Sociological Review* 44(4), 588–608.

Daly, Martin, and Margot Wilson. 1997. "Crime and Conflict: Homicide in Evolutionary Psychological Perspective." *Crime and Justice* 22, 251–300.

Erickson, Maynard L. 1971. "The Group Context of Delinquent Behavior." *Social Problems* 19, 114–129.

Gat, Azar. 2000. "The Human Motivational Complex: Evolutionary Theory and the Causes of Hunter-Gatherer Fighting." *Anthropological Quarterly* 73(1), 20–34.

Gottfredson, Michael R., and Travis Hirschi. 1990. *A General Theory of Crime*. Stanford, CA: Stanford University Press.

Harper, Cynthia C., and Sara McLanahan. 2004. "Father Absence and Youth Incarceration." *Journal of Research on Adolescence* 14(3), 369–397.

Hirschi, Travis. 1969. *Causes of Delinquency*. Berkeley: University of California Press.

Lafree, Gary, and Andromachi Tseloni. 2006. "Democracy and Crime: A Multilevel Analysis of Homicide Trends in Forty-Four Countries, 1950–2000." *Annals of the American Academy of Political and Social Science* 605(1), 25–49.

Lee, Richard B. 1979. *The !Kung San: Men, Women and Work in a Foraging Society*. Cambridge, UK: Cambridge University Press.

———. 1982. "Politics, Sexual and Non-Sexual, in an Egalitarian Society." Pp. 37–59 in *Politics and History in Band Societies*, edited by Eleanor Leacock and Richard B. Lee. Cambridge, UK: Cambridge University Press.

Levitt, Steven D., and Stephen J. Dubner. 2005. *Freakonomics: A Rogue Economist Explores the Hidden Side of Everything*. New York: Morrow.

Lowenkamp, Christopher T., Francis T. Cullen, and Travis C. Pratt. 2003. "Replicating Sampson and Groves's Test of Social Disorganization Theory: Revisiting a Criminological Classic." *Journal of Research in Crime and Delinquency* 40(4), 351–373.

Mackey, Wade C., and Bonnie Mackey. 2003. "The Presence of Fathers in Attenuating Young Male Violence: Dad as a Social Palliative." *Marriage & Family Review* 35(1/2), 63–75.

Pampel, Fred C., and Rosemary Gartner. 1995. "Age Structure, Socio-Political Institutions, and National Homicide Rates." *European Sociological Review* 11(3), 243–260.

Pratt, Travis C., and Timothy W. Godsey. 2002. "Social Support, Inequality, and Homicide: A Cross-National Test of an Integrated Theoretical Model." *Criminology* 41(3), 611–644.

Sampson, Robert J., and W. Byron Groves. 1989. "Community Structure and Crime: Testing Social-Disorganization Theory." *American Journal of Sociology* 94(4), 774–802.

Unnever, James D., Francis T. Cullen, and Travis C. Pratt. 2003. "Parental Management, ADHD, and Delinquent Involvement: Reassessing Gottfredson and Hirschi's General Theory." *Justice Quarterly* 20(3), 471–500.

van Wilsem, Johan. 2004. "Criminal Victimization in Cross-National Perspective: An Analysis of Rates of Theft, Violence and Vandalism across 27 Countries." *European Journal of Criminology* 1(1), 89–109.

Walmsley, Roy. 2009. *World Prison Population List*, 8th ed. London: King's College London.

West, Donald, and David Farrington. 1977. *The Delinquent Way of Life*. New York: Crane Russak.

BIOSOCIOLOGY OF HEALTH

15

EFFECTS OF BOTH GENES AND ENVIRONMENT ON HEALTH

The kinds of diseases you get, and what you are likely to die of eventually, are a result of both the **genetic predispositions** you inherited and the environment you live in. The environment includes your diet and lifestyle, as well as your social environment. Consider, for example, colon cancer. I have a family history of this disease. My grandfather died of it, and my dad has had it. If I am unlucky enough, I have inherited the gene for that particular cancer and may one day get it myself.

Genetic predisposition Having genes that predispose individuals to various diseases, traits, and behaviors.

You also probably know that many of the **genes** or gene complexes associated with various diseases can be determined ahead of time by DNA (genetic) testing, so you can find out what diseases you are likely to get. But do you really want to know? Having the gene predisposing you toward a certain disease is not enough. Also important are a host of environmental factors that began before you were even born, for example, the conditions in your mother's womb. Then there is your diet, lifestyle, whether you are overweight, whether you smoke, your exposure to stress, and so on. If you are unlucky enough to have had a poor environment before you were born, you may, for instance, have had a low birth weight. This, in and of itself, predicts many negative outcomes for you, including early death and a higher risk of disability (Conley, Strully, and Bennett, 2003).

Gene Basic unit of heredity; section of DNA that codes for proteins in the organism.

Sociologists and other scientists are just now identifying genes and gene complexes associated not just with disease but also with social behaviors. They have also investigated how genetic predispositions are influenced, to a greater and lesser degree, by an individual's environment. Consider, for instance, the number of sexual partners a person has. Guo, Tong,

Xie, and Lange (2007) found that men possessing a particular version of a dopamine transporter gene associated with reward-seeking behavior had an 80–100% increase in the number of (self-reported) sexual partners compared to men with other versions of the gene. This was true across all races and ethnicities. It was not changed by factors such as religiosity, family structure, parental education, marital and cohabitation history, and neighborhood poverty—factors that one would think would be associated with sexual history. However, the same association was not found among women.

Another study, by Shanahan et al. (2008), examined the associations between the dopamine receptor gene (DRD2) and educational continuation beyond secondary school. The dopamine receptor DRD2 gene encodes the dopamine D_2 receptor that plays a critical role in the functioning of many neural circuits in the human brain. A version of this gene is associated with inappropriate behavior in school and in school-related activities. Shanahan et al. found that boys with this version of the gene were less likely to attend college than were other boys. This was not true for those who also had high parental socioeconomic status, high parental involvement in school, and a high-quality school, showing how environment can modify the effects of a genetic predisposition.

Diseases in Different Areas of the World

Health is an interaction of genes and environment in cruder ways, also. Where you were born and where you live help determine what kind of infectious diseases you are likely to get and also what you are likely to die of. People born in poor countries are much more likely to die of violent causes and infectious diseases than are people born in rich countries. Infectious diseases include cholera, hepatitis, dysentery, malaria, tuberculosis, and influenza. People in rich countries are more likely to die of heart disease and cancer. Of course, life expectancy is much longer in rich countries, so in part what is going on is that people in poor countries are dying before they are likely to get diseases of old age such as cancer. There are some differences in the types of cancers people in rich countries get. Japanese people, for instance, are much more likely to get stomach cancer than are Americans (National Cancer Institute, 1999). These sorts of differences are likely related to both genetic and environmental causes (e.g., diet).

Differences across Developed Countries

Among the rich countries of the world, some do better at maintaining the health of their population than others. The United States does not do very well compared to other rich countries in Europe and elsewhere. **Infant mortality** is one of the factors that is most reflective of the health of a population: In healthier populations, infant mortality is low. Infant mortality is usually measured as the number of deaths of children younger than 1 year old per 1,000 live births. Figure 15.1 shows levels of infant mortality in the United States compared to other countries of the world and how they have changed since 1960. These data do not show the large differences between racial and ethnic groups in the United States. Non-Hispanic black, American Indian, Alaska Native, and Puerto Rican women have the highest rates of infant mortality, whereas Asian and Pacific Islanders, Central and South Americans, Mexicans, and Cubans have the lowest. Nevertheless, the United States ranks poorly compared to other countries. In 2009, the countries with the lowest infant mortality rates were Singapore, Sweden, and Japan. The countries with the highest infant mortality rates were Russia, Bulgaria, and Costa Rica. Omitted from this list were the less developed countries of Africa and Asia, which have the highest infant mortality rates of all, as discussed in Chapter 6.

Infant mortality The number of deaths of children younger than 1 year of age per 1,000 live births.

So why does the United States have comparatively high infant mortality rates? One reason is the high cost of medical care in the United States, which can make it difficult for less well-off people to afford. Even working people in the United States often have trouble paying for medical insurance for themselves. In many of the nations on the list in Figure 15.1, there is no need for medical insurance because the government pays for all medical services.

Sex Differences in Death and Disease

One's sex also influences what diseases one gets, and that interacts with the environment as well. In general, regarding death and disease, it is best to be female, and this starts early—*in utero* to be precise. Fewer female than male fetuses die in the womb. Females are much less likely to die of any cause than men, at least up until the age of approximately 50 years. The sex differential in mortality rates is greatest for young adults aged 15–24 years.

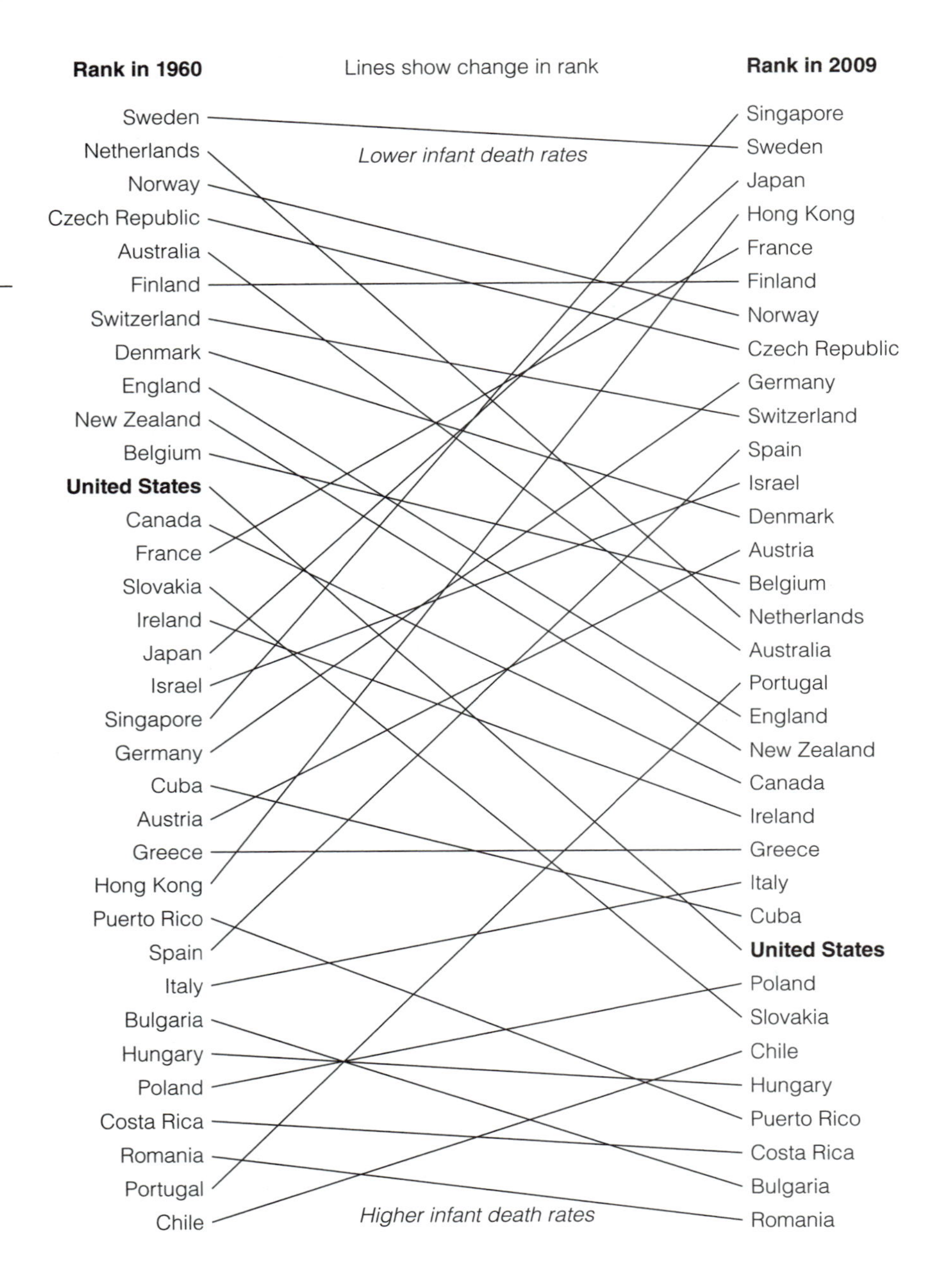

FIGURE 15.1 Levels of infant mortality in the United States compared to other countries of the world.

Source: Adapted from Bakalar (2009).

The death rate for 15- to 24-year-old males is more than twice that of their female counterparts. The major causes of death in these ages are accidents, suicide, and homicide, all of which tend to kill more young men than young women. Men are four times more likely to commit suicide than women and

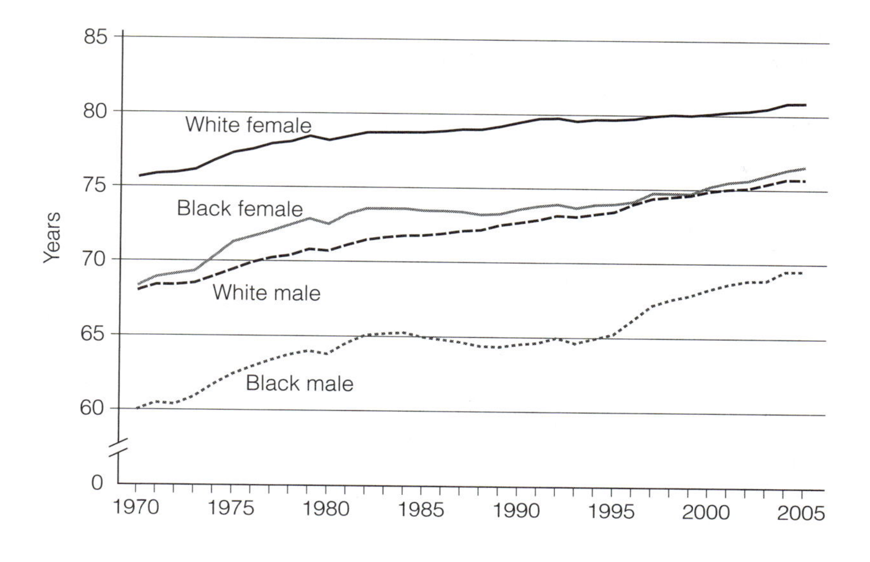

FIGURE 15.2 Life expectancy by race and sex, United States, 1970–2005.

Source: Centers for Disease Control and Prevention, National Center for Health Statistics, National Vital Statistics System, Mortality.

are six times more likely to die from homicide. Men of all ages are also more likely to die from disease than are women. Women are less likely to contract fatal diseases, but they are more likely to contract chronic but often nonfatal diseases such as lupus or multiple sclerosis. Life expectancy overall is greater for women than for men (Figure 15.2). In the United States, in 2004, life expectancy for women was 80 years, and for men it was 75 years.

Due to the sex difference in life expectancy, seniors are disproportionately female (Photo 15.1). Men are particularly outnumbered among the oldest old. Approximately 80% of people who have reached 100 years are women. The longest-lived person on record was Jeanne Calment, a Frenchwoman who died in 1997 at the age of 122. There have been undocumented reports of people living longer, but Jeanne Calment's birthdate has been authenticated.

The sex difference in life expectancy is found throughout the world. Why does it exist? Part of the reason is sex differences in lifestyle. Men are more likely to engage in risky and violent behaviors that can lead to accidental death. Men are less likely to eat well, exercise, and seek medical care than women. Men's health is generally more fragile than women's health. The evolutionary reason for the sex difference is that over evolutionary time it was more important for the well-being of offspring for women to stay alive than men. Women who lived longer lives had children who were more likely to survive and reproduce than women who lived shorter lives; hence, there has been selection for longevity in women.

PHOTO 15.1 Among seniors, women outnumber men, and the older people get, the greater the proportion of women. Source: iStockphoto.

Race and Ethnic Differences in Death and Disease

Table 15.1 shows the causes of death for the U.S. population in 2005 and gives ratios of male to female deaths, black to white deaths, and Hispanic to non-Hispanic white deaths. The top two causes of death in the United States in 2005 were heart disease and malignant neoplasms (cancer).

From Table 15.1, you can see that the ratio of male to female deaths of almost every cause is over 1, which means more men than women die from that cause. You can also see that African Americans are more likely to die of almost every cause than whites. This is not true for Hispanics. Why are African Americans more likely to die of all causes? The primary reason is that African Americans are disproportionately located at the bottom of the socioeconomic ladder, and all people with low socioeconomic standing tend to die sooner than those with higher socioeconomic standing. Education is

TABLE 15.1 **Percentage of Total Deaths by Cause, United States**[a]

					Age-Adjusted Death Rate				
						% Change	Ratio		
Rank[b]	Cause of Death (Based on ICD-10, 1992)	No.	% of Total Deaths	2005 Crude Death Rate	2005	2004 to 2005	Male to Female	Black to White	Hispanic[c] to Non-Hispanic White
...	All causes	2,448,017	100.0	825.9	798.8	−0.2	1.4	1.3	0.7
1	Diseases of heart	652,091	26.6	220.0	211.1	−2.7	1.5	1.3	0.7
2	Malignant neoplasms	559,312	22.8	188.7	183.8	−1.1	1.4	1.2	0.7
3	Cerebrovascular diseases	143,579	5.9	48.4	46.6	−6.8	1.0	1.5	0.8
4	Chronic lower respiratory diseases	130,933	5.3	44.2	43.2	5.1	1.3	0.7	0.4
5	Accidents (unintentional injuries)	117,809	4.8	39.7	39.1	3.7	2.2	1.0	0.8
6	Diabetes mellitus	75,119	3.1	25.3	24.6	0.4	1.3	2.1	1.6
7	Alzheimer's disease	71,599	2.9	24.2	22.9	5.0	0.7	0.8	0.6
8	Influenza and pneumonia	63,001	2.6	21.3	20.3	2.5	1.3	1.1	0.8
9	Nephritis, nephrotic syndrome and nephrosis	43,901	1.8	14.8	14.3	0.7	1.4	2.3	0.9
10	Septicemia	34,136	1.4	11.5	11.2	0.0	1.2	2.2	0.8
11	Intentional self-harm (suicide)	32,637	1.3	11.0	10.9	0.0	4.1	0.4	0.4
12	Chronic liver disease and cirrhosis	27,530	1.1	9.3	9.0	0.0	2.1	0.8	1.6
13	Essential (primary) hypertension and hypertensive renal disease	24,902	1.0	8.4	8.0	3.9	1.0	2.6	1.0
14	Parkinson's disease	19,544	0.8	6.6	6.4	4.9	2.2	0.4	0.6
15	Assault (homicide)	18,124	0.7	6.1	6.1	3.4	3.8	5.7	2.8
...	All other causes (residual)	433,800	17.7	146.4	...	...	...	...	...

... Category not applicable.

[a]Death rates on an annual basis are per 100,000 population: Age-adjusted rates are per 100,000 U.S. standard population.

[b]Rank based on number of deaths.

[c]Data for Hispanic origin should be interpreted with caution because of inconsistencies between reporting Hispanic origin on death certificates and on censuses and surveys.

Source: Kung et al. (2008).

FIGURE 15.3 Death rates for selected causes for adults 25–64 years of age, by education level and sex, 1995. Death rates are age adjusted.

Source: Centers for Disease Control and Prevention, National Center for Health Statistics, National Vital Statistics System.

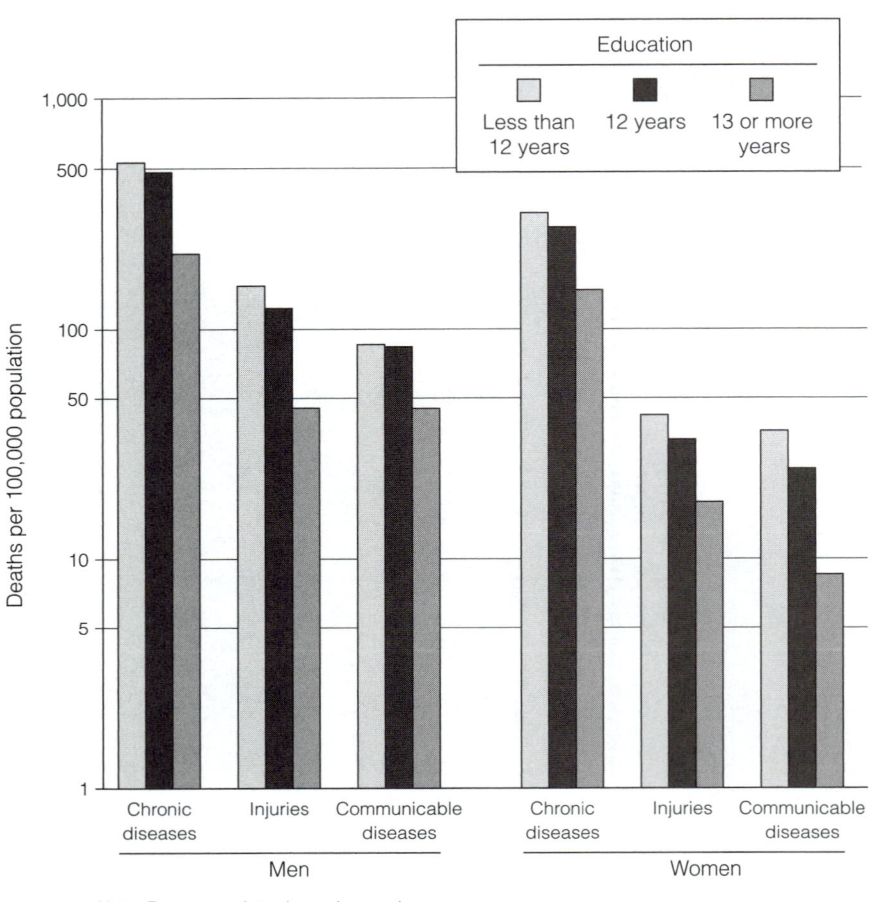

one measure of socioeconomic standing, and Figure 15.3 shows that those with less education are more likely to die from all causes than those with more education. This is discussed in more detail later.

Sex Differences in Mental Health

Men are more likely to get all kinds of mental diseases, except for depression and anxiety. They are also more likely to abuse alcohol. Women are more likely than men to be depressed or anxious. These differences are found in the United States and throughout the world (Figures 15.4 and 15.5; Table 15.2).

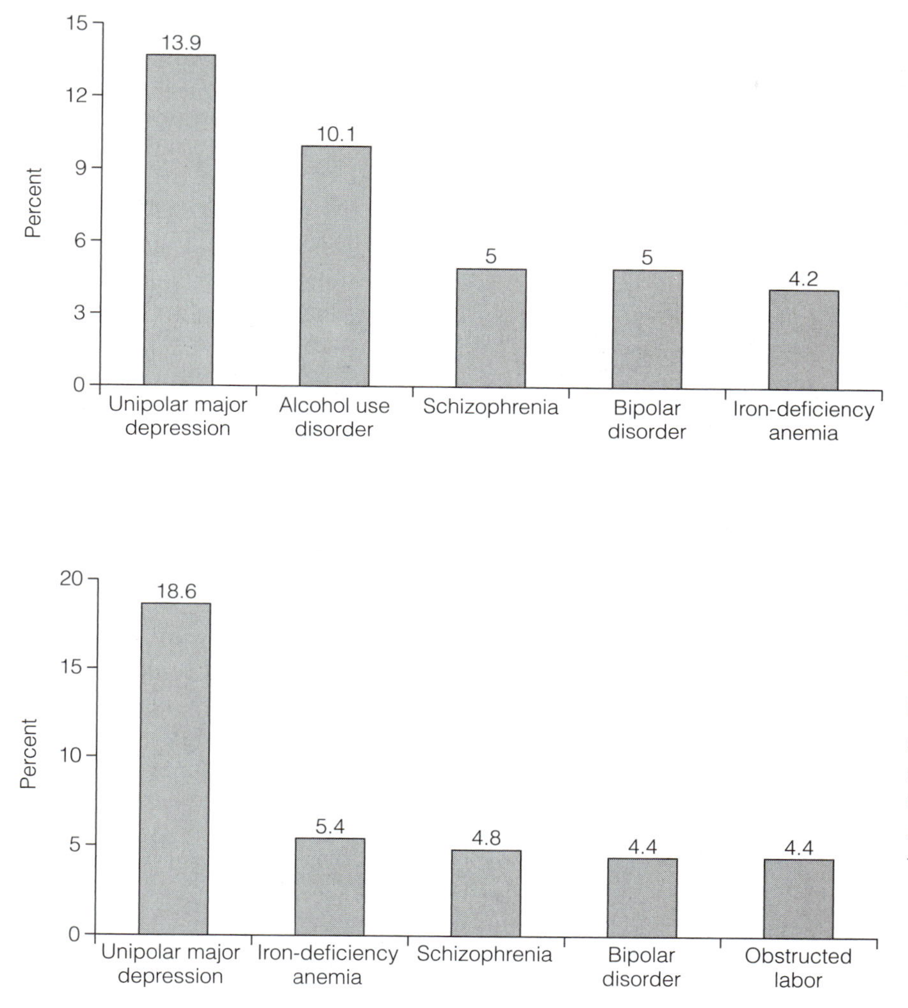

FIGURE 15.4 The top five leading causes of years lived with disability among 15- to 44-year-old men in the world.

Source: World Health Organization, World Health Report 2001 Statistical Annex (http://www.who.int/whr/2001/annex/en/print.html).

FIGURE 15.5 The top five leading causes of years lived with disability among 15- to 44-year-old women in the world.

Source: World Health Organization, World Health Report 2001 Statistical Annex (http://www.who.int/whr/2001/annex/en/print.html).

SOCIAL STATUS INFLUENCES HEALTH

Physical Health

In all countries of the world, people who have higher income and social status have better health and live longer than people who have lower income and social status (Commission on Social Determinants of Health, 2008). Much of this is because poorer people have less access to health care, eat lower-quality food, and are likely to have more dangerous jobs and unpleasant working conditions. They are also more likely to live in

TABLE 15.2 Leading Causes of Years of Life Lived with Disability (YLDs), in All Ages and in 15- to 44-Year-Olds, by Sex, Estimates for 2000[a]

	BOTH SEXES, ALL AGES	% TOTAL		MALES, ALL AGES	% TOTAL		FEMALES, ALL AGES	% TOTAL
1	**Unipolar depressive disorders**	**11.9**	**1**	**Unipolar depressive disorders**	**9.7**	**1**	**Unipolar depressive disorders**	**14.0**
2	Hearing loss, adult onset	4.6	**2**	**Alcohol use disorders**	**5.5**	2	Iron-deficiency anemia	4.9
3	Iron-defiency anemia	4.5	3	Hearing loss, adult onset	5.1	3	Hearing loss, adult onset	4.2
4	Chronic obstructive pulmonary disease	3.3	4	Iron-deficiency anemia	4.1	4	Osteoarthritis	3.5
5	**Alcohol use disorders**	**3.1**	5	Chronic obstructive pulmonary disease	3.8	5	Chronic obstructive pulmonary disease	2.9
6	Osteoarthritis	3.0	6	Falls	3.3	**6**	**Schizophrenia**	**2.7**
7	**Schizophrenia**	**2.8**	**7**	**Schizophrenia**	**3.0**	**7**	**Bipolar affective disorder**	**2.4**
8	Falls	2.8	8	Road traffic accidents	2.7	8	Falls	2.3
9	**Bipolar affective disorder**	**2.5**	**9**	**Bipolar affective disorder**	**2.6**	**9**	**Alzheimer's and other dementias**	**2.2**
10	Asthma	2.1	10	Osteoarthritis	2.5	10	Obstructed labor	2.1
11	Congenital abnormalities	2.1	11	Asthma	2.3	11	Cataracts	2.0
12	Perinatal conditions	2.0	12	Perinatal conditions	2.2	**12**	**Migraine**	**2.0**
13	**Alzheimer's and other dementias**	**2.0**	13	Congenital abnormalities	2.2	13	Congenital abnormalities	1.9
14	Cataracts	1.9	14	Cataracts	1.9	14	Asthma	1.8
15	Road traffic accidents	1.8	15	Protein–energy malnutrition	1.8	15	Perinatal conditions	1.8
16	Protein–energy malnutrition	1.7	**16**	**Alzheimer's and other dementias**	**1.8**	16	Chlamydia	1.8
17	Cerebrovascular disease	1.7	17	Cerebrovascular disease	1.7	17	Cerebrovascular disease	1.8
18	HIV/AIDS	1.5	18	HIV/AIDS	1.6	18	Protein–energy malnutrition	1.6
19	**Migraine**	**1.4**	19	Lymphatic filariasis	1.6	19	Abortion	1.6
20	Diabetes mellitus	1.4	**20**	**Drug use disorders**	**1.6**	**20**	**Panic disorder**	**1.6**

	BOTH SEXES, 15–44-YEAR-OLDS	% TOTAL		MALES, 15–44-YEAR-OLDS	% TOTAL		FEMALES, 15–44-YEAR-OLDS	% TOTAL
1	**Unipolar depressive disorders**	**16.4**	**1**	**Unipolar depressive disorders**	**13.9**	**1**	**Unipolar depressive disorders**	**18.6**
2	**Alcohol use disorders**	**5.5**	**2**	**Alcohol use disorders**	**10.1**	2	Iron-deficiency anemia	5.4
3	**Schizophrenia**	**4.9**	**3**	**Schizophrenia**	**5.0**	**3**	**Schizophrenia**	**4.8**
4	Iron-deficiency anemia	4.9	**4**	**Bipolar affective disorder**	**5.0**	**4**	**Bipolar affective disorder**	**4.4**
5	**Bipolar affective disorder**	**4.7**	5	Iron-deficiency anemia	4.2	5	Obstructed labor	4.0
6	Hearing loss, adult onset	3.8	6	Hearing loss, adult onset	4.1	6	Hearing loss, adult onset	3.6
7	HIV/AIDS	2.8	7	Road traffic accidents	3.8	7	Chlamydia	3.3
8	Chronic obstructive pulmonary disease	2.4	8	HIV/AIDS	3.2	8	Abortion	3.1
9	Osteoarthritis	2.3	**9**	**Drug use disorders**	**3.0**	**9**	**Panic disorder**	**2.8**
10	Road traffic accidents	2.3	10	Chronic obstructive pulmonary disease	2.6	10	HIV/AIDS	2.5
11	**Panic disorder**	**2.2**	11	Asthma	2.5	11	Osteoarthritis	2.5
12	Obstructed labor	2.1	12	Falls	2.4	12	Maternal sepsis	2.3
13	Chlamydia	2.0	13	Osteoarthritis	2.1	13	Chronic obstructive pulmonary disease	2.2
14	Falls	1.9	14	Lymphatic filariasis	2.1	**14**	**Migraine**	**2.1**
15	Asthma	1.9	**15**	**Panic disorder**	**1.6**	**15**	**Alcohol use disorders**	**1.5**
16	**Drug use disorders**	**1.8**	16	Tuberculosis	1.6	16	Rheumatoid arthritis	1.4
17	Abortion	1.6	17	Gout	1.3	**17**	**Obsessive-compulsive disorder**	**1.4**
18	**Migraine**	**1.6**	**18**	**Obsessive-compulsive disorder**	**1.3**	18	Falls	1.4
19	**Obsessive-compulsive disorder**	**1.4**	19	Violence	1.2	**19**	**Post-traumatic stress disorder**	**1.4**
20	Maternal sepsis	1.2	20	Gonorrhea	1.1	20	Asthma	1.3

[a]Neuropsychiatric conditions are highlighted.

Source: World Health Organization, World Health Report 2001 Statistical Annex (http://www.who.int/whr/2001/annex/en/print.html).

polluted and/or dangerous environments. In addition, they are more likely to experience stress associated with low-level jobs, low income, and irregular employment.

The stress of poverty even affects brain functioning. In 2006, Martha Farah et al. showed that the working memories of children who have been raised in poverty have smaller capacities than those of middle-class children. In 2009, Gary Evans and Michelle Shamberg showed that this is almost certainly the result of stress, which influences the way children's brains develop. In this study, the researchers studied 195 voluntary participants—all age 17 years, all white, with an approximately equal number of men and women. The researchers measured stress using an index known as **allostatic load**—a combination of diastolic and systolic blood pressure; the concentrations of three stress-related hormones; and the body mass index (a measure of obesity). A higher value on this index indicates a more stressful life. Poor children in the study had higher levels on this index, on average, than middle-class children. The researchers were able to estimate the proportion of each child's life that had been spent in poverty: The longer this time, the higher the allostatic load index, indicating more stress. In addition, the higher the allostatic load index, the smaller the child's working memory. Those who had spent their whole lives in poverty could hold an average of 8.5 items in their memory at a time. Those who had spent their lives in middle-class homes could hold an average of 9.4 items in their memory at a time.

Allostatic load A combination of diastolic and systolic blood pressure; the concentrations of three stress-related hormones; and the body mass index (a measure of obesity).

Other correlates of poverty, such as low birth weight, mother's age when the child was born, mother's level of education, her marital status, and mother's stress level, did not fully account for the correlation between allostatic load and working memory. This means that none of those factors were fully responsible for the stress a child experiences. The researchers concluded that children who are exposed to stress have smaller working memories and as a result find it more difficult to learn.

In the previously described study, the stress was a result of living in poverty. However, other adverse social situations create stress that in turn affects people's health. Even people who are economically well-off suffer from being low in a social hierarchy. Michael Marmot (2006) found that people low in the British civil service are more likely to die from all causes than people ranked a few grades higher in the British civil service, even though their incomes are not hugely different. Having to kowtow to higher-ups, it seems, is stressful and, therefore, damaging to one's health.

Mental Health

Social status not only affects physical health but also influences mental health. The lower your social status—measured as education, income, and occupational prestige—the higher your chances of being depressed or being diagnosed with another mental illness (Miech and Shanahan, 2000). This is true throughout the world for both men and women (Hopcroft and Bradley, 2007). In the United States, children from low socioeconomic status backgrounds are also at increased risk of poor mental health and depressive symptoms (Wickrama et al., 2008). In the United States, African Americans and Hispanics are more likely to experience poor mental health than are whites, and this is largely due to their low socioeconomic position in U.S. society (Mossakowski, 2008). As discussed in Chapter 11, poor families are often single-parent families, and people in single-parent families (as well as stepfamilies and single-parent families with other relatives present) tend to have worse mental health than people in intact families (Barrett and Turner, 2005).

HEALTH INFLUENCES SOCIAL STATUS

The relationship between social status and health is a two-way street. Not only does your social status influence your health but also your health (along with your other physical characteristics) can influence your social status. It is difficult to keep a high-status job if you are in poor health. It is also more difficult to do the things that are necessary to obtain a high-status job in the first place, such as obtaining higher education.

Height and Social Status

Health and nutrition as a child influence height, and this in turn has implications for one's social status as an adult. Tall people are granted higher status in interactions than short people. Tall people earn higher salaries. In all cultures, leaders are likely to be tall. For example, in U.S. presidential races, the taller of the two candidates has typically won the election (McGinnis, 1976). In the 2008 presidential race, the taller candidate, Barack Obama, won (Photo 15.2). The high social status granted to tall people in turn has implications for their health, as discussed previously.

PHOTO 15.2 In presidential elections, the taller man usually wins. This was the case in the 2008 election. You can see from the picture that Barack Obama is noticeably taller than John McCain. Source: Associated Press photo/ Charles Dharapak.

Lack of Deformity, Disability, and Status

Lack of good health, adequate nutrition, and proper medical care increase the chances of deformity and disability in adults. Just as height grants social status in all societies, deformity and disability lower social status in all societies. This lower status thus compounds the stress that people already experience as a result of living with disability.

Beauty and Status

Healthy people are also more likely to be good looking than unhealthy people. Good health and nutrition promote high-quality skin, hair, and general good health—all things that make people look attractive. Good health throughout childhood promotes symmetry in features, and symmetrical people are considered more attractive than less symmetrical people. Attractiveness has its own benefits. Teachers expect good-looking children to be more intelligent, sociable, and popular than less attractive children. Attractive children get better grades from their teachers. Beautiful people, both men and women, are more popular with the opposite sex. They have more dates and get more attention. Perhaps as a result, both good-looking men and women begin to have sex earlier. In the job market, good-looking men and women are more likely to be hired and receive higher salaries, on average.

Beautiful people are more likely to be helped by strangers. For example, in a staged experiment, a dime was planted in a phone booth. A pretty or an ugly woman approached the occupant of the phone booth and asked, "Did I leave my dime there?" Eighty-seven percent of the people returned the dime to the good-looking woman, but only 64% returned the coin to the ugly woman (Sroufe, Chaiken, Cook, and Freeman, 1977). In another study, bogus college applications were left in Detroit airports. A note attached to them suggested that the applications were given to fathers who had accidentally left them behind. Each had the identical application answers, but each had a different photo attached. People were much more likely to mail the applications of the better-looking applicants than the less attractive-looking applicants (Benson, Karabenick, and Lerner, 1976).

Beautiful people are more likely to be treated leniently in court. This effect is especially strong for good-looking women. They are less likely to be penalized for minor crimes. Beautiful people also expect better treatment from other people. In one study, people were asked to participate in an interview with a psychologist. During the course of the interview, the psychologist was interrupted and excused herself. Attractive people on average waited 3 minutes and 20 seconds before demanding attention. Less attractive people waited an average of 9 minutes (Jackson and Huston, 1975). These kinds of benefits mean that life is often less stressful for beautiful people, and lack of stress, as previously noted, in turn has health benefits.

CONCLUSION

Your health is a result of a complex interaction between your genetic predispositions and your environment. An important determinant of your environment is the type of country in which you live. If you live in a poor country, you are much more likely to get sick and die early than if you live in a rich country. The country in which you live also determines the type of medical care you receive, how much it costs, and how accessible it is. If you are female, you tend to live longer than if you are male, no matter what the environment. Your social status in your environment also has important effects on your health. In general, the lower your income and education, and the worse your occupation, the more likely you are to get sick and die. But like many things we have seen, the relationship between health and status is a two-way street: Not only does your status affect your health but also your health in turn influences your social status.

REFERENCES

Bakalar, Nicholas. April 7, 2009. "U.S. Still Struggling with Infant Mortality." *New York Times.*

Barrett, Anne E., and R. Jay Turner. 2005. "Family Structure and Mental Health: The Mediating Effects of Socioeconomic Status, Family Process, and Social Stress." *Journal of Health and Social Behavior* 46(2), 156–169.

Benson, P. L., S. A. Karabenick, and R. M. Lerner. 1976. "Pretty Pleases: The Effects of Physical Attractiveness, Race and Sex on Receiving Help." *Journal of Experimental Social Psychology* 12, 409–415.

Commission on Social Determinants of Health. 2008. "Closing the Gap in a Generation: Health Equity through Action on the Social Determinants of Health. Final Report of the Commission on Social Determinants of Health." Geneva: World Health Organization.

Conley, Dalton, Kate W. Strully, and Neil G. Bennett. 2003. *The Starting Gate: Birth Weight and Life Chances.* Berkeley: University of California Press.

Evans, Gary W., and Michelle A. Shamberg. 2009. "Childhood Poverty, Chronic Stress, and Adult Working Memory." *Proceedings of the National Academy of Sciences* 106, 6545–6549.

Farah, Martha J., David M. Shera, Jessica H. Savage, Laura Betancourt, Joan M. Giannetta, Nancy L. Brodsky, Elsa K. Malmud, and Hallam Hurt. 2006. "Childhood Poverty: Specific Associations with Neurocognitive Development." *Brain Research* 1110(1), 166–174.

Guo, Guang, Yuying Tong, Cui-Wei Xie, and Leslie A. Lange. 2007. "Dopamine Transporter, Gender, and Number of Sexual Partners among Young Adults." *European Journal of Human Genetics* 15, 3.

Hopcroft, Rosemary L., and Dana Burr Bradley. 2007. "The Sex Difference in Depression across 29 Countries." *Social Forces* 85(4), 1483–1507.

Jackson, D. J., and T. L. Huston. 1975. "Physical Attractiveness and Assertiveness." *Journal of Social Psychology* 96, 79–84.

Kung, H. C., D. L. Hoyert, J. Q. Xu, and S. L. Murphy. 2008. *Deaths: Final Data for 2005*, National Vital Statistics Reports Vol. 56, No. 10. Hyattsville, MD: National Center for Health Statistics.

Marmot, Michael G. 2006. "Status Syndrome: A Challenge to Medicine." *Journal of the American Medical Association* 295(11), 1304–1307.

McGinnis, J. M. 1976. *The Selling of the President*. New York: Andre Deutsch.

Miech, Richard Allen, and Michael J. Shanahan. 2000. "Socioeconomic Status and Depression over the Life Course." *Journal of Health and Social Behavior* 41(2), 162–176.

Mossakowski, Krysia N. 2008. "Dissecting the Influence of Race, Ethnicity, and Socioeconomic Status on Mental Health in Young Adulthood." *Research on Aging* 30(6), 649–671.

National Cancer Institute. 1999. "Cancer Death Rates among 50 Countries." Available at http://rex.nci.nih.gov/NCI_Pub_Interface/raterisk/rates50.html.

Shanahan, Michael J., Stephen Vaisey, Lance D. Erickson, and Andrew Smolen. 2008. "Environmental Contingencies and Genetic Propensities: Social Capital, Educational Continuation, and Dopamine Receptor Gene DRD2." *American Journal of Sociology* 114, S260–S286.

Sroufe, R., A. Chaiken, R. Cook, and V. Freeman. 1977. "The Effects of Physical Attractiveness on Honesty: A Socially Desirable Response." *Personality and Social Psychology Bulletin* 3, 59–62.

Wickrama, K. A. S., Rand D. Conger, Frederick O. Lorenz, and Tony Jung. 2008. "Family Antecedents and Consequences of Trajectories of Depressive Symptoms from Adolescence to Young Adulthood: A Life Course Investigation." *Journal of Health and Social Behavior* 49(4), 468–483.

World Health Organization. 2001. *The World Health Report: Mental Health: New Understanding, New Hope*. Geneva: World Health Organization.

ECONOMIC SOCIOLOGY

16

AN ECONOMY IS THE EXCHANGE of goods, rights, services, and money between people, so it is a social interaction. Like most social interactions, it is governed by social institutions or systems of rules. Sometimes those rules are *informal* or unwritten rules that everyone agrees on, such as norms of common courtesy or politeness. Sometimes those rules are *formal*, written down and enforced by law. Think about a simple economic exchange, such as buying your lunch in a coffee shop. First, when you approach the counter, in U.S. society the unwritten rule is that you stand in line. You do not try to elbow your way to be first at the counter. The next unwritten rule is you ask politely for what you want to eat, and the employee gets it for you. Next, you pay for your food—that is a written rule—and depending on where you are, there are a variety of ways you can pay. If you pay cash and you are in the United States, you must use American dollars, not the currency of another country. You cannot use play American dollars, either. Then the informal rule is you thank the shop employee and leave with your lunch. The shop employee obeys rules, too. The unwritten rule is that the employee is polite to the customer. Food is prepared following written rules laid down by health regulations for the hygienic preparation of food. If any of these rules are broken, people in the United States tend to become upset and say things such as the following: "That person was so rude!" "There was dirt in my sandwich!" "They gave me euros as change!" and "They tried to give me Monopoly money!" Worst comes to worst, they report the person to the police or sue the person.

Economy The exchange of goods, rights, services, and money between people.

Given the importance of rules to the operation of the economy, it is easy to see how the economy is socially created. If people break the rules, the economy breaks down because people take their goods/rights/services/money and go home. Many of the rules are meant to promote trust, and if

PHOTO 16.1 The dollar bill. Although intrinsically worthless, everyone in the United States accepts that a dollar bill has a certain value, and therefore it does. Source: iStockphoto.

trust breaks down, the entire economy breaks down. The credit crisis of late 2008 is an example of this. Banks were not willing to lend money to other banks because with all the bank failures they could no longer trust that the other institutions would be able to repay the money.

Paper money is probably the best example of a social construction that is essential to the working of a modern economy (Carruthers and Babb, 1996). Although the paper has little worth in and of itself, everyone in the society agrees to the value of the money, and there are strict rules governing its creation and use, and thus the paper has value. Everyone who uses money trusts that the rules are followed and therefore the paper is worth what they think it is worth (Photo 16.1).

ECONOMIES FROM SIMPLE TO COMPLEX

In the simplest societies, hunting and gathering societies, there is no formal economy. People provide for their subsistence needs, and any exchange is of gifts or favors that are likely to be repaid in the future. In hunting and

PHOTO 16.2 Several Roman coins. Source: iStockphoto.

gathering societies, tribal societies, and chiefdoms, there may also have been **bartering** as well as gift exchange. This is the exchange of goods between two individuals or groups. So I may give you some of my hen's eggs for some of your grain. The crucial point about barter is that money is not involved.

Bartering Exchange of goods between two individuals or groups with no money involved.

Real trade does not exist until money is involved. The use of proto-money probably dates back at least 75,000 years. Proto-money may include shell or ivory jewelry or metal (Wilford, 2004). Where metals were available, gold or silver were preferred. The first agrarian civilizations of the Middle East are also the first to have manufactured and used metal money—usually gold and silver. The Roman Empire also had metal money (Photo 16.2). The law codes of the king of Ur (ca. 2050 BC), the Code of Hammurabi (ca. 1760 BC), the Codex of Eshnunna (ca. 1930 BC), and the Codex of Lipit-Ishtar of Isin (ca. 1870 BC) all laid out rules for the use of money. They set amounts of interest on debt, fines for "wrong doing," and compensation in money for various violations of the law.

The Salt and Spice Trades

Our Paleolithic ancestors did not salt their food (MacGregor and de Wardener, 1998). Approximately 5,000 years ago, that changed. As people increasingly began to like salt, it became the most important object of trade. It may seem difficult to believe, but common salt—something that today is cheap and easy to come by—was once a highly valued commodity. When they could afford it, people also wanted other spices to season their food. It was for this reason that the spice trade became the driving force of the world economy from the end of the Middle Ages until the beginning of the modern era. America and the country I am from (Australia) were discovered by Europeans because of this trade. Christopher Columbus was searching for an alternative route to the Indies, where many valued spices grew. It was traders in search of spices in the East Indies who were blown off course and accidentally ran into the west coast of Australia.

In the early economies, most trade went by water. As a result, it was often coastal seafaring groups that specialized in trade. In classical times, it was the Phoenicians. In medieval times, the Frisians of northwest Europe (part of what is now The Netherlands and Germany) were important traders. Such traditions of seafaring often lasted into the early modern period. The Dutch people of The Netherlands in the early modern period were noted traders and seafarers. Abel Tasman, the man who discovered the island of Tasmania off the south coast of Australia, was a Frisian.

The Emergence of Complex Economies

The first really complex economies were those based in Italy during the 16th-century Renaissance and later in The Netherlands. New inventions such as bills of exchange and promissory notes helped facilitate long-distance trade. These devices were used instead of cash, so traders did not have to worry about carrying large amounts of different local currencies. North and Thomas (1973) discuss how in The Netherlands, other institutions emerged that further facilitated trade. Particularly important were the emergence of relatively impartial courts of law that served to uphold the law, protect property rights, and enforce contracts. **Property rights** are rights to make use of property such as real estate, buildings, animals, or vehicles. If you steal my vehicle, for instance, you have violated my property rights.

Property rights Rights to make use of property such as real estate, buildings, animals, or vehicles.

With the rule of law, enforcement of contracts, and protection of property rights, people could build their businesses without fear that others would renege on what they owed or take away the fruits of their labors.

Also important were institutions and social arrangements in the rural agricultural communities where the foodstuffs that were traded were produced. This includes the nature of property rights in land, the relations between lords (the owners of the land) and those who worked the land (peasants), and local trading relations (Emigh, 2009; Hopcroft, 1999; Lachmann, 2000). Institutions that provided certainty to producers and traders—certainty that they would own the results of their labors and certainty that they would get a fair price for their products—typically promoted the emergence of complex trading economies.

INSTITUTIONAL CREATION OF THE MARKET

The social institutions that underpin a market economy make it clear that a complex economy is fundamentally a social creation. The nature of social institutions determines whether the economy works or fails. Failures include **hyperinflation**, which occurs when governments try to buy their way out of financial crises by printing increasingly more money. The increased supply of money means that the value of each unit of currency declines to the point where each unit becomes almost worthless. The worst case of hyperinflation in human history was in Germany in 1923, which at that time had the third largest economy in the world. In August of that year, one dollar bought 620,000 German marks, and by November a dollar bought 630 billion marks (Ahamed, 2009). Such episodes of hyperinflation usually accompany social chaos, and this was the case in Germany in the 1920s. Adolf Hitler conducted his "Beer Hall Putsch"—his first failed bid for power—at this same time. Typically, when governments make such errors, they are ejected and new governments are less likely to make the same mistakes. In Germany in the 1920s, a new government introduced a new currency, the amount of which was strictly limited, and hyperinflation disappeared. Other countries have tried to minimize the risk of hyperinflation by making those responsible for the money supply (in the United States, the Federal Reserve) immune from government pressure, but this does not always work. Sometimes, governments make economic mistakes on a truly massive scale. One example is the Soviet experiment.

Hyperinflation The rapid rate of inflation that occurs when governments print increasingly more money.

PHOTO 16.3 Soviet stamp with picture of Joseph Stalin. Source: iStockphoto.

The Soviet Experiment

The Bolshevik Revolution in Russia (1917) ushered in a group of people led by Vladimir Lenin who were determined to turn Russia into the kind of socialist society that Karl Marx had once envisioned as a human utopia. This involved getting rid of private property—the private ownership of goods, land, vehicles, buildings, stocks, companies, etc. Thus, people of all classes and statuses found their land and possessions taken from them. Companies were taken over by the state. Supporters of the old regime of social democracy (white Russians) also had their possessions and often their lives taken. Many of the survivors ended up in America (where, ironically, one of them, Pitirim Sorokin, became a prominent early sociologist). After Lenin's death, Joseph Stalin was able to maneuver his way into power (Photo 16.3). Stalin turned the Soviet Union into an autocracy, with him in charge and everybody and everything subservient to him. Stalin instituted a command economy in which rules for what was to be produced, how much of it, and the price for which it was sold were dictated by the central government, not by the market.

Under Stalin, Russia was able to successfully industrialize its economy, simply by building factories and copying the industrial technology of the West. But it was at great cost. Particularly dreadful were the results of the collectivization of agriculture. In order to create communal farming, private farmers were thrown off their land and their land was taken. The initial result was a steep drop in agricultural production, which resulted in one of the most terrible famines of all time—the Ukrainian famine of 1932–1933. Soviet authorities set requisition quotas of grain and other agricultural products for Ukraine at an impossibly high level. Brigades of special agents were dispatched to Ukraine to collect the quotas, and homes were routinely searched and any foodstuffs found were confiscated. The rural population was left without enough food to feed itself. Estimates of the total number of deaths in Ukraine range from 4 to 5 million. The number of famine victims throughout the Soviet Union is estimated to be 6–8 million (*Encyclopedia Britannica*, 2009).

Not only did the economy of the Soviet Union provide poorly for its citizens but also its industry proved unable to innovate to keep up with the free-market West (including western Europe and the United States). Partly as a result, the Soviet Union ceased to exist in 1991 and splintered into many separate regional countries (including the Ukraine).

CONTEMPORARY ECONOMIES

Contemporary economies in rich countries run mostly on market principles, using the institutional descendants of those institutions pioneered in northern Italy, The Netherlands, and Britain. There are laws supporting property rights and enforcing contracts, and there are court systems and police forces to enforce these laws. Nevertheless, there are differences between rich world economies, most notably in the amount of state involvement in the market.

Differences between the United States and Europe

Labor market The market for workers.

The **labor market** is the market for workers. Labor market rules (rules on the hiring and firing of workers) are very different between the United

PHOTO 16.4 Young guests play with Barbie dolls at Barbie Shanghai flagship store Friday, March 6, 2009, in Shanghai, China. The six-story, pink and sparkling Barbie Shanghai flagship store opened on Saturday to the Chinese public. Source: Associated Press photo/Eugene Hoshiko.

States and those countries that make up the European Union. In the United States, it is comparatively easy to hire and fire workers, whereas this is not the case in the European Union. There are also fewer rules on what benefits are provided by the employer. In Europe, many benefits (medical care, child care, and unemployment compensation) are provided by the state. In some countries, trade unions are also involved in setting wages and benefits packages, which rarely happens in the United States. Although the influence of unions has recently been on the wane everywhere, some countries have more union involvement in deciding wages and benefits than do others (Western, 1995).

Development of a Global Economy

We now have a truly global economy. Certain products are sold throughout the world, such as Coke, Pepsi, Hollywood movies, and even Barbie (Photo 16.4). You can buy these products almost anywhere you travel.

In addition, many products are now *made* throughout the world. In his 2005 book *The World Is Flat*, Thomas Friedman describes the production of his Dell notebook computer as follows:

> My computer was conceived when I phoned Dell's 800 number on April 2nd, 2004, and was connected to sales representative Mujteba Naqvi, who immediately entered my order into Dell's order management system. He typed in both the type of notebook I ordered as well as the special features I wanted, along with my personal information, shipping address, billing address, and credit card information. My credit card was verified by Dell through its work flow connection with Visa, and my order was then released to Dell's production system. Dell has six factories around the world—in Limerick, Ireland; Xiamen, China; Eldorado do Sul, Brazil; Nashville, Tennessee; Austin, Texas; and Penang, Malaysia. My order went out by e-mail to the Dell notebook factory in Malaysia, where the parts for the computer were immediately ordered from the supplier logistics centers (SLCs) next to the Penang factory.
>
> So where did the parts for my notebook come from? . . . To begin with . . . the notebook was codesigned in Austin, Texas, and in Taiwan by a team of Dell engineers and a team of Taiwanese notebook designers. . . . Dell uses multiple suppliers for most of the 30 key components that go into its notebooks. That way if one supplier breaks down or cannot meet a surge in demand, Dell is not left in the lurch. So here are the key suppliers for my Inspiron 600m notebook: The Intel microprocessor came from an Intel factory either in the Philippines, Costa Rica, Malaysia, or China. The memory came from a Korean-owned factory in Korea (Samsung), a Taiwanese-owned factory in Taiwan (Nanya), a German-owned factory in Germany (Infineon), or a Japanese-owned factory in Japan (Elpida). My graphics card was shipped from either a Taiwanese-owned factory in China (MSI) or Chinese-run factory in China (Foxconn). The cooling fan came from a Taiwanese-owned factory in Shanghai (Quanta) or a Taiwanese-owned factory in Taiwan (Compal or Wistron). The keyboard came from either a Japanese-owned company in Tianjin, China (Alps), a Taiwanese-owned factory in Shengzhen, China (Sunrex), or a Taiwanese-owned factory in Suzhou, China (Darfon). The LCD was made in either South Korea (Samsung or LC Philips LCD), Japan (Toshiba or Sharp), or Taiwan (Chi Mei Optoelectronics, Hannstar Display, or AU Optronics). The wireless card came from either an American-owned factory in China (Agere) or Malaysia (Arrow), or a Taiwanese-owned factory in Taiwan (Askey or Gemtek) or China (USI). The modem was made by either a Taiwanese-owned company in China (Asustek or Liteon) or a Chinese-run company in China (Foxconn). The battery came from an American-owned factory in Malaysia (Motorola), a Japanese-owned factory in Mexico or Malaysia or China (Sanyo), or a South Korean or Taiwanese

> factory in either of those two countries (SDI or Simplo). The hard disk drive was made by an American-owned factory in Singapore (Seagate), a Japanese-owned company in Thailand (Hitachi or Fujitsu), or a Japanese-owned factory in the Philippines (Toshiba). The CD/DVD drive came from a South Korean-owned company with factories in Indonesia and the Philippines (Samsung); a Japanese-owned factory in China or Malaysia (NEC); a Japanese-owned factory in Indonesia, China, or Malaysia (Teac); or a Japanese-owned factory in China (Sony). The notebook carrying bag was made by either an Irish-owned company in China (Tenba) or an American-owned company in China (Targus, Samsonite, or Pacific Design). The power adapter was made by either a Thai-owned factory in Thailand (Delta) or a Taiwanese-, Korean-, or American-owned factory in China (Liteon, Samsung, or Mobility). The power cord was made by a British-owned company with factories in China, Malaysia, and India (Volex). The removable memory stick was made by either an Israeli-owned company in Israel (M-System) or an American-owned company with a factory in Malaysia (Smart Modular). . . . *The total supply chain for my computer, including suppliers of suppliers, involved about 400 companies in North America, Europe, and primarily Asia, but with 30 key players* [italics added]. (pp. 580–585)

Whew! These complex webs of supply chains and business relationships connect the world in one great global economy. Labor is so much cheaper in countries such as Malaysia than in places such as Europe that it is more economical for companies to locate production facilities close to the cheap labor.

Just as national economies work because of institutions, so does the global economy. In addition to the institutional rules of each country that companies must obey, there are also the rules laid out by the World Bank, International Monetary Fund, and the United Nations (Halliday and Carruthers, 2007). There are also international organizations to catch crooks and administer justice, including Interpol, the UN Security Council, and the International Criminal Court.

ORGANIZATIONS AND WORK

As discussed in Chapter 4, companies and other organizations are key players in a modern economy. The workings of any company or organization also rely on institutions—both formal and informal. These are the rules that people follow on a day-to-day basis at work. It also includes the informal rules, or culture, of the organization. Some institutions are hierarchical and formal, whereas some are egalitarian and informal. Consider, for example, the Las Vegas headquarters of Zappos.com, an Internet company that sells shoes and clothing (*The Economist*, 2009):

> There are outlandish decorations adorning the walls and cubicles, including jungle creepers that hang from the ceiling and a menagerie of toy monkeys and other creatures. There are the boisterous employees, some of whom rattle cowbells, shake pompoms, and bellow greetings as visitors pass their desks. And there are . . . a visiting masseuse and generous helpings of free food for "Zapponians."

Sometimes rules are specific to a particular organization. In other cases, there are similarities between organizations in the same industry or economic sector. Industries in U.S. society have been classified by the government using the Standard Industrial Code since 1937, and sociologists have often made use of these codes in their research. Since 1997, the U.S. government has used the North American Industry Classification (NAIC) system. The census uses the NAIC codes in its own industrial classification. See Table 16.1 for the major categories of the census industrial classification and the numbers employed in each industry in 2008.

Two leisure and hospitality firms are typically more alike than two manufacturing firms, for instance, but this is not always the case. Sociologists have also divided industries into sectors—often the **core** or **primary sector** and the **periphery** or **secondary sector**. The core is made up of industries dominated by a very few large firms. In these firms, wages tend to be high and job security is high. The periphery is made up of industries dominated by many very small firms. In these firms, wages tend to be low and job security is low.

Core or primary (sometimes monopoly) sector The core sector of the economy is made up of industries dominated by a very few large firms. In these firms, wages tend to be high and job security is high.

Periphery or secondary (sometimes competitive) sector The periphery sector of the economy is made up of industries dominated by many very small firms. In these firms, wages tend to be low and job security is low.

Not only the type of industry but also the size of the firm is important. Large, well-established companies in high value-added or core industries tend to have the most hierarchy and formality. Small, mom-and-pop shops in low value-added or periphery industries tend to be the most informal. Large firms typically pay their employees more than do small firms, but the difference is not as great as it once was (Hollister, 2004).

There can also be regional differences in the way firms operate, depending on local situations and local consumer markets (Otis, 2008). Some organizations in some regions become home to particular ethnic groups, and this influences the way each organization operates. The restaurant industry in New York City in the 1990s was dominated by workers from Ecuador,

TABLE 16.1 Major Categories of the Census Industrial Classification and the Numbers Employed

INDUSTRY (2007 CENSUS INDUSTRIAL CLASSIFICATION)	NO. EMPLOYED (1000s), 2008	% OF LABOR FORCE
Agriculture, forestry, fishing, and hunting	2,168	1.5
Mining, quarrying, and oil and gas extraction	819	0.6
Construction	10,974	7.4
Manufacturing	15,904	10.8
Wholesale and retail trade	20,585	14.0
Transportation and utilities	7,727	5.2
Information	3,481	2.4
Financial activities	10,228	6.9
Professional and business services	15,540	10.5
Education and health services	31,402	21.3
Leisure and hospitality	12,767	8.7
Other services	7,005	4.8
Public administration	6,763	4.6

Source: U.S. Census Bureau, Current Population Survey, 2008.

for example (Bourdain, 2000). In the United States overall, the construction, manufacturing, and retail industries with many service and blue-collar occupations are primarily occupied by indigenous African American and Hispanic groups. High-tech industries and industries with many professional and managerial occupations (e.g., banking, finance, health, and education) are occupied by groups of people from Europe, the Middle East, and India (Wilson, 2003). People from Russia, for example, are mainly concentrated in high-level occupations in health services, elementary–secondary education, and professional services.

In Which Organizations Are Co-workers Most Supportive?

Organizations with many jobs involving complex tasks have the most co-worker support. Based on a sample of employed residents of the city of Toronto, Canada, Scott Schieman found that jobs with high levels of authority and that involve complex tasks tend to be the ones in which co-workers are most supportive. Organizations with many menial jobs tend to be ones in which co-workers are least supportive (Schieman, 2006). Jobs that involve much autonomy tend to have more co-worker support among women. More demanding jobs tend to have more co-worker support among men. There is also evidence that it is more stressful for men to work with one male boss, whereas for women it is less stressful to work with one male boss (Schieman and McMullen, 2008).

Organizational Ecology

Organizational ecology examines the environment in which organizations compete and the process by which organizations emerge, grow, change, and die. Organizational ecologists have found that when a new technology is developed, such as television broadcasting or the Internet, many companies are set up to make use of the new technology. After a while, most of these new companies go out of business, resulting in only a few large, dominant companies in the industry (Hannan and Freeman, 1977). An example is all the Internet companies (dot-coms) that emerged in the 1990s. The bubble burst in early 2000, and half or more of all the dot-coms went out of business. Other examples in the past in the United States include the railroad boom in the 1840s, automobiles and radio in the 1920s, and home computers in the early 1980s.

Organizational ecology An area of study that examines the environment in which organizations compete and the process by which organizations emerge, grow, change, and die.

Women in Organizations

Institutions in businesses and companies also influence the integration of men and women into the workplace. Some organizations have the reputation of being "woman friendly" and some do not. Woman-friendly companies have programs such as paid maternity leave and flexible schedules. Organizations that have these policies tend to be those that employ women in higher-prestige, higher-earning jobs (Boushey, 2008). Industry also makes a difference. There is evidence that firms in more competitive industries are more likely to promote women into positions of authority, all else being equal, including the woman's type of occupation (Hopcroft, 1996).

TABLE 16.2 Proportion with Supervisory Authority by Country and Sex: Data for Paid Employees 20–60 Years Old

COUNTRY	TOTAL	MEN	WOMEN	WOMEN/MEN
Australia	0.533	0.559	0.503	0.899
U.S.	0.472	0.550	0.378	0.687
Great Britain	0.343	0.411	0.260	0.633
Canada	0.347	0.419	0.259	0.618
Denmark	0.275	0.351	0.202	0.575
West Germany	0.314	0.370	0.211	0.570
Sweden	0.317	0.394	0.221	0.561
Norway	0.331	0.421	0.207	0.492
Japan	0.363	0.535	0.117	0.219

Source: Rosenfeld et al. (1998).

Do women do better in organizations in other countries? As noted in Chapter 11, women in all countries earn less than men. The most equitable country for the wages of full-time workers is Australia. In terms of authority in the workplace, in most countries women have less authority on the job than do men (Rosenfeld, Van Buren, and Kalleberg, 1998). Table 16.2 shows that women have the most supervisory authority in Australia and the United States and the least in Norway and Japan. Strangely, those countries with a great amount of state intervention in the labor market and economy have many women working but few women in high-level managerial occupations (Mandel and Semyonov, 2006).

CONCLUSION

A complex economy only works because it is governed by formal and informal rules. In this way, we can see that the economy is a social construction. Similarly, group actors within the economy, including individual companies and organizations, only work because they are also governed by formal and informal rules. These rules differ across places and across time. In this chapter, we have seen that some sets of rules are more successful than others in promoting the functioning of the economy. Change the rules in the wrong way and the economy (or the company) can break down. We also discussed differences in rules across countries, organizations, and companies; why differences exist; and some of their effects.

REFERENCES

Ahamed, Liaquat. 2009. *Lords of Finance. The Bankers Who Broke the World*. New York: Penguin.

Bourdain, Anthony. 2000. *Kitchen Confidential: Adventures in the Culinary Underbelly*. New York: Bloomsbury.

Boushey, Heather. 2008. "Family Friendly Policies: Helping Mothers Make Ends Meet." *Review of Social Economy* 66(1), 51–70.

Carruthers, Bruce G., and Sarah Babb. 1996. "The Color of Money and the Nature of Value: Greenbacks and Gold in Postbellum America." *American Journal of Sociology* 101(6), 1556–1591.

The Economist. April 18, 2009. "Tony Hsieh of Zappos.com Keeps the Dotcom Spirit Alive."

Emigh, Rebecca Jean. 2009. *The Undevelopment of Capitalism*. Philadelphia: Temple University Press.

Encyclopedia Britannica. 2009. "Soviet Ukraine: The Famine of 1932–33." Available at http://www.britannica.com/EBchecked/topic/612921/Ukraine/30078/Soviet-Ukraine.

Friedman, Thomas. 2005. *The World Is Flat*. New York: Picador/Farrar, Straus and Giroux.

Halliday, Terence C., and Bruce G. Carruthers. 2007. "The Recursivity of Law: Global Norm Making and National Lawmaking in the Globalization of Corporate Insolvency Regimes." *American Journal of Sociology* 112(4), 1135–1202.

Hannan, Michael T., and John Freeman. 1977. "The Population Ecology of Organizations." *American Journal of Sociology* 82(5), 929–964.

Hollister, Matissa N. 2004. "Does Firm Size Matter Anymore? The New Economy and Firm Size Wage Effects." *American Sociological Review* 69(5), 659–676.

Hopcroft, Rosemary L. 1996. "Authority Attainment of Women: Competitive Sector Effects." *American Journal of Economics and Sociology* 55(2), 163–184.

———. 1999. *Regions, Institutions and Agrarian Change in European History*. Ann Arbor: University of Michigan Press.

Lachmann, Richard. 2000. *Capitalists in Spite of Themselves*. New York: Oxford University Press.

MacGregor, G. A., and H. E. de Wardener. 1998. *Salt, Diet and Health: Neptune's Poisoned Chalice: The Origins of High Blood Pressure*. Cambridge, UK: Cambridge University Press.

Mandel, Hadas, and Moshe Semyonov. 2006. "A Welfare State Paradox: State Interventions and Women's Employment Opportunities in 22 Countries." *American Journal of Sociology* 111(6), 1910–1949.

North, D. C., and R. P. Thomas. 1973. *The Rise of the Western World*. Cambridge, UK: Cambridge University Press.

Otis, Eileen M. 2008. "Beyond the Industrial Paradigm: Market-Embedded Labor and the Gender Organization of Global Service Work in China." *American Sociological Review* 73, 115–136.

Rosenfeld, Rachel A., Mark E. Van Buren, and Arne L. Kalleberg. 1998. "Gender Differences in Supervisory Authority: Variation among Advanced Industrialized Democracies." *Social Science Research* 27, 23–49.

Schieman, Scott. 2006. "Gender, Dimensions of Work, and Supportive Coworker Relations." *Sociological Quarterly* 47(2), 195–214.

Schieman, Scott, and Taralyn McMullen. 2008. "Relational Demography in the Workplace and Health: An Analysis of Gender and the Subordinate–Superordinate Role-Set." *Journal of Health and Social Behavior* 49(3), 286–300.

Western, Bruce. 1995. "A Comparative Study of Working-Class Disorganization: Union Decline in Eighteen Advanced Capitalist Countries." *American Sociological Review* 60(2), 179–201.

Wilford, John Noble. April 20, 2004. "Tiny African Shells May Be Oldest Beads." *New York Times*, p. F3.

Wilson, Franklin D. 2003. "Ethnic Niching and Metropolitan Labor Markets." *Social Science Research* 32(3), 429–466.

SOCIOLOGY OF THE ENVIRONMENT

17

IN RECENT YEARS, there has been much concern about global warming and climate change caused by human activities. There are related concerns about the loss of biodiversity, water shortages, and environmental pollution. Sociologists have only recently started examining these issues, but they are a "natural" area for sociologists (no pun intended) because all these problems stem from human activities and can only be solved by a change in human activities. In this chapter, we examine current environmental concerns and the contributions of sociologists (among other social scientists) to understanding the causes of environmental problems and to finding workable solutions.

CURRENT ENVIRONMENTAL CONCERNS

Climate Change

In the early chapters of this text, we discussed three major events in the history of human life on Earth. In Chapter 2, we discussed the diaspora of the human species out of Africa approximately 50,000 years ago. In Chapter 3, we discussed the Neolithic Revolution (the beginning of agriculture, approximately 15,000 years ago) and the Industrial Revolution (the beginning of large-scale manufacturing industries, approximately 200 years ago). The wealth of the rich world, our modern standard of living, and the rich/poor world divide are due to the changes brought about by the Industrial Revolution. The fuel of the Industrial Revolution in England was coal; unfortunately, burning coal (among other fossil fuels such as oil and gas) produces carbon dioxide (CO_2). From 1769 to 2006, world annual coal production increased 800-fold (MacKay, 2008). Coal production is still

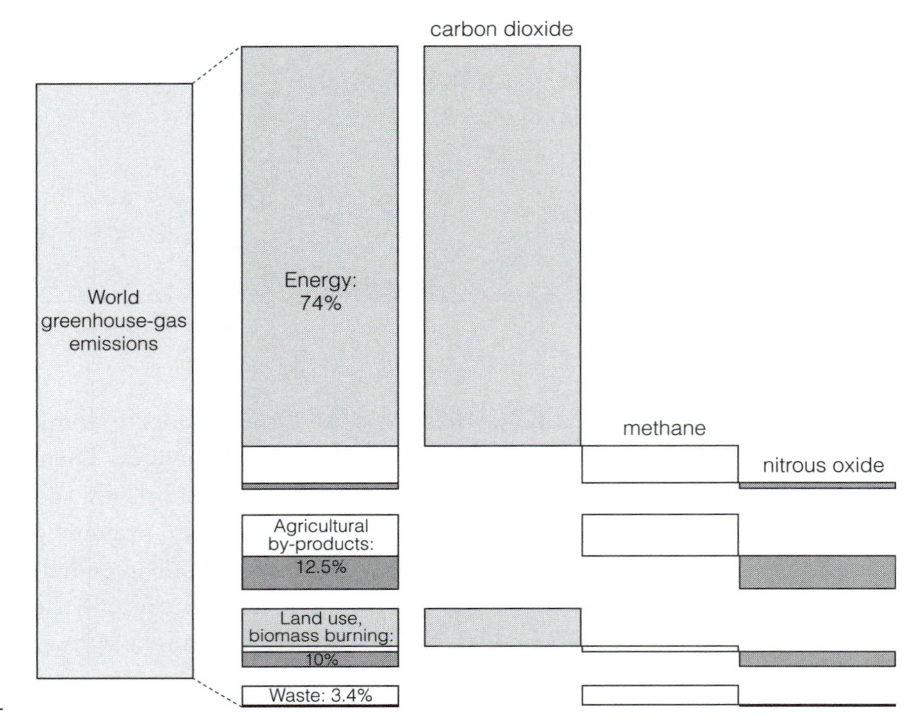

FIGURE 17.1 Breakdown of world greenhouse gas emissions (2000) by cause and by gas. "Energy" includes power stations, industrial processes, transport, fossil fuel processing, and energy use in buildings. "Land use, biomass burning" means changes in land use, deforestation, and the burning of unrenewed biomass such as peat. "Waste" includes waste disposal and treatment. The sizes indicate the 100-year global warming potential of each source.

Source: Emission Database for Global Atmospheric Research.

increasing today. Although the burning of other fossil fuels produces CO_2, burning coal still produces most of the CO_2 emissions.

"OK," you might say, "but I don't use any coal." Unfortunately, you do, even if you don't realize it. Most power stations that generate electricity are run on coal. So every time you turn on a light, switch on the air conditioner, plug in your hair dryer, turn on the oven, use a refrigerator, etc., you are indirectly using coal. Industrial production of all sorts of things (e.g., steel and automobiles) is still heavily dependent on coal. You also produce CO_2 when you use other fossil fuels besides coal. Driving a car, taking a bus, or flying in an airplane uses up fossil fuels and emits CO_2. For example, a round-trip intercontinental flight emits nearly 2 tons of CO_2 per passenger (MacKay, 2008, p. 16). Figure 17.1 shows the breakdown of the world's production of CO_2 and other greenhouse gas emissions by source. Figure 17.2 displays coal and oil production since 1700 in units of billions of metric tons (gigatons) of CO_2 released when the coal and oil were burned. Figure 17.3 shows the increase in CO_2 levels as measured from air trapped in ice cores and directly in Hawaii (from 1958 on).

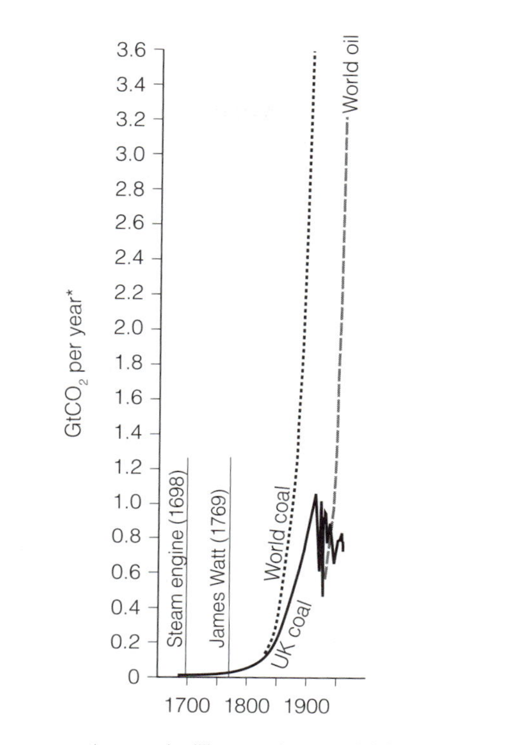

FIGURE 17.2 The history of UK coal production and world coal production from 1650 to 1960.

Source: MacKay (2008)

*A billion metric tons or one thousand million metric tons of CO_2 is 1 $GtCO_2$—one gigaton.

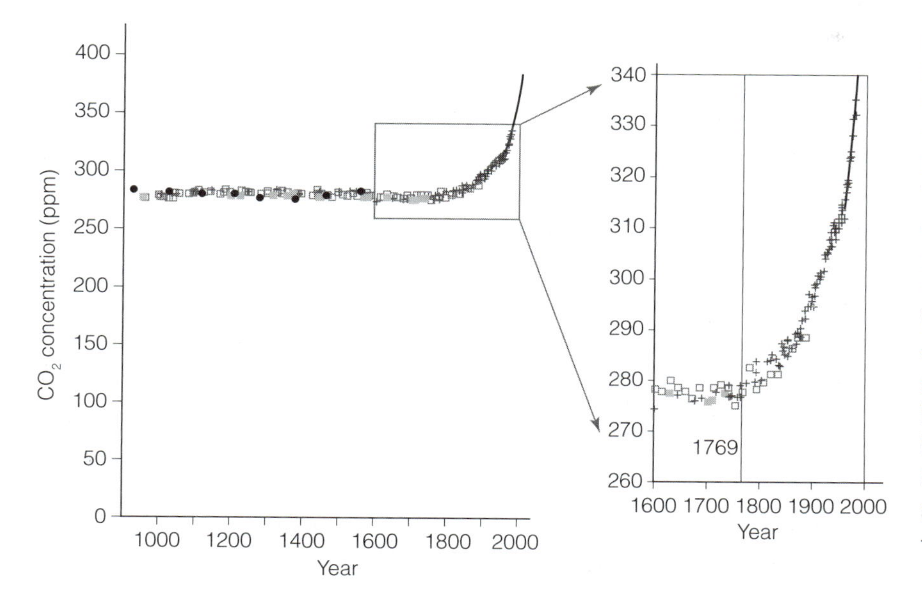

FIGURE 17.3 The increase in CO_2 levels as measured from air trapped in ice cores and directly in Hawaii (from 1958 on). This figure shows the effects of the industrial revolution. The year 1769 is when James Watt patented his steam engine. (The first practical steam engine was invented 70 years earlier in 1698, but Watt's was much more efficient.)

Source: MacKay (2008).

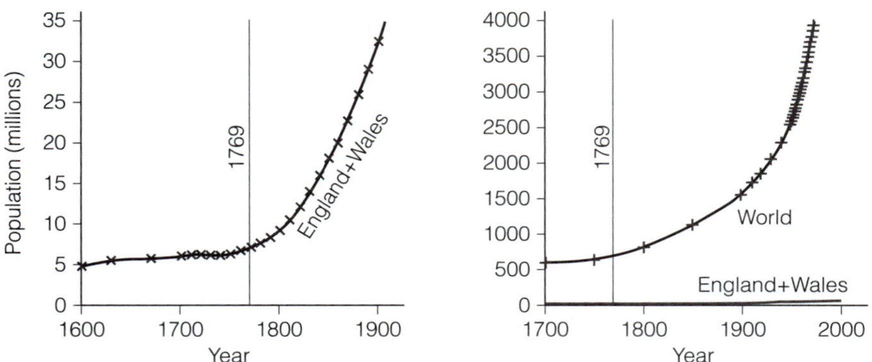

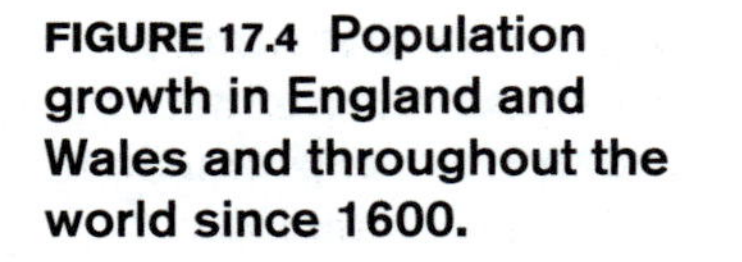

FIGURE 17.4 Population growth in England and Wales and throughout the world since 1600.

Source: MacKay (2008).

If you remember from Chapter 6 on demography, the Industrial Revolution and the increased use of coal are also associated with the major increase in the population of England and Wales. As the rest of the world has developed, the world's population has also skyrocketed (Figure 17.4).

The Industrial Revolution and its consequences allowed people to live longer and healthier lives, greatly increased living standards, and allowed us to live the lives we have all become accustomed to. So it was a good thing. The problem is that all the fossil fuels burned in the process released CO_2, a greenhouse gas. Greenhouse gases work like a quilt over the world, and CO_2 is one layer of the quilt. This quilt prevents heat from leaving the planet, and so the earth warms up.

What is the result of this? David MacKay (2008), a physicist at Cambridge University in the United Kingdom, notes the following:

> So, if humanity succeeds in doubling or tripling CO_2 concentrations (which is where we are certainly heading, under business as usual), what happens? Here, there is a lot of uncertainty. Climate science is difficult. The climate is a complex, twitchy beast, and exactly how much warming CO_2-doubling would produce is uncertain. The consensus of the best climate models seems to be that doubling the CO_2 concentration would have roughly the same effect as increasing the intensity of the sun by 2%, and would bump up the global mean temperature by something like 3 degrees C. This would be what historians call a Bad Thing. I won't recite the whole litany of probable drastic effects, as I am sure you've heard it before. The litany begins "the Greenland icecap would gradually melt, and, over a period of a few 100 years, sea level would rise by about 7 metres." The brunt of the litany falls on future generations. Such temperatures have not

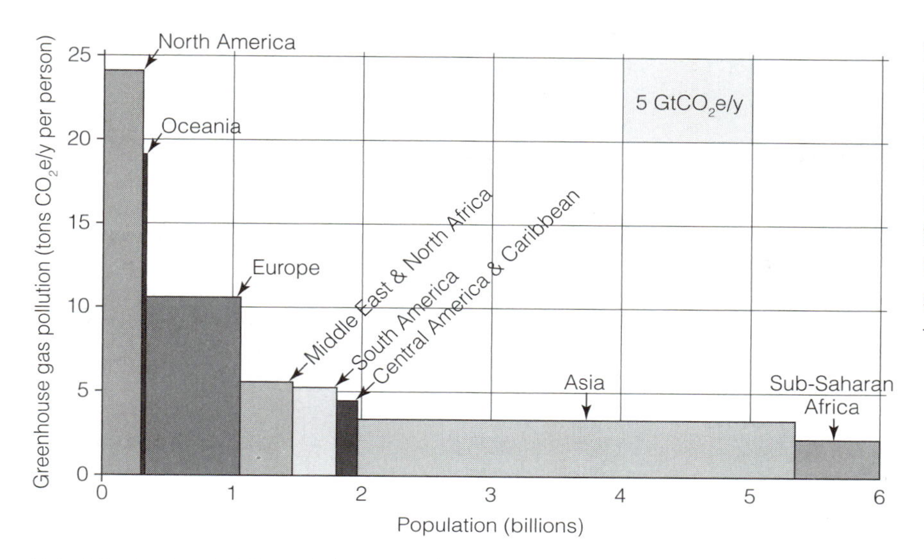

Note: CO_2e/y refers to CO_2 equivalent gas emissions per year. CO_2 equivalent gases are gases that have the same warming effects as CO_2 over a period of 100 years.

FIGURE 17.5 Greenhouse gas emissions per person per year by continent. The width of the rectangle is the population of the region, and the height is the average per-capita emissions in that region.

Source: MacKay (2008).

been seen on Earth for at least 100,000 years, and it's conceivable that the ecosystem would be so significantly altered that the earth would stop supplying some of the goods and services that we currently take for granted. (p. 10)

Which Places Produce the Most CO_2?

Just as North America is home to the highest incomes in the world, so it also produces the most CO_2 per year per person (Figure 17.5). However, it is instructive to look at the data by country. It is not just the United States producing lots of CO_2 (Figure 17.6). You can see that per person, the largest producers of CO_2 emissions are the oil-rich states of the Middle East, namely Qatar, United Arab Emirates, and Kuwait. They are followed by Australia and the United States. The developing countries, such as China and India, produce a lot of CO_2, but they are also the most populated countries in the world, and thus per capita emissions are not very high.

Generally, the consensus is that global warming is bad and that we all need to use fewer fossil fuels. This is a major social problem, and in the following sections we discuss social solutions to this problem. But for now, I mention a few things that you can do personally. Table 17.1 shows the power consumption of various gadgets you use on a day-to-day basis. This

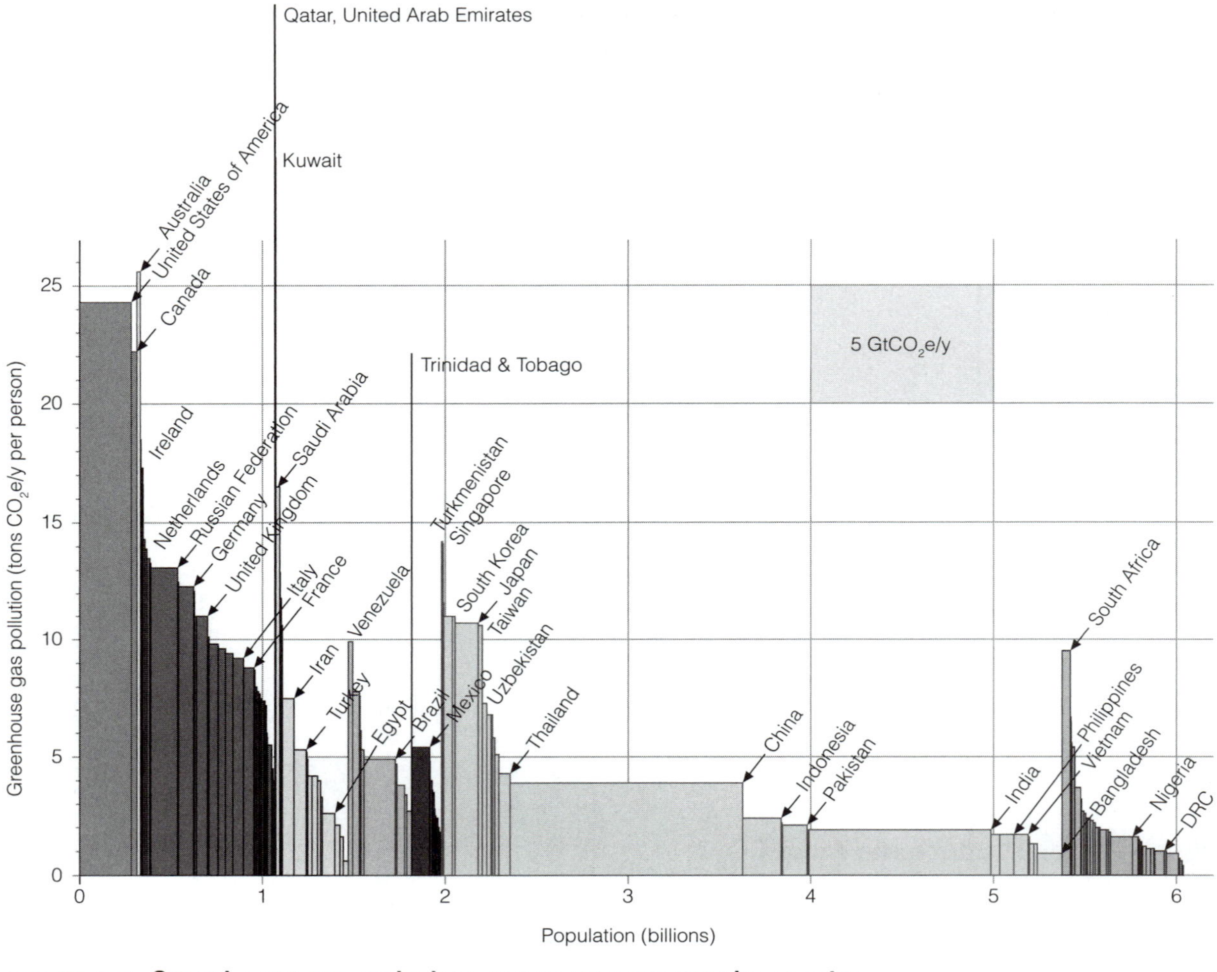

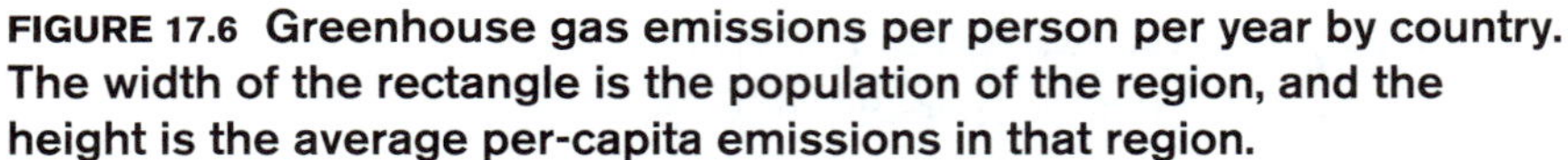
FIGURE 17.6 Greenhouse gas emissions per person per year by country. The width of the rectangle is the population of the region, and the height is the average per-capita emissions in that region.

Source: MacKay (2008).

table (and others) comes from David MacKay's (2008) clear book on the topic, which you can obtain free online at www.withouthotair.com (you can also buy a hard copy if you want).

Table 17.2 lists things you can do to save energy and thereby reduce CO_2 emissions. You can also buy a low-emissions vehicle. Figure 17.7 shows which vehicles have the lowest emissions. A U.S. version of the VW Polo is due out in 2010.

TABLE 17.1 Power Consumption of Everyday Gadgets

	POWER CONSUMPTION (W)			
GADGET	ON AND ACTIVE	ON BUT INACTIVE	STANDBY	OFF
Computer and peripherals				
Computer box	80	55		2
Cathode-ray display	110		3	0
LCD display	34		2	1
Projector	150		5	
Laser printer	500	17		
Wireless and cable modem	9			
Laptop computer	16	9		0.5
Portable CD player	2			
Bedside clock radio	1.1	1		
Bedside clock radio II	1.9	1.4		
Digital radio	9.1		3	
Radio cassette player	3	1.2		1.2
Stereo amplifier	6			6
Stereo amplifier II	13			0
Home cinema sound	7	7	4	
DVD player	7	6		
DVD player II	12	10	5	
TV	100		10	
Video recorder	13			1
Digital TV set-top box	6		5	
Clock on microwave oven	2			
Xbox	160		2.4	
Sony PlayStation 3	190		2	
Nintendo Wii	18		2	
Answering machine		2		
Answering machine II		3		
Cordless telephone		1.7		
Mobile phone charger	5	0.5		
Vacuum cleaner	1600			

Source: MacKay (2008).

TABLE 17.2 Things You Can Do to Save Energy and Thereby Reduce CO_2 Emissions

ACTION	POSSIBLE SAVINGS (KWH/DAY)
Simple	
Put on a woolly sweater and turn down your thermostat (e.g., to 59 or 62°F). Put individual thermostats on all radiators. Make sure the heating is off when no one's at home. Do the same at work.	20
Read all your meters (gas, electricity, water) every week, and identify easy changes to reduce consumption (e.g., switching things off). Compare competitively with a friend. Read the meters at your place of work too, creating a perpetual live energy audit.	4
Stop flying.	35
Drive less, drive more slowly, drive more gently, carpool, use an electric car, cycle, walk, use trains and buses.	20
Keep using old gadgets (e.g., computers); don't replace them early.	4
Change lights to fluorescent or LED.	4
Don't buy clutter. Avoid packaging.	20
Eat vegetarian, 6 days out of 7.	10
Major	
Eliminate drafts.	5
Double glazing.	10
Improve wall, roof, and floor insulation.	10
Solar hot water panels.	8
Photovoltaic panels.	5
Knock down old building and replace by new.	35
Replace fossil-fuel heating by ground-source or air-source heat pumps.	10
Minor	
Wash laundry in cold water.	0.5
Stop using a tumble dryer; use a clothesline or drying rack.	0.5

Source: MacKay (2008).

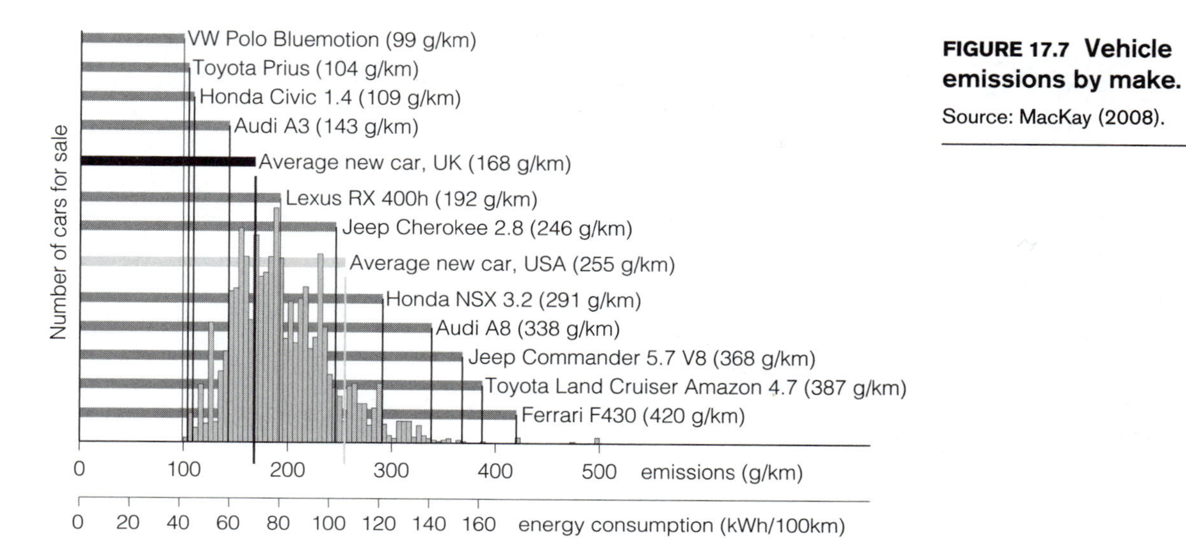

FIGURE 17.7 Vehicle emissions by make.

Source: MacKay (2008).

Water Shortages

Global warming appears to be speeding up the hydrolic cycle, the rate at which water evaporates and falls again (World Water Assessment Programme, 2009). This faster cycle is apparently making wet regions wetter and dry areas drier. In general, the result is longer droughts between more intense periods of rain. Boom and bust in water supply increases problems of water management because communities have to deal with both increased flooding and increased periods of drought. Longer periods of both wet and dry also change the way plants and trees grow. Periods of wet weather encourage spurts of growth. Then dry periods mean that crops wilt, and the trees dry out. A large number of dry plants and trees creates ideal conditions for forest fires. Photo 17.1 is a picture from the fires in Australia in early 2009. These fires were the result of unprecedented conditions: hot winds in excess of 62 miles per hour, all-time record high temperatures—46.4°C (115.5°F), and extremely low humidity. The fires led to the greatest loss of human life from fire in Australian history (Huxley, 2009).

Water shortages due to drought have been exacerbated by growing demand for water throughout the world. This is due to both population growth and economic development. As the population grows, the demand for agricultural products grows, and agriculture is the largest user of water. To grow a pound of wheat takes approximately 132 gallons of water, and to

PHOTO 17.1 A fire truck moves away from out-of-control flames from a bushfire in the Bunyip State Forest near the township of Tonimbuk, 125 kilometers (78 miles) west of Melbourne, Australia, on February 7, 2009. Source: Associated Press photo.

produce a pound of beef takes approximately 1,981 gallons of water (World Water Assessment Programme, 2009). As countries develop economically and people become richer, the demand for meat grows. As a result, water use intensifies. Figure 17.8 shows that the highest water usage is in the developed, richer areas of the world.

Furthermore, in an effort to stem climate change, interest has grown in the use of biofuels (from crops such as sugarcane, sugar beet, soybeans, and corn). Some governments are now giving incentives for farmers to grow such crops. Unfortunately, these crops require tremendous amounts of water to grow, thus exacerbating water shortages (Figure 17.9).

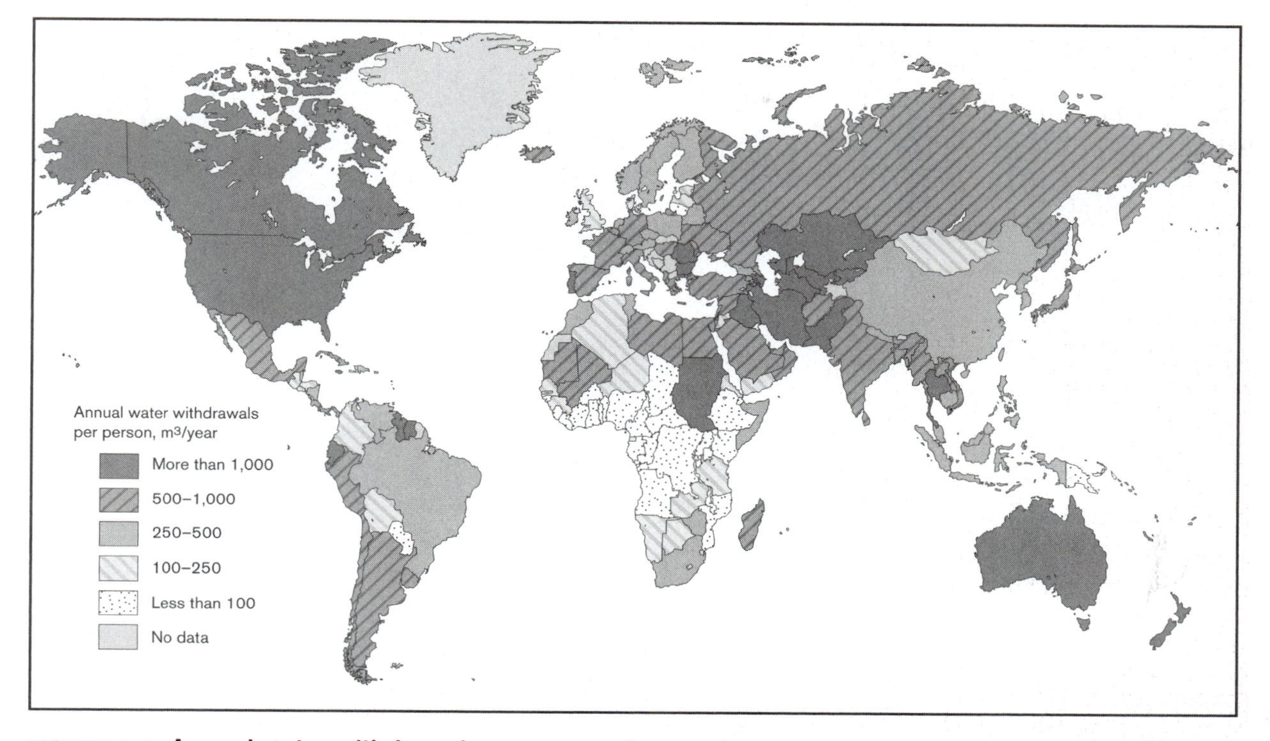

FIGURE 17.8 Annual water withdrawals per person by country, world view, 2000.

Source: Food and Agriculture Organization of the United Nations, World Water Development Report 2009.

As a result of both increased periods of drought and increased demand for water, local water shortages have increased in number throughout the world. In early 2009, Governor Arnold Schwarzenegger of California declared a state of emergency—California was running out of water. As of early 2009, Australia had been in drought conditions for approximately 10 years. Brazil and South Africa, both of which depend on hydroelectric power, have suffered problems with too little water to drive the turbines properly. A number of the world's great rivers no longer reach the sea, including the Indus, Rio Grande, Colorado, Murray-Darling, and Yellow Rivers. These rivers run though some of the world's main grain-growing areas (*The Economist*, 2009). In addition to shrinkage of rivers, during the 20th century, half the world's wetlands were drained.

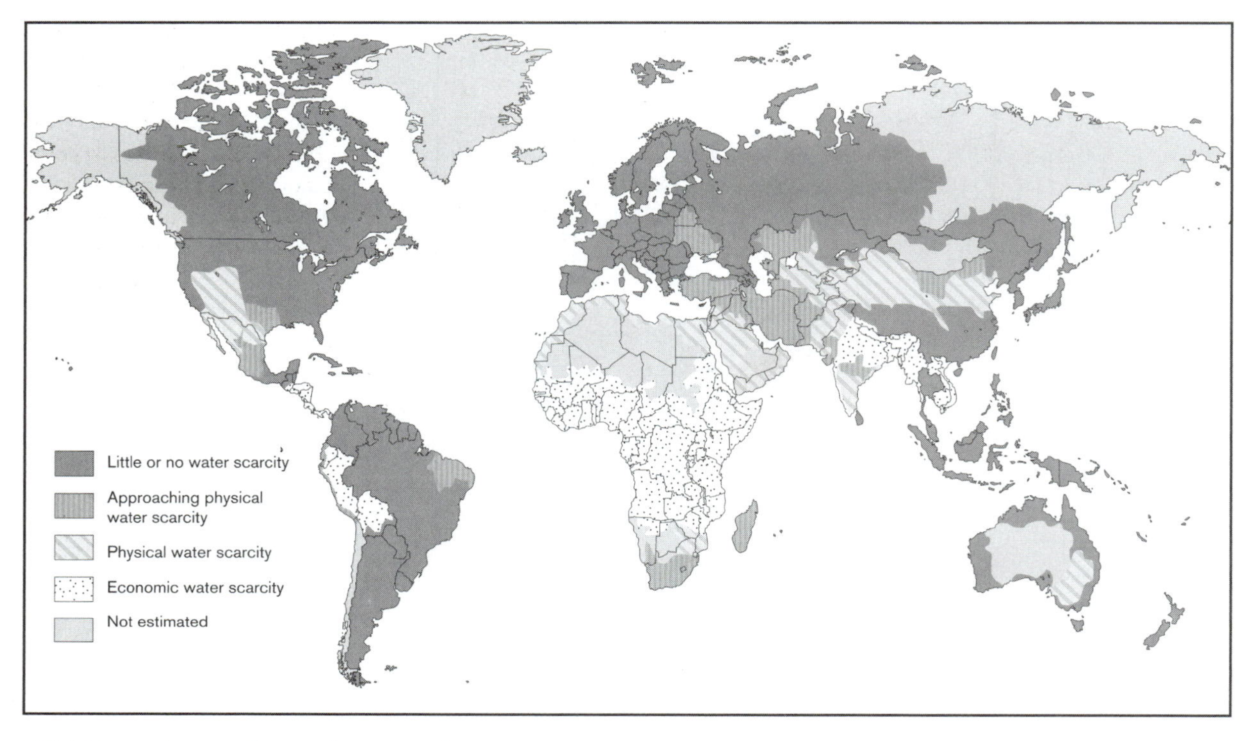

FIGURE 17.9 Increasing water scarcity.

Source: Food and Agriculture Organization of the United Nations, World Water Development Report 2009.

The loss of rivers and wetlands means that habitats for freshwater fish and other wetland species have declined. For example, freshwater fish populations are in decline. Since 1970, fish stocks in lakes and rivers have fallen by approximately 30%. Figure 17.10 shows that biodiversity in freshwater species has declined by half since 1970.

Deforestation and Decline in Biodiversity

Population growth in poor countries also contributes to deforestation. People cut down the forests to create agricultural land, and as the population grows more forests are cut down. Deforestation is a problem because the world's forests, particularly the world's rain forests, are important in pro-

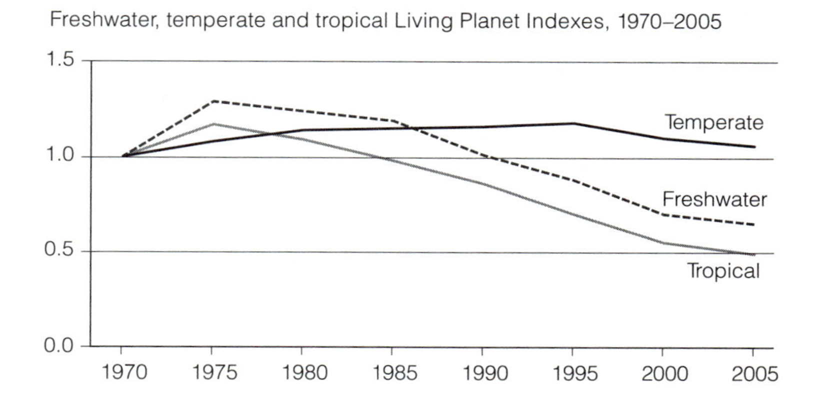

FIGURE 17.10 Biodiversity in freshwater species has declined by half since 1970. Note that the Living Planet Index tracks trends in populations of 1,313 vertebrate species throughout the world.

Source: World Wildlife Fund (2008).

viding oxygen for the atmosphere and mopping up CO_2. Without the rain forests, less oxygen is produced, and the less healthy we all are.

Deforestation is also associated with declines in biodiversity because the world's rain forests are home to a disproportionate number of species. Not only does deforestation lead to habitat loss but also it promotes fragmentation of habitats that reduces animal migration. This promotes species decline and also contributes to the collapse of whole ecosystems.

Deforestation in poor countries is partly compensated for by reforestation in many areas of the rich countries of the developed world. However, given that the rich countries of the world tend to be located in temperate climates, this does not prevent the decline in biodiversity in tropical areas.

The environmental problems of climate change, water shortages, deforestation, and decline in biodiversity are major problems, and they need major solutions. In the following section, we discuss some of the problems that such large-scale, social solutions are up against.

THE TRAGEDY OF THE COMMONS

Think of a common grazing land. Everyone in the local community is allowed to use the land for grazing their sheep, cows, and goats. However, if too many animals are put out to graze on the land, the grass is overgrazed and dies out. Say you are one of the people in the local community. You know that if there are too many animals put out to graze, the grass will disappear. So you decide to only put a few animals out yourself—fewer animals than you have to feed. But you notice everyone else is putting out more animals and taking advantage of the free food for their animals. So what do you do? You figure you may as well get free food for your animals while you can, so you put out more animals as well. Because everyone is putting too many animals out to graze, the grass is overgrazed and soon dies out. The lack of grass promotes erosion, so good soil is washed away and new grass does not grow. The free pasture is no more.

This is the classic *tragedy of the commons*. There used to be common lands all over western Europe (there still are in some places). How did people prevent the tragedy of the commons? In some places, they didn't, and common grazing land deteriorated and disappeared. In most places, however, local communities devised strict rules prohibiting people from putting out more than a certain number of animals into the common herd. However, there were always people who tried to cheat, or tried to slip a few more animals than everyone else into the common herd. That way, the cheaters would get just a little bit more free food for their animals than everyone else. Because there were cheaters, there were local people whose job it was to make sure the rules were followed, and if the rules were not followed, there were courts whose job it was to punish the cheaters.

Free rider Anyone who tries to take advantage of a common or public good without contributing to the cost or maintenance of the common good.

Common (public) good Something publicly available to all.

The cheaters figured it wouldn't hurt if they put just a few more animals into the common herd. Another term for the cheaters is "free riders." A **free rider** is anyone who tries to take advantage of something publicly available (often called a **common** or **public good**) without contributing to the cost or maintenance of the common good. A person who comes to a potluck and doesn't bring a dish to share is a free rider, as is a person who comes to a potluck with a bag of chips to share. These people are free-riding on the efforts of others. Things are fine if there are only a few free riders, of course—something the free riders are counting on. However, if everyone free-rides and no one contributes to the costs of the good, then the tragedy of the commons results—and nothing is available to anyone.

A modern example of the tragedy of the commons is carbon emissions and resulting climate change. Most people want lower CO_2 emissions, but almost everyone wants to keep the amenities of modern life, etc., and drive their own large, comfortable car. However, the amenities of modern life and large, comfortable cars produce a lot of CO_2 emissions. As long as everyone keeps doing things the way they have been doing, there will be no lowering of CO_2 emissions.

Problems related to public goods such as lower CO_2 emissions are often called *collective action* problems. The good, low CO_2 emissions, is only created and maintained if everyone limits their emissions. So how do you do this? Easy, you might say, have government make a law. What kind of law? Here is where things get sticky. Before we discuss laws and the issues associated with such laws, let's look at some of the possible ways to lower CO_2 emissions while not changing everyone's modern lifestyle too much. These ideas come from U.K. physicist David MacKay (2008), whose book on climate change I have already mentioned.

Possible Solutions to Climate Change

1. Electrify transportation. Electrification means that buses, cars, and trucks no longer use fossil fuel. Of course, the electricity has to be generated, but perhaps we can generate electricity without using coal (e.g., using wind, wave, or tidal energy).
2. Use electrical and solar heat for homes. Everyone would start using solar heating for their houses, supplemented with electric heat pumps, which are more efficient than electrical heaters.
3. Generate "green" electricity. We generate electricity from some combination of wind, solar, wave, tidal, or nuclear power. Solar power from deserts is the most plentiful option.

According to MacKay's (2008) calculations of energy that can be generated in "green" ways and energy required to sustain a modern lifestyle, the nonsolar renewable sources of energy (wind, wave, tide, etc.) are not large enough to cover modern energy needs. His calculations suggest that to obtain enough energy per person (he uses 195 kWh per day per person, although that is much lower than the average American's current use of 250 kWh per day), we will have to rely on solar energy, nuclear energy, or both.

Any of these options requires government laws, often massive changes, and large investments of time and money in alternative sources of energy as well as cars and other appliances designed to use these alternative sources of energy. How do we get such changes? We discussed laws previously, but we all have to agree on the laws. Many people do not want wind turbines to generate electricity in their neighborhood, lots of solar panels, or large

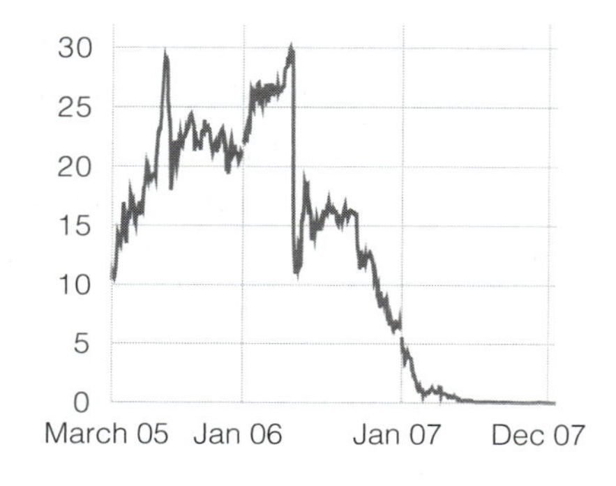

FIGURE 17.11 The price, in euros, of 1 ton of CO_2 under the first period of European emissions trading scheme.

Source: European Energy Exchange (www.eex.com).

hydroelectric plants. Many people do not want nuclear energy because of the real issues of safety and the problems of disposal of nuclear waste. In short, many people do not want to pay the costs of the change to "green" energy.

What about Carbon Trading as a Solution to Climate Change Problems?

You hear a lot about carbon trading, whereby people trade permits to emit CO_2 for permits to capture carbon, with one metric ton carbon-capture certificates being convertible to one metric ton CO_2 emission permits. This compensates individuals and companies for investing in carbon-capture technologies. The problem is that carbon-capture technologies are expensive, and coal power station owners are only likely to want to invest in carbon-capture technologies if they think the price of carbon is going to be high enough that the carbon-capturing facilities will then pay for themselves. Experts suggest that a long-term guaranteed carbon price of approximately $100 per metric ton of CO_2 will be enough, but that is difficult to attain (Figure 17.11). How can the government arrange this? One way is for the government to auction off CO_2 pollution permits with a fixed minimum price. The government could also offer to buy carbon-capture certificates for $100 per ton of CO_2, no matter what happens to the market price.

Many people think that such laws are the only solution to the problem of CO_2 emissions and global warming. Yet in a democratic society, such laws are difficult to enact, as previously discussed. Also, they may not always be the best way to achieve the desired result. In an article published in 1960 titled the "Problem of Social Cost," Ronald Coase pointed out that often such laws can be fraught with costs. Remember the need for people in preindustrial Europe whose job it was to make sure the rules were followed and, if they were not followed, the courts whose job it was to punish the cheaters? All these people must be paid, and in a modern society there would have to be many of them. The existence of such people also opens the door to corruption and bribery. Last, the laws themselves can have unintended costs. We previously noted one of these: Government support for the growing of biofuels has had the unintended consequence of helping exacerbate water shortages. Coase noted that laws affecting everyone are not the only way the tragedy of the commons has been solved. Lighthouses are often used as an example of a common good—a good everyone can benefit from. Ship owners who do not contribute to the cost of the lighthouse are free-riding: They get the benefits of the lighthouse without paying for them. In the early days of lighthouses in Britain, lighthouses were built and operated by a government authority. The money for the authority came not from general tax revenues but from dues paid by ships when they arrived at or deparated from a port (Coase, 1974). In this way free-riding was not possible.

It becomes more difficult in a large mass society such as our own, in which it is not always possible to make sure everyone who benefits from a public good contributes to it. Mancur Olson (1965/1971) pointed out in his classic book, *The Logic of Collective Action*, that one way collective action problems are solved is for the government to offer some kind of incentive to individuals for contributing to the common good. Thus, the state could offer a rebate on a small, fuel-efficient, less polluting car, for instance. Such incentives are referred to as **selective incentives**. Yet someone has to get the government to pass laws to provide such selective incentives. This is where lobbying organizations come in.

Selective incentive Some kind of incentive to individuals for contributing to the common cause or good.

Environmental Organizations as Public Goods

Organizations that lobby the government to pass laws aimed at lowering CO_2 emissions can be considered public goods in and of themselves. If an environmental group lobbies for government laws to promote lower CO_2 emissions, and such laws are enacted, everyone receives the benefit of lower emissions, regardless of whether or not they contributed to the costs of the lobbying effort. That is, if an organization lobbies the government to pass laws, then everyone benefits, so people may try to free-ride on the efforts of the organization.

In a democracy such as the United States, many organizations lobby the government for various causes—protection of the environment, protecting the rights of retired people, protecting the interests of doctors, etc. A number of organizations in the United States are designed to lobby the government in Washington, DC, about environmental concerns—for example, the Sierra Club, Nature Conservancy, and World Wildlife Fund. National activities to protect the natural environment are on the rise in all countries (Frank, Hironaka, and Schofer, 2000).

How do all these organizations get people to contribute to the cause? Organizations can (and often do) offer selective incentives to people who will join the organization and support the cause. Sometimes this may be something small such as a magazine subscription. Other organizations offer cheap life insurance and a plethora of discounts and other perks for membership. Another, less tangible selective incentive that organizations can offer is an atmosphere of camaraderie with other members. Environmental organizations can also offer a personal identity as an environmentalist (Vasi and Macy, 2003).

Mobilizer's dilemma People faced with a crisis message may become fatalistic and think there is nothing they can do to make a difference.

Other ways to encourage people to support conservation organizations, besides using selective incentives, include issuing crisis messages that call attention to impending disaster. However, this can create the **mobilizer's dilemma** (Vasi and Macy, 2003). People may become fatalistic and think there is nothing they can do to make a difference and thus not want to contribute to the organization. On the other hand, if people are told that positive change is possible and is in fact already happening, this may encourage people to free-ride and not support the organization. Vasi and Macy tested the effects of both crisis and empowerment messages in an experimental setting and found that although crisis messages tend to undermine the belief in the efficacy of the organization (as the mobilizer's dilemma suggests), they are less likely to do so when coupled with messages that reinforce a sense of efficacy (that the organization is having effects). Also, they found that providing a sense of identity to participants is key. They conclude,

> The implication for mobilizing strategy is straightforward: Underscore the gravity of resource depletion, but also point to successful conservation efforts wherever possible *while promoting identification with conservationists.* In groups with a conservationist identity, empowerment messages appear to enhance per-

> ceptions of collective efficacy and mitigate tendencies to view improving conditions as an opportunity to free ride. (p. 994)

Mancur Olson (1965/1971) also pointed out that sometimes just one person with enough incentive to do so can solve the collective action problem. For example, in 1907 there were runs on the banks in New York, and a banking crisis (in which banks did not have enough to pay out all the money asked for by depositors) was imminent. The banking system in New York was on the verge of collapse, and if the New York banks collapsed, the banks throughout the rest of the country would likely follow. Pierpont Morgan, head of the bank J. P. Morgan and Company, injected $3 million of his own money and raised more than $8 million from other bankers, $10 million from John D. Rockefeller, and $25 million from the secretary of the treasury, but this still was not enough to stop the panic. Finally, Morgan summoned the presidents of the major New York banks to his house and invited them into the library. "Once the moneymen had gathered, Morgan had the great ornamental doors to the library locked and refused to let anyone leave until all had collectively agree to commit a further $25 million to the rescue fund" (Ahamed, 2009, pp. 52–54). This did the trick. So one man's actions were able to save the New York banking system, including, of course, his own bank. Unfortunately, with climate change one person is probably not going to be able to do something comparable to solve the problem.

CONCLUSION

In this chapter, we examined the major environmental issues of the day, possible solutions, and the social issues involved with implementing these solutions. These issues are likely to be major social and political issues in the 21st century.

REFERENCES

Ahamed, Liaquat. 2009. *Lords of Finance: The Bankers Who Broke the World.* New York: Penguin.

Coase, Ronald H. 1960. "The Problem of Social Cost." *Journal of Law and Economics* 3, 1–44.

———. 1974. "The Lighthouse in Economics." *Journal of Law and Economics* 17(2), 357–376.

The Economist. April 11, 2009. "Sin Aqua Non," pp. 59–61.

Frank, David John, Ann Hironaka, and Evan Schofer. 2000. "The Nation-State and the Natural Environment over the Twentieth Century." *American Sociological Review* 65(1), 96–116.

Huxley, John. February 11, 2009. "Horrific, But Not the Worst We've Suffered." *Sydney Morning Herald*.

MacKay, David J. C. 2008. *Sustainable Energy—Without the Hot Air*. Cambridge, UK: UIT Cambridge. Available at www.withouthotair.com and www.uit.co.uk/sustainable.

Olson, Mancur. 1971 [1965]. *The Logic of Collective Action: Public Goods and the Theory of Groups*, rev. ed. Cambridge, MA: Harvard University Press.

Vasi, Ion Bogdan, and Michael Macy. 2003. "The Mobilizer's Dilemma: Crisis, Empowerment, and Collective Action." *Social Forces* 81(3), 979–998.

World Water Assessment Programme. 2009. "The United Nations World Water Development Report 3: Water in a Changing World." Paris/London: United Nations Educational, Scientific and Cultural Organization/Earthscan.

POLITICAL SOCIOLOGY AND SOCIAL MOVEMENTS

18

HUMAN POLITIES THROUGHOUT HISTORY

Polities in Preindustrial Societies

In the simplest societies, hunting and gathering societies, there is no government as such. Authority typically lies in a headman, but his power is limited to his personal influence and he cannot force others in the group to do things they do not want to do. The same is true in horticultural societies. It is only in agrarian society that a true government emerges, which is able to enforce its laws and decisions on the populace through the help of a full-time officialdom and a military force of some sort. This military force may be a police force or an army. In most agrarian societies, there is a monarch of some sort, and his authority (in theory) is absolute. I say "in theory" because in reality in agrarian societies, in which most of the populace work on farms scattered in villages across the countryside, it is difficult to enforce every single rule in every outlying area. Mountainous areas are notoriously difficult to police and control, and many mountainous areas of the world—the Alps in Switzerland, the Himalayas, the Basque country in southern France, and the mountainous areas of the Massif Central—have been home to groups of people who have guarded their independence fiercely.

The general trend has always been toward a concentration of authority and power in the state as societies became larger and more complex. Agrarian societies were once widespread throughout much of the world, and they were dominated by large kingdoms with a single ruler. In the 18th and 19th centuries, China was ruled by an emperor, Japan by a shogun and a puppet emperor, the various countries of Europe were almost all monarchies, Turkey was the center of the Ottoman Empire, which stretched into the Balkans, and much of the rest of the world made up the colonial empires

Democracy The form of government in which people are able to freely vote for their leaders and influence decisions that affect them.

of various European powers (England, France, Germany, Belgium, etc.). **Democracy**, in which people are able to freely vote for their leaders and influence decisions that affect them, has historically been rare. In ancient Greece and, for a while, in ancient Rome, democracy did exist. However, in each case it was limited to a small percentage of the population who were considered full citizens, and in each case it was eventually swallowed up by a monarchy—the Roman Empire.

Moore's Social Origins of Dictatorship and Democracy

Given that most states in advanced industrial societies in the contemporary world are democracies, the question is, How did this happen? How did democracies ever replace monarchies? This is the question that Barrington Moore tackled in his 1966 book, *Social Origins of Dictatorship and Democracy*, which is a classic of political sociology. In this book, Moore examined why democracy emerged in England and France and did not emerge, for instance, in China, which remained a monarchy into the early 20th century and to this day remains a one-party, Communist state.

Moore noted that the development of democracy in England was a gradual process, which was brought about by a coincidence of historical events. England started out as a monarchy under the Norman conquerors in the 11th century. William the Bastard of Normandy conquered England in 1066, and thereby was renamed William the Conqueror. From then on, England became home to a French-speaking aristocracy and king. (This is the reason why the fancy words in the English language all have a French origin.) However, England had many local grandees who were not always willing to obey the king. In the Magna Carta of 1215, these local grandees forced William's descendant, John, to state that he would not do things they did not approve of. In particular, it proclaims certain rights for nobles and barons, requires the king to respect the law and follow legal procedures, and gives all the king's subjects the ability to appeal unlawful imprisonment (the right of **habeas corpus**). The right to petition for a writ of habeas corpus is found in most contemporary democracies and has long been celebrated as the most efficient safeguard of the liberty of the individual. Anyone in prison can petition for a writ of habeas corpus that forces the prison to allow the person to appear in court and have the court decide whether the prison has the lawful authority to imprison the person. The Magna Carta is typically

Habeas corpus Ability to appeal unlawful imprisonment; dates to English Magna Carta.

considered the beginning of democracy in England. In particular, it created a "common council" made up of the most powerful grandees whose job it was to advise the king. Importantly, the common council was responsible for taxation. Although the council was not representative, it became the forerunner of the English parliament or representative body (and hence, indirectly, the forerunner of the U.S. Congress).

Moore (1966) noted that as time went on Parliament became stronger, particularly because it controlled the purse strings, and when the king wanted money he had to convene Parliament to ask for it. In addition, English society became a commercialized, market-oriented society, and agriculture in particular became oriented toward production for the market. Unlike in other countries in Europe, local grandees were often involved in agricultural production for the market, and they also had seats in Parliament. Consequently, they often pushed for the enactment of laws that favored commercial interests. The English Civil War (1642–1651) led to the victory of the Parliamentarians over the Royalists and consequently strengthened Parliament. The victory of the Parliamentarians meant that commercially oriented people had the upper hand in England. They further pushed for the rationalization of agriculture, for instance, by passing enclosure acts that helped eradicate traditional peasant subsistence farming. This led to the dissolution of this group of subsistence-oriented farmers—a group that often served as an impediment to democratization elsewhere.

In France, a powerful monarchy persisted into the 18th century. Unlike in England, the French aristocracy had never turned to commercial agriculture and, instead, made their living basically by squeezing the subsistence peasantry through taxes and other fees. This happened because the French peasantry had fairly secure property rights so they could not be evicted off their land. As a result, in France there were many small peasants farming small holdings and paying heavy taxes and dues. Eventually, however, the peasantry rebelled against heavy taxation and helped bring about the French Revolution. According to Moore (1966), the revolution was crucial for the development of democracy because it destroyed the overly large central state bureaucracy that had crippled economic progress. The revolution also destroyed the old feudal system. After some reversions to monarchy (e.g., the rule of Napoleon Bonaparte), France became a representative democracy in the 19th century.

Nearly 100 years after the French Revolution, the American Civil War set the stage for the further development of democracy in the United States.

According to Moore (1966), the American Civil War was crucial for the development of democracy in the United States because it meant the victory of the non-slave-owning North over the slave-owning South. In the South, the elites were an aristocratic class of slave owners. Slave owning was antidemocratic because the denial of citizenship rights to all people prevented the creation of a true democracy. In the North, the elites were the industrialists, who were against slavery and in favor of free labor; in the South there were few industries and few powerful industrialists.

Last, Moore (1966) examined why democracy did not emerge in China, a huge, comparatively sophisticated agrarian society. As in France, no commercialized agriculture ever developed in China. This is because the urban population was small, and the landlord/tenant relationship in the countryside led to the peasantry being heavily taxed, as in France. Eventually, as in France, the peasantry revolted against the burden of taxation. However, instead of ushering in a democracy, their actions helped usher in the Communist regime of Mao Tse-Tung (in office from 1943 to 1975).

In a later work, a student of Barrington Moore's, Theda Skocpol, in her book *States and Social Revolutions* (1979), further analyzed why revolutions brought down the state in China, Russia, and France but never did so in England during the English Civil War, Russia in 1905, Prussia during the Prussian Reform Movement of 1807–1815, and Japan during the Japanese Meiji Restoration. She concluded that in each case of successful revolution, some outside conflict had weakened the state. Furthermore, the military went over to the side of the revolutionaries in the cases of the successful revolutions, whereas this did not happen where the revolutions were unsuccessful. When the military deserted the state, peasant revolts went unchecked and helped bring about the fall of the state.

Democracy in the World Today

Most European states eventually became full democracies in the late 19th and early 20th centuries. All the English settler societies (Canada, Australia, New Zealand, and the United States) were established as democracies. As in most places, early democracy in the United States was confined to a small percentage of all adults. By 1920, however, women had won the right to vote. Unfortunately, in the South, Jim Crow laws effectively disenfranchised approximately half of the population. It took the civil rights movement of the 1950s and 1960s to eradicate Jim Crow laws in the southern states and bring about a full democracy of all citizens in the United States.

In the contemporary world, the majority of rich world countries are democratic to this day, although largely nondemocratic, authoritarian regimes are still found in many areas in the world today.

Freedom House conducts a yearly survey that assesses the extent of freedom throughout the world. Countries are divided into three categories: free, partly free, and not free. A free country is one in which there is broad scope for open political competition, a climate of respect for civil liberties, significant independent civic life, and independent media. Partly free countries are characterized by some restrictions on political rights and civil liberties, often in a context of corruption, weak rule of law, ethnic strife, or civil war. A not-free country is one in which basic political rights are absent, and basic civil liberties are widely and systematically denied. Figure 18.1 shows the results of Freedom House's 2008 survey of 193 countries and 15 related and disputed territories during 2007.

THEORIES OF THE CONTEMPORARY STATE

If you remember in Chapter 4, Karl Marx thought democracies were in actual fact not very democratic at all. He thought the state was the "handmaiden of the ruling class"—that is, state policies reflected the interest of the elite. For Marx, in a capitalist society the elite were the capitalists—the owners of land, property, and machines. This is what he saw in late 19th-century England, where he wrote his magnum opus *Das Kapital* in the beautiful domed Reading Room of the British Museum. Nearly 100 years later, C. Wright Mills continued this line of thought in his book, *The Power Elite* (1956). In this book, Mills argued that state policies reflect the interests of the **power elite**, leaders of what he termed the military-industrial complex: military leaders, government leaders, and the heads of large corporations. Although they do not necessarily get together and conspire (but they may), Mills claimed that these people have similar interests and support similar policies. He said these people tend to be male, white, and Protestant, have similar values, and have similar upbringings. They tend to have all gone to the same East Coast prep schools and Ivy League colleges. As adults, they mix socially and tend to be on corporate boards together, are involved in the same charity organizations, and they very often own

Power elite Leaders of what C. Wright Mills termed the military–industrial complex: military leaders, government leaders, and the heads of large corporations.

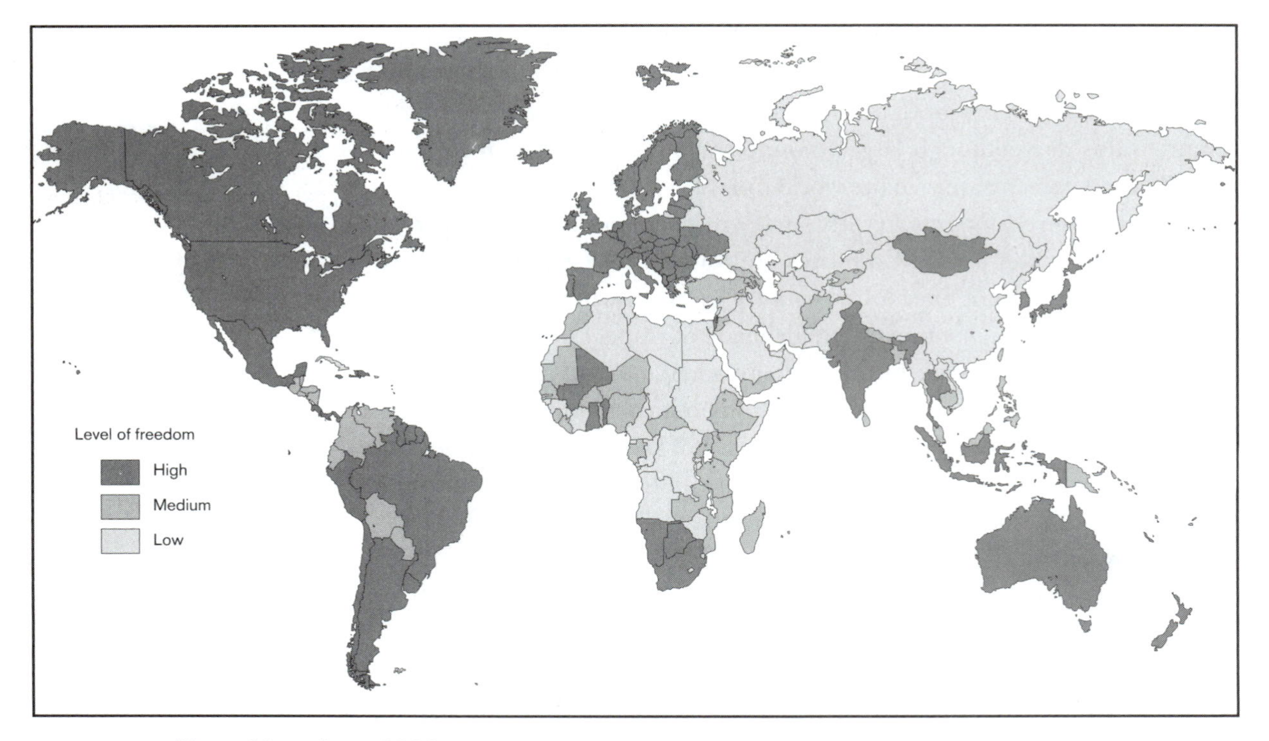

FIGURE 18.1 Map of freedom, 2008.
Source: Used with permission of Freedom House. www.freedomhouse.org

property in the same places (e.g., the Hamptons at the east end of Long Island, New York).

Pluralism The theory that democratic decision making is an outcome of competition between different groups with different interests.

Pluralists see that power is less concentrated in a democracy (Dahl, 1956). They suggest that rather than state policies meeting the set interests of just one elite, there are many elites and many political groups with different, conflicting interests. Thus, AARP (formerly known as the American Association of Retired Persons) wants cheaper prescription drugs, and the drug companies do not want drug prices regulated. Car makers want gas prices to be kept as low as possible, whereas oil producers prefer gas prices to be as high as possible. The political process becomes one of negotiation between all these competing groups and interests. This is the reason so many different groups hire lobbyists to lobby for their interests in Congress, for instance, to try to convince individual Congresspeople and Senators to support the legislation they favor.

SOCIAL MOVEMENTS

Peasant revolts in preindustrial Europe, which were so important for bringing down states in France, Russia, and China, were social movements of subsistence farmers. A **social movement** can be defined as a grassroots movement of many people aimed at political reform or social change. There have been many different types of social movements aimed at different types of change, including union, environmentalist, racist (e.g., Ku Klux Klan), animal rights, anti-abortion, women's rights movements. Not all of these movements are or have been successful.

Social movement A grassroots movement of many people aimed at political reform or change.

In history, some social movements have helped bring about major political change. The civil rights movement in the United States in the late 1950s and 1960s, the fall of communism in Eastern Europe, and the Iranian Revolution are relatively recent examples.

Civil Rights Movement

After the end of the Civil War and the end of the Reconstruction period from 1865 to 1877, white Southerners moved to deprive African Americans of the rights they had gained after the Civil War. Beginning in Mississippi in 1890, each state passed new constitutions, amendments, and laws that required poll taxes, literacy requirements or comprehension tests, and residency and record-keeping requirements in order to register to vote. Naturally, most African Americans as well as many poor whites failed such tests or failed to meet the requirements and thus were denied the right to register to vote. Voter turnout dropped drastically throughout the South as a result of such measures. In many areas in the South, not a single African American was registered to vote, even though they comprised as much as 45% of the population in some states.

Facilities became segregated on the basis of "separate but equal," but separate was never equal. African Americans had separate restrooms, drinking fountains, waiting rooms, and seats on trains and buses. They were excluded from white parks, swimming pools, playgrounds, schools, universities, hospitals, hotels, and restaurants. They were not allowed in most stores, and in some stores they were allowed to shop only if they came in the back door. The public money that went to the African American "equivalents" was always far less than the public money that went to white facilities, which is not surprising given that most African Americans

PHOTO 18.1 Rosa Parks, Montgomery, Alabama. Her refusal to give up her seat on a crowded bus to a white person when asked to do so by the driver precipitated the start of the civil rights movement in 1955. Source: Library of Congress.

could not vote. African Americans were also subject to a host of smaller indignities: They were expected to get off the sidewalk when a white person approached, tip their hats (if male) toward whites, and address all whites in a formal and deferential manner as Mr., Miss, and Mrs. even though all blacks were called by their first names (Box 18.1).

Then in 1955, a seamstress named Rosa Parks refused to give up her seat on a crowded bus to a white person when asked to do so by the driver (Photo 18.1). This precipitated the start of the civil rights movement, culminating in the Civil Rights Act of 1964 and the Voting Rights Act of 1965. Whereas state-sponsored school segregation had been declared unconstitutional by the Supreme Court of the United States in 1954 in *Brown v. Board of Education*, most of the remaining Jim Crow laws were overruled by the 1964 and 1965 Acts.

Fall of Communism in Eastern Europe

In 1989, East Germany was under Communist, totalitarian rule. Free movement to and from West Germany was restricted, and the Berlin Wall divided

BOX 18.1
EXPERIENCING THE CIVIL RIGHTS MOVEMENT

A. is an African American woman in her 70s who lives in Charlotte, North Carolina. She has cleaned houses for much of her life. Before the civil rights movement, she said, you never were allowed to come in the front door if you were going to clean a white person's house. You had to go around the back. Back in those days you didn't just clean–you washed clothes, cooked meals, and did everything else too. If you ate anything, you weren't allowed to sit with the family but had to stand while they sat. Your dishes couldn't be mixed with the white people's dishes. If you used the bathroom, you had to use the one in the basement. White people always had to be referred to with a Miss or Mister, never by their first name.

After the civil rights movement, she said, it felt like a skin came off. She felt that she didn't have to put up with bad treatment anymore. One time in the late 1960s, a woman whose house she cleaned left a key under the front doormat so A. could let herself into the house to clean. One day A. came in and started vacuuming the floor. The woman's sister was upstairs.

The sister came down and demanded: "How did you get in here?"

A. replied, "How do you think?"

"Are you trying to be smart with me?" said the sister sharply.

"What did you just say to me?" asked A.

"I cannot stand a smart-mouthed nigger."

"I am so sick of being called a nigger. If you don't call me by my name I will leave."

"Go ahead. And you don't have to come back."

"I won't," said A. Then she took the dustbag out of the vacuum cleaner and started throwing the contents all over the living room.

"I'll call the police if you do that."

"Call the police" said A., as she continued to throw dirt all over the house.

The woman who owned the house called A. later that evening and asked her to come back. A. refused. She never did go back to that house.

It was a liberating experience, she said.

East Berlin (under the control of the Communist government of East Germany) from West Berlin (under the control of the democratic government of West Germany). However, things had been changing in Eastern Europe since 1985 and the ascension to power in the Soviet Union of Mikhail Gorbachev. In the summer of 1989, Hungary opened its borders to the West, and 200,000 East Germans took advantage of this to flee to the West.

Protest demonstrations broke out all over East Germany in September 1989. Initially, they were of people wanting to leave to the West, chanting "Wir wollen raus!" ("We want out!"). Then protestors began to chant "Wir bleiben hier" ("We're staying here!"). This was the start of what East Germans generally call the "Peaceful Revolution" of late 1989. The most crucial moment happened in Leipzig on October 9, 1989. On the evening of this day, 70,000 East Germans, chanting "Wir sind das Volk" ("we are the people") called for democratic reform of the communist East German government. A first-hand observer (Crawshaw, 2009) described the events of that day as follows:

> Throughout 1989, weekly Monday demonstrations—prayers for peace in the Nikolaikirche, followed by a demonstration—gradually gained strength, despite constant beatings and arrests. Eventually, the authorities decided enough was enough. They would teach Leipzig, and thus all of East Germany, a lesson. A "reader's letter" (read: an officially sanctioned announcement) in the Leipzig local paper announced that "these counter-revolutionary actions" would be dealt with, "if need be, with weapons in our hands." In effect, the regime was publicly heralding its plans for a local reprise of the Tiananmen Square killings, which had taken place just 4 months earlier. Nor was this mere bluster. The city of Leipzig was closed off. Weapons and ammunition were handed out. Hospitals were cleared. Before the demonstration began, I counted 16 trucks with armed workers' militias in one side street alone. Inside the 13th-century Nikolaikirche, everybody knew what to expect once prayers were over. Through the tall windows, we could hear the echoing cries of the huge crowd outside, chanting, "No violence!" But it was clear to everybody: Violence there would be tonight, and it might be lethal. After the service, we moved outside. Presumably in common with many of those around me, I felt the tightening knot of fear as we waited for the shooting to begin. A few minutes passed, without violence. And then a few minutes more. And then—utterly dramatic and conventionally un-newsworthy in equal measure—it became clear that there would be no shooting tonight. No shooting, not even arrests or beatings. As one demonstrator said after it was all over: "I felt as if I could fly. It was the most fantastic day that I have ever known. Now, we knew that there was no going back." Even outsiders could share in the exhilaration of that achievement. The regime's threats of lethal action were intended to persuade the crowds to stay at home. Instead, more had come out that day than ever. (p. 42)

Whereas for years there had been virtually no challenge to the East German government, in the space of a few months the regime fell. The longtime leader of East Germany, Erich Honecker, resigned on October 18,

PHOTO 18.2 Berliners sing and dance on top of the Berlin Wall to celebrate the opening of East–West German borders, Friday afternoon, November 10, 1989. Source: Associated Press photo/Thomas Kienzle.

1989. After the Leipzig demonstrations, the size of demonstrations against the regime began to increase until on November 4, 1 million people gathered in Alexanderplatz in East Berlin. On November 9, the East German government made an announcement that was interpreted to mean that all GDR (German Democratic Republic) citizens could visit West Germany and West Berlin. In response, crowds of East Germans climbed onto and crossed the wall. They were joined by West Germans on the other side. During the next few weeks, the wall was chipped away by the public (Photo 18.2). The official destruction of the wall began June 13, 1990.

The mood in Berlin after the fall of the wall was celebratory. On Christmas Day, 1989, Leonard Bernstein performed a concert of pieces including Beethoven's 9th Symphony ("Ode to Joy"), with an international orchestra drawn from both East and West Germany, as well as the United Kingdom, France, the Soviet Union, and the United States. On July 21, 1990, Roger Waters of Pink Floyd performed songs from the Pink Floyd album *The Wall* in Potsdamer Platz, along with a variety of other Western singers and bands, including the Scorpions, Bryan Adams, Sinéad O'Connor, Thomas Dolby, Joni Mitchell, Marianne Faithfull, Levon Helm, Rick Danko, and Van Morrison. David Hasselhoff performed his song "Looking for Freedom," which was very popular in Germany at that time, standing on the Berlin Wall. The fall of the Berlin Wall paved the way for German reunification, which was formally concluded on October 3, 1990.

Islam and the Iranian Revolution

The revolution that led to the overthrow of the Shah in Iran was not just an Islamic revolution but a nationalistic protest against the perceived injustice and shortcomings of the government. The Shah had instituted economic policies that led to shortages of goods and inflation. In addition, the Shah was seen as a puppet of Western powers, particularly the United States.

The first demonstrations against the Shah began in 1978. The scale of further demonstrations and strikes into 1979 convinced the Shah to flee the country in January 1979. Eventually, the royal government fell when troops loyal to the Shah were overwhelmed by troops backing the revolutionaries. A national referendum was held on April 1, and Iran voted to become an Islamic republic. In December 1979, a theocratic constitution was also approved that made Ayatollah Khomeini—a prominent Shia cleric—Supreme Leader of the country. The new regime stifled dissent and instituted strict Islamic laws. The freedoms of women were severely curtailed, and all women were required to wear a head scarf and either a coat, black chador, or **burqa** covering the entire body. Sale of Western cultural goods (movies, CDs, etc.) was strictly limited because Western culture was considered to be a corrupting influence (Photo 18.3).

Burqa An outer garment (usually black) covering a woman's body from neck to toe. It is worn over the clothes.

Since the Iranian Revolution, Islamicist parties have risen throughout the Middle East. For example, in 2002, the Islamicist Justice and Development Party won a landslide victory in Turkey's elections. The head of the party, Tayyip Erdogan, became prime minister of Turkey in 2003.

Fundamentalist Muslim Organizations as Sponsors of Terrorism

More problematic is the rise of militant Islamic movements that sponsor terror. They include Al Qaeda (varied countries), the PKK (Kurdistan Workers' Party) in Turkey, Hezbollah (Lebanon), and Hamas (Palestine). All of these organizations are willing to use violence in pursuit of their goals.

PHOTO 18.3 Image from the film *Persepolis* (2007), a coming-of-age story about a girl growing up in Tehran (Iran) at the time of the Iranian revolution. Source: 2.4.7. Films/The Kobal Collection.

Many of these organizations capitalize on the fact that the Middle Eastern countries often have poorly functioning economies coupled with a lack of democracy. As a result, there are large numbers of young, unemployed or underemployed, disaffected men who are drawn to the rhetoric of fundamentalist Islam. Al Qaeda was the organization responsible for the attacks on the United States on September 11, 2001, which killed approximately 3,000 people. The vast majority of Muslims deplore the use of such violent tactics and note that killing is antithetical to the Muslim religion.

Why Do Social Movements Occur?

Stark (2004) suggests that for a social movement to occur, four conditions must be met. The first is that some members of the society must be unhappy with the existing state of things and want to change it. That is, they must have some *grievance*. The second is that people must think that they might be successful in an attempt to change things. They must have *hope* of success. In the East German case, Gorbachev's reforms in the Soviet Union and his reluctance to intervene in East German affairs gave some hope to demonstrators that success might be possible (Pfaff, 1996). Especially after the success of the Leipzig demonstration, people began to believe that the demonstrations could be successful and there was hope of change. Often, an *event* will precipitate the beginning of a social movement. In the case of the civil rights movement, it was the arrest of Rosa Parks. People must be connected through *networks* of attachments that serve to pull them into the movement. These networks may be informal, such as friends and relatives who are already involved with the issues of the movement. This was the case in the East German social movement (Opp, 1994). These networks may also be more formal, through established organizations such as churches. This was the case in the civil rights movement in the U.S. South: Many of the original protesters knew each other because they were members of the same churches.

When Do Social Movements Succeed?

Social movements succeed when, first, they achieve a successful *mobilization* of people and resources. It is not enough for people to come together with a shared grievance. There are logistical issues to address, such as how demonstrators will be fed, and these are only solved by money and/or resources. This idea is often referred to as **resource mobilization theory** (Zald and McCarthy, 1987). The social movement must be able to withstand or *overcome external opposition*. It is more likely to succeed if it enlists *external allies* from other powerful groups in or outside the society, or at least does not face strong opposition from such groups (Stark, 2004, p. 596).

Resource mobilization theory The theory that social movements can only succeed if they successfully mobilize both resources and money to solve logistical problems.

CONCLUSION

After the Neolithic Revolution and the beginning of settled agriculture, democracies have been rare in human history. They emerged sporadically and often disappeared, swallowed up by vast authoritarian states. In this chapter, we examined the contributions that sociologists have made to understanding the emergence of democracy and its establishment as the leading form of government in the rich countries of the world today. We also discussed sociological theories of democracy and social movements.

REFERENCES

Crawshaw, Steve. March 16, 2009. "Now We Knew That There Was No Going Back." *New Statesman*, p. 42.

Dahl, Robert. 1956. *A Preface to Democratic Theory*. Chicago: University of Chicago Press.

Mills, C. Wright. 1956. *The Power Elite*. Oxford, UK: Oxford University Press.

Moore, Barrington. 1966. *Social Origins of Dictatorship and Democracy*. Boston: Beacon.

Opp, Karl-Dieter. 1994. "Repression and Revolutionary Action: East Germany in 1989." *Rationality and Society* 6, 101–138.

Pfaff, Steven. 1996. "Collective Identity and Informal Groups in Revolutionary Mobilization: East Germany in 1989." *Social Forces* 75(1), 91–118.

Skocpol, Theda. 1979. *States and Social Revolutions*. Cambridge, UK: Cambridge University Press.

Stark, Rodney. 2004. *Sociology*, 6th ed. Belmont, CA: Wadsworth.

Zald, Mayer N., and John D. McCarthy. 1987. *Social Movements in an Organizational Society: Collected Essays*. New Brunswick, NJ: Transaction.

name index

subject index